Polis, Ontology,
Ecclesial Event

Polis, Ontology, Ecclesial Event

Engaging with Christos Yannaras' Thought

Editor
Sotiris Mitralexis

Associate Editors
Andreas Andreopoulos
Pui Him Ip
Isidoros Katsos
Dionysios Skliris

©

James Clarke & Co

James Clarke & Co
P.O. Box 60
Cambridge
CB1 2NT
United Kingdom

www.jamesclarke.co
publishing@jamesclarke.co

ISBN: 978 0 227 17671 9

British Library Cataloguing in Publication Data
A record is available from the British Library

First published by James Clarke & Co, 2018

Table of Contents

Part II
PHILOSOPHY

Part III
ECCLESIA

List of Contributors

Andreas Andreopoulos is Reader in Orthodox Christianity at the Theology, Religion and Philosophy Department of the University of Winchester.

Deborah Casewell is Postdoctoral Teaching Fellow in Philosophy at Liverpool Hope University. She completed her doctoral studies in systematic theology at the University of Edinburgh in 2015, writing on the theological and philosophical background and consequences of Eberhard Jüngel's theology of the cross. She has studied at Edinburgh, Oxford, Tübingen, and the Institut Catholique, Paris, working on continental philosophy of religion and modern German theology.

Jonathan Cole is a research member of the Centre for Public and Contextual Theology, Charles Sturt University (CSU), Canberra, Australia, and a doctoral candidate in political theology at the School of Theology CSU. He has an MA specialising in Middle Eastern politics and Islamic theology from the Australian National University. He also has a BA Honours in modern Greek language and history.

Brandon Gallaher is Lecturer of Systematic and Comparative Theology at the University of Exeter. From October 2011 to December 2014 he was a British Academy Postdoctoral Fellow at the University of Oxford.

Angelos Gounopoulos is a doctoral candidate at the School of Political Science of the Aristotle University of Thessaloniki specialising in political theory and philosophy. His PhD research focuses on political theology, and more specifically the historical experience of the Latin American liberation theology.

Pui Him Ip is a doctoral candidate at the Faculty of Divinity, University of Cambridge, after an MA in philosophy at Heythrop College, University of London, and an MSci in physics at Imperial College London.

Daniel Isai holds a doctorate from the Faculty of Theology 'Dumitru Stăniloae' at the 'Alexandru Ioan Cuza' University of Iasi. His research focuses on the dialogue between theology and phenomenology, and on the theological dimension of Jean-Luc Marion's phenomenology in particular.

Isidoros Katsos is a doctoral candidate at the Faculty of Divinity, University of Cambridge, after a doctorate in Law at the Freie Universität Berlin.

Nikolaos Koronaios studies philosophy at KU Leuven after receiving a degree in education from the University of Athens.

Marcello La Matina is Professor of Philosophy and Theory of Language at the Department of Human Studies of the University of Macerata in Italy.

John Milbank is Emeritus Professor of Religion, Politics and Ethics and President of the Centre of Theology and Philosophy at the University of Nottingham. He is the founder of the Radical Orthodoxy movement and author of many books, including *Theology and Social Theory: Beyond Secular Reason*.

Sotiris Mitralexis is Assistant Professor of Philosophy at the City University of Istanbul and Visiting Research Fellow at the University of Winchester. He received his doctorate in philosophy from the Freie Universität Berlin (2014), a doctorate in theology from the Aristotle University of Thessaloniki (2017), and a degree in classics from the University of Athens.

Dionysios Skliris is a Teaching Fellow at the University of Athens after receiving a doctorate from the Faculté des Lettres et Sciences Humaines of the University of Paris (Sorbonne-Paris IV). He studied classics and theology at the University of Athens and completed a masters degree in late antique philosophy at the University of London (King's College) and a masters degree in Byzantine literature at the University of Paris (Sorbonne-Paris IV).

Paul Tyson is the director of the Emmanuel Centre for the Study of Science, Religion and Society at Emmanuel College, University of Queensland, Brisbane, Australia.

Rowan Williams is Master of Magdalene College, University of Cambridge, and former Archbishop of Canterbury.

Preface
Hellenism in Motion
John Milbank

It is a pleasure to introduce this volume of probing essays concerning the work of one of the most important and insufficiently attended-to thinkers of our times, the Greek orthodox theologian and philosopher Christos Yannaras.

It might be more accurate to say that Yannaras is a Hellene, rather than a Greek. The position of Greece in modern Europe is curious: is its culture Eastern European or Mediterranean? Clearly, it is both and, as such, offers something of a bridge between East and West, Latin and Graeco-Slavic. Unlike Italy, however, it does not appear to offer a continuous historical link from antiquity to the present. There has been too much rupture, and often it has appeared to be a shadow of its former self. We now know that any notion that the modern Greeks are not of the same stock as the ancients to be an insidious myth and that the ruptures are largely to do with a violent history, not with ethnic and cultural legacy. Yet in this context Yannaras poses an awkward question: suppose that the oldest Greek legacy of the West has languished, not just in Greece but everywhere? Suppose that one aspect of the rupture is the departure of the West from the true Greek legacy, whereas the Roman legacy has been supported and sustained, just because it was already somewhat proto-modern? This explains much of his natural interest in Heidegger, even if his account of what has been crucially lost from the Hellenic legacy is in the end drastically different from that of the sage of the *Schwarzwald*.

It is this legacy that Yannaras celebrates, rather than that of modern Greece. For him, the emergence of Greece as a nation state involved capture by modern liberal notions of individualism, rights, social contract and absolute sovereignty. He regards this, despite my long-deceased Southwell neighbour Lord Byron's adventures, as an ironically imperial seizure, ultimately displacing the older imperial legacies of the Ottomans and Byzantium, where the attempted universalism of empire was, however problematically (as Eric Voegelin so brilliantly discusses in *The Ecumenic Age*), linked to the other universalism of the quest for truth. In this way, the apparent dynamism of modernity has, for Yannaras, in reality imposed a certain formal stasis, and has lost a more substantive cosmopolitan dynamic, linked to an always unfinished quest for goodness, truth and beauty in trust that they are nonetheless realities.

In this context the main charge of Yannaras against the Latin West is that it is twice-over solely focussed on the individual. Once, in terms of its sole spiritual concern with the individual soul, in ultimate disparagement of both *polis* and *cosmos*. Twice, in terms of its assumption that it is the lonely individual who knows, in objective detachment from nature, whose 'facts' and inevitable or observed laws it disinterestedly records. All this is based upon an impoverished metaphysics unable to perceive any dynamic, energetic third between essence and individual, and therefore doomed to sterile debates about the objective reality or mere human constructedness of such essences, in either case restricted by an ultimate focus upon lone, individual substance.

Many of the essays in this volume raise doubts about the extremity of this contrast, including the earliest by date, written by Rowan Williams, who rightly asks whether Aquinas' concern with existential being did not modify such essentialism, similar to how notions of 'energy' did within the Christian East? One could add that an entire set of questions of *translatio studii* between East and West now look far more complex in the wake of the work of Williams on Augustine and of Christoph Erismann in his *L'Homme Commun* on the continuities of metaphysical realism from the Cappadocians through Maximus in the East to Boethius and Eriugena and beyond in the West. This legacy is fully alive in the West, far from any 'individualism' prevailing. The doctrines of original sin, Christology, and Trinity all helped to sustain an absolute 'reciprocity' between universal and particular, and are also derived philosophically from Porphyry: Universal Man falls from grace in Adam alone; Christ in person is 'all' of human and divine natures in one; the Nature of God is fully and only found in the three hypostases/persons of his Trinitarian existence. Moreover, the relationality of personhood, deriving from the Trinitarian context initially, was further developed rather than abandoned by both Augustine and Aquinas, as Williams and others have argued.

However, I thoroughly agree with Brandon Gallaher in this volume that one cannot so easily dismiss the demonisation of the West in the case of Yannaras as one can in the case of some Eastern Orthodox genealogical mythologies. For one thing, he is fully alert to degeneracies within his own Orthodox tradition and fully prepared creatively to learn from modern Western thought in order to correct them. For another thing, and this one much more crucial, his most basic case is not that the West has suppressed apophaticism, personhood and relationality, but that it has forgotten the unity and dynamism of all truth-seeking and that it is a collective and natural endeavour. In this respect, he accuses his own tradition of having forgotten the true import of *apophasis* as well.

Perhaps his most crucial claim is that the apophatic legacy derives from classical Greece and was only consummated by the new, Christian context. It is by the same token that he rightly makes no real separation between theology and philosophy. This means that, for him, the ancient Greeks, like all other ancient societies (as none other than HRH Prince Charles has stressed), thought of their culture as seeking to reflect a cosmic order and thereby 'to be' in the truth. Yet in the Greek version of the 'axial' civilisational shift, this reflection was critically questioned and dynamised all the more as the cosmos itself was seen to reflect a transcendent, eternally truthful reality which was regarded by Socrates and Plato as 'good'. In this way, for Yannaras, the Western, critical, and 'enlightened' spirit was begun. But what the West and ultimately nearly all of us have forgotten was the link of critique to religion and a realist metaphysic of essence and participation, enshrined so acutely in Plato's 'Meno paradox', where we can only seek the truth if in some way we already share in it. Also forgotten is the fact that the Greek novelty remained rooted in a much more perennial human attitude that assumed a normative social 'representation' of reality, as Voegelin argued.

Viewed in this way, one can argue for the ultimate Western forgetting of the true Hellenic spirit, which also turns out to be much more 'ecumenically' related to other, far Eastern post-axial civilisations, as well as to purportedly 'primitive' human cultures. Perhaps this would serve both to confirm and adjust Heidegger's intuition of a forgetting – of both specifically Western authenticity and yet of the greater modesty of this intuition when compared to liberal and technocratic self-vaunting.

Of course, crucial stages of this forgetting now have to be dated much later than was once thought. The subordination of God to a flattened and abstract 'being' and ultimate, idolatrous reduction of him to the status of supreme single being occurred but gradually, from roughly 1300 onwards. It eventually brought in its wake the nominalist splitting of every reality between an 'empty' generalisation on the one hand and de-essentialised atomic individuals – who might potentially become anything and everything – on the other.

Nonetheless, the assumption that matters in the West were completely all right before that date, or that Aquinas unquestionably distilled the entire essence of Patristic wisdom, has to be called into question. Yannaras' understanding of the Hellenic spirit is that not only are theology and philosophy ultimately united, but so too are logic, physics, metaphysics and politics – a point admirably elucidated by Sotiris Mitralexis in this volume. However much they may also have been distinguished, especially by Aristotle, they were still only distinguished in order to be ultimately re-united – in a synthesis which the German Romantics and Idealists tried to reconstitute.

In Yannaras' terms, this means that all proper human thinking is dialectical, part of a conversation for which the provisional (and not, as for Habermas, ultimate) test of truth is its acceptability by the community, and not just in theory, but as the basis for a shared existence. In this way, truth is socially performed, but in faithfulness to nature and to what lies behind the natural. Such an exercise is cataphatic, but *cataphasis* involves, as for Dionysius the Areopagite, the articulation of enigmatic symbols that are subject to qualification and ultimate negation insofar as they necessarily involve divisions which cannot apply to the ultimate divine ground of reality. To articulate a logic is to seek to echo and repeat the structures of the cosmos and to propose an erotic and political practice which will test and revise this logic. Through this logic we can approach and recreate in ourselves (as Eriugena remarkably says) human, natural and angelic others without exhausting their reality.

Obviously the paradigm for this understanding of Hellenism is Plato, and not, as for Heidegger, the presocratics. Once more, one can argue that it was for long sustained in both East *and* West, thanks to the correction by Neoplatonism of any disintegrative, purely peripatetic tendencies and the overwhelming endorsement and elaboration of this project by the Church Fathers.

Yet one might call attention to the entire question of a mediating motion, which is clearly central for Yannaras. Energetic motion is linkage and all linkage is dynamic. It is the entire question of the 'third' or of the 'between' (as William Desmond calls it) that mysteriously links essence and individual. The Porphyrian legacy, much reinforced by Christian doctrine, deemed these two realities to be entirely coincident, without elaborating exactly how. It is this question which Russian sophiology tried to resume and which the Cappadocian-derived discourse of *dynamis* and *energeia* had already broached.

However, the Cappadocian efforts, and that of Maximus later, rested on Neoplatonic revisions of categorial doctrine, stemming ultimately from Plotinus. In Aristotle himself, as recent research has shown, the question of motion, of *kinesis*, is very difficult. As long as something is in motion it is apparently and contradictorily at once in potency and act – otherwise motion would be deconstructable into a series of stoppages. For this very reason Aristotle thinks all motion must be a teleological 'tending' to something, or else it would just be at an end. Similarly, he also sees in the *Physics* that motion is infinitely divisible. Although this is only a potential infinite, the potential infinite is ontologically actual (not just a mental projection), as long as motion is in being.

These latent conclusions in part permit Neoplatonism to radicalise *kinesis*. If, for Aristotle, both potency and act are fully real and movement is fully real as the transition between the two, then how can there be any clear division between metaphysics, the science of Being and God, and physics, the science of moving things? Much later, Eriugena elaborates a 'physics', or 'division of nature' (*natura* translates as *physis*), which includes even God. If motion and rest are equally natural, then the higher nature of intelligence must involve both a greater contemplative rest and a higher, more unfinished, spiralling motion. Beyond Aristotle, Plotinus sees understanding as *kinesis* as well as *energeia*: as a literally moving, transitional as well as completed, action. If, for him, the One is now infinite, that is because it is the infinite consummation of motion beyond motion, since it is the aporetic hesitation of motion between act and potential that opens up the irreducibility of the infinite and not a contradictorily infinite projection of inherently limited act, as it might seem to be for Aquinas.

For this reason Plotinus also relativises Aristotle's distinction between *poiesis* and *praxis* (and by implication between art and ethics). In every 'making' the mind itself fully goes out of itself and transits along with the external process of construction. Equivalently, in every 'action' some sort of expressive becoming must be also involved.

All this assumes that if motion is ontologically fundamental, then the priority of action over potential is questioned, though by no means reversed. By the same token, if transiting is ultimate, the process of differentiation involved suggests a certain mysterious reality of non-being, of the 'this is not that', on pain of denying alterity, as Plato had argued in the *Sophist*. It is for this reason that Plotinus places the transcendent One equally beyond rest and motion, act and potential, being and non-being. He fails to see, like some later writers as well as Aquinas, that thereby it could be said to be the infinite 'to be', which cannot have the same restrictions as a finite action. All the same, one can argue in a Plotinian (and Eckhartian) vein beyond Aquinas that this *esse* must be also and equally infinite potential, infinite spiralling motion and an infinite abyss (as it is for Buddhism, though too one-sidedly). It is indeed a transcendent One that is all these things and also an infinite plurality, even if the preference for the ultimate terminology of 'one' occludes the dimension of eminent actuality.

Such an intensified *apophasis,* inherently linked to an ontological heightening of *kinesis,* was sustained and elaborated by the Greek Fathers and even to a degree by Augustine – though much less so. Eventually their perspectives were incorporated by Eriugena and arguably with much later influence, now untraceable (in the early thirteenth century the burning of his books in all libraries was ordered). He also incorporated different and yet somewhat equivalent appropriations of Neoplatonism by Boethius, at least with regard to an ontologically-focussed version of Porphyrian dialectics and a 'reciprocal realism', whose influence remained official and sustained.

Most crucial here is the point that a greater apophaticism, of Plotinian derivation, more admitting of motion and non-being into ultimate reality, can much more naturally allow the thinking of the Trinity. Here one can at last see that Ralph Cudworth (and his Anglican successors) grasped just this point and was not trying to 'liberalise' Trinitarian thought, in his *True Intellectual System of the Universe,* as Douglas Hedley and others have well understood. Thus in a mysterious, eminent sense, there can be generation and further procession in God, even an eminent formative making and a 'dance-like' forming-motion beyond form towards, and in keeping with, the motion of the other. In this way indeed, above and beyond the cosmos, polity is shaped and sustained with the Godhead.

Likewise, as Piero Coda argues in his *Dalla Trinità,* the persons can only be differentiated if this motion in God twice crosses the abyss of non-being, fearful transitions that are the eternal ground of the finite suffering and seeming risk undergone on the Cross, besides the glorious novelty of Pentecost.

In this way then, the Neoplatonic heightening of *kinesis* permits for the Trinity the thinking of dynamic mediation between essence and person. Essence is also the transitional *dynamis* that is manifested and received, as Gregory of Nyssa understood it. Equally it is the 'stylistically' yet substantially fusing energy involved in the *enhypostasis* of the human nature in Christ. Likewise, it is the negatively moving 'transmission' of the sin of Adam which is the manifestation of his essence in identity with his singleness as the excess of contagion – something better brought out by Augustine.

This heightening also better permits the thought that the self-contained divine essence is paradoxically at one with its outgoing 'energies', as for Maximus the Confessor. God is in himself ecstatic. Or, as Eriugena has it, in radicalising the Greeks, God as infinite is not self-circumscribed, even as self-knowable, and *therefore* reaches beyond even the 'no beyond' into a circumscription where he creates, defines and knows himself in rendering something other to himself. This 'created God' is initially the core of the world beyond the world which the Bible names 'wisdom' and Eriugena the 'created and creating' 'Primordial Causes' which are the equivalent of Maximian *logoi* and Augustinian *rationes seminales*. The core of ontological reality is not just*ousia,* or essence, but also a moving, shaping and thinking process, which gradually flows down from the primordial causes through the universal *genera* and *species* that pre-include particulars (in a more passing and essential mode) to individuals that fully and reciprocally include their universals, though more in the mode of fully-realised substantive rest. Their basis is not, for Eriugena, a fixed material stability; rather, every instantiated *atoma* is a unique 'bundle' of the (ultimately divine) shaping and in-flowing thoughts, a singular combination of the 'alphabet' of inherently universal essential qualities.

What we can glimpse in all of this is the inherent link between a more radically apophatic doctrine of the divine simplicity on the one hand, and a more fluid ontology on the other. By comparison, even the restoration of metaphysical realism undertaken by Aquinas risked (for all the factors in his thought that massively qualify this) first, marginally reducing divine simplicity by entertaining some distinction between an absolute and ordained power (as the late John Hughes so brilliantly argued in pitting Bulgakov against Thomas) and concomitantly too much residual sense of a divine literal 'choosing' of one action rather than another. Secondly and simultaneously, this restoration risked losing some integral dynamism by not entirely preserving the unity of metaphysics, physics and logic – even though at several points he is close to reinstating it and even though one must admit that specific attention to logic and grammar yields ultimate ontological gains.

Aquinas' accounts of analogy and *convenientia* indeed involve a great fluidity, both vertical and horizontal. Yet he fails to be (and likely could not have been) aware of how the essentially Neoplatonic legacy of *paronomasia* and attributive analogy tends to displace the primacy of substance towards the co-primacy of *kinesis,* for two linked reasons. First, as Plotinus concluded, substance itself cannot be univocally predicated even within cosmic reality because one then faces an *aporia:*

either superior things (like intelligences and rational embodied beings) are included with one genus of substance with inferior things and hierarchy is thereby subordinated to a 'transcendental' universal class, or else there is no continuity of being and thinghood at all, which is clearly false. For this reason, substance itself and even within immanence is subordinated, beyond Aristotle, to *pros hen* predication, never mind in the case of being.

Secondly, this implies that such predication repeats and captures the reality of a moving ontological linkage between levels of substance, whereby higher generates lower, lower is at once same and different to higher, while it at once seeks to go out from and return to the higher reality. Such motion, like all motion, is inherently aporetic, indeed 'contradictory', as Aquinas does not allow, but Eckhart and Cusanus later will.

To contextualise these observations, in support of Yannaras' sense of a Latin deviation, one can point to the significance of Abelard's earlier parricide of his teacher, William of Champeaux, as newly discussed by Alain de Libera, John Marenbon and Christophe Erismann. As the latter suggests, Champeaux fully sustained the 'reciprocal realism' of the Greek and some Latin fathers, in his case as an isolated thesis, divorced from a wider metaphysical vision. In consequence, Abelard could readily treat it as a mainly logical thesis which was seemingly logical nonsense. The paradoxes and strange coincidences argued for by realism (and by Christian doctrine insofar as it is orthodox) all truly depend on the attempt to think and speak the strangeness of the *real world* and especially its curious 'connectedness'. It is then no accident that scholastic realism briefly returned to favour with the discovery of Aristotle's more natural and metaphysical writings. Yet without a strong Neoplatonic gloss (which is indeed to some degree present in Aquinas), this did not prove enough to head off the advocates of nominalism and 'disconnection', nor the corralling of logic and cosmology against the metaphysical.

There were still stronger counter-currents: the School of Chartres and the Albertine tradition; eventually Nicholas of Cusa, the heir of both; and other Renaissance thinkers like Pico and Ficino. There has been a tendency within Eastern Orthodoxy sometimes to view these figures, seemingly more sympathetic for Eastern Christian tradition, as 'too extreme' or even as heterodox. I would contend that often this extremity is precisely the result of a clearer sense, owing to direct experience, of where Western errors are likely to lead and the need to head them off by a still stronger thinking-through of the 'Hellenic' tradition. In the end then, Italy and the Rhine (and beyond!) do not represent solely a Roman continuation.

But what is the source of these errors? Perhaps one has to say that finally it is theological. The paradigm for the Western choosing individual, as for the Western sovereign pope and state, is the conception of God as a long, single, choosing, merely ontic being. He is not of course even remotely already there in Augustine, and yet Augustine's allowance of a seemingly non-synergic 'predestination', when taken alongside the Western (and indeed majority Eastern) allowance of a region of hell that can (somehow) prevail eternally alongside God, ultimately and fatally encourage the ideas of God and creation as ontically separate realms and of divine and human action as in competition with each other, – whether this ultimately ensues in semi-Pelagianism or in Lutheranism and Calvinism.

In many ways it would seem that the perverse desire to defend this false 'transcendence' was the factor that most powerfully lent to the disconnection of cosmos from God, and individual human thought from human involvement with nature and with political society.

As Yannaras says, however, the project of the Church – the ecclesial council of the cosmic polity on earth, the assembly of the wise under the guidance of the *Logos,* and the engraced restorers of a shattered nature – is precisely the reverse, Hellenic one of combining an integrated vision with a project of reintegration. With him, we must keep faith that a shattered Church still contains within these fragments the primordial seeds of restoration and renewal. With him, and inspired by his lead and example, we must take up once more this truly philosophical and political cosmic project.

Introduction
Sotiris Mitralexis

The recent translation of a number of Christos Yannaras' books in English prompted a new wave of international scholarly interest in his work. The present volume, emerging from the 'Polis, Ontology, Ecclesial Event: Engaging with Christos Yannaras' Thought' conference at the University of Cambridge,[1] is but one of the testimonies to this.

An academic philosopher, theologian, public intellectual and a profusely productive author with about seventy book titles[2] currently available in Greece, Christos Yannaras has authored treatises in philosophy (mainly ontology and epistemology), theology, and political science, while both his weekly newspaper *feuilleton* and his frequent public appearances establish him as a well-known figure in Greece's public sphere. His impact in Greece is undeniable,[3] but international engagement with his thought is steadily on the rise as well:[4] while his treatises 'began to be translated

---

1. 27-28 March 2017, Eastwood Room, Office of Post-Doctoral Affairs, University of Cambridge. Organising Committee: Dr Andreas Andreopoulos, Mr Pui Him Ip, Dr Isidoros Katsos, Dr Sotiris Mitralexis, Dr Dionysios Skliris. The conference concluded with a public discussion between John Milbank and Christos Yannaras.

2. Most of them, though not all, are listed in the last pages of his most recent book at the time of this writing, Christos Yannaras, Ἡ Ὀντολογία Τοῦ Προσώπου *(Προσωποκεντρικὴ Ὀντολογία) [The Ontology of the Person (Prosopo-Centric Ontology)]* (Athens: Ikaros, 2017), while two more are currently in press.

3. Russell notes that 'his books had huge sales' in Greece. Norman Russell, 'Christos Yannaras' in *Key Theological Thinkers: From Modern to Postmodern*, ed. Svein Rise and Staale Johannes Kristiansen (New York: Routledge, 2013), 725.

4. For a more or less full bibliography of studies on Yannaras up to 2014 see Basilio Petrà, *Christos Yannaras: L'Orizzonte Apofatico Dell'Ontologia* (Brescia: Morcelliana, 2015), 172-9. It should be noted that the emergence of secondary

into Western European languages in the early 1970s,[1] the first decade of the new millennium has seen most of his books in English come to print, with translations of his works currently appearing in twelve languages.[2]

He is considered controversial both as a philosopher and as a theologian for reasons that include his very approach to these disciplines, politics, and the relationship between them: '[I]t is difficult to categorise Yannaras' thought. His work proceeds as if there were little distinction in practice between theology and philosophy, and even political theory. In that sense he transcends what can still be in the West rather rigid conventional boundaries between disciplines,'[3] proposing an alternative understanding thereof, with all the controversy that such a move necessarily entails. This has led to mutually exclusive criticisms: Yannaras has been criticised *both* with subordinating theology to philosophy *and* with subordinating theology to philosophy, for exhibiting *both* a disregard for Orthodox Christianity's continuity in tradition[4] *and* a traditionalist fixation on the past, for maintaining *both* a Greek anti-Westernism[5] *and* a fervent, uncompromising cosmopolitanism that denies the Greek nation-state to the point of undermining it.[6]

Born in 1935, Christos Yannaras studied theology at the University of Athens and subsequently proceeded to study philosophy in Bonn, Germany (1964-67) and to undertake doctoral research in philosophy at Sorbonne

---

literature is increasing its pace, with new studies appearing in English and other languages.

1. Russell, 'Christos Yannaras', 725. See also Norman Russell, 'The Enduring Significance of Christos Yannaras: Some Further Works in Translation', *International Journal for the Study of the Christian Church* 16, no. 1 (January 2, 2016): 58–65, doi:10.1080/1474225X.2016.1152448.

2. Apart from English, these include French, Italian, German, Finnish, Polish, Slovenian, Russian, Romanian, Bulgarian, Ukrainian and Serbian, while some translations in other languages are underway.

3. Jonathan Cole, 'The Communo-Centric Political Theology of Christos Yannaras in Conversation with Oliver O'Donovan' in *Mustard Seeds in the Public Square*, ed. Sotiris Mitralexis (Wilmington, Delaware: Vernon Press, 2017), 62.

4. See, for example, the reactions to his *Freedom of Morality*, detailed in Christos Yannaras, *Τὰ Καθ' Ἑαυτόν [Autobiographical Sketch]* (Athens: Ikaros, 1995), 95-100.

5. Vasilios N. Makrides, 'Orthodox Anti-Westernism Today: A Hindrance to European Integration?', *International Journal for the Study of the Christian Church* 9, no. 3 (2009): 209-24; Pantelis Kalaitzidis, Ἑλληνικότητα Καὶ Ἀντι-Δυτικισμὸς Στὴ Θεολογία Τοῦ '60' ['Greekness and Anti-Westernism in the Theology of the '60s'] (PhD diss., Aristotle University of Thessaloniki, 2008), 209-584.

6. Yorgos Karambelias, Ἡ Ἀποστασία Τῶν Διανοουμένων [The Intellectuals' Apostasy] (Athens: Enallaktikes Ekdoseis, 2012), 229-71.

University–Paris IV (*Faculté des Lettres et Sciences Humaines*). A doctorate in theology from the University of Thessaloniki would follow. His visiting professorships in philosophy in Paris, Geneva, Lausanne, and Crete would be followed by a professorship in philosophy and cultural diplomacy at the Panteion University of Social and Political Sciences in Athens, which sparked an intense public debate on the relationship between philosophy and theology (1982). It would be safe to say that no other thinker has had such a profound influence on the development of modern Greek theology.

The rediscovery of the Patristic legacy, the engagement with the thought of the Russian diaspora (particularly Vladimir Lossky), the encounter with the corporeality of tradition and ecclesial life as well as the challenges put forth by the philosophical thought of Martin Heidegger and, later, Ludwig Wittgenstein are the elements that initially sparked Christos Yannaras' theological originality. Having already played an important role in the gradual turn from pietism and scholasticism to the new era of Orthodox theology in Greece through the publication of the journal *Synoro* (1964-67), Yannaras proceeded to receive theological stimuli such as Lossky's underscoring of the importance of personhood and to articulate an original synthesis, culminating in his *critical* and *relational* ontology of the person, which has yet to be systematically and comprehensively engaged with to an adequate degree.[1]

The title of this book, *Polis, Ontology, Ecclesial Event*, hints at its three parts: Yannaras' political thought,[2] his philosophy, and his theology respectively. The centre of gravity is on the first part, political thought, and the third part on the life of the Church is the shortest one, something which is *not* representative of the foci in Yannaras' oeuvre: there, philosophy would be ranked first and theology second – if we are, in an un-Yannaric way, to draw a line between the two – with political thought ranking third. This seeming lack of balance, owing to the conference's

---

1. Having first been translated in French, Yannaras' books started becoming available in English mostly after the 2000s, usually translated by the indefatigable Norman Russell. Consequently, an English *reception* of his thought (and not merely an overview) is still pending, despite Yannaras' enormous influence in Greece and Orthodox theology.
2. An important distinction needs to be made between Yannaras' treatises in political philosophy and theology, which will be discussed in the first part of this book, and his journalistic weekly *feuilletons*, first in the Greek newspaper *To Vima* and then in *Kathimerini*. While it should normally be obvious that weekly political commentaries and systematic political treatises are not the same thing and should not be treated as such, this distinction has not always been retained and respected (Kalaitzidis' Ἑλληνικότητα Καὶ Ἀντι-Δυτικισμός' is an example of such a confusion), leading to unavoidable yet systematic misreadings.

discussions, is rectified in treating this book as complementary to the forthcoming *Christos Yannaras: Philosophy, Theology, Culture*, edited by Andreas Andreopoulos and Demetrios Harper (London: Routledge, forthcoming in 2018), which emerges from the 2013 conference in Oxford[1] and focuses more on theology.

The book starts with **Dionysios Skliris**' take on Christos Yannaras' engagement with political philosophy and theology. Skliris observes Yannaras' complex relation not only with political theology, but with Marxism as well; Yannaras does assume a sort of humanist and Aristotelian Marx, by exalting the contribution of the German philosopher to a paradigm shift in the history of Western thought. The latter consists in situating man's essence in his praxis, his goal being the realisation of his specific difference, a view that brings Marx close not only to Aristotelian teleology, but also to the Greek Patristic tradition. However, according to Skliris, Yannaras also performs a deconstructive lecture of Marx, since he highlights the latter's contradictions, while trying to open the Marxist text to novel interpretations against the scientism and the positivism that prevailed in Marxism as an official ideology of socialist regimes. After Skliris' critical engagement with Yannaras' ideas, **Jonathan Cole** proceeds to question the charge of 'anti-Westernism' in Yannaras' thought. Cole places that purported 'anti-Westernism' in new perspective by considering the way that the problematic of contemporary Greek identity and the lived experience of Greek political disorder have shaped Christos Yannaras' critique of the 'West' and his political thought more generally. According to Cole, Yannaras' politico-ontological proposal to reconceive politics as the common human struggle for truth and authentic existence, which he retrieves from his Greek and Orthodox tradition, aims to resolve the problematic of Greek identity and Greek political order. Thus, although intimately bound to the particularity of the Greek context, Yannaras' political ontology offers a transcultural proposal that can provide a potent basis for dialogue with Western theologians.

In the third chapter, **Angelos Gounopoulos** explores further elements of political theology in the work of Christos Yannaras, which, as Gounopoulos contends, is based on the 'freedom of relationship' as the ontological foundation both of the *polis* and of the ecclesia of Christ. The author analyses the semantic content that the Greek philosopher ascribes to the terms 'polis' and 'ecclesia' and puts them in dialogue with other versions of Western political theologies in order to understand the

1. 'Conference dedicated to Christos Yannaras: Philosophy, Theology, Culture', organised by the Orthodox Theological Research Forum at St Edmund Hall, Oxford, 2-5 September 2013.

way Yannaras correlates theology, the ecclesial event and political life. In the last chapter of the first part, **Paul Tyson** applies Yannaras' insights to more contemporary concerns: he states that the *polis* is intended as a discursive deliberative community that pursues the common good as an act of human freedom. In our day, however, power is increasingly defined by the global non-political necessities of international force; whilst globalisation offers the hope of the first truly inclusive community of human communities, in practise human freedom – indeed the freedom to be human – is under threat. Tyson examines the Greek referendum of 2015 as a case study in the triumph of necessity over freedom and explores, with the help of Yannaras' critique, how appreciating the dynamics of the *personal*-relational mode of existence is vital in resisting the unreality and violent necessity of our times.

The second part of the book shifts the focus to philosophy. **Deborah Casewell**'s 'Loving in Relation to Nothing: On Alterity and Relationality' juxtaposes Christos Yannaras to Emmanuel Levinas. Casewell notes their similarity, as both Yannaras and Levinas base their thought on Heidegger in an effort to transcend ontotheology in different ways: Yannaras to regain an apophatic account of God as beyond being, and Levinas to avoid the totalising violence that he sees ontology is when defined as static, abstract being. Furthermore, she engages with Yannaras' relational philosophy of the person and compares it with Levinas, for whom it is the interpersonal relation in the encounter with the other rather than ontology that is 'first philosophy'. Casewell proceeds to determine what Yannaras' account of relationality through incarnation and love can add to Levinas' knowledge of God through absence, and whether, with their love of Heidegger's account of nothingness, Levinas or Yannaras presents a more inviting account of human interrelatedness and the being of God. Following this, **Sotiris Mitralexis** presents Yannaras' critical ontology by attempting a reading of his book of the same name via three 'triads': relation, *logos,* and consciousness; substance, particulars, and activities; and, lastly, otherness, art, and participation.

The succession of chapters continues with **Daniel Isai** bringing Yannaras' apophaticism in dialogue with Jean-Luc Marion's philosophy via the Dionysian corpus, also highlighting phenomenology's theological turn. In Chapter Eight, **Marcello La Matina** employs Yannaras' relational philosophy of language in order to apply it to *musical sound* and its philosophical implications, linking sound to ontology. The second part concludes with **Nikolaos Koronaios**' 'Education as Freedom: An Attempt to Explore the Role of Education through Christos Yannaras' Thought'. In order to clarify the 'meaning' of education, the author presents Yannaras' distinction between 'utilitarianism' and 'communal relations', leading to an enquiry into the relationship of education and freedom. Turning to the life of the Church, Part Three opens with **Andreas Andreopoulos'** critical view of the Council of Crete – i.e. the 'Holy and Great Council of the Orthodox Church' held in Kolymvari, Crete, from 19 to 26 June 2016, in which ten out of the fourteen autocephalous local churches of the Eastern Orthodox Church participated in dialogue with Yannaras' insights. In Chapter Eleven, **Brandon Gallaher** provides a re-evaluation of Christos Yannaras' theological critique to the West, not approaching it as triumphalist anti-Westernism anymore but rather as Yannaras' declared *self-critique* as a Westerner.

It is an honour and joy to be able to conclude this volume by reprinting Lord Williams' review article on 'The Theology of Personhood: A Study of the Thought of Christos Yannaras'. First published in 1972 in *Sobornost*, when **Rowan Williams** was a student at Oxford and Cambridge and before his 1975 DPhil thesis on Vladimir Lossky, this is a detailed engagement with Christos Yannaras' 1970 doctoral thesis in theology at the University of Thessaloniki entitled 'The Ontological Content of the Theological Notion of Personhood' (*Τὸ Ὀντολογικὸν περιεχόμενον τῆς θεολογικῆς ἐννοίας τοῦ προσώπου*), the first part of what would later become *Person and Eros*. While Yannaras was one of the first theologians to write theology in *demotiki*, the vernacular everyday form of the Greek language, the thesis was by necessity and university regulations written in the obscure and now abolished *katharevousa*, an artificial compromise between Ancient Greek and the vernacular of the time. Rowan Williams' article is thus one of the earliest (if not *the* earliest) cases of international engagement with Yannaras' theology that, to the best of my knowledge, has not been reprinted before. This truly indispensable paper for the study of Yannaras' thought is now made available again thanks to the kind permission of the author and *Sobornost*, with some minor adaptations in the footnotes' bibliographical information.

*

This volume is primarily aimed at scholars already possessing an overview of Yannaras' thought and is not necessarily meant as an introduction to his *oeuvre*. For the sake of those readers that have not read Yannaras' works before and in lieu of an introduction to their primary tenets, I will proceed to an attempt at recapitulating the main lines of his thought.[1]

---

1. The following is based on my paper 'Person, Eros, Critical Ontology: An Attempt to Recapitulate Christos Yannaras Philosophy', first published in *Sobornost* 34:1

Christos Yannaras has written extensively on ontology, epistemology, ethics, theology, and politics. He has been characterised as 'Greece's greatest contemporary thinker' (Olivier Clément)[1] and 'one of the most significant Christian philosophers in Europe' (Rowan Williams),[2] whereas Andrew Louth describes him as 'without doubt the most important living Greek Orthodox theologian.'[3] A simple categorisation of his voluminous *corpus* would be to classify his main works according to the branches of philosophy to which they pertain. Thus one may classify the works *Person and Eros, Relational Ontology, Propositions for a Critical Ontology* etc. under ontology/metaphysics, the works *On the Absence and Unknowability of God: Heidegger and the Areopagite, The Effable and the Ineffable: the Linguistic Limits of Metaphysics* under epistemology, and finally *The Freedom of Morality* under ethics. Other notable contributions include treatises on social philosophy (*Rationality and Social Practice*), political economy (*The Real and the Imaginary in Political Economy*), the relation between contemporary physics and philosophy (*Postmodern Metaphysics*), philosophy of religion (*Against Religion: the Alienation of the Ecclesial Event*), and the historical background of the clash of civilisations (*Orthodoxy and the West*).

Yet Yannaras himself has provided us with a much better approach than this arbitrary categorisation. In his latest book in Greek under the title *Six Philosophical Paintings*[4] – which I would describe as a 'philosophical autobiography' – he introduces us to his thought in a manner that reflects the whole spectrum of his contribution to philosophy. I shall attempt to present such a prioritisation here by primarily referring to that particular book as encapsulating Yannaras' most mature and recapitulatory thought, while considering other areas of his research such as his political philosophy or his purely ecclesial writings as a corollary of this main body of ideas.

To approach Yannaras' work we must first consider the importance and scope of the term 'apophaticism' for him, which is exhaustively grounded in the Greek Patristic corpus in both *On the Absence and Unknowability of God: Heidegger and the Areopagite* and *Person and*

(2012): 34-40.
1. In his preface to Christos Yannaras, *De l'absence et de l'inconnaissance de Dieu d'après les écrits aéropagitiques et Martin Heidegger*, trans. Jacques Touraille (Paris: Cerf, 1971).
2. See Rowan Williams' endorsement on the back cover of Yannaras' HC Press translations.
3. In his introduction to Yannaras' *On the Absence and Unknowability of God* (London: T. & T. Clark, 2005), 1.
4. Yannaras, Ἔξι φιλοσοφικὲς ζωγραφιές [*Six Philosophical Paintings*] (Athens: Ikaros, 2011).

Eros. It is the Areopagite corpus and Maximus the Confessor's works that provide Yannaras with primary sources for the most explicit elucidations of apophaticism in the Patristic tradition.

The term 'apophaticism' is usually understood as a method to speak about God in theology, as the 'via negativa', that is to say by defining God not through the characteristics that God has, but through the characteristics that God *does not* have (in-effable, etc.). Yannaras, however, saw in apophaticism something immensely wider in importance, namely the epistemological tendency of the whole of Hellenic/Greek civilisation from the time of Heraclitus (with his famous quote, 'for if we are in communion with each other, we are in truth, but if we exist privately, we are in error')[1] to that of Gregory Palamas. As an overall *stance* and *attitude* towards the question of the nature of knowledge and truth, towards epistemology, and not as a *theory* on epistemology, explicit formulations concerning this apophatic *stance* can only be found in fragmentary form in the corpus of Greek texts and seldom as a systematic exposition. As is almost always the case with the epistemological attitude of a civilisation, this attitude cannot but be *implicit*, as it is taken for granted in the context of that civilisation itself.

According to Yannaras, apophaticism is the stance towards the verification of knowledge that underlines every facet of this civilisation and can be defined as 'the refusal to exhaust truth in its formulations, the refusal to identify the understanding of the signifier with the knowledge of the signified.'[2] Formulations of truth can only *refer* to the signified truth or knowledge, not exhaust it. By coming to know the formulations that refer to truth, one does not *know* truth – truth can only be lived, experienced, and as such it is not static. There is a gap of crucial cognitive importance between the signifier and its signified reality.

In an apophatic epistemology, the individual cannot conceive truth individually as a finite formulation. Truth lies in the field of experience and, more specifically, shared experience because 'there is no relation that does not constitute an experience and there is no experience . . . not arising from a relation or establishing a relation. Moreover, relation is the foundational mode of the human logical subject: the way in which Man exists, knows and is *known*.'[3]

Truth can only be attained through shared experience, communed experience, or life in communion, and cannot be confined in finite formulations.[4] This excludes the possibility of *a priori* truths, prescribed

---

1. Diels-Kranz, *Fragmente der Vorsokratiker*, Band I, 148, 28-30.
2. Yannaras, Ἕξι φιλοσοφικὲς ζωγραφιές, 32.
3. Ibid., 58.
4. Yannaras often reminds us of Democritus' example about the 'bitter honey', Diels-Kranz, II, 119, 22-6.

doctrines and axiomatic theories.[1] Yannaras writes: 'Prerequisite and criterion for critical thinking (that is, thinking that strives to discern right from wrong, truth from falsehood) was the communal verification of knowledge.'[2] According to him, 'communed experience and not the accuracy of the individual's intellectual faculty verifies knowledge, even if proper communion of experience presupposes the accuracy of intellectual faculties'.[3] These signifiers allow us 'to share our common reference to reality and experience, but cannot replace the cognitive experience itself. This obvious difference can only then be understood when the criterion of the critical function is the communal verification of knowledge.'[4]

I must here note that Yannaras' apophatic epistemology and the usual understanding of apophaticism (in the context of the study of religion and theology) as the *via negativa* that banishes knowledge to the realm of mysticism are not merely different, but can be seen as polar opposites of each other. The cataphatic approach (either to the understanding of God in theology or of *anything else* in general) would be to attribute characteristics to something and attest that these characteristics truly reflect the nature of their object or phenomenon. *Via negativa* is the choice of negative attributes or of non-attributes in our attempt to encircle reality and knowledge with our intellect. The *via negativa* consists in the attempt to progressively claim the knowledge of an object or phenomenon by *rejecting* certain characteristics or attributes, by defining it in terms of what it is *not*, in order to arrive at a closer intellectual understanding that excludes certain errors and misconceptions. In this context, true knowledge – and above all transcendental knowledge – can only be achieved in the realm of radical subjectivity, in the realm of 'mysticism', without any possibility of sharing it effectively through language and without any vital reference to the community that would exclude the transmutation of radical subjectivity into radical individualism. However, apophatic epistemology, i.e. the refusal to exhaust truth in its formulations and the refusal to identify the understanding of the signifier with the knowledge of its signified reality, lies beyond this polarisation between cataphaticism and *via negativa* and beyond a choice of negations rather than affirmations: it is based on the symbolic character of every epistemic expression. Apophaticism sees language as *referring to* truth and reality, *signifying* reality and *iconising* it,[5] while not exhausting it. It is not *negation*,

1. Ἔξι φιλοσοφικὲς ζωγραφιές, 26.
2. Ibid., 25.
3. Ibid.
4. Ibid., 27.
5. On the iconising function, cf. Yannaras, *Person and Eros* (Brookline, MA: Holy Cross, 2007), 184-7.

but the *signifying/semantic function* that characterises the relationship between language and reality. As such, language is not an obstacle hindering us from achieving an individualistic 'mystical' knowledge, but a medium to share, to commune knowledge and truth and an attempt at a communal participation to it. This elevates the communal verification of knowledge to a criterion of knowledge itself.

So, whereas the *via negativa* is usually understood as *anti-realism*, apophaticism for Yannaras is the prerequisite for realism and realism is the goal of apophaticism. Or rather realism is the *stance and attitude* that is guaranteed by a consistent apophaticism.

Knowledge emerges from participating in experience, not from the understanding of a linguistic formulation. 'And the experience is not exhausted in what is affirmed by the senses,' writes Yannaras. 'Nor is it simply an intellectual fact – a coincidence of meaning with the object of thought. Nor is it even an escape into a nebulous "mysticism", into individual existential "experiences" beyond any social verification. By the word *experience* I mean here the totality of the multifaceted fact of *relation* of the subject with other subjects, as also the relation of the subject with the objective givens of the reality surrounding us.'[1]

For Yannaras, every ontological system or statement presupposes and is based on the epistemology on which it is built, i.e. the criteria through which knowledge is considered as valid or invalid.

That is why, he remarks, 'we conclude from history that common epistemology (incorporated in the everyday life of the people) and not common ontology constitute a common civilisation, i.e. the otherness of common way of life: it is not the content we attribute to truth, but it is the way in which cognitive validity is confirmed that confers otherness in shaping public life, identity of civilisation, and ensures the historical continuity of that cultural otherness.'[2] Therefore, the criterion of the communal validation of knowledge is a crucial prerequisite for the understanding of the ancient Greek ontology and the early Christian ontology as well.

This apophatic epistemology, this communal epistemology, refers the possibility of 'existence in truth' not in the individual level, but in the field of the relations between logical 'othernesses', relations that manifest the 'other' in these 'othernesses'. The most suitable term for the will-to-relate, not as a quality of the individual but as a way of being, a mode of existence, is ἔρως. 'For Plato, the fullest knowledge is love, ἔρως: a relationship that attains freedom from all selfishness,

---

1. Yannaras, *Person and Eros*, xiii-xiv.
2. Yannaras, Ἔξι φιλοσοφικὲς ζωγραφιές, 45.

that attains the offering of the self to the other.'[1] If valid knowledge and truth can only be attained through a self-transcendent relation with existence, then the mode of truly existing is the transcendental relation, ἔρως according to the Greek language and the Platonic and Areopagite writings.

With the word ἔρως, we are introduced to the first of the two elements that constitute Yannaras' ontology of the person (or more precisely, *prosopocentric ontology*, as it is termed in proposition 12.3.2 of *Relational Ontology*; I use this term in order to discern it from personalism),[2] the 'person' (πρόσωπον) being the second.[3] 'The replies given to the ontological question, as I have identified them in the particular philosophical tradition that I have studied, may be summarised under two basic terms: person and ἔρως,' Yannaras writes. 'In the Greek philosophical literature of the early Christian and medieval periods, the starting-point for approaching the fact of existence in itself is the reality of the *person*. And the mode of this approach which makes the person accessible to knowledge is ἔρως.'[4]

Ἔρως here means what it meant for the author of the Dionysian corpus or for Maximus the Confessor, i.e. self-transcendence, the offering of the self to the other. If we define the subject merely as

1. Ibid., 26.
2. Cf. Zizioulas' distinction between personalism and the ontology of personhood (*prosopocentric ontology*) in his *The One and the Many*, 19-24. Zizioulas regards their comparison as a 'superficial association in terminology' (p. 20), noting that no substantial similarities exist between these two approaches, as the term 'person' bears a different semantic content in each case. As such, references to an 'Orthodox personalism' remain unsubstantiated. I would say that Zizioulas' explanation is wholly applicable to Yannaras' works as well; the ontology of personhood (*prosopocentric ontology*) is not to be regarded as a stream of thought within (or parallel to) personalism in which the term 'person' denotes an individual – instead of a being of relations and otherness.
3. After the publication of Yannaras' breakthrough studies on the importance of the notion of πρόσωπον for philosophy through Patristic thought in 1970, Zizioulas' 'Personhood and Being' (first published in 1977 in Greek and subsequently in English in *Being as Communion*, 27-65) offered a comprehensive analysis of the development, content and importance of the term from ancient Greek philosophy to Patristic thought and came to be recognized as a landmark publication on this ontological proposal in the English-speaking world. Confusingly enough, this contains a long footnote (in 44-6) downgrading Yannaras' 1970 dissertation, i.e. the very source of this prosopocentric understanding of theology and philosophy of which 'Personhood and Being' is such a fine specimen, as wholly subjecting Patristic thought to Heidegger's ontology, thereby alienating it from its source. In my opinion, the cited arguments bear little or no relevance to Yannaras' actual text.
4. Yannaras, *Person and Eros*, xiii.

an individual, as ἄτομον, as an undifferentiated unit of a whole that cannot be further divided,[1] then by definition it cannot manifest ἔρως.

In this semantic frame, only the person (πρόσωπον) can manifest ἔρως, and πρόσωπον is a word with an absolutely unique semantic content. It is constituted of the words πρὸς (towards, with direction to) and ὤψ/ὤπὸς (face, eye), so that it defines someone whose face looks at, or rather is directed towards, someone or something.[2] Someone that exists in-relation-to, only in relation and in reference to other beings, someone who refers his existence to the other, coming out of his existential individuality; someone who exists only by participating in relations and relationships.[3] So, πρόσωπον is not merely defined as reference and relation but it defines a reference and relation itself.[4] This entails that personhood is the only possible relationship with beings, as beings are 'things set opposite', 'ἀντι-κείμενα' in Greek, 'Gegen-stände' in German, etc. Being is manifested only in relation to the person and as such beings emerge as phenomena, they appear/are disclosed in the horizon of personal relation.[5] Yannaras adds, in a Heideggerian tone, 'beings are (εἶναι) only as phenomena, only insofar as they become accessible to a referential relation or disclosure. We cannot speak of the *being-in-itself* of beings; we can speak only of being-there or being-present (παρ-εἶναι), of co-existence with the possibility of their disclosure. We know beings as presence (παρ-ουσία), not as substance (οὐσία).'[6]

From early Christian times the word person, πρόσωπον, was very wisely identified with the word hypostasis, meaning actual existence. 'The fact that the identification of the terms person and hypostasis was originally used to logically clarify meta-physical references of the ecclesial experience does not restrict this identification from being used in the field of anthropology. However, a prerequisite for that would be to retain the communed experience of relations as the criterion of the formulations in language.'[7] These pairs of terms, person/hypostasis (πρόσωπον/ὑπόστασις) and substance/nature (οὐσία/φύσις) were first defined and at some point agreed upon and elaborated (as there were many different schools of terminology before the Cappadocians) in

1. See Yannaras, Ἔξι φιλοσοφικὲς ζωγραφιές, 61.
2. Ibid., 63.
3. Ibid., 103.
4. Yannaras, *Person and Eros*, 5.
5. Ibid., 6.
6. Ibid. This first chapter of *Person and Eros* provides a thorough analysis of the signifier πρόσωπον and its implications for philosophy.
7. Yannaras, Ἔξι φιλοσοφικὲς ζωγραφιές, 104.

relation to God and Christology. This, however, only reflects the way in which the philosophers and Church Fathers articulated their understanding of the world in language: these terms cannot be reserved exclusively for Christology, as they also reflect the Church Fathers' approach to ontology.

Yannaras observes that 'self-transcendent love, ἔρως, was recognised in the philosophical language of the Christianised Hellenic and Byzantine civilisation as the highest existential attainment (or fullness and causal principle) of freedom'.[1] Freedom, because self-transcendence is not really self-transcendence until the subject is freed even from the necessities and prerequisites of his own substance (οὐσία).[2] This can only happen if the hypostasis of the subject, the actual and specific manifestation of its substance, has an ontological priority over its substance and is not restricted to the constraintments and prerequisites of its substance.

According to the Patristic corpus, the testimony of the ecclesial experience identifies such a priority in the case of God, a trinity of persons/hypostases with common substance. It is being testified in the case of Jesus Christ, who transcends the necessities/prerequisites of his divine substance/nature ('logical' necessities of being outside the boundaries of time, space, the cycle of life and death) without losing it or impairing it by being incarnated as a human being, a crying baby in the manger, in a very specific time and place, and by dying on the cross. He transcends the necessities/prerequisites of his acquired human substance/nature through the resurrection. Ecclesial experience testifies man as being made 'in the image of God' and in the image of this triune existence-as-πρόσωπον, establishing man's capability to transcend by grace the necessities/prerequisites of his substance and nature through its hypostatic manifestation.[3]

With the co-ordinates of person, ἔρως and otherness, Yannaras builds a 'relational ontology'. He states 'otherness is realised and known in-relation-to-the-other, always relationally. It is an outcome and an experience of relation and relationship. Through this perspective, we can speak (with logical consistency) of a relational ontology.'[4] Relation and relationship is never granted or finite, but a dynamic event which is continually found or lost, a fact which can be traced in our human

---

1. Ibid., 60.
2. There is a crucial difference between being freed from the *necessities* and *prerequisites* of one's own substance and being freed *from the substance itself*: overseeing this difference has led to much confusion.
3. Ibid., 74.
4. Ibid., 58.

experience. Given the apophatic nature of the epistemology on which we base 'propositions for an ontological interpretation of existence and reality that are subject to critical verification or refutation',[1] Yannaras concludes a relational ontology can only be a 'critical ontology'.[2] He defines 'critical ontology' as follows:

> We term onto-logy the theoretical investigation of existence (τὸν λόγον περὶ τοῦ ὄντος), the logical propositions for the interpretation of reality. We try, with our rational faculties, to interpret reality and existence as to the fact that it is real and that it exists. We try to interpret the meaning of existence, the cause and purpose of existence.
>
> With the word 'critical' we term the process of evaluating ontological propositions, evaluating the logical accuracy of these propositions on the grounds of κοινὸς λόγος (i.e. common sense, word, rationality, language and understanding), evaluating the capability of the ontological propositions to be empirically verified through shared, communed experience accessible to all.[3]

Propositions of a critical ontology are never finite, granted, or 'closed': they are always subject to communal verification or refutation, to the communal criterion of truth, due to the fact that there is no way of individually 'securing the truth' of said propositions.

According to Yannaras, every attempt to continue the philosophical tradition of the ancient Greek or Christianised Hellenic and Byzantine civilisation without the fundamental prerequisite of apophaticism is inherently dysfunctional. He writes 'despite the post-Roman West's boasting of inheriting and continuing the ancient Greek tradition of philosophy and science, the refutation of the fundamental characteristics of Hellenism, i.e. apophaticism and the communal criterion, leaves no room for the validity of such a claim'.[4] Based on this, Yannaras argues the reception of classical and Christian thought in the West was crucially undermined by the reversal of its epistemological preconditions and their replacement with epistemological criteria that are entirely based on the individual's capacity to think rationally (*facultas rationis*), a criterion that the West ascribes to the philosophical legacy of Aristotle.

---

1. Ibid., 54.
2. As such, I will use these terms interchangeably, as synonyms. To be precise, a relational ontology is the outcome of a consistently critical stance towards ontology.
3. Yannaras, Ἕξι φιλοσοφικὲς ζωγραφιές, 51.
4. Ibid., 35.

I will come to the philosophical importance of the activities (ἐνέργειαι) for Yannaras and their relation to the hypostatic manifestation of the substance in Chapter Six of this book. But I must stress here that Yannaras regards the activities as absolutely important for a coherent ontological terminology. He remarks that '[A]n ontology which (out of conviction or ignorance) denies to discern the substance/nature and the hypostasis from the activities of substance/nature, which are hypostatically manifested is condemned to an irreversible deficit of realism; it is trapped in the separation and dissociation of thinking (νοεῖν) and existence (εἶναι).'[1] This insistence in the *concreteness* and realism of philosophical reasoning remains a priority throughout Yannaras' work.

*

As noted in the beginning, we are currently witnessing the *beginning* of a more sustained and systematic engagement with Yannaras' multifaceted work in Anglophone scholarship: a new phase, in which many of Yannaras' books are finally available in English, putting an end to the monopoly of second-hand engagement with his thought, mediated mainly through Greek scholars writing in English,[2] which was so often the case until recently. Even though a collective volume such as this constitutes by definition secondary literature on Yannaras (and even though some of the contributors are indeed Greek), we remain with the hope that this book can act as a 'bridge' to this new era.

---

1. Yannaras, Ἔξι φιλοσοφικὲς ζωγραφιές, 101.
2. Apart from the few books by Yannaras that were indeed available in English in previous decades, and apart from Francophone scholarship, an exception to this would include Anglophone scholars reading Yannaras through French translations, which were in relative abundance, with six major titles available prior to the 1990s.

Part I
POLIS

Part I

POLIS

Chapter One
Christos Yannaras' Political Ontology:
An Introductory Sketch
Dionysios Skliris

Christos Yannaras' stance toward political theology is ambivalent. However, his reluctance does not concern the possibility of political theology as such. On the contrary, he wonders if there can be any Theology in the authentic sense of the word that is not *already* political in character. Yannaras' scepticism rather concerns the redundancy of the adjective 'political' in the expression 'political theology', since politics is anyhow included in theology. One of the first and most important mentions of the expression 'political theology' takes place in the title of an early book named precisely *Chapters in Political Theology*. It is a collection of articles in the daily newspaper *To Vima*, written during the period 1974-1975; that is, just before and after the fall of the military junta of the colonels (1967-1974). Greece had recently emerged from a far-right military regime, which had served the purposes of the Cold War, having also played a very negative role in the crisis of Cyprus which led to the occupation of a large part of the island by Turkey. The ideological alibi of the dictatorship was a sort of oversimplified moralist fusion of Christianity and Greek nationalism, which was supposed to counterbalance the ideology of internationalist – and therefore supposedly 'anti-Greek' – communism. During the dictatorship, Yannaras felt the need to claim an alternative version of synthesis between Hellenism and Christianity that was contrary to the official state ideology, the latter serving a naïve and more or less fascist anticommunism.

During the first years of the rehabilitation of democracy, Yannaras felt an opposite obligation. This was an age of a long hoped for democracy, as the fall of the junta had inaugurated a new prestige for the Left. The latter equally meant a deferred transfer to Greece of the spirit of a whole European generation, which had May 1968 as its point of reference. In this context, Yannaras engaged in a serious theological dialogue with the thought of Karl Marx, focusing on the most humanistic aspects of an early period. He equally assumed the method as well as the findings of the Frankfurt School (thinkers like Theodor Adorno, Herbert Marcuse or Jürgen Habermas were the favourite interlocutors in his writings). At the same time, Yannaras did not completely follow the spirit of a subversive euphoria which prevailed, neither did he agree with all the causes of the longed for 'Change' (the slogan which prevailed in Greece during the 1970s and 1980s). He was engaged rather in an effort to criticise the shortcomings of his contemporary Modern Greeks, a critique which is nevertheless exercised with love for his compatriots and which regards Modern Greek civilisation as the last offspring of a long political tradition encompassing both the ancient polis and the communities of the Byzantine and Ottoman Empires. This is a narrative of continuation not in a national sense, as in most nationalistic ideologies, but in a civilisational one, focusing on the political significance of civilisation. This consideration of Modern Greece as the last descendant of a long tradition, which was both continued and negated as Greece was turned into a tiny nation-state which betrayed the ecumenical character of Hellenism, makes Yannaras both severe and tender with his compatriots. He criticises them for new shortcomings, like the combination of a new consumerist spirit with an ideology of easy leftism. At the same time, he is trying to detect the genealogy of Modern Greeks' hostile attitude toward the State in the historical experience of Modern Greece between the Byzantine tradition, the Ottoman past and the ambiguous relationship with the West. It is thus in this context that Yannaras' ambivalent dialogue with 'Political Theology' takes place.

By putting the term 'political theology' in the title of his work *Chapters in Political Theology*, Yannaras is entering into dialogue with an emphasis on political theology that we find mostly in leftist movements of this age, such as the 'Theology of Liberation'. Yannaras is sceptical toward such movements. While he does have sympathy for the struggle of oppressed people against colonialism or the consequences of dominant capitalism in geopolitical matters, he thinks that political theology is a new form of ideology which originates from the Western metaphysical tradition. The basic subject of Yannaras' thought during the whole decade is the Eastern Orthodox comprehension of the person in contradistinction with Western individualism and, correspondingly, the ethos of the community in opposition to an impersonal and objectified intellectualistic morality. At a more theological level, Christos Yannaras is trying to bring the attention back to the ecclesial mode of existence which is to be found in the ecclesial community, i.e. in the life of the parish. The latter was threatened by religious organisations which spread a spirit of pietistic moralism in the post-war decades in Greece. Yannaras views the success of religious organisations of Pietistic leanings as a symptom of large-scale urbanism and of the subsequent loss of communitarian life. But another symptom of this same urbanism which deconstructed the communitarian tradition was exactly this combination of a leftist dominant discourse with a new tendency for uninhibited consumerism.

It is in this historical context that Yannaras is sceptical toward the 'Theology of Liberation'. Even though Yannaras, with his major book *The Freedom of Morality*, is seen himself as a principal theologian of liberation in post-war Greece, especially concerning ethics,[1] he would like to see the 'Theology of Liberation' complemented by an opposite 'Theology of Engagement'; that is, an engagement in the net of relations which constitute a living community and its communion with the transcendent other. Yannaras' critique toward a prevailing form of political theology[2] could be summarised in the following four points:

i) At a more fundamental level, Christos Yannaras is distinguishing between different metaphysics, which constitute the presuppositions of different civilisations. He thus thinks that the current versions of political theology are based on a special mentality of claiming individual rights. The notion of human rights is generally considered to be one of the greatest contributions of Western civilisation to a progressive potential of emancipation. But, already in this early work Yannaras regards the notion of human rights as the most characteristic symptom of a civilisation, which he chose to criticise for its impact. For Yannaras, the logic of human rights entails an individualist vindication which alienates man, turning him into an 'impersonal social unit, a neutralised object of economic and cultural amelioration'.[3] This critique will be developed thoroughly in his later work about *The Inhumanity of Right*,[4] but it can be found in this early work in a seminal form. For Yannaras, the ideology of human rights is the backbone of Western civilisation, since the kind

1. See Yannaras, *The Freedom of Morality* (Crestwood, NY: St Vladimir's Seminary Press, 1984).
2. For a brief sketch of this critique, see Yannaras, 'A Note on Political Theology', in *The Meaning of Reality: Essays on Existence and Communion, Eros and History*, ed. Gregory Edwards and Herman A. Middleton (Los Angeles; Athens: Sebastian Press ; Indiktos, 2011), 149-52.
3. Yannaras, *Κεφάλαια Πολιτικῆς Θεολογίας [Chapters in Political Theology]* (Athens: Grigoris, 1983), 11.
4. Yannaras, Ἡ Ἀπανθρωπία Τοῦ Δικαιώματος *[The Inhumanity of Right]* (Athens: Domos, 1998).

of person who claims rights is the individual which is separated from the community and vindicates them in the name of an abstract version of his nature. It is to be noted that Yannaras is here a brave and counter-intuitive thinker: when he wishes to criticise a civilisation, he does not point to its obvious shortcomings but to what is generally considered its main achievement.

ii) There seems to be an even deeper problem from a Christian point of view. This refers not only to the individualist vindication of rights in the context of Western or globalised civilisation, but to the practice of *social denunciation* as such. In a slightly posterior work, Yannaras makes a contradistinction which is very important for understanding his stance:

> A true witness of the truth of the Church denounces social injustice and lack of freedom, knowing that the root of evil is inside him, in human nature itself. He is thus not opposing adversaries, but strives for the healing of our common nature and bears as his personal cross both the existence of the oppressed and that of the oppressor. When a true faithful criticises evil, his speech does not have the relentlessness of the ideologist who wants to annihilate his adversary in order for his just cause to shine through; on the contrary, his speech has the sincerity of love that is ready for sacrifice in order to save the reproached one. This reception and affirmation of the other even through the most violent criticism is the crucial difference between one the one hand the true ecclesial person, and, on the other, the ideologist of Christian Socialist or Christian Democratic leanings.[1]

Yannaras is more radical here: it is social denunciation *per se* which is deemed incompatible with the ecclesial way of life, especially if such a denunciation is committed in the name of an ideology which judges the other persons outside me and divides persons into good oppressed ones and bad oppressors. Of course, an ulterior question which might be posed here is what happens when omitting social denunciation de facto puts the ecclesial man on the side of the oppressors inside a system of structural exploitation. It is to be noted that Yannaras' stance is in no way the classic right-wing argument that one should search for evil primarily in the private sphere of individual psychology and only consequently in the public one. Quite the contrary: Yannaras thinks that leftist social denunciation is after all a form of ideological judgment (κατάκρισις), which is not fundamentally different from right-wing private moralism.

---

1. Yannaras, Ἡ Νεοελληνικὴ Ταυτότητα [*Modern Greek Identity*] (Athens: Grigoris, 1978), 198-9.

This question has a special acuteness for the ecclesial person who is called 'not to judge, for he too will be judged' (Matthew 7:1). The question is thus whether or not one could combine the need for social and political denunciation with an ecclesial mode of existence which consists exactly in abstaining from judging, so that a person can assume the cause of evil in his own self. Yannaras' answer is that one should avoid ideological denunciation from the stance of righteousness. In a sense, being always right is being always *right*: ideological self-righteousness is always a sort of right-wing moralism, even if it chooses to point to the social level instead of the private/psychological one which is usually the favourite target of typical right-wing ideologists.

iii) Another reproach is that political theology is more or less integrated inside 'Apologetics'; that is, a sort of rear-guard combat of a Christianity that is losing its influence and thus tries to keep pace with the evolutions of Modernity. In this sense, it could be viewed as originating in an inferiority complex, as Christians try to reformulate their faith in a secularised context without having the self-confidence of the past. Christianity's historical defeat sometimes leads to a need for a psychological overcompensation, as Christians try to convince atheist thinkers that everything of value already exists inside Christianity. Yannaras describes in a vivid way this 'novel interpretation' (or should one say 'alienation'?): '[E]ngaged theologians try to interpret the Gospel of man's salvation borrowing the categories of Marxist and Neo-Marxist Left.' The Bible is thus turned into a 'text of political morality or a theory of revolution, in order to bring classless society'; 'a political demonstration is regarded as an act of worship, a political placard becomes a symbol of faith, unity in political action is considered as the new form of ecclesial communion'.[1] Yannaras is not against actualisation of faith, as such. He is reacting against efforts of a re-actualisation of Christian faith which stay at the level of ideological variation and do not delve into ontology.

iv) To make a long story short, Yannaras' problem seems to be the adjective 'political' in 'political theology'. He considers the term 'political theology' to be an effort to bridge *a posteriori* a certain dualism between the political and the transcendent, which is typical of Western Christianity.[2] But this need for bridging presupposes an inherent split between theology and politics. This means that the bridging cannot but be ideological, that this is an attempt to hide the fact that at the deeper ontological level the realities of secular politics and transcendent theology are radically alien to one another. In his 'Note on Political Theology' Yannaras asks

1.   Yannaras, *Κεφάλαια Πολιτικῆς Θεολογίας* [*Chapters in Political Theology*], 10.
2.   Ibid., 9.

the question: 'Why isn't it sufficient for me – purely and simply – to register myself with a political party or become a revolutionary? Why is it necessary that I be, in addition, also Christian?'[1] In a civilisation where theology is opposed to secular politics at a deeper ontological level, trying to rediscover the theological character of politics acts as an alibi or as an a posteriori justification for a political activity that we would pursue in any case, even if we were not Christians. Yannaras' own bent is for a version where politics and theology would be interwoven in such a way that theology itself would be already political in character. In other words, he aspires for a paradigm where it would suffice to say the word 'theology' and politics would be immediately entailed.

Yannaras' critique of what he perceives as the prevailing way of doing political theology is quite interesting, but it is also very harsh. One could say that it is interesting precisely because it is very harsh. A number of objections could be raised when replying to it. It could be argued that political theology is not exhausted to the extent Yannaras presumes, but includes other forms or touches upon matters that ought to be treated. For example, one might argue that there can be a non-individualistic theory of human rights, in which the latter would originate in a sense of human dignity, which is not given in nature, but emerges inside a community. In this sense, one does not vindicate something that is considered as inherent in her abstract nature, which she possesses as an individual. On the contrary, she claims a dignity coming not from an essentialist past, but from a future horizon of values to which humanity is progressing. The question of whether human rights can be conceived only in an individualistic way or if there could be ground also for a communitarian understanding is an open issue and Yannaras' critique should be taken into account in this on-going debate. With regard to social denunciation, it could be argued that what Political Theology brings is exactly the possibility to criticise the structural and institutionalised sin, which is quite different from the personal one. The structural and institutionalised sin takes the form of what is called 'facticity' (facticité, Faktizität) in existentialism, ossifications of human freedom which become an obstacle for future human freedom, due to which human persons cannot but be sinful as well as unfree. Structural and institutionalised sin cannot be generalised to personal sin. For example, it is different to be a hateful egoist in one's personal life and to follow politics and practices as a member of one's social class or as a participant in a colonialist power or an international institution which perpetuates oppression. The problem with Christianity is that on many occasions Christians do show love at a personal level, for example

1. Yannaras, 'A Note on Political Theology', 150.

through loving charity, while they let themselves be integrated inside the practices of a capitalistic system, which perpetuates exploitation. At other times, Christians might preach the gospel of salvation, while letting themselves become instruments of a colonialist power which uses them for its own purposes. In some cases, institutionalised and structural sin might coexist with good personal intentions, even with sincere love at the personal level. For example, a philanthropist might sincerely love the recipient of charity while contributing to his further exploitation. Such cases might be seen as a serious reason for a distinct political theology to engage in a special form of denunciation. It is to be noted that Yannaras himself speaks of a 'political sin', as when 'the polis is extinct and the citizen becomes alienated by turning into a passive partisan of ideologies or an objectified component of totalitarian mechanisms'.[1] The problematic of a distinct 'political sin' is present in Yannaras' thought, but he is anxious not to turn social denunciation into yet another form of a Pharisean moralism. It could also be argued that political theology might be not only a re-actualisation of Christian tradition in a new secularised context, but also Christianity's self-reflection or self-criticism about its complicity with practices and systems of oppression and exploitation. The latter are necessary not only in the West, but also in the Orthodox world, where Christianity often allowed itself to be used by autocratic forms of power.

Yannaras seems to follow a particular logic, according to which a Christian might engage in political acts, such as defending powerless and underprivileged people who suffer injustice, so long as she does not turn this engagement into an ideology proper. He insists on the need to avoid the self-righteousness of the ideologist, which is incompatible with the ethos of continuous repentance found in the ecclesial mode of being, in which persons are called to assume evil in themselves instead of projecting it to others. This theological stance is indeed very precious and can hardly be exaggerated. On the other hand, we should not be led into a kind of phobia of consciousness and self-reflection. If Yannaras' logic is followed literally, Christians could be engaged in politics and act, as long as they do not consciously justify this act and engagement. This could indeed mean an authentic ecclesial ethos of constant repentance without self-righteousness. It could also lead to a phobia toward or even an eclipse of any reflection and, even worse, self-reflection on Christian political acts and commitments. Political theology is thus needed as such a critical self-reflection. It is important to avoid a sort of Modernist Neo-Apollinarianism, according to which everything could be received in ecclesial life except consciousness and self-reflection. On the contrary, an anti-Apollinarian Christian

1. Yannaras, Ἡ Νεοελληνικὴ Ταυτότητα [The Modern Greek Identity], 220.

stance could mean an abiding assumption of self-reflection, thought and awareness about participation in political debates. Yannaras does himself stress the importance of self-consciousness, as we shall observe later.

What is much more interesting than defending political theology against Yannaras' criticism is to examine how he himself articulates an alternative kind of political theology, in the name of which he criticises its current versions. After all, Yannaras does not reject political theology altogether. The title of his work remains *Chapters in Political Theology*, which means that he affirms political theology as an endeavour. He just tries to propose an alternative type of political theology, which could be termed an 'ontological', 'prosopo-centric' and 'apophatic' political theology. Yannaras' stance could be summarised in the view that every genuine political theology is already political in character. Instead of opposing theology and politics as two distinct domains of transcendence and secular immanence and then try to reunite them a posteriori at the ideological level, one should rather focus on how theology could describe the ecclesial event and thus on how the Church is already a political community, albeit a peculiar one which is alternative to the world while at the same time responding to its existential thirst. Nikolai Fedotov once said that 'the political theory of the Church is the truth of the Trinity'. The Church is, however, a divine-human community: it is both an image of the Trinitarian life as it was revealed by the head of the Church, i.e. the Christ, and a community which engages human persons in an organised as well as a dynamical way of life, in which dangers of new sin and failure might emerge.

The three fundamental dimensions of a particularly ecclesial political theology would thus be ontology, respect for personhood and apophaticism. The emphasis on ontology means that political theology is examined as a mode of existence that focusses on what the human person is in her 'nature' and 'truth' ('κατὰ φύσιν, κατ' ἀλήθειαν ἄνθρωπος').[1] Political theology is thus not an ideological statement but a response to the human person's deepest political nature, to her drive for love which constitutes the presupposition for every political communion. It is true that the Eucharistic community is an eschatological reality, but this eschatological reality responds to the deepest ontological demands of human nature, to which the polis also tries to respond. The polis and the Ecclesia endeavour to respond to the same quests of humanity, even if the former constitutes a historical articulation whereas the latter an eschatological anticipation. Politics is the struggle for living according to truth ('ἄθλημα τοῦ κατ' ἀλήθειαν βίου'[2]) and the Ecclesia is the eschatological end to this

1. Yannaras, *Κεφάλαια Πολιτικῆς Θεολογίας [Chapters in Political Theology]*, 12.
2. Yannaras, *Ἡ Εὐρώπη Γεννήθηκε Ἀπὸ Τὸ Σχίσμα [The Great Schism Engendered*

struggle, which guides us already inside History. An ecclesial political theology entails a 'radical rejection of the objectification of man and the world and thus a spectacular change in the function of economy as well as of the political and social structures'.[1] Ecclesial ontology is thus necessarily based on the truth of the person, in the sense that 'salvation does not concern the impersonal historical becoming, but a personal struggle with our own nature and its passions: salvation belongs to man's dynamical truth and not to the logic of History'.[2]

This emphasis on the truth of the person means that when Yannaras is writing his works in the 1970s and 1980s, he assumes a double struggle against the totalitarian practices of both capitalism and communism. In fact, an ecclesial political theology would be called to transcend the polarisation between individualism and collectivism inherent in Western modernity.[3] In the fundamental modern dilemma, capitalist individualism sacrifices equality in the name of freedom, whereas socialistic collectivism sacrifices freedom in the name of equality.[4] Behind this false dilemma, Christos Yannaras discerns a common tendency of modernity to objectify and quantify the world and the human person, the latter being related to the modern turn towards mechanical causality.[5] Yannaras' critique takes place in the name of a traditional civilisation. However, his position does not entail the return to a medieval past. Yannaras' stance is rather that of a man of post-war modernism, who experiences the impasses of modernity from the inside and who thus searches for a way out of modernity's constitutive dilemmas. Yannaras engages in dialogue mostly with thinkers who are critical of modernity from the inside, such as Friedrich Nietzsche, Karl Marx, Martin Heidegger, Hannah Arendt, Jean-Paul Sartre, Ludwig Wittgenstein, Karl Popper, thinkers of the Frankfurt School such as Theodor Adorno, Herbert Marcuse and Jürgen Habermas, etc. Yannaras receives the critical and humanistic aspect of Marxism, but he rejects the scientism and positivism of the supposedly 'scientific Marxism'. He notes that it was Engels who saw Marxism as the scientific equivalent of Darwinism.[6] In other words, during the nineteenth century Darwinism emerged as a capitalist imaginary of a Hobbesian war of all against all. Conversely, Marxism claimed to be another, more scientific world-view,

---

Europe] (Athens: Ikaros, 2015), 32-5.
1. Yannaras, Ἡ Νεοελληνικὴ Ταυτότητα [*The Modern Greek Identity*], 106.
2. Yannaras, Κεφάλαια Πολιτικῆς Θεολογίας [*Chapters in Political Theology*]. 101.
3. Yannaras, Ἡ Νεοελληνικὴ Ταυτότητα [*The Modern Greek Identity*], 10.
4. Ibid., 89.
5. Ibid., 15-16.
6. Ibid., 21-31.

imposing its own particular determinism. For Yannaras, both disregard the dynamical freedom of human personhood in its ontological stance toward the mystery of death. In his opinion, capitalism and Marxism constitute two complementary dimensions of one sole civilisation of repression of death and of the person's ontological truth in her struggle with it.[1] It is to be noted that Yannaras was writing these texts at the end of the Cold War in Greece, which was a borderline country between the capitalist West and the socialist East. Greece was thus a peculiar space where the question of transcendence of a false dilemma could be put with a specific acuteness.

Consequently, the third dimension of an ecclesial political theology is apophaticism. The latter means the denial to identify God with the intellectual idols and imaginary fictions that we employ in order to approach God through our reason. The political dimension of an apophatic ecclesial theology would be to equally deny what the human person has committed inside History. Apophaticism entails an eschatological 'do not judge, or you too will be judged' (Matthew 7:1), by which we avoid the demonisation of political opponents and their moralist/ideologist denunciation. Consequently, apophaticism opposes any form of totalitarianism by attributing a special importance to the respect of human failure. The quest for an apophatic political theology took the form of what Christos Yannaras has termed 'Critical Ontology'. Before examining the latter, it is crucial to examine Yannaras' dialogue with Marxist thought and the way in which he utilised elements of the latter in the direction of an ontological political theology.

Christos Yannaras' Dialogue with Karl Marx: Towards an 'Aristotelian Marxism'

The dialogue with Marxism took place at the end of the 1970s and the beginning of the 1980s, during the period after the fall of the military junta of the colonels in 1974 when Marxism had a renewed influence in Greek society. Some important currents were the supposed rediscovery of an early 'humanistic' Marxism as well as novel readings, such as the one by Louis Althusser and by the Frankfurt School. A part of this influence was a special Christian-Marxist dialogue which culminated in 1983. Christos Yannaras was one of the most prominent figures of this dialogue, but his stance toward Marxism was ambivalent. On the one hand, he exalts Marxism's critical function and the fact that it constituted one of the first efforts in the West to articulate an ontology of relation

---

1. Ibid., 19.

and activity (in the sense of the Aristotelian ἐνέργεια). Yannaras thus claims a Neo-Aristotelian Marxism that emphasises praxis and energeia as the specific difference of human beings. On the other hand, he criticises the positivism or even scientism of official Marxism: the latter was the *post mortem* fate of Marxist thought as the official ideology of socialist states. In an ironic twist, Yannaras views this Marxistic scientism as another form of the same alienation discerned by Marx himself in capitalist society. What Yannaras strives for is thus a rediscovery of an 'Aristotelian' Marxist dynamic and a consequent novel interpretation of Marxism in the direction of a neo-Marxist humanism of relation and activity (ἐνέργεια). This project is summed up in the following points:

i) Yannaras most enthusiastically endorses Marx's critique of the alienation which takes place in the frame of the capitalist mode of production, focusing on the remark that the latter deprives man of the specific features of his way of acting.[1] At the same time, Yannaras wishes to follow a much broader genealogy of alienation. Following Max Weber, he explains alienation by a 'certain religious conception of an abstract version of life and the world'.[2] The root of alienation is thus not the capitalist-industrial mode of production, but rationalism, the latter having appeared already at the time of Thomas Aquinas and scholasticism. Rationalism begins with the meaning of *ratio* as a 'capacity of the subject to recognise the essence of things and to conceive the being of beings in itself'.[3] Industrial capitalism might be linked with the emergence of a new emphasis on mechanical causation in the beginning of modernity, but the latter is not only related to nominalism, but also to intellectualist realism. According to Yannaras, behind false dualisms, such as nominalism versus realism or voluntarism versus intellectualism, there is a common background: rationalism as a whole, entailing an alienation of man by admitting him as an abstract unit. The result of rationalism was an ongoing quantification to the detriment of qualitative criteria. The false dilemma between capitalism and socialism is thus but a late offspring in a long history of Western dualisms having rationalism as their core[4] and totalitarianism as the necessary result. Totalitarianism is something different from autocracy, despotism or

---

1. Yannaras, Ὀρθὸς Λόγος καὶ Κοινωνικὴ Πρακτικὴ *[Rationality and Social Practice]* (Athens: Domos, 2006), 34.
2. Ibid., 37.
3. Ibid., 15.
4. For an evaluation of the Marxist version of quantification, see Yannaras, Προτάσεις Κριτικῆς Ὀντολογίας *[Propositions for a Critical Ontology]* (Athens: Domos, 1985), 125-6.

tyranny, which are to be found in many traditional societies, including orthodox ones. Totalitarianism emerges as a meeting between rationalism and historicism,[1] i.e. on the one hand, the abstract version of the human individual and, on the other, the consideration that there is an inherent meaning in human history which is intended by this rationalism. Even though this combination took place already in the late Middle Ages and early modernity, what we find in late modernity is the 'rational-scientific perfection of methods of imposing power and the development of a technology of controlling individual and collective activity'.[2] Yannaras follows a deconstructive reading of Marxism. He assumes the Marxist critique of alienation, but he turns this same critique against official Marxism. It could also be said that he points to an internal contradiction between the early emancipatory Marxism of the nineteenth century and its later evolution in the twentieth. Yannaras' endeavour is to save the freedom of human personhood against two opposite totalitarianisms, namely the capitalist one, justly criticised by Marx, and the socialist one.

ii) The importance of Marxist thought lies in the fact that the critique of alienation takes place in the name of a very concrete consideration of the human condition, nature and historicity. Yannaras expresses his agreement with fundamental features of this consideration. What Marx brings to the history of Western thought is the consideration of human existence as a relation,[3] as well as the position that the human creativity which distinguishes man from animals is also an event of relation.[4] In his reading, Yannaras vindicates an 'Aristotelian' Marx, or, if you wish, a 'Hellenic' Marx. The question put by Yannaras after Marx, Aristotle and the Greek Patristic tradition is what constitutes the specific difference of man ('τὸ ἰδιαζόντως ἀνθρώπινον'); that is, his difference from animals. A Marxist answer would be that whereas animals are identified with their vital activity, the vital activity of man is an object of his will and consciousness.[5] This means that man produces in a way that is free from natural necessity and he thus confirms himself as a specifying essence through the formation of the external world. The nature is thus presented as the work of man who can discern himself in a world that he has himself

1. Yannaras, Ὀρθὸς Λόγος καὶ Κοινωνικὴ Πρακτικὴ [*Rationality and Social Practice*], 59. In these observations about totalitarianism, Yannaras is influenced by Karl Popper.
2. Ibid., 46.
3. Ibid., 103.
4. Ibid., 122.
5. Ibid., 124.

created.[1] Aristotle and Marx coincide in a peculiar teleology, according to which the goal of man is the realisation of his specific difference. This would also be the position of the Greek-speaking Patristic tradition, from which Yannaras is inspired. For Marx this specific difference consists in man's productivity and creativity, namely in the fact that man is the only being that can form the world through his act and work. In this sense, the world as man's work objectifies man's specific difference from animals, whereas 'man's creative relation with matter verifies man's particularity, man's humanness'.[2] Marx thus begins from a critique of alienation inside capitalism in order to arrive at a teleological theory about the specific difference of man from animals. It is here that a dialogue with the Greek Fathers could prove very fruitful. One equally observes in Marx an emphasis in historicity: being as a meaning of beings is identified to their own historicity, comprehension of which can only be achieved by men.[3] But Marx is a materialist philosopher in that this particularly human historicity is based on man's body as a dynamical event of acted relations,[4] which include consciousness itself. Yannaras celebrates Marxist materialism, finding affinities with the Hellenic Patristic tradition, which supposedly emphasises concrete corporeality,[5] and with the participation of matter to the full actualisation of man's capacities. He adds that by considering corporeality as an acted relation, Marx introduces the notion of activities (Energien – Kräfte – Tätigkeiten) as a third ontological category next to those of essence and substance, which were the only ontological categories recognised by the Western philosophical tradition.[6] This means, according to Yannaras' lecture, that Marx rediscovers the 'energeia', i.e. the third pole of the Greek Patristic tradition, which was lost when Thomas Aquinas identified essence and act. What is more, human activity is considered not in its individual but in its collective form in the context of the communist vision. This Marxist vision of communism seems to achieve the most important demand raised by Yannaras in view of a genuine Political Theology, namely the realisation of what man is in his true nature ('κατὰ φύσιν καὶ κατ' ἀλήθειαν ἄνθρωπος').[7] In other words, communism entails an

---

1. Ibid., 126.
2. Ibid., 127.
3. Ibid., 100.
4. Ibid., 105.
5. See Yannaras, Ἡ Μεταφυσικὴ τοῦ Σώματος [The Metaphysics of the Body] (Athens: Dodoni, 1971).
6. Yannaras, Ὀρθὸς Λόγος καὶ Κοινωνικὴ Πρακτικὴ [Rationality and Social Practice], 115.
7. Ibid., 136.

ontology and not only an ideology or morality. The 'ought' of morality is reunited with the 'being' of ontology[1] and the latter is understood in a communal dimension.

iii) The endeavour to retrieve an Aristotelian Marxism which would revive the most fundamental ontological categories of the Greek Patristic tradition, such as *energeia*, seems to imply that a certain interpretation of Marxism fulfils most of the demands for a genuine political theology that were made by Yannaras in the early 1970s. This is only one part of Yannaras' reading, however. A second part consists of what one might term a 'deconstructive' reading of Marx by Yannaras. In other words, Yannaras tries to highlight the internal contradictions of Marxist thought, which might annul the liberating character of some initial intuitions. The most fundamental contradiction discerned by Yannaras is the following:

> In Marx man's specific difference is that he is producing in a way that is free from natural necessity. This means that freedom from natural necessity precedes and defines the reaction to natural necessity; it determines every reaction, including the formation of the superstructure. The sole basis of material needs is not a necessary and sufficient condition for the emergence of creative productivity and of the concomitant superstructure, since this same basis does not lead animals into relations of creative production and the concomitant superstructure.[2]

In other words, Marx insists on human freedom from natural necessity when trying to discern the human specific particularity. Conversely, he also supports a quasi-deterministic relation between base and superstructure, which seems to refute this initial human freedom. Consequently, consciousness acquires in Marx the form of an instinct.[3] But the notion of human particularity, in the name of which Marx criticised the alienation caused by industrial capitalism, seems to be eliminated. On the one hand, Marx

> attributes an ontological content to human relations, since it is they that constitute subjective otherness as an existential even. He thus distinguishes the freedom of relation from its

1. Yannaras, *Τὸ Πραγματικὸ καὶ τὸ Φαντασιῶδες στὴν Πολιτικὴ Οἰκονομία [The Real and the Imaginary in Political Economy]* (Athens: Domos 2006), 151.
2. Yannaras, *Προτάσεις Κριτικῆς Ὀντολογίας [Propositions for a Critical Ontology]*, 84.
3. Ibid., 85.

alienation into dependency, absorption, subordination and exploitation. On the other, Marx interprets conscious relations as well as the total becoming of historical relations through a blind and mechanistic determinism, which eliminates every possibility of human freedom.[1]

Yannaras distinguishes between two aspects of Marx. On the one hand, we find the ontologist who discovers human particularity in creativity and its teleology and thus criticises alienation as a form of deep existential failure. On the other hand, we find the determinist who seeks a scientific understanding of the history of relations which are constituted through creativity. The latter ends up refuting the notion of freedom which was the point of departure of the Marxist critique: Marx 'introduces the most radical break with Western metaphysics by attributing an ontological content to the activities of the subject, thus interpreting reality as an event of relations'.[2] At the same time, Marx remains imprisoned in some ontological presuppositions of this same metaphysics, as though he 'hesitated to draw the conclusions of the new ontological perspective that he himself had opened'.[3] It should be noted that the position of Marx in the history of thought is a borderline one. He could be considered as a predecessor of the critical stance of Modernist thinkers who have showed the impasses of Modernity. He is equally very well placed in the context of nineteenth-century positivism or even scientism. This contradiction became too obvious in Marxists of the Middle-War period, who had to remain faithful to a sort of Marxist positivist determinism at the same time as the modern scientific paradigm was being shattered due to the fascinating new evolution, in the theory of indeterminacy or relativity, e.g. in quantum mechanics.

What should be our stance toward this contradiction today? Yannaras agrees with Popper that scientific Marxism is now dead. For Yannaras, however, the Marxist contradictions constitute points of departure for new dynamical understandings of the human existential adventure.[4] What Yannaras proposes is a new connection between Marxism and the findings in the realm of linguistics, psychoanalysis and the sciences of consciousness. This endeavour was popular at the time when Yannaras was writing his major works on political philosophy. One can remember for example the connection between Marxism, Lacanian psychoanalysis and structuralist linguistics in the thought of Louis Althusser. The particularity of Yannaras' effort is that these connections are brought

---

1. Ibid., 88.
2. Ibid., 122.
3. Ibid., 122.
4. Ibid., 90.

into contact with Greek Patristic thought. In the latter, the praxis and the *energeia* also constitute expressive 'logoi' (see, for example, the thought of Maximus the Confessor or Gregory Palamas). Creative acts are thus 'signifiers of the subjective otherness of the actor';[1] they are *logoi* in the sense that this notion bears in Maximus the Confessor. If man's creative act is such a 'logos', then Yannaras feels entitled to ask what the criterion is for the real needs that move history. If human needs are not exclusively material but rather are linked to the creative and expressive character of the productivity of the human person, then the consciousness of a need precedes its satisfaction and thus a consciousness of the insufficiency of the current system of productive relations might lead to the assumption of revolutionary initiative.[2] Consciousness is thus a constitutive feature and not a superstructure. The determination of real needs is linked not only to consciousness but also to language and its symbolic systems. It is thus the semantic of needs which precedes and determines a common revolutionary dynamic of subversion in the current system of productive relations.[3] The underestimation of language by Marx leads him into contradictions, such as when he speaks of 'commodity fetishism'. But how can fetishism emerge without language and its significations?

In conclusion, Yannaras points to the need not to stay at the level of simple production, but proceed to that of the act (πρᾶξις). The latter is a significant activity which includes language (or an *energeia* including the *logos* in a Patristic idiom). Through his deconstructive reading of Marx, Yannaras tries to open up the texts in the direction of a less positivist and more apophatic interpretation of Marxism concerning the act inside history. This is linked to a more general project that Yannaras terms 'Critical Ontology', the latter being close to what one could name an 'apophatic' version of political theology.

Critical Ontology: Toward an Apophatic Political Theology

In his endeavour for a critical ontology, Yannaras is inspired by a quest of Western Modernity that goes back as far as Immanuel Kant, even though his immediate sources are Karl Popper and Jürgen Habermas. Criticism highlights the social valorisation of critical thought as an intersubjective function of verification resulting in attributing a social

---

1. Ibid., 96.
2. Ibid., 99.
3. Ibid., 100.

character to the Kantian critique of pure reason.[1] Yannaras' further goal is to link criticism to the apophatic and communal ontology of the Greek Patristic tradition. For Yannaras, criticism consists in the 'possibility to use reason in a way that is subject to verification or falsification, thus avoiding the subjection of knowledge to dogmatism'.[2] Yannaras insists on the principle of falsifiability formulated by Karl Popper: the perpetual possibility of experimental control entails a permanent possibility of falsification, i.e. the possibility of replacing one scientific hypothesis with another which can in turn be falsified.[3] Falsifiability is thus the ultimate criterion of rationality. Yannaras concedes to Popper's principle, but he remarks that it lacks an ontological foundation. He is interested in a criticism that would not only be a gnosiological method, but also a stance and a way of life.[4] If one extreme to be avoided is dogmatism and a priori intellectualism, the other is the degeneration of criticism into relativism and a priori agnosticism. Yannaras is again engaged in a double struggle following a project with an interior tension. Criticism and ontology might be considered contradictory, as was the case in Post-Kantian thought. Yannaras tries to combine them, a fact that provokes a tension in his thought. The same is true with the more general tendency of his thought to articulate a phenomenological metaphysic.[5] Ontology is based on a 'version of the existence of the subject and its cognitive function as an event of relation and a dynamic of communion'.[6] This consideration can be 'an ontological foundation of criticism, a critical stance which verifies knowledge with the criterion not of methodological correctness . . . but of that of saving the relationship and avoiding the alienation of the subject and its cognitive function'.[7] If ontology helps criticism to avoid turning into relativism, conversely criticism helps ontology to be critical toward truth by adopting the falsifiability of knowledge.[8] Yannaras thus reaches critical ontology by following an internal critique on criticism: 'A consistent

---

1. Yannaras, Ὀρθὸς Λόγος καὶ Κοινωνικὴ Πρακτικὴ [Rationality and Social Practice], 82.
2. Ibid., 210.
3. Ibid., 87.
4. Ibid., 91.
5. For ways in which metaphysics could be admitted in the context of a critical ontology, see Yannaras, Προτάσεις Κριτικῆς Ὀντολογίας [Propositions for a Critical Ontology], 47.
6. Yannaras, Ὀρθὸς Λόγος καὶ Κοινωνικὴ Πρακτικὴ [Rationality and Social Practice], 180.
7. Ibid., 180.
8. Ibid., 92.

criticism would lead us to be critical toward itself as well and thus pose the question: Is criticism a truly liberating project in all its aspects?'[1] For Yannaras, philosophy must continue posing the ontological question at all costs, or risk becoming an *ancilla scientiae*.[2] He wishes to combine the best features from different worlds. For example, he searches for an overcoming of the opposition between causality and freedom by asking the following questions:

> Is it possible to have an ontological interpretation of existence without explaining it by a causal principle of Being and Becoming, a principle which nevertheless would not constitute an a priori necessity that would predetermine the being and the becoming, but would critically verify the event of existence as an achievement of freedom? Is it possible to explain being by an otherness to every predetermination and by freedom from every necessity? Is it possible to overcome the opposition between freedom and causality, to consider a dynamical realisation of the event of existence which would exclude every aprioristic version of truth?[3]

In his work *Propositions for a Critical Ontology* Yannaras defines the latter as an 'answer to the ontological question which is subject to critical verification, thus responding to the principle of falsifiability of knowledge, by transferring the possibility of verification of cognitive propositions to experience'.[4] Yannaras' version of empiricism is not exhausted in the data of the senses, but includes the entirety of givenness as it is offered in relation,[5] rather reminiscent of a phenomenological approach. In his own terms he is following a 'revisionist empiricism'.[6] The latter is also linked to ancient Greek thought, in which truth is approached through 'theory' (θεωρία) in a rather optical sense of the term.[7] Truth thus becomes an event of relation, which is offered through an intersubjective experience of relation, according to the 'common logos' referred to by Heraclitus. Yannaras understands the 'apophatic' approach to truth in the following way:

1. Ibid., 95.
2. Yannaras, Προτάσεις Κριτικῆς Ὀντολογίας [Propositions for a Critical Ontology], 64.
3. Yannaras, Ὀρθὸς Λόγος καὶ Κοινωνικὴ Πρακτικὴ [Rationality and Social Practice], 98.
4. Yannaras, Προτάσεις Κριτικῆς Ὀντολογίας [Propositions for a Critical Ontology], 21.
5. Ibid., 38.
6. Ibid., 135.
7. Ibid., 28.

the formulations of meaning point to the experience of relationship without exhausting it, since relation is acted as a manifestation and revelation of the existential otherness of the subject. Every semantic formulation of the common experience is symbolical in character, since it puts together (συν-βάλλειν) subjective experiences.[1]

Conceptual formulations do not conquer an idol or a fiction of truth. On the contrary, truth is identified with communion and knowledge becomes the event of an empirical relation which is subject to the verification of its authenticity or its alienation through an ongoing widening of communion.[2] When Yannaras speaks about verification, he does not merely mean a cognitive confirmation, but an ampler affirmation of ontological authenticity:

> The interpretation of the existential reality of the subject is open to a verification or falsification through the critique of relations that manifest subjective existence. If the dynamic of relation is altered, if it turns into non-relation, that is to subordination, subjection and exploitation, then the subjective existence is not true anymore, it becomes alien to its own self. . . .[3]

The subjective existence thus suffers alienation in an ontological sense of the word. In this sense, critical ontology presupposes freedom; only if we are free can there be a contingency between existential authenticity and alienation. At the end of his propositions, Yannaras recapitulates his endeavour as follows:

> Critical ontology founds its propositions on the existential self-consciousness of the subject as an experience of freedom and otherness. Freedom and otherness are approached as cognitive and empirical events through relation and its dynamic indeterminacy. The criterion of reality is the experience of relation with reality and the verification of this relation through a widening of communion – it is thus the indeterminate dynamic of the event of communion which constitutes History and civilisation. But for critical ontology truth is tantamount to relation. It is an achievement.[4]

---

1. Ibid., 23.
2. Ibid., 37.
3. Ibid., 81-2.
4. Ibid., 156.

Critical ontology thus presupposes a community that achieves its meaning in a metaphysical way,[1] but is at the same time apophatic in its definition.[2] Yannaras would rather regard this community in the context of the direct democracy of the ancient polis, since it is only the latter that is addressed to people who refuse to surrender their responsibility to representatives.[3] At the same time, the apophatic character of community implies the need to avoid a tyranny of the democratic majority. For Yannaras, apophaticism means that every institutional factor should be ready to be revoked.[4] The most important feature of an apophatic community would be respect for its members' failures to achieve the truth that it embodies.

A Critical Dialogue with Critical Ontology: Possible Objections and Possible Answers to These Objections

Given that the most important characteristic of critical ontology is its being perpetually open to critique following the principle of falsifiability, I think that the best way to honour this specific endeavour of Christos Yannaras is to enter into a critical dialogue with it. I would thus like to raise a series of objections, noting however that Yannaras' own work possesses the antidotes for some of them, if it is carefully read.

i) A first objection that could be raised is whether the communitarian version that critical ontology takes in the thought of Christos Yannaras could lead to a sort of what one could term 'gnosiological populism' or even 'ontological populism'. If truth is verified and falsified in a communal way according to the Heraclitean notion of the common *logos*, then what could prevent a gnosiological tyranny of the majority, in which the experience of the many would be the norm, whereas the experience of the few would be excluded? One must raise the obvious example: if the multitude of people have the experience that it is the sun that rotates around the earth, then the experience of a scientist that it is actually the earth that rotates around the sun would contradict a common experience and could thus be rejected. This Copernican example constitutes a usual initial objection to Yannaras' 'communal empiricism', but it is to be noted that Yannaras' work contains answers to such objections. Yannaras is by no means a 'populist', given

---

1. Yannaras, Πολιτιστικὴ Διπλωματία [*Cultural Diplomacy*] (Athens: Ikaros, 2001), 94.
2. For an apophatical understanding of rationality, see Yannaras, Ὀρθὸς Λόγος καὶ Κοινωνικὴ Πρακτικὴ [*Rationality and Social Practice*], 230.
3. Ibid., 285-6.
4. Ibid., 302.

a specific ontological and gnosiological meaning of 'populism'. It is true
that some positions in his work could give the impression of a populist
mindset; equally, other expressions could give the impression of elitism.
What is crucial is Yannaras' insistence on quality over quantity. In his
thought, truth is by no means located in the majority. On the contrary,
it could be saved by a small minority. It is to be noted that this was also
the stance of Heraclitus, the ancient Greek philosopher who is Yannaras'
source of inspiration. Heraclitus is famous for his formulation of the
theory of the 'common logos', according to which truth is tantamount to
communion and falsehood to seclusion in a private sphere. But he is also
notorious for his distrust of (or even misanthropy towards) the people of
Ephesos, making it hard to believe that he would locate truth in a simple
majority of its citizens. The priority of quality over quantity in the thought
of Yannaras is so fundamental that it makes it hard to believe that truth
in his thought would be a mere function of the quantitative majority of a
community. Besides, since truth is also referred to future experience, there
can always be a possibility that a truth which is preserved in the few will
be revealed in the future as more important than the truth of the majority.

A similar objection would be whether we find in Yannaras a sort of
'ontological populism', in which a minoritarian stance in a community
would be thrown to a sort of ontological Kaiadas. But here Yannaras
is even more explicit in the direction of a total respect of those who
have failed inside a community. The apophatic community entails a
'respect in act not only for disagreement and dissent, but also for
failure, deviation, inability of participation in the social relations, even
for a conscious effort of undermining them. Only such a total respect
can guarantee subjective freedom and the true salvation of subjective
otherness and the dynamics of relations that it constitutes.'[1] One should
not forget that the context of the early development of Yannaras'
thought is the struggle against totalitarianism, in what he perceived
as the two complementary versions of it, both the socialist/collectivist
and the capitalist one. The respect for failure is the touchstone for the
manifestation of truth as a constant struggle ('ἄθλημα') which takes
place through the active respect for personal otherness and subjective
differentiations.[2] 'Failure and deviation,' insists Yannaras, 'is an inherent
feature of the dynamic of relations; it is not the exception, but a symptom
that always follows us.'[3] There is thus plenty of room for failure in the
apophatic community.

---

1. Ibid., 315.
2. Ibid., 317.
3. Ibid., 318.

A similar but distinct question is what happens not with blatant failure, but with simple disagreement and especially with different experiences, which could lead to a novel value in the future. Let's give some well-discussed examples: what happens when a community regards slavery as a natural event and builds around it the net of relations that constitute its truth? Or, to bring a timely example, if a community considers that only heterosexual marriage can achieve truth, how can an alternative experience, namely the truth of a homosexual relationship, emerge? In general, what happens with minorities, the truths of whom are silenced and suppressed by the community? One can better follow Yannaras' position when truth resides in the dynamically acted relations of the community and an individual fails to co-ordinate himself with this truth. Problems emerge when an individual or a minority proposes an alternative truth, or, at least, an alternative experience which is in clash with the dominant one. Another question is how new truths and novel values might emerge inside a community like the one described by Yannaras, and how individuals might express divergent experiences which are not co-ordinated with those of the totality. In any case, it should be noted that Yannaras' emphasis on apophaticism includes an answer to such objections, but one would wish a more explicit development of thought about cases where alternative values emerge inside a community.

ii) The latter leads us to a second critical question: if a disagreement inside the community does emerge, what should be the criterion for solving it? Yannaras emphatically rejects the principle of majority. Truth is a question of quality and it can be saved in the few or even in one sole person. It can even temporarily eclipse. But what is then the criterion of truth? Traditional communities, such as those often referred to by Yannaras, had some specific procedures. For example, one can think of ecclesial communities, especially in the first millennium before the Schism. If some individuals or groups did not co-ordinate with the truth of the ecclesial body and expressed a heretical experience, there was a certain procedure which involved convening a synod of bishops so that each one expresses his local Church in the Spirit as well as the historical reception of the decisions of the Council by the totality of the ecclesial body. There are indeed striking cases in Church history where truth was preserved by a very small minority. One cannot help but remember Maximus the Confessor, who died in 662, being expelled from communion by all the Patriarchates of his age, but his theology triumphed two decades later in the Sixth Ecumenical Council (680-681). There was, however, a concrete procedure for judging the truth of the experience. Similar concrete procedures were the case in the democracies of ancient Greek cities. A related question is what happens with communities with epistemological value. Would we be ready to accept modern ways of verification and falsification such as the scientific experiment which usually takes places in the special conditions of a laboratory? Would we affirm such ways and methods of verification or falsification which are sometimes not immediately approachable by the totality of the community? In general, one cannot but admire Yannaras' capacity for pointing to the ontological depth of the questions and the way in which he is formulating them following a methodology of exposition drawn by Ludwig Wittgenstein. At the same time, Yannaras' reader might sometimes wish a greater concreteness about the criteria of truth, especially in cases of disagreement or split inside a community. And especially about cases where this disjunction is not only a matter of theoretical difference, but arises from a polyphony of different experiences inside a community.

iii) Another problem that arises in the communitarian critical ontology is that at some points one finds references to communion or communal verification or falsification without precisely defining the form of community referred to. Yannaras' critical ontology certainly makes sense as an ecclesiology. In the latter, the basic principles of critical ontology can be understood. It is true that in ecclesiology (at least an orthodox one, which is probably implied) truth arises through a co-ordination of experiences, whereas falsehood is the case with heresies which choose a partial (this is the etymological sense of αἵρεσις) experience to the detriment of the catholicity of experience. In the ecclesial community, truth is indeed not a matter of majority or numerical quantity but of quality. But in some mysterious way, the quality of truth is ultimately recognised even if it is abandoned by the great majority of the Church members and is saved only in the case of, perhaps, a sole hermit. One could equally say that the true Church is the opposite of totalitarianism, since it accepts its failed and sinful members through the mystery of repentance.[1] Yannaras states this in an even more provocative way by saying that the Church is built on the material of human failure and sin as the incarnated Wisdom of God takes this material to construct the new 'polis of the Kingdom, the body of the Resurrected Adam, the immediacy of the relation between the created and the uncreated, time and eternity'.[2] Here one could pose a series of new questions: are we entitled to identify (or to bring so close) the Ecclesia and the polis? The Ecclesia is a divine-human institution

---

1. Yannaras, Ἡ Νεοελληνικὴ Ταυτότητα [The Modern Greek Identity], 200.
2. Ibid., 221.

with Christ at its Head. It is open in the Spirit to the eschatological future of the Kingdom, where it is expected to achieve the truth of the goodwill of the Father. A question that is thus posed is what space is there for a sort of 'self-regulation' of the community (or 'self-institution', as Cornelius Castoriadis would put it). When Yannaras uses an abstract philosophical or ontological discourse, he may give the impression that it is the community and the sum of acted relations that realise truth. But in this sense the Ecclesia and the polis cannot be subsumed under the same generic category 'community' or 'communion'. In the Ecclesia, truth is achieved in a synergistic way through the co-operation of God and man; for example, in the decrees of ancient Church Councils we find expressions such as 'ἔδοξε τῷ Ἁγίῳ Πνεύματι καὶ ἡμῖν'. The ultimate truth is only eschatological. The cosmic polis does not always present this tension between history and eschatology or between the 'betrothal' and the 'marriage', to use the relevant imagery. It could of course be argued that the ancient polis also had a sacred character; it was not a product of convention as in the modern social contract, but reflected the cosmic relations of the 'mode of the articulation of the universe' ('τρόπος τῆς τοῦ παντὸς διοικήσεως', in the expression of Heraclitus). If we choose to subsume the Ecclesia and the polis under a common category of 'community', 'communion' or 'communal verification' then we risk two opposite things: either losing the eschatological character of the Church, which would be turned into a community of verification of historical truths; or, inversely, implying that the democratic polis too would have to wait for its truth to come from the outside, in full opposition to Castoriadis' famous notion of 'democratic self-institution'. (The latter would arguably be a very significant correction of Castoriadis by Yannaras.) The general issue that needs clarification is the relation of the community to otherness during the communal verification of knowledge. What could be meant by an eschatological character of the communal verification of knowledge as a synergy in the Spirit with the eschatological Christ who fulfils the goodwill of the Father? Meanwhile, in every polis, what is the importance of otherness, of the Other with a capital 'O', for its truth?

Such objections could be answered by pointing out that this is precisely what Yannaras' project of political theology is all about. An Ecclesial political theology means exactly this: to see the polis under the light of the Ecclesia and to observe the ecclesial responses to the ontological demands put forward by the polis. If we don't do this, we will either fall into a secularised political theology, which will be solely based in abstract moral and ideological principles, that is, in politics without theology, or we will inversely follow a 'celestial' and 'transcendental' theology referring to a parallel universe that does not relate to the thirst and desire of man's political nature. Those are exactly the two dangers that Yannaras wishes to avoid. A certain fusion between the Ecclesia and the polis is inevitable and inherent in the project of political theology put forward by Yannaras. It is also in some sense desirable as an important and interesting alternative to prevailing forms of political theology. At the same time, we must find ways to express a certain dialectical tension between the historical and the eschatological mode of the Ecclesia as a novel polis, as well as the relation between the human community and the divine otherness in their synergetic way of achieving truth. In any case, it could be argued that both eschatology and synergy are implicit in the notion of apophaticism as developed by Yannaras, so his work does include answers to such objections, if carefully read.

iv) But otherness is to be found also in cases of borderline subjects within the community. The notion of 'communal verification' in the thought of Yannaras gives the impression of quite a solid community which confirms or rejects the experiences of its members, even if this sometimes takes the form of a future 'truth-achievement' perpetually subject to falsifiability. But what happens when the truth is saved by someone who is outside the community or at its threshold? One can here think of the Greek communities during the Ottoman occupation, which is a favourite example of Yannaras. In these communities, it could be argued that the truth was saved by people who were outside them or had a complex relation with them, by being both inside and outside them. One can think of the 'kleftes', the 'brigands' who practised a sort of guerrilla warfare in the mountains outside the villages, thus preserving the spark of freedom. At another level, the truth of communities could be said to be achieved by the poets who often resided abroad and sometimes could not properly use the Greek language. George Seferis has famously spoken of 'our three great poets who did not know Greek', meaning the national poet Dionysios Solomos, Andreas Kalvos and Konstantinos Kavafis. Both the 'kleftes' and the poets could be said to be modally inside the community, even if they were spatially outside it. Their relation with the rest of the community, however, was a dialectical one, such as with the peasant who was a reaya (i.e. the subject of heavy taxation and oppression). Even inside the community there existed borderline subjects. For example, the elders in charge of the communities (δημογέροντες) and the Orthodox bishops could be seen both as the first representatives of the Greeks and as the last representatives of the Turks. On the one hand, their contribution was crucial for the maintenance of an order which would ensure tax collection, among other things. On the other hand, they represented the interests of Greeks before the Turkish authorities and it was they who were executed in case of rebellions, in which they sometimes wholeheartedly engaged. Even the 'kleftes' could change sides and become place-keepers for the Ottoman rule (ἀρματολοί) and vice versa. The Greek communities during Turk occupation were thus constituted by borderline subjects who were simultaneously inside and outside the community. What can this mean for the communal achievement of this community's truth?

Even in the Byzantine community one can pose the question of the dialectic between the empire and the desert. When Christianity was assumed by the Roman Empire, some Christians felt the need to abandon the cities and become anachorets, in order to save the eschatological perspective of the Christian vision. Eventually, new communities were developed around these hermits, the latter being alternative to the communities of the cities. (A similar question that emerged was whether it was the Emperor who should convene and preside over an Ecumenical Council or the first Patriarch in order, as the need for Church independence gradually emerged.) Anachoretism also took the form of 'fools for Christ' who could live inside the community but challenged its norms of conventional morality. All these are favourite topics in the works of Christos Yannaras. One would like him to examine in greater detail their significance for the achievement of truth in the community, in cases when some of its members are abandoning the official or the spatially defined community in order to achieve its profoundest truth in an alternative way. Even in cases of failures, one would wish to see a more lengthy discussion about what happens with different forms of sinners and outcasts such as the 'repentants' with a temporary privation of communion, the heretics, the provisionally schismatics or ethnic groups like the Jews and the Samaritans. Even in the ancient polis, it would be interesting to observe the significance of those who were ostracised for the truth of the community, since they were often expected to return to the city and play an important role in it, even if they were provisionally expelled. Besides, what was the importance of women, children, foreigners and slaves for the community? Or, at a political level, what was the dialectic relation between the 'first man' ('πρῶτος ἀνήρ' according to Thucydides), who was often a renowned general and/or orator like Pericles, and the people who would make the decisions in the context of immediate democracy? All these are questions which would be crucial in the discussion of how specific communities achieve their truth.

v) Fusion between the polis and the Ecclesia in the thought of Christos Yannaras poses one more problem which is pertinent to political theology. The secular polis, even a democratic one (in both the ancient and modern sense of democracy) cannot but be related to the 'kratos', i.e. power and domination. ('Kratos' is anyway to be found in the word 'democracy' itself.) On the contrary, the Ecclesia is constituted as a community of people who enter it freely with their baptism (without this free entrance totally excluding problems of power inside the Church; quite the contrary). The issue of power in the polis and the Ecclesia, as well in their relation, is linked to the question whether the Ecclesia could be conceived as a 'resistant' community in its relation to the states of this world; and to questions of resistance to domination inside the ecclesial community. Yannaras does have a lot to say about cases where freedom and relation are alienated and turned into relations of suppression and domination. But it would be equally crucial to develop the dialectical relation of the Ecclesia to the power of the world, as well as the question what happens when the Ecclesia itself or a part of it becomes a power of this world.

Conclusion

In concluding this paper, I would like to sum up what is the general stance, the philosophical gesture of Yannaras as a political philosopher and theologian. One could say that he initially puts himself in a position from which he could denounce false dualisms. He does for example denounce the false dualism between capitalism and socialist collectivism by discerning in both an underlying totalitarianism. The latter is supposedly inherent in Western rationalism and in a historicist approach which is tantamount to historical pantheism. He equally denounces the false dualisms between idealism and materialism,[1] transcendence and immanence, realism and nominalism, discerning in all of them mutilations of human experience which feed one another. Yannaras' care is, on the contrary, for a Eucharistic conciliation of divided realities and for eminent syntheses which preserve inside them important tensions between the different components that are brought to unity. Yannaras' philosophical project is thus a *phenomenological metaphysic*, in which the priority of catholic experience (that would not be reduced to the data of the senses) is not exhausted to the immediacy of its evidence, but would raise a true metaphysical contemplation as to its reason (λόγος)

---

1. Yannaras, *Προτάσεις Κριτικῆς Ὀντολογίας [Propositions for a Critical Ontology]*, 41.

and goal, so that philosophy regains its specific difference and stops being an *ancilla* of other studies. At a metaphysical level, Yannaras unites the notions of *stasis* (repose) and *energeia* (activity). We thus find in his thought a community in repose, i.e. one which has found its meaning, a meaning perpetually acted and realised as relation, thus reminding us of the notion of the '*ever-moving repose*' (ἀεικίνητος στάσις) in Maximus the Confessor. One of Yannaras' important syntheses is of course the way he views the Ecclesia as integrating the Hellenic polis, by responding to the deepest hunger and thirst[1] of the political animal that is man. It is in this sense that Yannaras supports a unity between politics and theology which is so deep that it arguably does not need political theology as special branch with an ideological/moral priority. Perhaps it would suffice to show the ways in which every genuine theology is profoundly political in character, as it expresses the realisation of man's innermost desire to live inside a political community.

---

1. See Yannaras' first work: *Πείνα καὶ Δίψα* [*Hunger and Thirst*] (Athens: Grigoris, 1969).

Chapter Two
The Problematic of Greek Identity and Christos Yannaras' Quest for a Politics of Authentic Existence
Jonathan Cole

Christos Yannaras has a reputation in the English-speaking world for being an unreconstructed and unbalanced critic of the 'West'. At least, that is the impression one gets reading some Orthodox accounts of Yannaras in English. Norman Russell, for example, has speculated that Yannaras' 'reputation for rebarbative anti-Westernism has probably put off scholars from engaging with him'.[1] Marcus Plested, who finds 'much of value in Yannaras' work' and describes him as a 'brilliant thinker', nevertheless finds him 'unduly dialectical and unwontedly oppositional'.[2] He thinks that Yannaras' work contains too many 'sweeping historical judgments and impossibly simple dichotomies'.[3] Andrew Louth has referred to the presence of a 'fierce anti-Western polemic' in Yannaras' work, though he, too, is sympathetic to Yannaras' overall contribution.[4] Pantelis Kalaitzidis has described Yannaras' 'systematic and structural anti-Westernism' as 'a contrived new version of Church history and theology' and 'a mocking caricature of the real West'.[5]

1. Norman Russell, 'The Enduring Significance of Christos Yannaras: Some Further Works in Translation', *International Journal for the Study of the Christian Church* 16:1 (2016), 59.
2. Marcus Plested, '"Light from the West": Byzantine Readings of Aquinas' in *Orthodox Constructions of the West,* ed. George Demacopoulos and Aristotle Papanikolaou (New York: Fordham University Press, 2013), 62-3.
3. Ibid., 63.
4. Andrew Louth, 'Some Recent Works by Christos Yannaras in English Translation', *Modern Theology* 25, 2 (2009), 331.
5. Pantelis Kalaitzidis, 'The Image of the West in Contemporary Greek Theology' in *Orthodox Constructions of the West,* ed. George Demacopoulos and Aristotle Papanikolaou (New York: Fordham University Press, 2013), 153, 155. Kalaitzidis' substantive criticism is that Yannaras too naively draws 'a direct connection

If Catholic and Protestant opinion of Yannaras mirrors Orthodox anxieties about his 'anti-Westernism', there is little evidence to show for it. Admittedly, the overwhelming response of Western theologians has been one of silence, so it is difficult to make categorical judgments about their reaction to Yannaras' critique of the West. It is noteworthy, however, that those Western scholars who have engaged with Yannaras' work in English have displayed far less anxiety about his supposed anti-Westernism than some of their Orthodox counterparts.

Catholic priest and academic Basilio Petrà, in his essay 'Christos Yannaras and the Idea of "Dysis"', went no further than acknowledging an 'East-West dualism' in Yannaras' thought and conceding that his book *Orthodoxy and the West* contains 'many provocative aspects'.[1] Former Anglican Archbishop of Canterbury Rowan Williams, in his essay 'The Theology of Personhood: A Study of the Thought of Christos Yannaras', concluded that the 'onesidedness' of Yannaras' arguments was perhaps justified in order to 'provoke Western readers to question the presuppositions of their own theology'.[2] Austrian scholar Kristina Stoeckl, however, has found Yannaras' 'anti-modern and anti-Western tone and the very clear assumption of superiority of his "Orthodox" standpoint' exasperating.[3]

It is therefore possible that Orthodox reactions to Yannaras' work have done more to cement his anti-Western reputation in English-language scholarship than either Protestant or Catholic responses. It is important to note, however, that not all Orthodox responses to Yannaras' work in English have exhibited concern about his anti-Westernism.[4]

Yannaras' portrayal of the West is certainly open to charges of being too generic, simplistic and lacking in subtlety.[5] But his critique has been

---

between texts and social reality'. Pantelis Kalaitzidis, *Orthodoxy and Political Theology,* trans. Fr Gregory Edwards (Geneva: World Council of Churches Publication, 2012), 41.

1. Basilio Petrà, 'Christos Yannaras and the Idea of "Dysis"' in *Orthodox Constructions of the West*, 176-7.
2. Rowan Williams, 'The Theology of Personhood: A Study of the Thought of Christos Yannaras', *Sobornost* 6 (1972), 423.
3. Kristina Stoeckl, 'The "We" in Normative Political Philosophical Debates: The Position of Christos Yannaras on Human Rights' in *Orthodox Christianity and Human Rights,* ed. Alfons Brüning and Evert van der Zweerde (Leuven: Peeters, 2012), 192.
4. For a sympathetic Orthodox engagement with Yannaras' critique of the 'West', see Sotiris Mitralexis, 'An Ontology of the Historico-Social: Christos Yannaras' Reading of European History', in *Mustard Seeds in the Public Square: Between and Beyond Theology, Philosophy, and Society,* ed. Sotiris Mitralexis (Wilmington, Delaware: Vernon Press, 2017).
5. It is interesting to note that in *Six Philosophical Paintings* Yannaras concedes that

misconstrued in some quarters as a form of ideological 'anti-Westernism', rather than the ontological critique it in fact represents.[1] Yannaras offers a political ontology that seeks to address tangible and pressing existential political problems in the Greek context. Although Yannaras' critique of the West is in many respects highly context-dependent, his political ontology promises a transcontextual and transcultural reconception of politics as the common human relational struggle for truth and authentic existence that has application well beyond the borders of Greece and the confines of Orthodox theology.

The Challenge of Yannaras' Corpus

A significant constraint on the evaluation of Yannaras' critique of the West in English language scholarship is the fact that only a relatively small proportion of his large corpus has been translated.[2] A particular gap is Yannaras' substantive body of work in political theory and his voluminous commentary on Greek politics, which are currently only available in Greek.[3] The works that have been translated into English happen to be in the fields of philosophy and theology, leading to the common characterisation of Yannaras as a philosopher-theologian, when in fact he is more accurately described as a philosopher, theologian *and* political theorist *and* political commentator. Yannaras is actually best known in Greece as a political commentator, not a theologian or philosopher.[4]

'an evaluation and comparison of civilisations is not feasible' because it is difficult to identity 'commonly accepted criteria'. But this does not prohibit him from making numerous categorical judgments about the 'West' and contrasting it with the 'East'. For example, he argues several sentences later that 'the civilisation of the post-Roman West . . . never recognised the need to move from the *community of necessity* to the *community of truth* [emphasis original]'. Christos Yannaras, Ἕξι φιλοσοφικές ζωγραφιές: σύνοψη εἰσαγωγικὴ καὶ πάντως αὐτεξεταστικὴ [Six Philosophical Paintings: Synoptic Self-Examination] (Athens: Ikaros, 2011), Chapter 6 Ἑλλάδα καὶ Δύση: ἡ διαφορά' [Greece and the West: The Difference], section 'Ἡ μεταφυσικὴ γεννάει τοὺς πολιτισμούς' ['Metaphysics begets civilisations'].

1. Both Petrà and Mitralexis have alluded to the ontological basis of Yannaras' critique of the West. Petrà, 'Christos Yannaras and the Idea of "Dysis"', 176; Mitralexis, 'An Ontology of the Historico-Social', 95.
2. An even smaller proportion has been translated into other European languages.
3. See, for example, Christos Yannaras, Ὀρθὸς λόγος καὶ κοινωνικὴ πρακτικὴ [Rationalism and Social Practice] (Athens: Domos, 1984), Chapter 6; Christos Yannaras, Ἡ ἀπανθρωπία τοῦ δικαιώματος [The Inhumanity of Right] (Athens: Domos, 1998).
4. Sotiris Mitralexis, 'Person, Eros, Critical Ontology: An Attempt to Recapitulate Christos Yannaras' Philosophy', *Sobornost* 34:1 (2012): 33.

While knowledge of Greek opens access to Yannaras' entire corpus, it brings with it its own challenges: the sheer size of the corpus. Yannaras has 69 Greek titles to his name and has published regular newspaper columns since the early 1970s.[1] Interestingly, Greek academics have thus far shown more interest in Yannaras' theological and philosophical writings than his political writings.

The integrated nature of Yannaras' thought makes it essential to consider his political theory and political commentary when evaluating his critique of the West. This work makes it much clearer than some of his theological and philosophical work that his critique of the West has an objective basis and validity in the contemporary Greek context that has not been appreciated by all English-speaking readers and, more surprisingly, by some Greek critics. This objective basis is the problematic of Greek identity and the problematic of Greek political order, both of which provide impetus for Yannaras' critique of the West.

Yannaras' Conception of the 'West'

Petrà has observed that the idea of the 'West' 'comes up in many different contexts and plays a variety of roles' in Yannaras' work.[2] Yannaras' critique of the West is broadly set within the framework of an East-West civilisational dichotomy. 'Civilisation' (*politismos*) is a central concept in Yannaras' political thought. It is given different, albeit coherent, definitions across his work, including 'a mode of life, a mode of individual and collective existence' and 'a central axis that ascribes meaning to reality and life.'[3] The mode of common life represented by Western civilisation, according to Yannaras, consists of capitalism, consumerism, materialism, utilitarianism, individual rights, nationalism and ideology.[4] Yannaras further identifies 'Western Christianity' and 'political liberalism' (*politikos fileleftherismos*) as important elements of Western civilisation.[5]

---

1. These titles include two autobiographies and a number of anthologies of his newspaper columns.
2. Petrà, 'Christos Yannaras and the Idea of "Dysis"', 161.
3. Christos Yannaras, Ὁ Καπιταλισμὸς καὶ ἡ συνείδηση τῆς θνητότητας' ['Capitalism and the Consciousness of Mortality'] in Ἡ Νεοελληνικὴ Ταυτότητα [*Modern Greek Identity*] 4th ed. (Athens: Grigoris, 2001), 15; Yannaras, Ἕξι φιλοσοφικές ζωγραφιὲς [*Six Philosophical Paintings*], iBooks, Chapter 6 Ἑλλάδα καὶ Δύση: ἡ διαφορά' ['Greece and the West: The Difference'], section '«Καθολικότητα»: οἱ συνέπειες τῆς ἀμφιλογίας' ['"Catholicity": the consequences of the dispute'].
4. Yannaras, Ὁ Καπιταλισμὸς καὶ ἡ συνείδηση τῆς θνητότητας' ['Capitalism and the Consciousness of Mortality'], 16-19.
5. Yannaras, Ἡ ἀπανθρωπία τοῦ δικαιώματος [*The Inhumanity of Right*], 167. I refer

It is interesting to note that the East-West dichotomy at the heart of Yannaras' thought is not predicated on a contrast between 'Western civilisation' and 'Byzantine civilisation'. The latter receives little emphasis in Yannaras' work. Rather, the Eastern part of the civilisational dichotomy relates to what Yannaras calls 'the Orthodox ecclesial tradition' and 'the civilisation of ecclesial Orthodoxy'. This is not an entirely idiosyncratic distinction. Peter Mackridge, for example, claims that 'in post-medieval Europe, language became the chief defining factor of collective identity in the West, while religion remained the defining factor in Eastern Christendom'.[1] It is not entirely clear whether Yannaras makes an implicit distinction between Byzantine political order and ecclesial Orthodox tradition, or whether he views them as indistinguishable.

It is helpful to make two distinctions related to Yannaras' critique of Western civilisation for the purposes of its evaluation. First is the distinction between his critique of Western theology, on the one hand, and Western liberal political order on the other. The second is between Yannaras' portrayal and critique of Western civilisation as it currently exists and his account of its historical development. These distinctions are important because it appears to be Yannaras' portrayal and critique of Western theology, much more than his critique of Western liberal political order, which has produced the charge of anti-Westernism.

It is noteworthy that Yannaras' critique of capitalism, consumerism, materialism, utilitarianism, individual rights, nationalism and ideology has deep synergy with critiques one can find in Catholic and Protestant political theology.[2] Moreover, these characteristic features of Western civilisation routinely come under strident criticism from secular intellectuals in the West, like Noam Chomsky. It is also relevant to note that the connection between Protestantism, in particular, and many features of Western liberal political order has long been investigated and debated in *Western* scholarship.[3]

---

to 'political liberalism' as 'Western liberal political order' in this paper.

1. Peter Mackridge, *Language and National Identity in Greece, 1766-1976* (Oxford: Oxford University Press, 2009), 13.
2. For 'Western' critiques of Western liberal political order that share some affinity with Yannaras' critique, see John Milbank and Adrian Pabst, *The Politics of Virtue: Post-Liberalism and the Human Future* (London: Rowman & Littlefield, 2016); William T. Cavanaugh, *Theopolitical Imagination: Discovering the Liturgy as a Political Act in an Age of Global Consumerism* (London: Bloomsbury; T. & T. Clark, 2002); and Stanley Hauerwas, *After Christendom? How the Church is to Behave If Freedom, Justice, and a Christian Nation are Bad Ideas* (Nashville: Abingdon, 1991).
3. John Coffey, for example, notes that 'Puritanism has been credited (and blamed)

The contentious point of difference is that Yannaras thinks Western theology is a primary cause of the pathologies of Western liberal political order and that there is a demonstrable historical causal connection between the two. He maintains, for instance, that 'the civilisation of capitalism and consumption has Christian roots, born of the alteration of Christian truth in the realm of the medieval West'.[1] It is no small irony that Western theological voices supportive of Western liberal political order also perceive a direct causal link between Western theology and Western civilisation. The difference is that they regard this link as positive *contra* Yannaras.[2] It is also worth noting, however, that some contemporary Protestant theology with roots in the radical reformation finds points of convergence with Yannaras' contention that Western theology has produced many of the woes of Western civilisation. But this is attributed to 'Constantinianism', something of which the Orthodox tradition is deemed to be equally guilty with Catholicism (along with the magisterial reformed traditions).[3]

One of the weaknesses of Yannaras' critique of the 'West' is that he does not engage any contemporary Catholic or Protestant political theology. Such an engagement might have given him a more nuanced understanding of the complexity of contemporary Catholic and Protestant attitudes to Western liberal political order and its historical development.

For the sake of clarification, the focus of this paper is Yannaras' critique of the Western liberal political order as it currently exists. It is not a critical evaluation of Yannaras' portrayal and critique of Western theology or of his account of the historical development of the Western liberal political order.

for bequeathing a puzzling set of legacies, including the spirit of capitalism, scientific enterprise, Anglo-Saxon sexual repression, companionate marriage, liberal democracy, American exceptionalism and religious bigotry'. John Coffey, 'Puritan Legacies' in *The Cambridge Companion to Puritanism*, ed. John Coffey and Paul C.H. Lim (Cambridge: Cambridge University Press, 2008), 327.

1. Yannaras, Ὁ Καπιταλισμὸς καὶ ἡ συνείδηση τῆς θνητότητας' ['Capitalism and the Consciousness of Mortality'], 20.
2. Anglican theologian Oliver O'Donovan, for example, argues that 'the liberal achievement' is 'the victory won by Christ over the nations' rulers' and that 'a Christian political theologian can venture to characterise a *normative political culture* broadly in continuity with the Western liberal tradition [emphasis original]'. Oliver O'Donovan, *The Desire of the Nations: Rediscovering the Roots of Political Theology* (Cambridge: Cambridge University Press, 1996), 229-30.
3. See, for example, John Howard Yoder, 'The Constantinian Sources of Western Social Ethics' in *The Priestly Kingdom: Social Ethics as Gospel* (Notre Dame: University of Notre Dame Press, 1984).

The Objective Problematic of Greek Identity
and Greek Political Order

The problematic of Greek identity is a prominent and consistent theme in Yannaras' political writings. A recent work that contains some of his most personal and searching reflections on Greek identity is Ἀόριστη Ἑλλάδα: Κοντσέρτο γιὰ δυὸ ἀποδημίες [*Indefinite Greece: Concert for Two Emigrations*].¹ The book closes with an amusing anecdote that encapsulates the problematic of Greek identity as Yannaras understands it. The scene is set early into a return flight from America to Greece, and Yannaras finds himself sitting across the aisle from a well-known Greek politician. Upon hearing Yannaras speaking Greek with his wife, the politician asks him in English: 'You are Greek?' Yannaras replies in English: 'We try to be, we try. It's not easy, you know.' The politician, looking rather perplexed, asks in Greek: 'From the homeland or the diaspora?' Yannaras replies: 'τῆς ἀόριστης Ἑλλάδας' (from indefinite Greece), and then adds, 'I mean the real homeland.' The politician didn't make a sound for the rest of flight.²

The problematic of Greek identity and Greek political order find their origin in the creation of what Yannaras refers to as the 'alien' Greek state in 1830.³ This development marked a complete innovation and turning point in the long and variegated history of Hellenic civilisation, and, according to Yannaras, marked the beginning of the Western corruption of Greek political life.⁴ In a 2014 newspaper column, Yannaras wrote that 'in form, mode, and institutional shape the "nation-state" was something foreign to Greeks, unrelated to their experience, untested: it hadn't emerged from their needs, their historical norms, their priorities or aspirations'.⁵ In the same column Yannaras identified three constitutive

---

1. Christos Yannaras, Ἀόριστη Ἑλλάδα: Κοντσέρτο γιὰ δυὸ ἀποδημίες [*Indefinite Greece: Concert for Two Emigrations*] (Thessaloniki: Ianos, 2016). This book contains Yannaras' reflections on visits to Australia in 1984 and the United States in 1993.
2. Ibid., 227-8.
3. Christos Yannaras, 'Συνεπάγεται ἀχρείωση ὁ ἀφελληνισμός' ['De-Hellenisation implies infamy'] *Kathimerini*, 10 August 2014, http://www.kathimerini. gr/779516/opinion/epikairothta/politikh/synepagetai-axreiwsh-o-afellhnismos.
4. The corruption of Greek thought began much earlier, according to Yannaras, with Demetrios Kydones' translation of Aquinas' *Summa contra Gentiles* into Greek in 1354. Christos Yannaras, *Orthodoxy and the West: Hellenic Self-Identity in the Modern Age,* trans. Peter Chamberas and Norman Russell (Brookline, Mass.: Holy Cross Orthodox Press, 2006), 3.
5. Yannaras, 'Συνεπάγεται ἀχρείωση ὁ ἀφελληνισμός' ['De-Hellenisation implies infamity'].

elements of Western liberal political order that were foreign to Greek thought and political praxis: 'freedom', construed as 'the freedom of unbridled individual choice', 'equality', construed as 'individual rights', which elsewhere Yannaras argues are little more than the security of private interests,[1] and 'brotherhood', construed as a conventional form of cohesion through a social contract.[2]

The emergence of the Greek state forced Greek-speaking Christians of the Ottoman Empire to contend with two difficult syntheses simultaneously. Greek historian Nikos Svoronos articulated the first synthesis in the following way:

> In order for Hellenism to . . . synthesise the elements of its national consciousness and to present itself as an autonomous historical entity, it had to try to reconcile and harmonise its multifarious, and often contradictory, traditions.[3]

Svoronos identified four such traditions: 'Ancient Greek civilisation', 'Orthodox Christianity', 'Byzantine Empire' and 'popular tradition'.[4] Svoronos described the second synthesis as 'the incorporation of [Greece] into the united current of European civilisation.'[5]

In reality, the nascent Greek state was incorporated into European civilisation in the best traditions of European colonialism. In 1831, the first leader of an independent Greece, Ioannis Kapodistrias, was assassinated in a portent of the political instability and division that would dog Greece throughout its contemporary history. In 1832 the short-lived indigenous Greek *politeia* was replaced by the establishment of the Kingdom of Greece at the behest of Europe's great powers. Catholic Bavarian prince Otto Friedrich Ludwig, at the time still a teenager, was installed on the newly minted throne, and he and his Bavarian officials ran Greece as an effective Bavarian protectorate – a period known in Greece as the *Vavarokratia* (the 'Bavarianocracy'). One of the most controversial Western institutions created during Otto's reign was a national church, the Church of Greece, unilaterally carved out of territory that had belonged to the Patriarchate in Constantinople for centuries. [6]

1. Yannaras, Ἡ ἀπανθρωπία τοῦ δικαιώματος *[The Inhumanity of Right]*, 15.
2. Yannaras, 'Συνεπάγεται ἀχρείωση ὁ ἀφελληνισμός' ['De-Hellenisation implies infamy'].
3. Nikos G. Svoronos, Τὸ Ἑλληνικὸ Ἔθνος: Γένεση καὶ Διαμόρφωση τοῦ Νέου Ἑλληνισμοῦ *[The Greek Nation: The Genesis and Development of Neo-Hellenism]* (Athens: Polis, 2004), 107.
4. Ibid.
5. Ibid., 108.
6. Giorgos Kokkolis, 'Τὸ νομικὸ καθεστὼς τῶν σχέσεων ἐκκλησίας-κράτους:

The philosopher and diplomat Ion Dragoumis evocatively captured the difficult integration of neo-Hellenic identity to the current of European civilisation in the following observations he made in 1904:

> Before 1821 the Greeks had *one* life, with *one* ideal. They had an Eastern life, with the goal of being liberated from the Turks and reclaiming Constantinople... everything then was certain, put in its place, remnants of Byzantium, a life settled, the product of older civilisations and times. Then, suddenly, with 1821, a Greek state was liberated, and everyone realised that things could change. They saw the Europeans, they brought new clothes from Europe, new systems of governance...and a greater revolution occurred than the revolution against the Sultan. After everything had been turned upside down, nothing remained in its place and so we find ourselves now unable to find our new form, our point of rest. ....[1]

Svoronos and Dragoumis remind us that the problematic of modern Greek identity has a widely attested synchronic and diachronic basis. It is not a contrived problematic of 1960s neo-Orthodox zealots or nostalgic Greek intellectuals living in the shadow of Ancient Greek and Byzantine glory. The degree to which the Eastern mode of life has been successfully integrated with the Western mode of life in contemporary Greece is still subject to debate. Tziovas, for example, regards 'Greek culture . . . as a hybrid construct that did not emerge from the synthesis of opposites but from the tensions between East and West, Enlightenment and Orthodoxy, Antiquity and Tourkokratia'.[2] Yannaras regards contemporary Greek culture as 'schizophrenic'.[3]

εἰσαγωγὴ στὶς νομικὲς διαστάσεις τῶν σχέσεων ἐκκλησίας-κράτους στὴν Ἑλλάδα καὶ στὴν Κύπρο' ['The Legal Framework of Church-State Relations: Introduction to the Legal Dimensions of Church-State Relations in Greece and Cyprus'] in Ἀπελευθέρωση τῆς Ἐκκλησίας ἀπὸ τὸ Κράτος: οἱ σχέσεις Ἐκκλησίας-Κράτους καὶ ἡ μελλοντικὴ μετεξέλιξή τους [*Liberating the Church from the State: Church-State Relations and Their Future Evolution*], ed. Sotiris Mitralexis (Athens: Manifesto, 2015), 62. The Patriarchate did not recognise the autocephalous Church of Greece until 1850. It is important to note that Greek intellectual and cleric Theoklitos Farmakides was a key instigator in the creation of the Church of Greece.

1. Ion Dragoumis, Ὁ Ἑλληνισμός μου καὶ οἱ Ἕλληνες [*My Hellenism and the Greeks*] (Athens: Pelekanos, *n. d.*), iBooks, Chapter 2, 3:2, 1904, Athens.
2. Dimitris Tziovas, 'Beyond the Acropolis: Rethinking Neohellenism', *Journal of Modern Greek Studies* 19 (2001), 203.
3. Yannaras, Ἡ ἀπανθρωπία τοῦ δικαιώματος [*The Inhumanity of Right*], 136-7.

Yannaras has clarified that his critique of the West is not that of a superior non-Western Orthodox other.[1] In the preface to the English translation of *Orthodoxy and the West,* for example, Yannaras wrote that 'my critical stance towards the West is self-criticism; it refers to my own wholly Western mode of life'.[2] More recently, Yannaras has made his personal 'Western' frame of reference even more explicit:

> My entire work and life are a dialogue with my Western self, searching my Greek ecclesial roots for serious . . . solutions to the problems of Western modernity, which is the flesh of my everyday life.[3]

Yannaras points out that he received a 'Western education'.[4] He also explains that he once had a 'typically Western religiosity', in reference to his formation in the extra-ecclesial *Zoe* movement, which was modelled on Protestant pietism.[5] Indeed, one of the great ironies of the discourse about Yannaras' anti-Westernism is just how many of Yannaras' major influences are Western: Martin Heidegger, Ludwig Wittgenstein, Jean-Paul Sartre, Jacques Lacan and Karl Marx.[6]

What hasn't been sufficiently taken into consideration in the critical evaluation of Yannaras' work in English-language scholarship is just how dysfunctional that Western mode of life has been for Yannaras living in the

1. Yannaras, Ἔξι φιλοσοφικές ζωγραφιές *[Six Philosophical Paintings],* iBooks, Chapter 6 Ἑλλάδα καὶ Δύση: ἡ διαφορά' ['Greece and the West: The Difference'], section Ἡ μεταφυσικὴ γεννάει τοὺς πολιτισμούς' ['Metaphysics begets civilisations']. Yannaras says 'it is dangerous to speak of "superior" and "inferior" civilisations, of "better" and "worse"'.
2. Yannaras, *Orthodoxy and the West,* ix.
3. Christos Yannaras, Ὀξφόρδη, Σεπτέμβριος *2013* [Oxford, September 2013] in Ἡ ἑλληνικότητα ὡς ποιότητα καὶ ὡς ντροπή *[Greekness as Quality and Shame]* (Thessaloniki: Ianos, 2014), 300. This is an anthology of Yannaras' columns from 2013. The citation is from remarks Yannaras made at 'A Conference Dedicated to Christos Yannaras: Philosophy-Theology-Culture', 2-5 September 2013, Oxford, St Edmund Hall.
4. Ibid., 296. Yannaras did doctoral research at the Sorbonne (Paris IV) after graduate studies in Bonn, Germany.
5. Ibid; Yannaras, *Orthodoxy and the West,* 226. Of *Zoe,* for example, Yannaras says '[its] preaching was to be based on Scripture, but Scripture was used in the Protestant manner introduced into Greece by missionaries. Protestant pietism provided the model'. For a personal account of Yannaras' life in the *Zoe* movement, see Christos Yannaras, Καταφύγιο Ἰδεῶν *[Refuge of Ideas]* 8th ed. (Athens: Ikaros, 2011).
6. Yannaras describes Heidegger as the 'decisive encounter of my life'. Yannaras, Ὀξφόρδη, Σεπτέμβριος *2013* [Oxford, September 2013], 296.

Greek state, and the way that this experience has shaped his perception of the 'West'. It would not be an act of hyperbole to describe Greek political order as 'disorder'. When Yannaras describes Greek political order as 'endemic divisions, civil war, gross government incompetence, economic dysfunction, a top-heavy and ineffective civil service, a feeble system of education, shortsighted diplomacy, an uncritical pedalling of ideologies, a jejeune nationalism and a provincial internationalism,' he is describing a lived personal experience and pressing existential political problems that demand resolution.[1] As he wryly noted in his autobiography *Τὰ καθ᾽ἑαυτὸν* [*Personal Matters*], during the military junta (1967-74) Greek intellectuals began decrying 'the dismantling of freedoms, the Greek polity and the principles of democracy, as if modern Greece had ever known democracy and a political order that wasn't rotten.'[2]

The problematic of Greek political (dis)order has profoundly shaped the sense of alienation at the heart of Yannaras' critique of the West. In *Orthodoxy and the West,* he argued that 'although content to be de-Hellenised through accepting the Western model, the Greeks did not achieve a real assimilation but remained in a disorganised state of alienation'.[3] Yannaras' personal sense of alienation, however, runs deeper than the widely-felt alienating effects of Greece's political dysfunction, and the more generic alienating pathologies, as he sees them, of Western civilisation, such as individualism, consumerism and utilitarianism. It is also a consequence of the problematic of Greek identity; not for the reason Svoronos identified – the 'contradictions' of Greece's multifarious cultural legacy – but for precisely the opposite reason: Yannaras' strong sense of continuity and coherence in Helleno-Christian ontology, epistemology and political thought, a continuity and coherence severed by the creation of the Greek state.

Helleno-Christian Political Ontology

Yannaras contends that Greek politics, in its Helleno-Christian conceptual form, and in its praxis from Athens to Constantinople, and even to the self-governing communities of the Ottoman period, was characterised by the common communal struggle for truth and authentic existence.[4] Yannaras speaks of a meeting of Hellenism and Christianity,

1. Yannaras, *Orthodoxy and the West,* 251.
2. Christos Yannaras, *Τὰ καθ᾽ἑαυτὸν [Personal Matters]* 4th ed. (Athens: Ikaros, 2005), 67.
3. Yannaras, *Orthodoxy and the West,* 252.
4. Yannaras, 'Συνεπάγεται ἀχρείωση ὁ ἀφελληνισμός' ['De-Hellenisation implies

of a connection between the Greek polis and the Christian ecclesia (of the 'ecclesia of the citizens' and the 'ecclesia of the brothers'), which, he contends, both had as their telos the pursuit of truth as a mode of existence.[1] Yannaras maintains that Greek politics was about ontology, whereas Western politics (including contemporary Greek politics) is about ideology.[2] Yannaras understands ideology as the interpretation of reality and organisation of communal life on an *a priori* basis, rather than the basis of the communally verified experience of the community.[3]

Accordingly, Yannaras' response to the problematic of Greek identity, and of Greek political disorder and the alienation wrought by the Western political model, is a reconception of politics from the Western paradigm of ideology to the Greek paradigm of ontology. Yannaras' Helleno-Christian-inspired political ontology envisions a politics that is personal, relational, communo-centric and participatory.[4] It is also ultimately a theological political ontology, one might even say a 'theotic' political theology, because the free, loving community of persons that constitutes the Trinity is both the source and telos of existence, and ergo of political life.[5] This is why the Trinity functions as a foundational political concept in Yannaras' political thought. Conversely, the Western political paradigm of ideology, rights, utility, nationalism and totalitarianism not only alienates the person from community, the citizen from authority, and the person from real existence, but crucially also the person and community from communion with God.

---

infamity'].

1. Ibid.
2. Christos Yannaras, 'Τὸ σήμερα ἔρχεται ἀπὸ τὸ χθές' ['The present comes from the past'], *Kathimerini*, 12 February 2017, http://www.kathimerini.gr/896065/opinion/epikairothta/politikh/to-shmera-erxetai-apo-to-x8es; Yannaras, 'Συνεπάγεται αχρείωση ο αφελληνισμός' ['De-Hellenisation implies infamity'].
3. Yannaras, *Ἕξι φιλοσοφικές ζωγραφιές [Six Philosophical Paintings]*, iBooks, Chapter 5 'Τὸ ἀδιάρρηκτο Φιλοσοφίας καὶ Μεταφυσικῆς' ['The Indivisibility of Philosophy and Metaphysics'], section 'Στοὺς ἀντίποδες τῆς ἰδεολογίας' ['In opposition to ideology'].
4. Petrà, 'Christos Yannaras and the Idea of "Dysis"', 162.
5. 'Theotic' here is used as an adjective of *theosis*. Mitralexis says that: 'Yannaras' attempt at a comprehensive narrative on European history, leading to a political theology, can be categorised as *an ontology of the historico-social* [emphasis original].' Mitralexis, 'An Ontology of the Historico-Social', 97. For an overview of Yannaras' political theology in English, see Jonathan Cole, 'Personhood, Relational Ontology, and the Trinitarian Politics of Eastern Orthodox Thinker Christos Yannaras', *Political Theology*, published online 22 February 2017, http://dx.doi.org/10.1080/1462317X.2017.1291127.

Greek Political Ontology or Greek Cultural Imperialism?

Some Greek scholars have interpreted Yannaras' political ontology as a form of Greek cultural imperialism. Kalaitzidis, for example, has charged Yannaras with propagating a notion of 'Greek cultural superiority over the West' and Sotiris Gounelas of 'cultural totalitarianism'.[1] Even more surprisingly, they fail to recognise the objective problematic of Greek identity and Greek political (dis)order that Yannaras' political ontology seeks to address. Yannaras is resigned to the existence of a Greek nation-state as an unavoidable necessity in today's global order.[2] However, he repudiates the 'statist nationalism' that comes with it. Moreover, there is nothing superior about contemporary Greek culture as far as Yannaras is concerned. His is a project of cultural retrieval from a lost past, and what is to be retrieved is a conception of politics as the common human struggle for truth and authentic existence, which by necessity is a Christian existence. As he asked rhetorically in one of his columns:

> Are we the continuity of the Greco-Roman 'oikoumene'? A cosmopolitan civilisation, a mode of life – language, art, communo-centric politics, prioritising relationship over utility? Do we seek the truth, not as a code of rationality, but as an experience of participation, in unbroken organic continuity from Heraclitus to Gregory Palamas? Or are we the racial potpourri of schismatic Greeks (Γραικών – Grekon), as the West would have us be . . . ?[3]

Thus while Yannaras' political ontology finds its impetus in the problematic of Greek identity and Greek political (dis)order, and finds its resolution in Helleno-Christian ontology, it is not, contra Greek critics, either a form of Greek cultural imperialism or a Greek Orthodox nationalist ideology. As a political ontology that has truth and authentic existence as its telos, with personhood, relationship and community as its means, it is a vision of transcultural and transcontextual scope and application, as indeed any ontological proposal must be by its nature. One of the recurring themes in Yannaras' work is the notion that Helleno-Christian political ontology represents a 'pananthropic' gift, i.e. for all humanity.[4]

1. Kalaitzidis, 'The Image of the West in Contemporary Greek Theology', 158. Gounelas quoted in Kalaitzidis, 153.
2. Christos Yannaras, 'Σωτηρία, ἴσως, ὁ κοσμοπολιτισμός' ['Perhaps our salvation is cosmopolitanism'], *Kathimerini*, 23 January 2017, http://www.kathimerini.gr/892825/opinion/epikairothta/politikh/swthria-isws-o-kosmopolitismos.
3. Yannaras, 'Τὸ σήμερα ἔρχεται ἀπὸ τὸ χθές' ['The present comes from the past'].
4. Christos Yannaras, Ἑλλαδισμὸς τὸ τέλος τοῦ Ἑλληνισμοῦ; [*Is the Greek Nation-*

Having said that, there is some ambiguity in Yannaras' Helleno-Christian politico-ontological proposal: the role of the Greek language and the Orthodox ecclesial tradition. While Yannaras on many occasions opens the door to the transcultural, or at a minimum multi-ethnic, adoption and practice of Helleno-Christian political ontology, his priority is to address pressing Greek political and cultural problems, in which case he does not indicate the extent to which he believes non-Greek speakers can adopt and implement his political ontology without any knowledge of Greek. Nor does he clarify whether he thinks Western Christians could embrace his reconception of politics without becoming Orthodox. In principle, there is no reason why the non-Greek speaking Western Christian could not embrace Yannaras' politico-ontological vision.

Yannaras' 'Anti-Westernism' in Perspective

Yannaras' ontological critique of the Western liberal political order, a key component of his wider critique of the West, finds an objective basis in the problematic of Greek identity and the lived experience of Greek political (dis)order. If there is an error on Yannaras' part, it is to overgeneralise a valid critique of Western liberal political order in the Greek context to contexts where the Western liberal political order is more functional and less alienating. Australians, Americans and English of Anglo-Saxon descent, for example, do not have to contend with the equivalent of the problematic of Greek identity. Western liberal political order is their indigenous political tradition.

Yannaras is well aware of the criticisms regarding his reading of the 'West' and his 'idealisation' of Hellenism.[1] He has even conceded that there might be some truth to such criticisms.[2] But his view of the 'West' is not as dogmatic and unnuanced as the impression sometimes given by his own prose. In his newspaper columns, for example, Yannaras habitually qualifies his characterisations of the 'West' as 'schematic'. In the prologue to an anthology of his articles published in newspaper *Vima* between 1975 and 1977, he made the following revealing comments:

> The antithetical contrast of Greece and Europe, of the Orthodox East and the Roman Catholic or Protestant West, perhaps reaches levels of exaggerated sharpness in the pages

---

State the End of Hellenism?], in Ἡ ἑλληνικότητα ὡς ποιότητα καὶ ὡς ντροπή *[Greekness as Quality and Shame]* (Thessaloniki: Ianos, 2014), 289.

1. Yannaras, Ὀξφόρδη, Σεπτέμβριος *2013* [Oxford, September 2013], 295.
2. Ibid.

that follow – often giving the appearance of unbridgeable polarity. The reader must not forget that they are reading discrete newspaper articles that unavoidably schematise problems in order to highlight them within the constraints of the format. What we here call the 'West' does not, of course, exhaust its history, nor the spirituality of Europe or Western Christianity. It merely highlights those factors that indisputably assumed prominence in the development of what is today called Western civilisation, at the expense of more positive elements of the Western tradition. The object of this book is not to render historical judgment, but to indicate to some extent the potential of Hellenism vis-à-vis the consumerist and technocratic 'West'. . . .[1]

The point to bear in mind is that Yannaras does not pretend to write historiography or theological history. The preoccupation that drives all his work, and which provides its unifying framework across the disciplines of theology, philosophy and political theory, is the problematic of existence. The East-West dialectic is the framework through which Yannaras has sought to understand the problematic of his own personal existence: that of a Greek man with an Orthodox ecclesial consciousness living in a dysfunctional Western nation-state. It is tempting to regard this framework as contrived. But the evidence suggests that this very personal struggle with identity and community is entirely authentic on Yannaras' part, irrespective of whatever valid criticisms can be levelled at his historiography and understanding of Western theology.

It is also important to recognise that the East-West dichotomy has been reinforced by both 'civilisations'. The historical Western stereotypes of Byzantium as backward and inferior are well known and need no rehearsing here. Samuel Huntington's famous and controversial thesis about the 'clash of civilisations', including between what he characterised as a 'Western civilisation' and 'Slavic-Orthodox civilisation', was not lost on Orthodox scholars, including Yannaras, who critically engaged Huntington in *The Inhumanity of Right*.[2] Dimiter Angelov has decried the West's 'simplistic, essentialist generalisations about such a sophisticated civilisation as Byzantium, and the drawing of causal connections between

1. Yannaras, preface to Ἡ Νεοελληνικὴ Ταυτότητα [Modern Greek Identity], 9-10.
2. Samuel Huntington, 'The Clash of Civilizations?' *Foreign Affairs* 72, 3 (1993), 25. Huntington was writing in the wake of the fall of communism in Eastern Europe, which undoubtedly influenced his conception of a separate non-Western contemporary 'Slavic-Orthodox civilisation'. Yannaras, Ἡ ἀπανθρωπία τοῦ δικαιώματος [The Inhumanity of Right], 239-48.

the Middle Ages and modernity'.[1] This mirrors the criticisms levelled at Yannaras' reading of the West. Dimitris Tziovas has further highlighted the way that certain Western prejudices have shaped the entire field of Modern Greek studies (the only European nation and culture to be qualified by 'Modern' in Western scholarship):

> Thus modern Greek culture has occupied an ambivalent position in Western scholarship; while classicists sought in it traces of survivalism, in order to understand and explain ancient cultural practices, others rejected its claims to be either modern or fully European. This epistemological prejudice made Modern Greek Studies seem an 'exotic' option for those interested in ethnic studies rather than a serious academic discipline.[2]

On a more minor note (though not an entirely trivial one), it is worth being mindful of rhetorical differences between Greek and English when evaluating Yannaras' 'anti-Westernism'. Greek discourse can lack the nuance and qualification of English discourse. Greeks tend to take categorical positions and then express them with what can strike an English-speaker as hyperbole and unnecessary polemic. It is easy to forget that Yannaras writes in Greek for a Greek audience. His language can sound more inflammatory and impolitic to an English-speaker than it might for a Greek-speaker.

Conclusion

The plausibility of Yannaras' critique of the Western liberal political order in the Greek context and its commensurate appearance of exaggeration in the English-speaking context raise interesting questions for political theology. It is indicative, for instance, of the fact that much English-language political theology works with far too thin a conception of 'Western liberal political order'. English-speaking Protestant political theology is a particular culprit in this regard, often restricting its interest to the place of just a handful of stable, prosperous and functional Anglo-Saxon states in the divine economy. Yannaras' uniquely Greek experience of, and perspective on, the Western liberal political order can provide important counterbalance to a Western Christian view of it that in some cases can verge on the naïve and unduly optimistic.

1. Dimiter G. Angelov, 'Byzantinism: The Imaginary and Real Heritage of Byzantium in Southeastern Europe' in *New Approaches to Balkan Studies*, ed. Dimitris Keridis, Ellen Elias-Bursac and Nicholas Yatromanolakis (Dulles, VA: Brassey's, 2003), 5.
2. Tziovas, 'Beyond the Acropolis: Rethinking Neohellenism', 191.

Moreover, a more sensitive understanding of the profound ways in which the very real problematic of Greek identity and Greek political (dis)order have shaped Yannaras' life's work could facilitate a critical evaluation of his politico-ontological proposal unburdened by questions of his supposed 'anti-Westernism'. Yannaras believes the problems and challenges of Western civilisation are common challenges for Orthodox, Catholic and Protestant Christians. He has long craved a critical dialogue with Western theologians and philosophers on these common problems.[1]

Yannaras' proposal to reconceive and reorient Western political thought and praxis away from the current paradigm of individualism, consumerism, utilitarianism, materialism, freedom of choice and ideology to a new ontologically-grounded paradigm of personhood, community, relationship and communion with God represents a transcultural and transcontextual foundation for dialogue that many Protestants and Catholics should be able to support.

---

1. Yannaras, Ὀξφόρδη, Σεπτέμβριος 2013 [Oxford, September 2013], 295-6.

Chapter Three
The Freedom of Relationship
as the Ontological Foundation in
Christos Yannaras' Political Theology
Angelos Gounopoulos

The Ecclesia of Christ as Polis

Christos Yannaras clarifies that 'politics is not a noun but an adjective; it is the political life, the life of the polis'.[1] The Greek Christian philosopher explains:

> *Polis* for the ancient Greeks was not a settlement that had grown to a quantifiable size. It was a *common struggle*, the struggle aimed at attaining life *according to truth*. What it wanted was that social coexistence should have truth as its goal, that it should not simply have a utilitarian purpose . . . . Moreover, they located truth in the common *logos*/mode (the given rationality) . . . of the relations that make the universe a *cosmos*, an ornament of harmony, order, and beauty. Such a mode of existence *according to truth* was what the city, or *polis*, sought to imitate and realise.[2]

According to Yannaras, the same choice is made in Christianity concerning the way believers (the disciples of Jesus Christ) meet and coexist in order to manifest their own truth. This is called the *ecclesia* (church). Furthermore, Christianity is understood as an ecclesial/Eucharistic event. Ecclesia is an ecclesial event; it is not a building, a denomination or an institution. As Yannaras argues:

---

1. Christos Yannaras, *Τὸ Προνόμιο τῆς Ἀπελπισίας* [*The Privilege of Despair*] (Athens: Grigoris, 1983), 29.
2. Christos Yannaras, *Against Religion: The Alienation of the Ecclesial Event*, trans. Norman Russell (Brookline MA: Holy Cross Orthodox Press, 2013), 21-2.

> The Greek word ἐκκλησία (*ecclesia* in its Latinised form) was chosen to express not a new religion but a social event – a *mode* of relations of communion . . . a mode of human existence and coexistence.[1]

Theology itself, as an expression of the ecclesia, is also an expression of the common life of the polis in which Christians take part and also participate creatively in the way that common life is constituted. Theology can therefore be characterised as a political theology, among other things. In addition, theology is considered 'political' as an expression of the ecclesial event in the common life of the polis, and does not only participate in the manifestation of the polis, but also has political consequences for it.

This connection of the polis/state and the ecclesia/church or the complex of politics and theology or Eucharistic event has been expressed in three main currents in modern theological thought. The first current supports the idea that a political theology can be directly produced from the Gospel of Christ and the witnessing of His Church in the world.[2] According to this logic the Church understands itself and is constituted as an 'alternative polis' with the mission to reveal to the world through its example the way the world exists. In this way it shows the existence of two distinct empirical ways of life, which also constitute distinct political experiences.[3] This separation of the two experiences of the Church and the state does not mean that the Christian underestimates the worldly. The people of God manifest their 'good news' into the world as an 'alternative polis' (church); they do not deny the world or withdraw from it.[4] The politics of the Christian are the political life of the Church-polis, which is distinct from the political life of the state-polis.

---

1. Ibid., 21.
2. A characteristic sample of this view is found in John Howard Yoder, *The Politics of Jesus* (Grand Rapids: Eerdmans, 1972).
3. J. Alexander Sider, *To See History Doxologically, History and Holiness in John Howard Yoder's Ecclesiology* (Grand Rapids: Eerdmans, 2011), 20-1, as cited in Fr Evangelos Gkanas, ʿΗ Πολιτικὴ τοῦ Ἰησοῦ καὶ ἡ Προσδοκία τῶν Ἐθνῶν: Θέτοντας τὸν Τζὸν Χάουαρντ Γιόντερ καὶ τὸν Ὄλιβερ Ὁ Ντόναβαν σὲ Διάλογο' ['The Politics of Jesus and the Expectation of Nations: Bringing John Howard Yoder and Oliver O'Donovan in Dialogue'] in *Θρησκεία καὶ Πολιτικὴ [Religion and Politics]*, ed. Stavros Zouboulakis (Athens: Artos Zois, 2016), 355-6.
4. John Howard Yoder, *For the Nations: Essays Public and Evangelical* (Grand Rapids: Eerdmans, 1997), 6, as cited in Gkanas, ʿΗ Πολιτικὴ τοῦ Ἰησοῦ καὶ ἡ Προσδοκία τῶν Ἐθνῶν' ['The Politics of Jesus and the Expectation of Nations'], 359.

The second current is a correlation between the two fields, the spiritual and the secular or the ecclesiastical and the political. According to this position, the Church must not show arrogance by trying to exist as a distinct and superior witnessing about the world but it needs to relate with it, to ideologise it through its spirituality, to provide it with an ethical dimension through the incarnated and democratised *Logos* of God.[1]

The third current supports that the models of distinct or of separate fields are obsolete because the Christian lives and becomes a Christian inside the world and with it. A characteristic example thereof is Gustavo Gutiérrez, a Peruvian Dominican priest and professor of theology, considered as one of the main founders of Theology of Liberation, who rejected any problem of dualism and added that the 'natural and the supernatural orders are therefore intimately unified.'[2]

Independently of whether someone supports the distinction or the separation of the ecclesial and the political event, their direct correlation or even their total identification, one cannot deny the political dimension of theology and the Church. Because of this fact, the German Reformer theologian, Jürgen Moltmann, argues:

> Political theology was not understood as a theology of the political, but rather it was a designation for every Christian theology and a hermeneutical or fundamental-theological category. There is consciously political theology, there is politically un-conscious theology, but there is no such thing as an un-political theology, at least not on this earth and presumably not even in the heavenly *politeuma*.[3]

1. A characteristic case of this position, according to the professor of theology William T. Cavanaugh, is the French Catholic philosopher Jacques Maritain. Cf. William T. Cavanaugh, 'Church' in *The Blackwell Companion to Political Theology*, ed. Peter Scott et al. (Malden: Blackwell, 2007), 400-1, as cited in Gkanas, Ἡ Πολιτικὴ τοῦ Ἰησοῦ καὶ ἡ Προσδοκία τῶν Ἐθνῶν' ['The Politics of Jesus and the Expectation of Nations'], 357.
2. Gustavo Gutiérrez, *A Theology of Liberation. History, Politics, and Salvation*, ed. and trans. Sister Caridad Inda et al. (Maryknoll, NY: Orbis Books, 1973), 70. Regarding the problem of history and ontology and the interpretation by the Latin American theology of liberation, see also Angelos Gounopoulos, 'The Common Path of Ontology and History: Orthodoxy and Theology of Liberation in Dialogue' in *Mustard Seeds in the Public Square: Between and Beyond Theology, Philosophy, and Society*, ed. Sotiris Mitralexis (Wilmington, Delaware: Vernon Press, 2017), 165-89.
3. Jürgen Moltmann, 'Political Theology in Ecumenical Contexts' in *Political Theology: Contemporary Challenges and Future Directions*, ed. Francis Schüssler Fiorenza et al. (Louisville, KY: Westminster John Knox Press, 2013), 2.

According to Moltmann, theologies can be categorised as 'church', 'state' or 'prophetic'. The first distinguishes the ecclesial from the political event without totally separating them; the second transforms Christianity into a state or political ideology and power practice, while 'Political Theology as prophetic theology is liberation theology, and liberation theology, is Political Theology'.[1] Moltmann argues that after Auschwitz the privatisation of the faith is no longer possible for Christian life and 'theology belongs in the realm of the public discussion of political freedom, social justice, and the future of the earth'.[2]

Moreover, the German Catholic theologian Johann Baptist Metz argues about the distinction between the 'old' or 'classical' political theology and the 'new' one. The 'old' or 'classical' political theology understands the 'political' in terms of national and legal policy, as an ideology of statism (from Roman political metaphysics until Machiavelli, Thomas Hobbes, Carl Schmitt and the 'Catholic State').[3] On the contrary, the 'new' political theology uses the term 'political' in 'a strictly theological intention',[4] which knows how to 'distinguish between the secularisation of the state and the dialectic of secularisation in society'[5] by strengthening Reason (*logos*) 'alive in the Public Sphere'.[6]

As a result, it makes sense to claim that political theology is distinguished from political philosophy, ideology or social theory, because it is a theology and Christology of a special mode of life, inspired by the life of Jesus Christ, faith in God and the freedom of love. As a conclusion, every Christian has a political life, even though they don't exhaust their mode of existence in the political dimension, and because of that every theology is a political theology. Following this logic, people became Christians because, although they lived a political life and had a great interest in it, they put at the centre of their existence the Eucharistic and ecclesial event. In this way they combined the polis with the Ecclesia.

---

1. Ibid., 11.
2. Jürgen Moltmann, 'European Political Theology' in *The Cambridge Companion to Christian Political Theology*, ed. Craig Hovey et al. (New York NY: Cambridge University Press, 2013), 3.
3. Johann Baptist Metz, 'Two-Fold Political Theology' in Fiorenza, *Political Theology*, 13.
4. Ibid., 14-15.
5. Ibid., 16.
6. Ibid.

Christos Yannaras' Criticism of Western Political Theology

Christos Yannaras sets the framework for his critique of Western political theology in a work from 1983. He argues:

> The term 'political theology' in the West today has taken a very special content: it means a group or school of theologians that try to interpret the message of the gospels for the salvation of man with the instruments of modern political theories, mostly from the Marxist and neo-Marxist left. The main endeavours of this 'political theology' vary from a purely theoretical-scientific attempt of political interpretation of the biblical texts to an immediate and practical involvement of theologians and priests in radical movements.[1]

Yannaras takes a critical stance towards political theology: in his view, conservative, liberal and revolutionary political theology belong to the same 'coin' of Western theology, not because they have the same political practices, ideologies and modes of life, but because they are based on the same faulty ground of Western logic. This ground is traced by Yannaras through two basic problems: the problem of the polarisation between the transcendental and the worldly, and the problem of political commitment as a mechanism of individualistic over-compensation.

The Problem of the Polarisation between the Transcendental and the Worldly

According to Yannaras, political theology in the context of the Western world becomes one pole in the conflict between an intellectualist, academic and scholastic theology on one side, and a practical, hyper-politicised and committed, or 'militant' theology on the other. Western political theology belongs to the second pole,[2] where the emphasis on

---

1. Christos Yannaras, Κεφάλαια Πολιτικῆς Θεολογίας [*Chapters of Political Theology*] (Athens: Grigoris, 1983), 9. Yannaras, in this text of 1983, argues that this interpretation of the gospels' message through the modern theories was mostly made with instruments from the Marxist and neomarxist left. It is important to understand, that even though nowadays almost no one can use Marxism as the hermeneutical horizon of reality, Yannaras' criticism of political theologies has not lost its value.
2. Clodovis Boff and Leonardo Boff, *Introducing Liberation Theology* (London: Burns & Oates, 1987), 19. The term 'Militant' is used by Leonardo and Clodovis

the practice and social radicalism of revolutionary political theologies is a natural response to and a negation of the centuries-old dominance of intellectual Scholasticism and the absolute truth that stems from this mode of metaphysical thinking.

The context of academic and scholastic theology identified the truth with the *Idea* of it and God with the *Noesis*. As American philosopher Charles Taylor added, 'the space of disclosure is considered to be *inside*, in the "mind"'.[1] According to Yannaras, this pole found in Aquinas and Descartes the climax of its metaphysics, in which faith is understood as an achievement of internal thinking and individual logic.

In this context, idea produces idea, thought produces thought, theory produces theory, independently of the total experience of the whole person and the experience of its relationship with others and the incarnated world, with which it constitutes a community or society. The development of this metaphysical understanding of the relationship between the transcendental and the worldly transforms theology into a philosophical system and faith becomes ideology. This intellectual logic thus leads to a problematic understanding of incarnation and history. As the French Catholic theologian Jean Daniélou points out, there is a distinction between Thomism and Patristic theology. In his own words, 'the concept of history is not part of Thomism. On the contrary it is central to the big patristic systems'.[2]

According to Yannaras, political theology, transformed through materialism and historicism into a revolutionary political movement, came into conflict with Western metaphysical Christianity, which was politically harmless. As a result, transcendental theologies deal with a 'God-Idea' that does not relate with the incarnated experience and its history, while the secularised theologies of praxis focus on a history rid of the eschatological experience. In many cases, political theology becomes so obsessed with changing social structures and political institutions that it seems like a 'theology without God'.[3]

However, the following must be made clear: Yannaras does not criticise theologies of political praxis or theologies of history. Quite the contrary, since incarnation and historical experience form a basic

Boff to describe the commitment to the poor by the Christians of the Latin American movement of 'Theology of Liberation'.

1. Charles Taylor, 'The Person' in *The Category of the Person: Anthropology, Philosophy, History*, ed. Michael Carrithers et al. (Cambridge: Cambridge University Press, 1985), 277.

2. Rosino Gibellini, Ἡ Θεολογία τοῦ Εἰκοστοῦ Αἰώνα [Twentieth Century Theology], trans. Panagiotis Yfantis (Athens: Artos Zois, 2009), 240.

3. Apostolos Nikolaidis, Κοινωνικοπολιτικὴ Ἐπανάσταση καὶ Πολιτικὴ Θεολογία [Socio-Political Revolution and Political Theology] (Katerini: Tetrios, 1987), 107.

pillar of his ontology and theology. The problem for him is that in many cases political theologies develop an historic devotion in which they underestimate the Resurrection and the Eucharistic dimension in their emphasis on social and political activism. In these cases, Yannaras wonders: 'why is theology needed in this context? Why is it not enough just to be politically or to be a revolutionary?'[1]

The Problem of Political Commitment as a Mechanism of Individualistic Over-Compensation

According to Yannaras, the main problem of the person who is socially and politically committed (or militant), while basing his activity on biblical tradition, is demonstrated in the fact that for this person Christianity is conceived and experienced as a religious and not as an ecclesial event. The religious event is individualistic, connected with commitment of any kind, including political and social commitment. On the other hand, the ecclesial/Eucharistic event as the Christian event per se, refers to the human person who related with others, with nature and God, in the freedom of Love.

But why does an individualistic religious logic lead necessarily to any kind of commitment, while an ecclesial logic leads to the freedom of relationship? Yannaras argues:

> Religion is another kind of event: it has a codified 'faith' which it demands from others, it has 'dogmas,' which the individual has to accept as his own beliefs. . . . The subordination of the individual to the 'right' beliefs and the upholding of norms of 'divine validity' exclude communal participation and make up another kind of event: a commitment that secures ego, through 'eternal' security.[2]

In this normative religious framework the Western Church is understood as an 'acropolis under siege' from the powers of evil and sin. The dogma of ideas and practices that offer salvation has been definitely given; its truth has been certified by the hierarchy of the Church or through the mystical experience of the inner self and the believer is now called upon to defend it individually. Christianity becomes a religion, and religiousness as an

---

1. Christos Yannaras, *The Freedom of Morality*, trans. Elisabeth Briele (Crestwood, NY: St.Vladimir's Seminary Press, 1984), 200; Yannaras, Κεφάλαια Πολιτικῆς Θεολογίας [*Chapters of Political Theology*], 9-10.
2. Christos Yannaras, Ἡ Εὐρώπη Γεννήθηκε ἀπὸ τὸ Σχίσμα [*The Great Schism Engendered Europe*] (Athens: Ikaros, 2015), 114.

individual choice and a mechanism of belonging serves the psychological defence that seeks existential security and certainty.[1] Every other person who questions their beliefs and axioms is thus seen as a threat and an enemy.

According to Athanasios Papathanasiou, a theologian and editor of *Synaxi*, a major theological journal in Greece, the belief that orders have a value in themselves leads to a loveless competition for self-justification about which the Apostle Paul spoke, presenting it as a twist of faith.[2] A good example of this attitude, according to Yannaras, is 'Pietism',[3] an expression of Protestantism at the end of the seventeenth and beginning of the eighteenth century, which understood the Gospel more as a code, as a practice of ethics, or as a moralistic duty and not as an *Ethos* of freedom, which means a mode of life inspired by freedom.[4]

The distinction between the religious and the ecclesial event as a distinction between individualistic and relational existence, or between abstract ideology and salvific experience, is made clear in the issue of faith. Yannaras argues:

> The Church speaks about *faith* in the Greek sense of the word: Belief in Greek means *trust*, and to *believe* means *to trust*. . . . Faith is an experience of a *relationship* and has the dynamic of the relationship. It is continuously conquered without it ever ending. . . . On the contrary, *faith* for the holy Augustine is an individual belief of principles and values.[5]

Yannaras follows the French theologian Marie-Dominique Chenu, pointing out that mental faith as a psychological belief objectifies faith into rules and values, thus turning its experience into an idol. 'Idols' of religiousness are the enemies of the Eucharistic event which makes up Christianity.

The religious event as an objective truth did not avoid being directly influenced by the dominant social, political and cultural relations of its time. Religiousness was expressed inside the feudal world as

1. Ibid., 123.
2. Athanasios Papathanasiou, Ἀχαμένοι στὴν Ἠθική: Στάσεις τῆς Σύγχρονης Ὀρθόδοξης Θεολογίας' ['Lost in Ethics: Stances of Modern Orthodox Theology'] in Ἡ Ἐπιστροφὴ τῆς Ἠθικῆς [*The Return of Ethics*], ed. Stavros Zouboulakis (Athens: Artos Zois, 2013), 282.
3. Yannaras, *The Freedom of Morality*, 119-36; Christos Yannaras, Καταφύγιο Ἰδεῶν: Μαρτυρία [*Refuge of Ideas: Testimony*] (Athens: Domos, 1987), 119-36.
4. Christos Yannaras, *On the Absence and Unknowability of God: Heidegger and the Areopagite*, trans. Haralambos Ventis et al. (London, NY: T. & T. Clark International, 2005), 32.
5. Yannaras, Ἡ Εὐρώπη Γεννήθηκε ἀπὸ τὸ Σχίσμα [*The Great Schism Engendered Europe*], 130.

a 'conservative theology'. With the passage of time and the rise of liberalism, the absoluteness of religion turned into a liberal stance, with 'theological Kantianism' as its climax. This historical phase, as Taylor claims, 'involves the interiorisation of personhood: it starts with the definition substantia rationalis individual and ends up generating the modern notion of the individual, as monad'.[1]

The historical reaction to both the conservative and the liberal political theology, when the labour movement arose into the mass societies of the industrial revolution worldwide, came from the 'militant' Marxist revolutionary theology, mostly in Latin America and the rest of the colonised world, which opposed abstract universal values with concrete historical action. But for Yannaras, all these historical forms are into the same context of transforming Christianity into a religion when social openness maintains an individualistic basis.

Individualistic religious logic reveals a need for psychological security. Sigmund Freud wrote about different kinds of love. One of them is the kind of love he senses in many persons who attempt to disengage from the pressures of an immediate relationship with others. Many of these people exchange the experience and the need of loving and being loved personally with the experience of a general offer towards the public. In this way they 'transfer' their love to people in general and not to certain persons, where they would risk being rejected.[2] This way of life, which Freud describes as a 'mechanism of overcompensation' is what Yannaras means when he talks about the 'psychological overcompensation of Western Christians' and the 'psychological motives of political theology'.[3] In these cases, love and faith is used as a political ideology for social practice; as a commitment and ethical system.

The Problem of Political and Social Violence

Another issue for political theology is the problem of the relationship between Christian life and political and social violence. Historical oppression and injustice in many cases has led to the development of radical political theologies, such as the theologies of revolution or liberation theologies in Latin America. According to Fr George Metallinos, a Greek theologian, historian, author and professor, radical

1. Taylor, 'The Person', 281.
2. Sigmund Freud, *Civilization and Its Discontents*, trans. James Strachey (New York: W. Norton & Company Inc., 1962), 48-9.
3. Yannaras, *Κεφάλαια Πολιτικής Θεολογίας [Chapters of Political Theology]*, 10.

political theologies are the result of the Western feudal system, which has been particularly cruel to the lower classes and culturally racist. That led to social and political polarisation in Western societies as well as in their colonies. The Roman Catholic Church in some cases took the place of the European feudal elite, sometimes supporting servitude with theological arguments. Moreover, it legitimised colonisation and imperialism as the divine order of things.[1] Fr Metallinos concludes that the revolutionary movement in the European colonies is an effort to restore the theology of the Christian world and discover the true spirit of theology in the Christian Third World, as well as the discovery of the real spirit of Christianity of the Bible in society.[2]

Christos Yannaras recognises the problem of historical violence and the choice for a Christian whether to undertake the responsibility to struggle with the people against a conqueror or an exploiter, or to participate in a common effort with others with the purpose of changing the oppressive political and social structures and establishing liberated social relationships and political institutions. The problem, according to the Greek Christian philosopher, is detected in the fact that the radical political theologies of revolution justify social and political violence with theological arguments. Because of this, political theologies serve the psychological reassurance of individual political choices and hopes. Moreover, Papathanasiou argues, these Christian acts were understood by Yannaras as attempts to replace the ethos of personal endangerment inside the tragic imperfectness of the world through a 'morality' of 'objective reassurance'; for example, through basing revolt on the Bible.[3]

Yannaras' main problem is neither the political stance of these Christians nor the fact that some of them revolt or resort to violence. His problem is with basing and justifying these actions on God's will, on the Holy Scriptures or on Christian traditions. A Christian should know that no psychological or spiritual reassurance exists when he takes the responsibility to act politically and use violence. Taking political responsibility, even through murder, with the purpose of changing social and political structures or of deposing a tyrant, mobilises many Christians in the so-called theologies of revolution and liberation. But

---

1. George Metallinos, 'Θεολογία Ἐλευθερίας καὶ Θεολογία Ἀπελευθερώσεως' ['Theology of Freedom and Liberation Theology'] in Τὸ Δικαίωμα τῆς Ἀντίστασης: Δικανικοὶ Διάλογοι III [The Right to Resist: Juridical Dialogues III], ed.Kostas Beys (Athens: Kentro Dikanikon Meleton, 1995), 369-70.
2. Ibid., 370-1.
3. Papathanasiou, 'Χαμένοι στὴν Ἠθική' ['Lost in Ethics'], 296-7.

when violent political action of the Christian is based on the Bible or on Christ, argues the theologian and researcher Christine Schliesser, it reaches its highest contradiction.[1]

Yannaras takes the *drama* of political and historical life a bit further. According to him, a Christian cannot take part in violence and murder and wonder if this mode of life is the mode of Christ; for it is not. In violence, people risk their soul, not just their biological existence. However, this is a danger that a believer accepts for the sake of the people, as the price of being one of them and of fighting with them, and not because Christology demands it. As a consequence, even if such a political stance cannot be totally isolated or distinguished from the spirituality and Christology of its actor, it also cannot be based on it, on the Bible or on some moral teaching of the Church.

It is accurate if we claim that the critical position of Yannaras does not reject any political theology but only the one that is 'á priori dedicated to individual claims'.[2] He rejects a political theology that transforms Christianity into an individualistic and egocentric religion and an ideology for specific uses inside the social and political sphere.

Moreover, Yannaras' criticism is not the kind of elitist view that underestimates everyday praxis from the standpoint of an aesthetically superior spirit.[3] His criticism is directed on those social actions of any political theology which although claiming to base themselves on the life of Christ and the Holy Scriptures, they actually have nothing to do with the Eucharistic event. This Christianity ends up as a romantic ideology and a moralistic aretology. Therefore, Yannaras' criticism does not question political theology; it clarifies it.

---

1. Christine Schliesser, *Everyone Who Acts Responsibly Becomes Guilty: Bonhoeffer's Concept of Accepting Guilt* (Louisville: Westminster John Knox Press, 2008), 175-205, as cited in Stavros Zouboulakis, ʾΝτήτριχ Μπονχαῖφφερ: ἡ Χριστιανικὴ Ἠθικὴ ὡς Ἠθικὴ τῆς Εὐθύνης' ['Dietrich Bonhoeffer: Christian Ethic as an Ethic of Responsibility'] in Zouboulakis, *Ἡ Ἐπιστροφὴ τῆς Ἠθικῆς [The Return of Ethics]*, 345.

2. Yannaras, *Κεφάλαια Πολιτικῆς Θεολογίας [Chapters of Political Theology]*, 10-11.

3. This critical view against Yannaras cited in Papathanasiou, ʾΧαμένοι στὴν Ἠθικὴʾ ['Lost in Ethics'], 294-5; Marios P. Mpegzos, *Τὸ Μέλλον τοῦ Παρελθόντος [The Future of the Past]* (Athens: Armos, 1993), 86-92; Stavros Zouboulakis, ʾΤὸ 'Σύνορο' καὶ ὁ Χρῆστος Γιανναρᾶς. Ἡ Θεολογικὴ Πρόταση τῆς Ἀποηθικοποίησης τοῦ Χριστιανισμοῦ' ['The "Border" and Christos Yannaras: The Theological Proposal of Demoralizing Christianity'] in *Ἀναταράξεις στὴ Μεταπολεμικὴ Θεολογία: Ἡ Θεολογία τοῦ '60 [Turbulence in Post-War Theology: The Theology of the 60s]*, ed. Athanasios Abatzidis et al. (Athens: Indiktos, 2009), 315-26.

Yannaras' Political Theology of the Eucharistic Event

Yannaras, by quoting Khomiakof, argues that 'the political theory of the Church is the truth of the holy Trinity',[1] since ecclesial ethic lies in the secret life of the Eucharistic event. This event is the generative cause and source of Christian ethos, which ontologically transfigures the human person,[2] the community and the polis.[3] Yannaras accepts the communal, social and political change that occurs when human existence responds to ontological originality, which is incarnated as an expression of love's freedom. This freedom will be put at the epicentre of Christian and political life as an event that takes place through the freedom of relationship.

This love is a catholic experience of the human being that transfigures the person's will and the mode of his other life. Distinguished from this experience, according to Yannaras, liberation in Western logic expresses a situation of sentimental love and rational management of egoistic passions that starts and ends with the inner self. Sometimes it is an 'internal' exhaustive fight with and against one's own self and, at other times, it is the 'external' struggle against social and political structures and the attempt to change them, as an expression of individual responsibility towards the world.[4]

However, by the ecclesial logic, the experience of freedom is expressed in history through relationships with others, with nature and with God, and not as a self-referring, individualistic and internal struggle. Human persons don't change first internally and personally and then open themselves to the world; on the contrary, they change inside the relationship, by communicating with the world.

Yannaras detects this change in Christians and their polis in the ecclesial/Eucharistic event, which is the expression of a special mode of being; the Christian act per se. This mode of being does not confine itself within the limits of a Church as a place of liturgy, but it spreads all

---

1. Yannaras, *Κεφάλαια Πολιτικῆς Θεολογίας* [*Chapters of Political Theology*], 12. Papathanasiou mentions that there are similarities with the views of many Russian orthodox, such as the Metropolitan Anthony Khrapovitsky, Vladimir Lossky or Sofronios of Essex, about the political dimension of the Christian life, in Papathanasiou, 'Χαμένοι στὴν Ἠθική' ['Lost in Ethics'], 289.
2. Yannaras, *The Freedom of Morality*, 16-17.
3. Ibid., 219-23. A similar view is shared by John Zizioulas, the Metropolitan of Pergamos. Zizioulas, 'Θεία Εὐχαριστία καὶ Ἐκκλησία' ['Eucharistic Event and Church'] in *Τὸ Μυστήριο τῆς Θείας Εὐχαριστίας [The Mystery of the Eucharistic Event]* (Athens: Apostoliki Diakonia, 2004), 34.
4. Yannaras, *The Freedom of Morality*, 204.

over the world as a social and political event, in this way becoming the beginning of social, political and cultural transformation and a cause for historical change.[1]

Because of this logic, Yannaras does not criticise the practising of solidarity and social justice,[2] but makes clear that taking care of the hungry, the thirsty, the foreigners, and so on, is an achievement and an indication not of moral behaviour but of a *mode of existence*, a transfiguration of personality that ripples throughout one's social and political relations.[3] Moreover, Papathanasiou mentions Fr Alexander Schmemann, according to whom the Eucharistic event does not only witness to the world its experience but is also baptised in the world.[4] The teachings of Maximus the Confessor are also similar in this aspect. In addition, Papathanasiou argues that for Fr Dumitru Staniloae, Maximus the Confessor finishes his work with praise for compassion and love for others, setting this task above everything else.[5]

In the same vein, Archbishop of Tirana and all Albania, Anastasios (Yannoulatos), in 1975 stated his famous thesis on political and social life as a 'liturgy after the liturgy'. He called for spreading the Eucharistic experience on everyday life as a kind of ministration, 'with the purpose of liberating humanity from all its demonic structures of injustice, exploitation, agony, loneliness and the creation of a real society that live in love'.[6] This ministration does not mean that the Church must have a political programme for social and institutional structural changes. It is clear for Archbishop Anastasios that the creation or destruction of social structures is a political and not a theological or ecclesial task. In the same vein, Gutiérrez makes clear:

1. Ibid., 216-23.
2. Yannaras was deeply influenced by the Russian Christian philosopher Nikolai Berdyaev, in Yannaras, *Καταφύγιο Ἰδεῶν [Refuge of Ideas]*, 256-7.
3. Christos Yannaras, *Τὸ Ρητὸ καὶ τὸ Ἄρρητο [The Sayable]* (Athens: Ikaros, 1999), 222. Papathanasiou, 'Χαμένοι στὴν Ἠθική' ['Lost in Ethics'], 295.
4. Athanasios Papathanasiou, Ἡ Ἐκκλησία ὡς Ἀποστολή. Ἕνα Κριτικὸ Ξανακοίταγμα τῆς Λειτουργικῆς Θεολογίας τοῦ π. Ἀλεξάνδρου Σμέμαν' ['The Church as a Mission: A Critical Review of the Liturgical Theology of Fr Alexander Schmemann'], *Theology* 80 (2009): 67-108; Papathanasiou, 'Χαμένοι στὴν Ἠθική' ['Lost in Ethics'], 303-4.
5. Fr Dumitru Staniloae, 'Introduction' in *Mystagogy* by Maximus the Confessor, trans. Ignatios Sakalis (Athens: Apostoliki Diakonia, 1973), 48, as cited in Pathanasiou, 'Χαμένοι στὴν Ἠθική' ['Lost in Ethics'], 306-9.
6. Anastasios of Androussa (Yannoulatos), *Ἱεραποστολὴ στὰ Ἴχνη τοῦ Χριστοῦ [The Mission on the Traces of Christ]* (Athens: Apostoliki Diakonia, 2007), 129-32; Papathanasiou, 'Χαμένοι στὴν Ἠθική' ['Lost in Ethics'], 301.

> My purpose is not to elaborate an ideology to justify postures already taken, or to undertake a feverish search for security in the face of the radical challenges that comfort the faith, or to fashion a theology from which political action is 'deduced'.[1]

Freedom of Relationship
as a Foundation of Political Practice

According to Yannaras, the ontological potential and the empirical reality of 'freedom of relationship' sets the ontological foundation for the ecclesia as well as for the polis as a community of persons. Theology and Christian life are also characterised as political, among other things, since the common life of the Christians among each other and with others manifests neither the ecclesia as polis, nor the polis as an entirety. In addition, 'freedom of relationship' means that no subjective or objective á priori truth precedes the relationship. Truth manifests itself to the world through the relation. Human persons find their common truth when they freely associate with others, converse with them with honesty and good intentions and without dogmatic ideas and absolute axioms.[2]

The 'freedom of relationship' is expressed by *apophatic rationality*, which Yannaras distinguishes from *cataphatic rationality*. Apophatic rationality refers to people who, as unique persons, meet to manifest in their common life the truth as it results from dialogue and social experience as an exercise in relationship.[3] This rationality is therefore apophatic exactly because it does not establish dogmatic truths and non-negotiable axioms, nor does it pursue domination upon others.[4] The apophatic *Relational Ontology*, according to which the being 'is not', but

---

1. Gutiérrez, *A Theology of Liberation*, ix.
2. Christos Yannaras, Ὀρθὸς Λόγος καὶ Κοινωνικὴ Πρακτικὴ *[Rationality and Social Practice]* (Athens: Domos, 2006), 303.
3. Charles Taylor goes so far as to write: 'I become a person and remain one only as an interlocutor', in Taylor, 'The Person', 276.
4. Christos Yannaras, Ἕξι Φιλοσοφικὲς Ζωγραφιές *[Six Philosophical Paintings]* (Athens: Ikaros, 2011), 32. Sotiris Mitralexis argues that, according to Yannaras, 'apophaticism is the stance towards the verification of knowledge . . . and can be defined as "the refusal to exhaust truth in its formulations, the refusal to identify the understanding of the signifier with the knowledge of the signified"' in Sotiris Mitralexis, 'Person, Eros, Critical Ontology: An Attempt to Recapitulate Christos Yannaras' Philosophy', *Sobornost* 34:1 (2012), 35.

'becomes', sets the foundation for theological and political praxis.[1] On
the flipside, cataphatic rationality of the individualistic and egocentric
logic acts as if the individual possesses the absolute truth of things or as if
it has the possibility to conquer it as a result of objective logic (*Ratio*). But
the meaning of the polis is manifest as a common *Logos* on the *ecclēsia
tou dēmou*, in the public sphere, and not as an individual rationality,
produced in the inner-self through intellectual abilities. The person of
apophatic rationality opens up to the world on the basis of a continuous
relationship of freedom, in constant co-creation and communication
with the historical evolution.

These distinct kinds of logic of apophatisism and cataphatisism
express distinct modes of life. For Yannaras, if freedom is understood
cataphatically, which means as freedom of action in order to fulfil the
requests of the individual for its own happiness, then social competition
and political struggle is unavoidable. The conflict will either take place
in order to acquire more and more consumer goods to serve constantly
increasing individual needs, or for the sake of social power and political
sovereignty. The egocentrism of individualism cancels the dynamic of
freedom in the relationship with the result of intensifying political hostility
and class conflict. When a similar individualistic and cataphatic logic
appears as an alternative in order to face this social and political division,
it will necessarily attempt to level and equate all possibilities of individual
fulfilment with the result of restricting or repressing personal liberties.[2]

Individual certainty in the possession of the truth destroys the
freedom of the relationship and any critical scrutiny to verify knowledge.
Critical scrutiny is only developed through the participation of many in
common decisions and through respect. This potential is only possible
with apophatic rationality, where freedom is understood as the negation
of necessity, as a dynamic of free relationships.[3]

Yannaras considers that the people who seek to live freely will have
to live with others in such a way that they are liberated from alienation,
which is caused by their natural impulses (e.g. instincts, uncontrolled
passions, unconscious impulses) as well as through social and political
restrictions (e.g. social and political relations, institutions and collective
views).[4] The social and political relationships that promote the unique

1. Christos Yannaras, *Relational Ontology*, trans. Norman Russell (Brookline, MA:
    Holy Cross Orthodox Press, 2011), 112-20.
2. Yannaras, Ὀρθὸς Λόγος καὶ Κοινωνικὴ Πρακτικὴ [*Rationality and Social Practice*],
    280, 290.
3. Ibid., 283.
4. Ibid., 284.

personality of every person, by helping him to exceed the bonds of nature and social restrictions, need to grow and develop through a non-dogmatic and non-individualistic rationality.

Epilogue

Since history never ends, nor is ever utterly fulfilled, and since no one possesses absolute truths, no statement should be rejected in advance. Instead, they should rather be put to scrutiny while they converse with each other. Because of this fact, Yannaras talks about a 'dynamic freedom' of apophaticism. The 'dynamic of freedom' and apophatic rationality should not demand perfection and absolution that anyway do not seem to appear anywhere in our historical existence. Moreover, it is Yannaras' central thesis that people organise their societies according to their needs. Radically different needs lead to different historical solutions.[1] History, society and politics always remain open to creation; always remain apophatic.

In conclusion, the experience of the mystery of 'freedom of relationship' expresses a revolutionary dynamic for the creative reforming of social relationships and political institutions, where each citizen takes his or her own responsibility for this effort. Nothing in this political and historical process can ensure the achievement of personal aims or a definite and successful historical transformation. The revolutionary explosion of collective imagination and creativity grows based on the 'freedom of ethos' alone.[2] The 'freedom of relationship' and the meaning of the mode that originated through this experience sums up the political event as 'polis' for Christos Yannaras. If 'freedom of relationship' refers to a life of trust in God and love for each other inside the polis, then this experience sums up the political theology of Christos Yannaras.

---

1. Ibid., 293-4.
2. Ibid., 288.

Chapter Four
Freedom and Necessity:
Yannaras and the Global Struggle for Life
Paul Tyson

This paper is divided into three sections. Firstly, the Greek referendum of 2015 will be examined as a case study in the triumph of necessity over freedom. Secondly, I will creatively unpack Yannaras' understanding of what freedom and necessity are in order to show how problematic dominant Western conceptions of both of these terms now are. Thirdly, I will briefly explore how appreciating something of the dynamics of the free mode of existence of persons is vital in resisting the unreality and violent necessity of our times.

Greece and Post-Political Power

The irrelevance of democratic politics to power in our times is demonstrated very clearly in the aftermath of the decisive victory of *oxi* over *nai* in the Greek referendum of 2015. This event unveils the now acute difference between pragmatic international necessity and state-located political freedom in the modern world. In that referendum the Greek people stood with their government in insisting that the imposition of deep austerity measures on their state by the Troika[1] was an economically self-defeating act of inexcusable brutality. However, even though the people stood with the government, the government did not stand with the people after the referendum. To save Greece from being ejected from the Eurozone, Prime Minister Alexis Tsipras

---

1. For brevity I will use 'the Troika' as a label signifying the three transnational institutions implementing the key financial decisions that govern the economic concerns of small and financially troubled states within the Eurozone: the European Commission, the European Central Bank, and the International Monetary Fund.

fully acquiesced to the demands of European financial and bureaucratic power, against the express political will of the people he was elected to represent. This was the end of the short power play between the Syriza government and the Troika which had been going since January of 2015 when Syriza was elected on a platform of re-negotiating crushing austerity demands with the Troika. Tsipras' surrender has resulted in deeper debt for Greece, deeper austerity for the poor, and has totally demoralised the political will of the Greek people as expressed in the 2015 referendum.

Tsipras' action was understandable. His choice was a function of the logic of realism as defined by relative size and financial dependence. Greece is a small power whose economic miracle in the early 2000s was a direct result of entry into the Eurozone.

That entry into what was originally the European Coal and Steel Community – a Western European heavy industry cartel – was a decisive turning point for the Greek people. In 2000 the ratio of household debt to a rather modest GDP was around 10%.[1] Yet, with a new and strong currency, Greece's twenty-first century boom period – 2003 to 2007 – was strongly debt enabled in both the public and private spheres. By the time the global financial crisis hit, the ratio of household debt to a greatly expanded GDP was 55%.[2] Profligate debt, producing speculative bubbles in real estate, tourism and luxury ventures, was enabled by a willing supply of foreign credit. Banks make money out of debt and they had been making it hand over fist in Greece in the boom time. When the global financial crisis of 2008 hit, and foreign credit took flight, this left Greek businesses and debtors in serious trouble. The good times rapidly turned into an unending nightmare of economic contraction, widespread poverty, unemployment, tax hikes, service cuts and an ever increasing mountain of unpayable debts accrued against the Greek government.

After 2008 the deeply unsound political and financial architecture of the Eurozone became unavoidably apparent. That architecture is defined by the absence of genuinely political controls over Eurozone finance, by the inability of weak national economies to depreciate their currency to solve regional problems, and by the determination of high finance not to pay the price of profligate lending.

---

1. Trading Economics, 'Greece Households Debt To Gdp, 1994-2018'; http://www.tradingeconomics.com/greece/households-debt-to-gdp. Accessed on 20 November 2017.
2. Ibid.

Greece's official unemployment rate is now at 23%.[1] The actual size of the Greek economy has shrunk by 25% since 2007.[2] At the same time as the Greek economy is in deep depression, taxes have been steeply raised and social benefits for the poor have been savagely cut, all in the name of necessary austerity.

Because Greece is a small economy that willingly sought union with European financial power, Tsipras obviously thought he had no choice but to give that power what it demanded. Fear is also a key component of this dynamic. History indicates that if you are a small power and you defy great powers, you can expect merciless reprisals. Indeed, in an overt siege move, the Greek banks were closed down during the 2015 referendum campaign. Who wants to stand up with the voice of the people and doom their entire nation to oblivion? Ironically, the destruction of Melos by the Athenian empire may well have been going through Tsipras' head once it became clear that the 'No' vote had won.[3]

Transnational instrumental financial and technocratic power, driven by an amoral pragmatic conception of numerically defined significance, now governs the material conditions under which we live. Such power has no regard for human needs or political deliberations. Michael Hauser has insightfully described this dynamic as the depoliticisation of power *within* states that are liberal democracies.[4] Whilst depoliticised power is far from just a Greek problem – it is a truly global feature of the world order in which we all now live – the anti-political and inhumane nature of this power is illustrated very clearly in the Greek referendum of 2015.

I want to bring Yannaras' understanding of freedom and necessity to bear on our present globally depoliticising context, but, before I do, let us unpack what is going on here a little more carefully in regards to our use of terms surrounding freedom and necessity.

---

1. Unemployment statistics - Statistics Explained - European Commission, 'Greece Unemployment rates, seasonally adjusted, January 2017'; http://ec.europa.eu/eurostat/statistics-explained/index.php/File:Unemployment_rates,_seasonally_adjusted,_January_2017_(%25)_F2.png. Accessed on 20 November 2017.
2. 'Countries of the World: Greece'; http://www.theodora.com/wfbcurrent/greece/greece_economy.html. Accessed on 20 November 2017.
3. Thucydides, *History of the Peloponnesian War*, 5: 84-116, trans. Rex Warner (London: Penguin, 1972), 400-8. It seems like Tsipras took the advice of the Athenians in this Melian dialogue in relation to the threat of siege and destruction by the Troika.
4. Michael Hauser, 'The Twilight of Liberal Democracy: A Symptomatic Reading of Depoliticization', *Décalages* 1 (2014). http://scholar.oxy.edu/decalages/vol1/iss3/4.

There are a range of very different meanings that the word 'indeterminate' can signify. The type of indeterminacy that Paul Virilio discusses concerns the removal of those factors that make a collectively reasoned determination within politics possible.[5] As a result, for example, of high-speed automated computerised stock market trading, the dominance of interconnected and algorithmically pre-determined responses so governs the world of international finance that the directional dynamic of the system as a whole is beyond human control. It has become indeterminate and vulnerable to accidents derived from its extraordinary speed, power and ubiquity. Here the velocity of interactive automated decision making is so much faster than the tempo at which thoughtful human decisions can be reasonably made that thoughtful human decisions are removed from the overarching dynamic of how the system works. In terms of how I wish to speak of freedom and necessity, this form of indeterminacy is the same thing as necessity. Necessity implies the absence of meaningful human deliberation, the powerlessness of chosen value directed action in the face of inhuman forces, even (actually, particularly) if those forces are entirely man-made. But there are other ways of thinking about the indeterminate.

In political economics it is usually understood that there are some things that are determinate, calculable and manipulable, and other things that are indeterminate and outside of economic calculation or manipulation. Neoliberals like to think that common values defining a common good must be seen as indeterminate in any aggregate of free and economically rational (that is, self-interested) individuals. On the other hand, this ideology believes in the existence of strict econometric laws governing 'the market', laws that must be liberated from the unnatural political constraints of 'excessive' government regulation, interference and taxation. These laws are determinate and objective, and hence calculable and subject to rational manipulation. We will explore the grounds of such neoliberal thinking later in this paper.[6] For now, and in stark contrast to Chicago School thinking, I wish to touch on Yanis Varoufakis' fascinating exploration of economic indeterminacy.

According to Varoufakis, economics is a human and political activity, conducted not by isolated algorithmic rationally self-interested machines, but by persons in solidarity.[7] As such, it is a free activity. In

5. Paul Virilio, *Negative Horizon* (New York: Continuum, 2005), 166. Paul Virilio, *The Administration of Fear* (Los Angeles: semiotext(e), 2012), 34-5, 86.

6. For an excellent introductory outline describing what neoliberalism is, see Manfred B. Steger and Ravi K. Roy, *Neoliberalism* (Oxford: Oxford University Press, 2010).

7. Yanis Varoufakis, *Economic Indeterminacy* (Abingdon: Routledge, 2014), 182-

the Greek polis tradition, Varoufakis sees indeterminacy and creativity within a community of un-coerced and discursive collaborators as the hallmark of human freedom and of good political economics. However, some aspects of human community life are materially constrained, and these are determinate factors which impinge on human freedom. To Varoufakis, there is a dialectic between the determinate and the indeterminate in economic activity.[1] The trick is to understand what is determinate and what is indeterminate and to order the political economy accordingly.

For example, it is a determinate reality that if you do not eat you die. However, financialised trade is an entirely human construct and its operational modes are thus indeterminate and are generated by our own creativity and the collective conventions that we ourselves invent. Where there is physically enough food to feed everyone, and yet some people starve because they have no money, we have treated the indeterminate (money) as determinate, and the determinate (the need for food) as indeterminate. In effect, when money serves human needs it is a good thing and material and determinate reality as well as human creativity and freedom are properly respected. But where human needs are subordinate to money as a reified reality, when money is treated as a determinate necessity, a natural kind with its own ontological essence, then the political economy has failed to be both realistic and human.

In our era of currency and derivative trading, astonishingly complex financial instruments, tax havens as central features of global high finance, and the fiat generation of enormous sums of money out of nothing – as seen in banking leverage and quantitative easing – clearly the unreal and the humanly constructed define modern finance.[2] Modern finance is indeterminate both as an entirely man-made construct (that, in reality, we could change) and, in Virilio's sense, as a power that – via technologies that overcome space and time – now controls us, removing our freedom to act politically. The fact that derivative and currency trading now moves inordinately larger sums of money than are circulating in the global economy in real goods

---

204, 338-42.

1. Yanis Varoufakis, 'Yanis Varoufakis: Confessions of an Erratic Marxist in the Midst of a Repugnant Eurozone Crisis', http://www.nakedcapitalism.com/2013/12/yanis-varoufakis-confessions-erratic-marxist-midst-repugnant-eurozone-crisis.html. Accessed on 20 November 2017.

2. See Satyajit Das, *Extreme Money: Masters of the Universe and the Cult of Risk* (USA: Financial Times Press, 2011); Nicholas Shaxson, *Treasure Islands: Tax Havens and the Men who Stole the World* (London: Vintage, 2013); Joseph Stiglitz, *Globalization and its Discontents* (London: Penguin, 2002).

and services, and that the super-rich can pay no taxes at all if it suits them, shows us that high finance is an artificial system of necessity unconnected to both human realities and political deliberations, in the extreme.[1]

In the case of the 2015 referendum in Greece, the artificial realm of finance was treated by the governing powers of the Eurozone as a realm of hard necessity. In contrast, the physical needs and political deliberations of real people were treated as a function of a neoliberal conception of indeterminate and unreal dreams that were of no concern to those financial institutions holding Greece to impossible austerity. The Eurozone finance sector must be saved and the Greek people must be sacrificed. This is where the depoliticisation of power has taken us in the realms of finance, economics and so-called politics.

I greatly admire thinkers such as Hauser and Varoufakis who have clearly identified the anti-political and anti-human trajectories of power within our times. Even so, they are not theologians and have not thought about the Western theological roots of this dynamic. Nor do they give much thought to the religious nature of the financialised world. Nor do they seem aware of the extent to which modern Western understandings of knowledge, power and reality potently enable this anti-political lifeworld of inhuman and artificial necessity. As a result they are struggling valiantly for solutions but they are still locked within the meta-cultural framework of what is possible for Western modernity.

At its most fundamental level, it is the assumed boundaries of what is possible and what is impossible within our life-world, and modern Western modes of existence, that have generated the problems we now face. Centrally, there is a profound ontological inadequacy at the core of the modern Western understanding of personhood that shapes the norms of our modes of existence. At these most fundamental levels of analysis, Yannaras helps us where few others can.

---

1. Susan George, *Shadow Sovereigns* (London: Polity Press, 2015), 25. George's information is drawn from the 2014 Bank of International Settlements Triennial Survey: 'Derivative trading has reached $2,300,000,000,000 per day [about $700 trillion a year].... How much is that? The GDP of the entire world is estimated at about $70 trillion [per annum], so the circulation of this single class of financial products is 10 times greater.' George notes on the same page that 'currency trading is at well over five trillion dollars a day', which is more than twice the size of derivative trading. That is, the real global economy in actual goods and services – and the vast majority of the livelihoods of the people of the world – is dwarfed by the immense speculative power of a relatively tiny group of global financial institutions and individuals.

Engaging with Yannaras
on Freedom, Necessity and the West

I should preface this attempt to engage with Yannaras' writings by pointing out that I am a Western Christian embedded in a set of terminologies, formations, sources and lifeforms largely alien to Eastern Christianity. No doubt my engagement will entail category errors, terminological mangles and misappropriations. I will risk this endeavour and accept a degree of failure for two reasons.

Firstly, I have not read Yannaras as a sectarian Orthodox theologian, but as a catholic (*katholikos*) theologian whose voice concerns the whole rather than just Eastern concerns. As a catholic thinker, I find that his problems with the West are in many regards also my problems with my own culture. The reverse is true as well. I have no difficulty in believing him when he claims that his critique of the West is self-critique.[1] Due to the global power of Western culture and its instrumental life-form, we all now live in the same macro life-world context, and we all now struggle with much the same problems, whether we are native Westerners or not.

Secondly, and in apparent contradiction to what I have just said, I have found Yannaras' critique of the West to be located within a context that does not directly concern me as a Western Christian, the context of the destructive appropriation of Western influences within Eastern Orthodoxy. That is, Yannaras' reading of Augustine, Aquinas and Luther are carefully constructed and well-justified in the context of their Eastern appropriation, but they are not persuasive for contexts they are not intended for. For that reason I do not feel offended as a Western Christian by what would be unfair readings if they were directed at a Western Christian audience. Even so, returning to the catholic significance of Yannaras, it is genuinely the case that the West has profound internal theological problems, and Yannaras' voice is very helpful for troubled Western Christians seeking an outsider's eye that can reveal what it is that we don't know about ourselves.

Because Yannaras is an insightful catholic theologian, I can take what I think I understand from his insights and reframe them in the context of my own Western theological critique of the post-Christian West. This is not going to work on all levels, but it is my engagement with Yannaras, and I think it is the only sort of engagement I, as a Western Christian, can do.

---

1.   Christos Yannaras, *Orthodoxy and the West* (Brookline: Holy Cross Orthodox Press, 2006), ix.

Let us now turn from the preface to examine the matter of freedom. It is important to understand the specific meaning that Yannaras gives to freedom. Freedom here is a function of the unique ontology of persons.[1] That is, persons are always located within relations of love that are not mechanically necessary, and the essence of any person is not determined by necessity either. In other words, love and personhood are essentially free. Creativity and goodness require this freedom from determinate necessity, such that the bonds of love and the mystery of personhood can never be defined in terms of determinate necessity. For example, a mother has strong natural instincts to care for her child, but she is in fact free to negate those instincts, and also free to love her child and follow those instincts. Determinate instinctive urges do not define the love of a mother for her child, even though those instincts really are there.

As I understand Yannaras, this way of thinking about what it means to be a person – and in our case, human – is an ontological outlook embedded in the Palamite distinction between essence and energy. God, in essence, is not knowable by us, but God's energies reveal God as Trinity of Persons, manifesting goodness and creative love and – in an apophatic but none-the-less revelatory manner – the wondrous *mystery* of the distinctive personal essence of the divine. As created in God's image – the image of persons in relations of love – there is thus also a distinction between essence and energy regarding our own personhood. There is some essentially mysterious essence at the core of the personhood of each of us, which is partially, creatively and apophatically revealed in our energies. I think of the image in the Apocalypse of John where the saints from the Church in Pergamum receive from Christ a white stone with a name on it known only to God and the one who receives it (Revelation 2:17). There is a unique personal essence – a divinely given name – defining each person, but it is not an essence that any determinate definition located in the realm of things and concepts can contain; it is a unique personal name. Love itself, without persons who love, cannot be love. Love is as dependent on Persons as Persons are on love. Persons must have a distinctive and unique essence, but that essence – as with all essence proper – remains the mysterious source of all particular things

---

1. Christos Yannaras, *The Freedom of Morality* (New York: St Vladimir's Seminary Press, 1984), 42-6. Christos Yannaras, *Elements of Faith* (Edinburgh: T. & T. Clark, 1991), 35-6. An excellent complement to Yannaras' understanding of freedom, embedded in a similar Christian reading of Classical Greek understandings, is Simone Weil's understanding of the opposite of freedom, the necessities of the existential mode of violent force. See Simone Weil, 'The Iliad or poem of force' in *War and the Iliad*, Simone Weil and Rachel Bespaloff (New York: New York Review of Books, 2005), 1-37.

manifest within the realm of energetic existence. That is, the realm of energies is populated by defined, finite and determinate beings, as well as necessary determinate causal relations manifest as universal laws and concepts. Yet, that which is below determination – chaos, flux and contingency – and that which is above contingent necessity – transcendent essence – are also partially manifest in the energetic realm. Indeed, this realm of energies is derivative of both chaos and nothing on the one hand, and unknowable essence on the other. In the energetic realm, those beings and universal laws that appear defined and determinate provide us with a useful intelligible framework for understanding and reasoned action within the energetic realm, but the realm of energies emanates from the realm of essence and so the energetic realm is not finally real in itself. Its reality is derivative of the ineffable Goodness Beyond Being of the Divine Trinity that is the source of all creative energies and all determinate and defined manifestations of particular material existence within created reality.

While, in the derivative realm of energies, the determinate and the defined can be known, such knowledge is knowledge of the surface and shape of an icon – it is not knowledge in itself of that which the icon participates in, of that which shines through the icon, of that which cannot be contained in the terms of the determinate and the defined.

The premier classical statement of the apophatic sensibility is Plato's *Theaetetus*. Allow me the anachronistic liberty of re-phrasing Plato's arguments in Palamite terms.

Because it is only possible to experience the energy of knowledge, not to know the essence of knowledge itself, we experience the mystery of truth *grasping us* from beyond the realm of determinate, particular and immediate experience, when we know. We cannot master knowledge, but knowledge invades us in its mysterious way. The point of *Theaetetus*, clearly laid out in the conclusion of the dialogue, is to affirm appropriate epistemic humility in doing justice to the actual experience of knowledge. What we always truly know is beyond determinate mastery. We do experience true knowledge, but that experience is itself mysteriously open: it is love, not mastery. Determinate, final, defined and certain knowledge is only ever partial, and is always false if taken as definitively true and mastered. True knowledge is found in the mystery of an apophatic openness to the essential mystery at the source of any energy producing knowledge within us. Our immediate knowledge is always of icons. These icons participate in the divine truths that are the unknowable essences of the created realm of being, but the essences of those divine gifts are mysteries.

William Desmond's recovery of Plato's *metaxu* is very helpful here.[1] Any metaphysics that does not take into consideration that the context of human existence is firmly situated *between* transcendence and immanence, ruling out any final epistemic mastery, will falsely seek to reduce reality to either a pure immanence or a pure transcendence in the quest for determinate intellectual closure. This is exactly what has gone on in the main currents of Western philosophy since at least the seventeenth century. The implications for a Western understanding of personhood are tragically clear. The philosophical failure of both a reductively empirical immanentism and a pure transcendental rationalism has left Western philosophy with a metaphysically vacuous pragmatism that has no viable way of understanding the very notion of being a person. These failed philosophical enterprises resulted from the shift away from the Christianised Aristotelian knowledge and wisdom synthesis of the medieval era and towards the modern Western mathematico-experimental understanding of instrumentally effective knowledge. That shift to modernity entailed an explicit commitment to firstly quarantine religiously-sanctioned theological and metaphysical meanings off from observable knowledge and mathematical logic, and then – after various attempts to generate new theological frameworks for modern natural philosophy – to redefine theology and metaphysics in the terms of supposedly hermeneutically obvious objective knowledge and necessary logic. The final effect of this complex process was to couple the astonishing instrumental power of modern science with a staggering ontological blindness to the very experience of being human.

In the West, it is only thinkers who have refused to embrace the principle of epistemic closure and have yet held onto the mystery of truth grasping us that have spoken clearly against the ontological, existential and moral pathologies of the West. The trajectory of Hamann, Kierkegaard and Ellul is one example of a powerful counter voice to these de-personising trends within the modern West.[2]

---

1. William Desmond, *The Intimate Strangeness of Being* (Washington D.C.: The Catholic University of America Press, 2012), 36-7.
2. See Johann Georg Hamann, 'Metacritique on the Purism of Reason' in *Hamann Writings on Philosophy and Language*, ed. Kenneth Haynes (Cambridge: Cambridge University Press, 2007), 205-18. On Hamman see John Betz, *After Enlightenment* (Oxford: Wiley-Blackwell, 2009). See Søren Kierkegaard, *Concluding Unscientific Postscript to Philosophical Fragments* (New Jersey: Princeton University Press, 1992). On Kierkegaard see Christopher Ben Simpson, *The Truth is the Way. Kierkegaard's Theologia Viatorum* (Oregon: Cascade, 2011). See Jacques Ellul, *The Presence of the Kingdom* (Colorado Springs: Helmers & Howard, 1989). On Ellul see Jacob Van Vleet, *Dialectical*

In large measure due to the absence of a meaningful ontology of the person, Western religion has become profoundly destructive. Here I am speaking of the religion of the post-Christian secular West: Mammon.[1]

Yannaras' understanding of religion as a basic psycho-social necessity makes very good sense.[2] The post-Christian secular West is a profoundly religious culture. As William Cavanaugh has pointed out,[3] people do not stop being religious just because they become secular materialists; rather, the site of the holy migrates from overtly religious institutions to other sites more organically integrated with the public cultus of the secular state and the shopping mall. Of course, forms of institutional religion that pride themselves on moving with the times readily adapt to the sites of value and purpose orientation within the larger culture.[4] Secularised liturgical practises signifying meaning, fulfilment, reality and a dependable common cosmology are integral with the modern Western lifeform. Notably, the central object of worship in this culture is monetary power.[5] Strong gnostic aversions to matter are also present in this culture. The significance of virtuality, the overcoming of space and time, the refusal to accept any natural boundary as given, and, most centrally, the immateriality of finance are all significant features of the religious lives of people who live within the Western lifeform. None of us can escape the pervasive influence of this lifeform now. Wealth and power for the individual, in a competitive agonism of endless struggle for dominance, is now central to our education, our entertainment, our commerce, and our governance. Scientism – notably as an assumed survivalist and competitive social Darwinism – is intimately entangled in the ontological barrenness and religious narratives and practices of modern secular Western society.

In this Mammon-centric, ontologically-barren context, economists are dispensers of orthodox doctrine and the guardians of right collective morality. It is economic doctrine that defines who are the worthy and justly remunerated and who are the unworthy and rightly punished

Theology and Jacques Ellul (Minneapolis: Fortress Press, 2014).

1. Jacques Ellul, *Money and Power* (Southampton: Marshall Pickering, 1986), 73-116.
2. Christos Yannaras, *Against Religion* (Brookline: Holy Cross Orthodox Press, 2013), 1-6.
3. William T. Cavanaugh, *Migrations of the Holy* (Grand Rapids: Eerdmans, 2011).
4. Marion Maddox, 'Prosper, Consume and Be Saved', *Critical Research on Religion* 1(2013): 108-15.
5. See the Archbishop of Canterbury's Lent reflections for 2017; Justin Welby, *Dethroning Mammon* (London: Bloomsbury, 2017).

in our lifeform. The super-rich, merely by virtue of being super-rich, are the aristocracy of a global order established around the worship of money. The public cultus of the global emporium is expressed in the gods, liturgies, disciplines of desire, and assumed centre of highest value manifest in the shopping mall. Unsurprisingly, high finance expects the priesthood of economics to legitimate its power, which – against the most obvious witness of observation and logic – the priesthood usually does. The priesthood depends on the palace for its status and role, so any preaching of a heretical economic gospel that challenges the aristocracy can expect the same treatment that the prophets received in ancient Israel.

Importantly, the absence of a viable ontology of humanity within the econometric doctrines and aristocratic power centres of the religious norms and certainties of Western culture does not imply the absence of metaphysical conviction; it implies wrong and degrading metaphysical convictions. Notably, in the place and even in the name of freedom, there is Necessity. In the place and even in the name of reality, there is Fantasy.

To neoliberalism, freedom is an arbitrary individualist voluntarism located in self-determination, self-sufficiency and the instrumental manipulation of the mathematico-legal constructs of power that enable a monetised mastery of physical needs and desires. This is a religious iron maiden designed with diabolical genius to torture and kill human freedom. To neoliberalism reality is an amoral system of interlocking forces entirely defined by an unbreakable causal chain of necessity. There is no 'ought' or 'ought not' to power: there is only 'is' as defined by 'can' and 'is not' as defined by 'cannot'. That such 'realism' is never manifest in the healthy human realities of our existence, but only in pathological and dysfunctional human contexts, does not seem to worry modern 'realism' at all. We thus call oppressive necessity freedom and pathological fantasy reality. This could not happen if our ontology of personhood was primary, and our epistemology, politics and economics was then constructed to be compatible with the realities of being human.

In stark antipathy to the prevailing conception of neoliberal negative freedom, Yannaras maintains that freedom is a function of the ontology of humanity and is expressed in liberation from the forces of necessity, as found among persons within the community of love. What it means to be human is denied without the freedom of being in relations of love. The very Life of the Trinity is the fount of true freedom, and the source of a community's mode of existence as liberty from mute and violent necessity. The ecclesia is a polis, and the polis is a body bonded in love, and love is grounded in the persons of the Trinity, whose energies are the fount of all creation. In this sense, true politics participates in the life of the Church, which is only living because of the divine gift of Life, beyond all dead necessities and determined needs.[1]

Modes of Existence and the Global Struggle for Life

The destruction of human freedom, of humanity, of life, is – in our day – being achieved through the creation of an ontologically blind, technologically enabled, financialised global grid of post-political power.[2] Resisting this destruction is the struggle for life. But the weapons of the struggle for life used by Christ's ecclesia are not carnal (2 Corinthians 10:4). This needs to be understood if the mode of the ecclesial event's way of life – true politics – is to engage with what is usually thought of as 'the political'. For 'the political', as defined by power relations within the context of globalised, Westernised, technologised, naturalised, individualised, socialised, securitised and financialised secular modernity, is not true politics at all. If the Church has 'a politics' that is recognizable in the terms of the above context, she has lost her way.

To use New Testament terms, Christ's ecclesia is the gathering together of those who live in the Life of Christ to be built up as one body in the communion of love, to be empowered by the Holy Spirit and sent out as emissaries of the mode of Life that overcomes the

---

1. This could be phrased more universally the other way around. The Church is an eschatological sign of the true politics of love and freedom that is the foundation of all human communities, and, hence, of humanity itself. That the Church often fails to reveal something of the true politics of love and freedom means that, like every other community, it also stumbles along in a yet to be eschatologically transformed manner. However, unlike communities that theorize their unity in terms of individual self-interest or collective violence, the Church is always subject to internal critique when it manifestly fails to reveal a telos of Christ-like love and freedom in its existential mode of life.

2. See Jacques Ellul, *The Technological Society* (New York: Vintage, 1964). I would like to see comparative work done on Yannaras and Ellul, as Ellul is often wrongly thought of as a technological determinist because he follows the sociological logic of necessity within the telos of mere instrumental efficiency so fearlessly. Like Kierkegaard, one needs to read the very different sort of texts produced by Ellul to get a full picture of his thinking. Freedom is only examined in his theological and biblical works; necessity is only examined in his sociology texts on technology and propaganda, but often his readers look only at one or the other body of texts that make up his entire work. See Van Vleet's fine text integrating the different dialectical voices of Ellul's full corpus: Van Vleet, *Dialectical Theology and Jacques Ellul*.

necessities, bondages and pathologies of the mode of anti-life ('death') that prevails in 'The World' (the arena of human action resistant to the divine gift of Life).

In New Testament terms, what St Paul in 1 Corinthians 2:14 calls the natural man (ψυχικὸς ἄνθρωπος) is unable to discern spiritual truth. That is, the natural man's outlook is limited by material necessity, artificial possibility and demonic bondage. The natural man's understanding of the material necessity is defined by physical need and the structures of irresistible force channelling human action. This necessity is a violation of the free ontology of human personhood; this is the arena of Death. The natural man's conception of the possible is defined by the artificial and unreal power structures of our own making (fantasy); this is the arena of false worship, the idolatry of worshiping artefacts of our own making. The natural man is shaped by the power-defined collective sublimations of unique relational personhood into the atomic false consciousness of the self-interested individual on the one hand, and the stratified exploitative power structures of the status quo and the seething dark energies of the mob on the other hand; this is the arena of the demonic energy of bondage and evil.[1] That is, the natural man is a slave of death, sin and the Devil: the fundamental enemies of humanity that Christ came to save us from.[2]

Death, to reiterate, is the final principle of determinate material necessity. Sin is an ontologically delusional existential falling short of life, which is always entangled in false worship. The Devil is the demonic energy of evil embedded in ontologically distorted collective human action. When the saints are sent out into the world as emissaries of the Life of Christ given to the world, the natural man will not readily desire freedom, reality and deliverance, though it is what he needs. But the thing is to live life, to demonstrate the mode of life. The good demonstration of life is always manifest in communal relations of the love of persons – the Life of the Trinity incarnate in human community – and such Life is always in opposition to the mode of existence that is centred around

1. The place of exorcism in the ministry of Jesus, in the New Testament and in the life of the Early Church is no longer well understood in the modern secular West, even though – as Peter Berger pointed out – the occult is the pornography of the modern mind. See Peter L. Berger, *Facing Up To Modernity* (New York: Penguin, 1979), 253-7. Here are a couple of excellent texts pointing out how pertinent this theological category is to an understanding of modern times. Chanon Ross, *Gifts Glittering and Poisoned: Spectacle, Empire and Metaphysics* (Oregon: Cascade Books, 2014); Walter Wink, *Engaging the Powers: Discernment and Resistance in a World of Domination* (Minneapolis: Fortress Press, 1992).
2. See Gustaf Aulen, *Christus Victor* (Oregon: Wipf & Stock, 2003).

the wealth and power interests of the individual or the conformist mob acting as a collective individual, the mode of being that is governed by the principalities of necessity, idolatrous fantasy, and demonic evil. The good and true demonstration of life will always produce a crisis between Life and death resulting in either the violent rejection of Life or the redemptive and existentially transformative acceptance of Life. This crisis is played out in its archetypal form in the passion of Christ.

Yet, bearing in mind that the nature of Christ's ecclesia's struggle for life is not, in the reductive and delusional terms of secular naturalist thinking, 'political', one must also be aware that the ecclesial event is not 'religious' – again in 'natural' terms – either.

To Yannaras, the ecclesial event is like a field of wheat growing with its roots entangled in the weeds of religious needs.[1] In practice, religion and the ecclesial event cannot be separated out before the eschatological harvest. Even so, the ecclesial event as a mode of existence, and the feeding of religious needs as a mode of existence, are as opposite as life and death.

The gift of Life is from God. As Life is not interested in the meeting of religious needs, religion should have nothing to do with the mission of Christ's ecclesia to be alive beyond the dead confines of determined necessity as a sign of the present and yet to come Kingdom of Heaven in our midst. The thing that matters is the partial expression of Life as the mode of existence that demonstrates the freedom and reality found in the love of persons; this can only be the gift of Christ, for it is not a necessity and we do not have life within ourselves.

For the 'political' to work towards true goodness, 'political' actors must be redeemed from the grip of death, sin and the Devil in order to free up a genuine community of political action: a real polis. The forms of power, the ideologies of power, the structures of wealth, production and social stratification etc., are all secondary. Any system of communal organisation must presuppose and promote some measure of genuinely human telos, or else it could not function, just as every system of communal organisation will fail to achieve a genuine flourishing of the human telos in all regards. What causes human organisation to work or fail is not firstly its structure and ideology, but the mode of existence of its participants. The language of Christ in referring to His ecclesia is thus the language of salt and light; of preservation against the 'natural' ways in which wealth and power go off, and of truthful and transformative illumination. The Church is for the world by not being of the world, and yet by being in the world.

1. Christos Yannaras, *Against Religion* (Brookline: Holy Cross Orthodox Press, 2013), 203.

To speak negatively, then, the Life that overcomes death is not 'religious' or 'political' in what St Paul calls natural terms. The Life of Christ is freely given as the centre and source of the life of the City of God (the true polis) but any human attempt to make this Life into a religion and a politics is a corruption. Can we then speak positively about the ecclesial event in such a way that enables us to define and control it, to plan programmes and technologies of advancement premised on it, to strategise and deliberate and advance the cause of the Kingdom of Heaven on earth? No; we cannot. As much as my Western cataphatic will to epistemic mastery would love to turn divine apophatic truth into an implementable human solution to the problem of global anti-politics, this simply cannot be done. There is the human silence and the human weakness that must be respected if we are to seek that divine freedom which is beyond the confines of determinate necessity. In this respect, Yannaras has many cataphatic critiques to offer on the ways of death, but it is only in existential demonstration that the way of Life is revealed. The apophatic cannot be said, it can only be existentially gestured towards, as the eschatological hope partially expressed in the oh-so-human walk of faith in the common life of the ecclesial event. The work of God, the reconciliation by Christ of all things back to the Father, is not a human work. Life is something we cannot manufacture. Christ, who is the Life, alone gives Life to the world and is the power of Life wherever death is resisted and overcome.

Practically, then, where does this leave us? No natural politics and no natural religion will deliver us from death, sin and the Devil. Divine grace can be expressed through almost any human politics and human religion nevertheless, for the Spirit blows where it wills and cannot be boxed in or out of the human world. Whilst any human politics and any human religion treated as ultimate in itself would be a demonic idolatry, any human politics and any human religion seen as a partial and fragile human construct open to the gift of Life from God can be a means of grace and a powerful force against death, deceptive illusion and demonic power.

Yannaras is a great admirer of Kierkegaard.[1] The melancholy Dane

---

1. I have not found any cited reference to Kierkegaard in my reading of Yannaras in what is available in English. I presume this is because the terminology Kierkegaard uses is one of 'the individual', a terminology that jars deeply with the ontology of relational persons in Yannaras' work. In the one brief discussion I have had with Professor Yannaras, he asked me how I came to read his work and I told him that Kierkegaard's Christian existentialism had been my pathway in. Professor Yannaras beamed warmly, telling me how, as a young man, he had gone to Copenhagen to walk the streets that Kierkegaard had walked. Kierkegaard is, in fact, highly relational, and his ontology is essentially grounded in an entirely orthodox personhood of the Trinity. Kierkegaard's terminology must

brings out the penultimate nature of all human ventures brilliantly in his *Two Ages*.[1] Looking back on the turn of the nineteenth century, Kierkegaard admires the revolutionary age where people ventured great things for great transformative ideals, and gained a deep fellowship with other revolutionaries as they were united in a high ideal bigger than each of them. Yet such glory was idolatry, which spawned the terrors of violent upheaval and the betrayal in practice of the very ideals pursued. The existentially insipid age of comfort and security-driven conformist and competitive bourgeois individualism which followed the revolutionary age is no less an idolatry – and an idolatry without any high glory or genuine community – but it has more regard for human stability and safety; genuine human goods which should not be despised. Both ages seek ultimate meaning in either political ideology, or in practical social and economic conditions, without regard for that which matters most: the eternal responsibility of each person before God – do I exist in the Life of Christ?[2] The penultimate treated as ultimate binds us to that which always falls short of true humanity. Any social, political, economic or religious work directed beyond itself towards love and truth will be graced by God.

This, then, is how the people of Christ's ecclesial should engage the so called political arena of our times. Wherever there is good work being done, the children of light should be there, but should never give themselves to any human cause as ultimate. Indeed, this is what every human cause – be it political, intellectual, economic, artistic or religious – needs. Here, liberalism is half right. Modern liberalism has failed terribly because the principle of no final unifying centre to society has become the final unifying centre of modern Western individualist society. The idol unifying Western culture – its doxological core – is the individual voluntarist self. Nevertheless, the commitment to hold no human principle or unifier as final out of deference to the divine horizon standing over all human constructs is entirely valid and is as old

---

be read in the context his antipathy to his reading of the Hegelian sublimation of persons into the ethical community as an impersonal expression of Geist. As Kierkegaard's *Sickness unto Death* and *Two Ages* point out, it is only the self who rests transparently in the relational power that establishes the self who can relate to others in love as a person.

1. Søren Kierkegaard, *Two Ages* (New Jersey: Princeton University Press, 1978).
2. Kierkegaard, *Two Ages*, 86. 'The idolized positive principle of sociality in our age is the consuming, demoralising principle that in the thraldom of reflection transforms even virtues into glittering vices. And what is the basis of this other than a disregard for the separation of the religious individual before God in the responsibility of eternity?'

as the ancient Greek concept of hubris and the ancient Hebraic refusal to make idols. This ancient doxological irreverence towards all human constructs, this refusal to take any work of our own hands as of final value, it is no modern idea, but it is the best spirit in modern liberalism and can only be adhered to in any time out of deference to the divine beyond all human saying, all human controlling, or all human interests.

But what can we think and do now about the reduction of power to the terms of fantastic necessity, the global sublimation of life to death?

Let us conclude by considering one concrete arena for resisting false necessity and fantastic reality within the realm of 'the political'. For example, at the time of writing, the Democracy in Europe 25 movement, spearheaded by Yanis Varoufakis, is seeking to make false financial necessity accountable to real political freedom in Europe. These are aims compatible with a Christian understanding of freedom and necessity. Whilst this movement may rapidly pass into historical oblivion – if, for example, the European Union implodes – let us conduct a thought experiment on what Christian participation in this movement might entail.

Christians should seek to be salt and light in any such a political movement. As well conceived and insightful as a movement such as DiEM25 may be, it will fail from within, even as it succeeds externally, precisely as the first Syriza government did, given the nature of natural politics. Human energy alone cannot realise sustainable partial political manifestations of the Good. Here, at the failure of human politics, the Church is to blame. Where was the salt and light that could preserve and illuminate the good in any political movement? The 'natural man' can see death, sin and the demonic as fundamental principles of natural power, but they cannot see beyond them; they are spiritually discerned. If one is to fight those powers of 'natural politics' without being drawn into the existential mode of death which those powers define, one needs both discernment and the mode of life-enabling power, the very things that should be found within the Church. Resisting 'natural power' tendencies and the modes of existence dictated to by them is best done by those who refuse to be defined by natural necessity. Who better to do that than those who believe that Christ has overcome death itself? It was C.S. Lewis who famously observed that those who are heavenly minded have done the most for earthly justice, for they were not committed to what is possible within natural terms, but to what is eschatologically right.[1] Freedom, as the martyrs have witnessed, is the courage to defy the necessity of death for the sake of a hope that cannot be contained by the determinate. The

1. C.S. Lewis, *Mere Christianity* (Glasgow: Fount, 1977), 116-7.

mode of Life that expresses this courage is the only freedom that can overcome the principalities of determinate force and fantastic necessity in our times. This mode of existence – as Yannaras understands – is not available to the categories of cataphatic epistemic mastery. For life cannot be said or manufactured or rendered as a technique or made into a religion or ideology; it can only be lived.

Part II
PHILOSOPHY

Chapter Five
Loving in Relation to Nothing:
On Alterity and Relationality
Deborah Casewell

The failures of the Western philosophical tradition, especially in regards to metaphysics, have long been discussed and dissected in continental philosophy, and one diagnosis of their failure comes from Martin Heidegger, who decries the way in which talk of being was grounded outwith being in itself, and found in God, in onto-theology.[1] In his lecture *Introduction to Metaphysics,* Heidegger outlines what he sees as the central question of metaphysics: why there is something rather than nothing. Throughout the text he works through what being is, understanding in relation to the concepts in question; that of being and nothingness. We thus find Heidegger vehemently opposed to

1. For Heidegger, Being (i.e., Being in general) has been represented in many ways in the history of philosophy, as the logos, the principle of reason, the *causa sui*, and such representation treats Being as just another thing in the world, albeit a very unique thing. In onto-theology, being is seen as the ground of all things, and God as the Being of all being; thus, in onto-theology, God is the ultimate foundation of metaphysics as *causa sui* (cause in itself, unmoved mover). As *causa sui* God is the Highest Being. Heidegger argues that, from Plato onwards, (Western) philosophy has forgotten the question of being. The question of Being is not what kinds of beings are there but what Being is in itself. Heidegger sees that being has become confused with presence, with actual, determinate things (beings) that are present before us (before our intellect). We have forgotten the question of Being; the various possibilities Being offers us. Hence Heidegger's stress on embodied 'being-in-the-world', 'being-with-others', i.e. Dasein is our (human beings) practical involvement with people and things. This is linked to critiques of a metaphysics of presence, where Being is understood in terms of presence, and truth claims must correspond to this presence. A metaphysics of presence secures a foundation for knowledge, but postmodern thought criticizes the belief in such foundations, thus questioning the assumption that reality can be (or become) fully present to thought.

this grounding of being in the being of God. In this text, a Christian philosopher is a round square and a misunderstanding,[1] as 'anyone for whom the Bible is divine revelation and truth already has the answer to the question "Why are there beings at all instead of nothing?" before it is even asked: beings, with the exception of God Himself, are created by Him. God Himself "is" as the uncreated Creator.'[2] For Heidegger, the horizon (that which we orient and relate our being towards) is nothingness and this nothingness is part and parcel of our existence and how we understand being. In his later lecture, *What is Metaphysics?*, Heidegger outlines more clearly what he understands as nothingness and how humanity is related to it. Moving on from his focus on death in *Being and Time*, nothingness terrifies us, but we are still intimately related to nothingness, and from nothingness we understand our being. Heidegger sees that nothingness is what creates anxiety in us, an anxiety that enables us to live authentically, as

> in anxiety occurs a shrinking back before . . . which is surely not any sort of flight but rather a kind of bewildered calm. This 'back before' takes its departure from the nothing. The nothing itself does not attract; it is essentially repelling. But this repulsion is itself as such a parting gesture toward beings that are submerging as a whole. This wholly repelling gesture toward beings that are in retreat as a whole, which is the action of the nothing that oppresses Dasein in anxiety, is the essence of the nothing: nihilation. It is neither an annihilation of beings nor does it spring from a negation. Nihilation will not submit to calculation in terms of annihilation and negation. The nothing itself nihilates.[3]

This is useful for Heidegger as this 'makes possible in advance the revelation of beings in general. The essence of the originally nihilating nothing lies in this, that it brings Dasein for the first time before beings as such.'[4] Nothingness is now what makes possible the openedness of beings as such, and thus Nothingness is the condition of possibility, in that 'the nothing is the negation of the totality of beings; it precedes every

---

1. Martin Heidegger, *Introduction to Metaphysics*, trans. Fried and Polk (Yale: Yale UP, 2000), 8.
2. Ibid., 8.
3. Heidegger, *What is Metaphysics?*, http://naturalthinker.net/trl/texts/Heidegger,Martin/Heidegger.Martin.. What%20Is%20Metaphysics.htm, 31. Accessed 19 May 2017.
4. Ibid., 32.

negation; it is even more original than the "not". It is not only that the nothing makes possible the negating of everything; it makes possible the thinking of everything – it is the transcendental condition.'[1] In Heidegger, nothingness is foundational and directional for being.

It is this movement towards nothingness, of using nothingness as the basis of talking about lived existence in the world, that is noted by and critiqued by Christos Yannaras, who proposes an account of existence in the world that sees this turn to nothingness as a mere step on the way to knowledge of God and other persons as Other. This turn to the alterity of the Other echoes the thought of Emmanuel Levinas, and these two thinkers have been linked briefly by Andrew Louth in his introduction to *Heidegger and the Areopagite*, with Louth noting that Levinas would be a better ground for Yannaras' thought than Heidegger.[2] On that ground, I am interested in bringing the thought of these two thinkers together, as they both find a similar inadequacy in Heidegger; an inadequacy of nothingness as the basis for life in the world. For both Yannaras and Levinas, life, interaction, and lived existence ensues from an encounter with the Other, out of the individuality of one's own lived existence. Whilst they certainly diverge in their accounts of personhood and relationality, I am not interested in seeing which one presents a better account of being in the world but in seeing how, using their rejection of previous categories of being, their thought can inform each other. I am interested in exploring what kind of vision of life they each present, and if there is a lack in one, can the other, considering their similar starting points, be used to augment and broaden the first? Following an analysis of the thought of Yannaras, Levinas' ethics as first philosophy shall be outlined. Finally, using the work of feminist philosophers on vulnerability, a mediating path between the two thinkers shall be outlined.

---

1. S.J. McGrath, *Heidegger: A (Very) Critical Introduction*, (Grand Rapids, MI: William B. Eerdmans, 2008), 69.
2. 'It is in a relationship, in coming face-to-face with another (or an other) that I realise what is meant by being a person. In that relationship I discover not what it is to be human in general – what human nature is in abstract terms, as, for instance, a rational being – but the different ways of being human that are summed up in the notion of being a person. Yannaras' analysis here is in many respects much closer to that of Emmanuel Levinas here, than to Heidegger's; it is arguable that Levinas could provide a much better philosophical foundation for the position Yannaras embraces than Heidegger himself.' Andrew Louth, 'Introduction to Christos Yannaras', in Christos Yannaras, *On the Absence and Unknowability of God: Heidegger and the Areopagite* (London: T. & T. Clark, 2005), 8.

Personhood and Relationality in Yannaras

Yannaras' account of personhood is incredibly rich and complex, engaging both Western philosophy and Greek Orthodox theology. In *Heidegger and the Areopagite* Yannaras sees himself as taking up an account of God after detailing how Heidegger's *Destruktion* leads to nihilism;[1] a nihilism that is the fault of the tradition itself; it sowed the seeds of its own destruction.[2] Focusing largely on Heidegger's lecture on Nietzsche, Yannaras sees that Heidegger presents Nietzsche's thought as 'the inevitable climax of a long historical process in European metaphysics.'[3] This nihilism entails a cancelling of all idols, offering nothing in their place, and it is seen by Yannaras as a starting point from this inner crisis of Western metaphysics.[4] Nihilism, as Heidegger understands, leads to either the absence or the unknowability of God, and Yannaras sees that Heidegger's

> determination of nothingness as an unrestricted limit of questioning thought is manifest as the starting-point of an ontology which presupposed both theism and atheism. . . nihilism, as the denial of the equation of Being and God (the denial of their subjection to conceptual fabrications) or as the reference of God to nothing (with the concept of indeterminism or of the emptiness that persists in thought when it defines *mode* of *being*) – such a nihilism seems more 'theological' than rationalist metaphysics.[5]

Yannaras eschews an apophaticism that says that solely the being or the essence of God is unknowable, as 'the *apophaticism of essence* in the Western metaphysical tradition, with its negative definition of God's

---

1. 'Early on he seized on Heidegger's analysis of the development of philosophy in the West as a kind of stick with which to beat the West.' Andrew Louth, 'Some Recent Works by Christos Yannaras in English Translation', *Modern Theology* 25:2 (2009), 331.
2. 'Precisely because it offers an absolutized rational affirmation of God, European metaphysics prepares for the possibility of its own rational refutation. The "death of God" is but the end-result of the historical unfolding of this absolutized and double-edged rationalism.' Yannaras, *On the Absence and Unknowability of God: Heidegger and the Areopagite*, 22.
3. Ibid., 21.
4. 'We speak then of an *apophaticism* destructive of idols, which under the guise of nihilism is manifest as the "inner crisis" of Western metaphysics. And we are indebted to Heidegger for seeing in this crisis the starting point for its historical understanding.' Ibid., 22.
5. Ibid., 54.

essential otherness, or with its mystical expressions of the *essential* indefinability of the impersonal absolute, not only failed to check the historical advance of relativism and agnosticism (which ended in atheist nihilism), but was organically implicated in their advance'.[1] Using the work of Dionysius the Areopagite,[2] Yannaras sees that the apophaticism, as understood in the Greek East, is one that is not the negative theology of the West but a more positive account of non-knowledge. Yannaras sees that 'the semantics of knowledge (the conceptual designations – affirmations, negations and the way of causality) is, for apophaticism, only a dynamic starting-point for realisation of an empirical *relationship* with the designated reality'.[3] The word *relationship* is key here, as the apophaticism of the person that Yannaras espouses depends on humanity wanting to relate, to know that which is outside of itself, and, for Yannaras:

> the catholicity of the event of knowing through *relationship* preserves the chief elements (otherness and freedom) with which we mark out the *personal* existence of human kind – man or woman as person/personality, with greater ontological meaning offered by this definition. Apophaticism, then, as an active *abandonment* of the consolidation of knowledge in conceptual categories, is the epistemological position that leads to the dynamics of the ontology of personhood.[4]

In short, because relationships can never be exhausted, knowledge of another person can never be complete. Yannaras sees that any other person is the Other, and cannot be fixed or determined the way that we fix and determine concepts.[5] Yannaras sees the apophaticism of the

---

1. Ibid., 30.
2. 'Yannaras found an answer to Western ontotheology in the apophatic theology of the East, notably that of Dionysios the Areopagite, according to which God utterly transcends being, so that none of our concepts can apply to the reality of God himself. It is only through the relationship that God has established with humankind, through the Incarnation and in the Church, that we can come to knowledge of God, a knowledge that is ineffable and inexhaustible. In that relationship with God, we encounter his love, which draws from us an answering love in which, no longer defined by the constraints of human nature, but transcending them in ecstasy, we discover ourselves as free persons, free in the love of God and other persons, defined by relationship, rather than fitting into preset patterns.' Andrew Louth, 'Some Recent Works by Christos Yannaras', 332.
3. Yannaras, *On the Absence and Unknowability of God*, 71.
4. Ibid.
5. 'The Person of God – not to mention any human person – cannot be fixed or known by objective definitions, analogical correlations or conceptual

person, rather than the essence, as what can emerge from the nihilism of Heidegger.[1] This apophaticism of the person incorporates God, in that whilst we are unable to know *what* God is, we know the *mode* of God's existence, which is that of personal energies: 'God is active as a *person* (a Trinity of Persons), that is to say, as a *hypostasis* of relative, self-consciousness, revealed with absolute otherness in ec-static relationship.'[2] Nothingness is the condition of God's ec-static existence; the way in which God's existence stands outside itself and enables participation in God. Nothingness is part of the energies of God, which we can know and participate in, rather than in the ever-unknowable essence.[3]

Yannaras' account of being is further explicated in his work *Person and Eros*. Echoing the reasoning in *Heidegger and the Areopagite*, Yannaras writes in *Person and Eros*, that 'the West was trapped in a polarised view of Being as either analogically absolute and ontic or else mystical.'[4] Whilst the Western tradition had some kind of understanding of alterity and otherness, it was always an apophaticism of essence, not of the person.[5] Yannaras sees that:

---

assessments. For every person is a unique, existential reality, unlike any other and unrepeatable, a reality of absolute existential otherness, refractory of any objectivity that could be defined by the utterances of human language. Our existential otherness becomes known and participated in only in the immediacy of *relationship*.' Ibid., 78.

1. 'The nihilism of Heidegger, as a respect for the unrestricted limits of questioning thought – as refusal to subject God and Being to conceptual constructs – seems provisionally to fit in with what we have here called, in reliance on the Areopagitical writings, apophatic *abandonment*. It differs crucially from the apophaticism of the Areopagite both in its presuppositions and consequences that make up the *ontology of the person*, the linking of apophaticism to the existential principle of freedom and otherness.' Ibid., 72.
2. Ibid., 78.
3. 'For Orthodox-Christian theology, God is not primarily a substance, but a Person, the Father: an identity of initial, ec-static relationality (also the Son and the Holy Spirit indicate relational entities). What makes Divinity exist is the Father, not only in his Economic dimension, but also in the very reality of the Trinity. This means that relationality does not restrict being, on the contrary, it is the very site of being as being, i.e. as God's image, an image of absolute personal freedom, an incarnation of truth.' Ilias Papagiannapoulos, 'Re-appraising the Subject and the Social in Western Philosophy and in Contemporary Orthodox Thought', *Studies in Eastern European Thought* 58 (2006), 318.
4. Christos Yannaras, *Person and Eros*, trans. Norman Russell (Brookline, MA: Holy Cross Orthodox Press, 2007), 21.
5. 'Scholastic analogy ignored the personal mode of existence, not only as an ontological reality but also as a means of cognition. It ignored the cognitive power of personal relation, the disclosure – the unmediated knowledge – of the person through the energies of the essence, which are always personal. It ignored the immediacy and universality of the knowledge, beyond any conceptual

> Heidegger's approach showed clearly how the apophaticism of essence defines and respects the limits of thought, and consequently the limits of metaphysics or of the ineffable, but leaves the problem of ontic individuality on the borders of a possible nihilism, reveals Nothingness as an eventuality as equally possible as Being, and transposes the ontological question to the dilemma between being and Nothingness.[1]

So whilst Heidegger saw us as relational, our relation is to nothingness, and Yannaras understands that in Heidegger 'humanity's relation with the world is only the anguish of being faced with nothingness.'[2] Yannaras then refocuses nothingness not as an empty void, but as the possibility of relationality, as nothingness 'is the absence of relation which leaves ontic individuality existentially suspended – it is that which is outside personal reference.'[3]

Again, relationality is the real question of being, rather than what being is. Being is relational, but the relation to nothingness only shows the greater relationality there is than a person has. Akin to the Trinity, the person is a relational event, and the Person is the power of the disclosure of being.[4] To be a being, to be this embodied existence in the world, one is relational; for Yannaras, personal existence is to be understood as ek-static, to have the ability to stand outside itself. In Yannaras, this ek-staticness is 'here is identified with the actualisation of the person's otherness, that is, with the essential presupposition itself of the person, which is also a unique ability to approach the mode of existence of the existence of beings.'[5] To be a person, you have the capacity to stand and exist, and you want to exist outside yourself, as 'ek-stasis, or ecstasy, signifies self-transference from the naturally given capacity for intellectualisation to the otherness of its personal actualisation, from the self-evidentness of noetic-conscious conceptualisation of objective conventionality and the naturally given common understanding of objective essences to universal existential relation.'[6] The ecstatic character

---

    signification that accompanies erotic "astonishment", the unexpected revelatory cognition of personal uniqueness and dissimilarity that arises in the relationship of love.' Ibid., 211.

1. Ibid., 23.
2. Ibid., 13.
3. Ibid., 226. In many ways this is similar to Sartre's nothingness as a lack, as shown in his example of Pierre not in the café.
4. Yannaras, *Person and Eros*, 19.
5. Ibid.
6. Ibid., 20.

of human existence is the 'recapitulation and self-transcendence of essence or nature in the fact of personal otherness, the disclosure of the essence only through the essence's *energies*, which are always personal. The person is the better of the essence's energies, which means that the essence's mode of existence is personal otherness'.[1] As noted earlier, there is this separation between the essence of the person and their energies, which enables the apophaticism of the person.[2]

This drive in our lives to not just be in ourselves, not just relating ourselves to nothingness, is for Yannaras *eros* as understood in the Patristics, where

> the dynamic and always unachieved consummation of this relation is the *eros* of the Greek Church Fathers, the loving impetus and movement of exodus from individualised existence in the realm of objects, for the sake of the actualisation of *relation* in the highest sense. Eros is the dynamics of ecstasy, which finds its consummation as personal reference to supreme Otherness.[3]

Whilst the Otherness of the Other remains, in Yannaras, he understands that 'every human person is the possibility of the universal disclosure of the *mode* in which human existence *is* and, at the same time, the presupposition of universal *relation*, in the context of which beings become true (*a-letheuousi*), that is, they are disclosed as that which they *are*'.[4] It is 'the ec-stasy of the person, the actualisation of otherness, is the *mode* by which humanity *is* as a "universal"'.[5] This leads to Yannaras' version of Heidegger's fallenness. Whilst for Heidegger Dasein falls through moving away from self-actualisation into everydayness through the They, Yannaras moves away from seeing self-actualisation as positive. Due to our desire to be relations and the ecstatic character of our existence, we must be in relationships with others, but that 'relation, however, as ecstatic self-transcendence, constitutes an existential potentiality, not a given existential necessity. The potentiality also implies the possibility of failing to transcend nature through personal relation'.[6] This entails the loss of the ecstatic character of the relation, 'a character

---

1. Ibid., 22-3.
2. 'The way of existence, which is personhood, is not predetermined, like our human nature, as a collection of properties, but is the way our human nature is lived out, or expressed, in a personal way of existence experienced as self-transcendence – an ecstatic moving beyond oneself in loving freedom.' Louth, 'Some Recent Works by Christos Yannaras in English Translation', 336.
3. Yannaras, *Person and Eros*, 20.
4. Ibid., 25.
5. Ibid., 26.
6. Ibid., 224.

that underlines personal otherness and makes erotic participation and communion possible.[1] Falling becomes alienation, the estrangement into an 'undifferentiated individuality, intellectually in terms of mental capacity and psychologically in terms of a self-conscious ego.[2] This falling, incidentally, seems to return to the metaphysics of presence,[3] where 'existential otherness gives way to a static individual self-consciousness, which sets the nature of the atomic individual, as the ego, against other natures of atomic individuals.[4]

Instead of this, as Rowan Williams notes:

> man experiences a divine call, an invitation to enter into relation, and so to become truly personal: personhood is known as response to the invitation of the Divine Person, its 'truth' is to be found outside the mere 'givenness' of finite facts. In this invitation, this outgoing of personal energy, the unknowable Divine essence becomes known as content of person (not known 'in itself'): the mode of God's being is personal communion.[5]

Thus, for Yannaras, as in Heidegger, nothingness is an essential part of knowing being, but in Yannaras Heidegger's orientation towards nothingness is only the beginning, and Heidegger does not have the tools to go beyond it.[6] The self-actualisation and individualisation in Heidegger is thus inadequate, as 'the person is the only ontological reality which counters the antithetical correspondence of being and nothingness, since the absence of the person does not negate its existential immediacy, and the "opposite" of the person is not its ontic negation but the existential fact of non-relation, or neutralise ontic individuality.[7] Instead of the call being the call of one's conscience, to be true and self-actualise, the drive out of fallenness is a kind of loneliness,[8] and Yannaras writes that 'the fact itself of

---

1. Ibid.
2. Ibid., 224-5.
3. For an account of the evils of a metaphysics of presence, refer to footnote 1 on p. 119.
4. Ibid., 234.
5. Williams, 'The Theology of Personhood', 419.
6. '[T]he experience of "Nothing" is revealed finally as a confirmation not only of human freedom but also of the personal reality of God: Christ's descent into Hell is "the transformation of Nothingness, of the abyss of human failure, into a triumph for the love and benevolence (φιλανθρωπία) of God". Williams, 'The Theology of Personhood'.
7. Yannaras, *Person and Eros*, 230.
8. '[T]he capacity for this sort of relatedness is a possibility, not an automatically

existential loneliness, which preserves the potentiality for ecstasy, although as the impossibility of universal personal relation, presupposes a second person to whom the ecstatic reference is directed as failure of relation – a person and not an atomic individual at a distance.[1] The relationality that the Trinity is, is the blueprint of the relationality of ourselves, and, as Williams writes, 'it is an attempt to show how personhood as we know it is grounded in Being, and so in God, and because we begin from a particular notion of personhood (existence-in-communion) we are obliged to postulate "internal" personal communion in God'.[2]

While it presents an account of human relations and knowledge of God that is dynamic and gives space to the desire of humans for one another, *eros* as the move outside oneself, this account of relationality and personhood has its critics. Paul Gavrilyuk sees that Yannaras' emphasis on Dionysius as a cure for the Western misinterpretation of philosophy[3] is mistaken in itself,[4] and that Dionysius may not provide the resources that he needs, in that 'according to Yannaras, the knowledge acquired in an ineffable personal encounter with God surpasses propositional knowledge. Whether the emphasis upon the non-propositional personal knowledge of this sort can be credibly derived from the CD is rather

---

realised necessity: we must reckon with the fact of human fallenness, the empirical fact that man exists in a state of "atomistic" self-consciousness, connected to other such consciousnesses solely in virtue of a shared objective relation to the "world," or to "absolute reality". The idea of Being is thereby reduced to that which exists, opposed to that which does not exist – Nothing (Μηδέν, Sartre's "Neant"): nothingness is, as it were, introduced into the definition of Being, as a possibility; the possibility of the universality of Being-as-relation is denied. There are only individual entities existing in "distance" (απόστασις) from the whole: mutual absence is the basic ontological category, Being is identified with Nothingness. Hence the problem in contemporary art and philosophy of "one-dimensional man", existing in alienation, in the absence of relation: the reality of the person is wholly obscured, and there is thus nothing to bridge the gulf between the individual and the whole, the mass. Yet we can only understand this "fall" as a personal decision, the result of the ability of freedom to deny itself, to subordinate itself to "nature"'. Williams, 'The Theology of Personhood'.

1. Yannaras, *Person and Eros*, 246.
2. Williams, 'The Theology of Personhood'.
3. 'Lossky, and Yannaras, are deeply invested in "de-Westernising" Dionysius and presenting his theology as an authentic form of Christian Hellenism'. Paul Gavrilyuk, 'The Reception of Dionysius in Twentieth-Century Eastern Orthodoxy', *Modern Theology* 24:4 (2008), 720.
4. 'Yannaras mistakenly, but confidently, reduces all forms of Western apophaticism to the method of correcting the limits of analogical predication in natural theology'. Ibid., 713.

dubious.'[1] However, as he notes, ultimately, 'the God of Dionysian apophaticism cannot be conceptually attacked, because this deity cannot be conceptually expressed. It is impossible to prove or disprove the existence of a God who surpasses being, as well as all other categories of human thought.'[2] Nicholas Loudovikos, including Yannaras in his critique of Zizioulas sees that the focus on the person rather than on nature leads to a separation of the two, with personhood considered against and as an escape from nature. His thought leads to a full ontologisation of the person against nature,[3] a critique that Torrance does agree with.[4] Intriguingly, Loudovikos issues a challenge to personalist theologians,[5] that

---

1. Ibid.
2. Ibid., 714.
3. 'Here we have not only a full ontologisation of the person, as the sole image of God in creation, against nature, but also an unavoidable identification of it with grace.' Nicholas Loudovikos, 'Person Instead of Grace and Dictated Otherness: John Zizioulas' Final Theological Position', *Heythrop Journal*, LII (2011), 686.

   Zizioulas thereby creates two beings: nature and personalized nature; substance/nature as a non-relational entity, and a mode of existence that relates and can also make substance a relational reality. But it is because logos is a relational reality that it is always ontologically connected with a mode of existence, which is the personal realisation of the dialogue that accompanies logos – because logos ultimately is a concrete koinonetic event. Logos is a personal divine creative proposal that awaits a response – the human personal logos – and this dialogue represents a nature's personal status of communion with God, that is, the mode of (dialogical) existence of this being. This means ultimately that each mode of existence (tropos hyparxeos) is a personal mode of realising the en-hypostatic logos/vocation inscribed in nature, in a dialogical/synergetic/analogical way, and not a liberation from nature.

   Nicholas Loudovikos, 'Person Instead of Grace and Dictated Otherness', 687.
4. 'Becoming a person, that is, being incorporated into Christ, is never described by Zizioulas as an escape or release from nature per se, but it is the personalisation and/or liberation of nature; in short, one could say the fulfilment of nature (though Zizioulas shies from such terminology).' Alexis Torrance, 'Personhood and Patristics in Orthodox Theology: Reassessing the Debate', *Heythrop Journal*, LII (2011), 700-7, 702.
5. *Editor's note*: Both Yannaras and Zizioulas have repeatedly voiced their detest for the label 'personalism', which forces them into a tradition of thought, or as a variation of it, from which they do not originate and with which they do not really converse: the notion of person in personalism and its philosophy (i.e. individualism, human subjectivity, free will, internalisation, 'only persons are real', Roman Catholic personalism of the Wojtyłan variety, etc.) and their use of the term πρόσωπον point, as they argue, to two substantially different and largely unrelated realities. We thus propose the terms *prosopocentrism*

in any case, it would be useful for all Orthodox personalists to read Paul Ricoeur's *Soi-me^me comme un autre*, in the tenth study of which he criticises the Levinasian priority of the Other which tends to become an absolute heteronomy, where the call of the lover cannot be distinguished from that of the executioner, unless we admit an opposite movement from the self towards the Other that recognises and accepts him.[1]

It is this relation to the Other in Levinas that I would like to explore further, and contrary to Loudovikos, explore how it can inform and augment this personalist account. Yannaras, in *Heidegger and the Areopagite*, sees the step beyond Heidegger's nihilism as an apophaticism of the person, and an apophaticism that encompasses both God and the human Other. Yannaras is seeking to preserve the alterity of the other, but in such a way that does not leave the other as merely outside self but as an other that relates to and augments the self; the participation in the social reality, in the energies of the other, does not totalise the other by assuming the other as an atomic individual. Reading this account of humanity, and appreciating how it understands and wants to provide the grounds for inter-personal relations, one notes the similarities to the work of Emmanuel Levinas. In examining Levinas' account of the Other, we can see the main difference between the two accounts and how Levinas' account of the Other could augment Yannaras'.

Levinas' Account of the Other

Emmanuel Levinas, the French Jewish philosopher, was also heavily influenced by Heidegger, studying with him in Freiburg. In Levinas there is an agreement with Heidegger's critique of Western philosophy as obsessed with presence, as noted earlier. Levinas sees that this is in part due to how we understand the role of reason in philosophy, where the way in which we use reason has become in a sense technological; such that consciousness directs itself towards the world in order to master it, to shape it, and to use objects for the subject's own projects. Whilst Levinas takes his cue from Heidegger there, Levinas is also critical of Heidegger's account of being. Much as Heidegger critiques the category of being

and *prosopocentric ontology* for Yannaras' thought, which retain Yannaras' insistence on the etymological implications of the Greek πρόσωπον and abstain from confusing Yannaras' thought with currents of personalism.
1. Nicholas Loudovikos, 'Person Instead of Grace and Dictated Otherness', 695.

as understood, abstracted and totalised from everyday lived existence, Levinas makes the same critique of Heidegger, being even warier of the totalising category of Being. Instead of focusing on the question of being, of why there is something rather than nothing, Levinas says we need to ask what there is *other* than Being. This emphasis leads Levinas to see that 'while Heidegger heralds the end of the metaphysics of presence, he continues to think of Being as a coming-into-presence; he seems unable to break away from the hegemony of presence he denounces'.[1] This reliance on presence in Heidegger is representative of this totalisation of being against otherness, where 'Western philosophy coincides with the disclosure of the other where the other, in manifesting itself as a being, loses its alterity. From its infancy philosophy has been struck with a horror of the other that remains other – with an insurmountable allergy.'[2]

Levinas sees that what philosophy has done is to seek knowledge of the Other, but through this process 'knowledge seizes hold of its object. It possesses it. Possession denies the independence of being, without destroying that being – it denies and maintains.'[3] For Levinas, ontology, in seeking to answer the question of *what* being is, is seeking knowledge of the object, and to do this is to become involved in a violence of sorts. This is a violence in that it denies the other the chance and freedom to be other. Levinas sees that 'Western philosophy has most often been an ontology: a reduction of the other to the Same by interposition of a middle and neutral terms that ensures the comprehension of being.'[4] This Same, for Levinas, is the thinking subject; and the reduction of the other to Same presumes that all who exist are just like us, that they can be classified according to our own category system and understood in terms of our own familiar concepts acquired by way of our own perspectively conditioned experience of the world.[5]

Ontology is thus a denial of the otherness of the other; a failure to allow the other to appear on their own terms. Ontology, as a question of metaphysics, and thus as a focus of philosophy, takes its methodological

1. Emmanuel Levinas, 'Ethics of the Infinite' in *Debates in Continental Philosophy: Richard Kearney in Conversation with Contemporary Thinkers* (NY: Fordham University Press, 2004), 71.
2. Emmanuel Levinas, 'The Trace of the Other' in *Deconstruction in Context*, ed. Mark C. Taylor (Chicago: University of Chicago Press, 1986), 346.
3. Emmanuel Levinas, *Difficult Freedom,* trans. Sean Hand (Baltimore: Johns Hopkins UP, 1997), 8.
4. Emmanuel Levinas, *Totality and Infinity: An Essay on Exteriority*, trans. Alphonso Lingis (Pittsburgh: Duquesne University Press, 2005), 33-4.
5. Ibid., 45-6.

starting point in the idea that the other (anything or anyone who is not myself) is similar enough to myself to be categorised by my own concepts and categories. Philosophy is violence in that it denies the otherness of the other and does not allow the other to transcend those categories or elude characterisation within one's own familiar conceptual scheme. In doing this, philosophy has forced the Other into a pre-determined mould, and does not let the Other be Other. Thus violence, for Levinas, 'does not consist so much in injuring and annihilating persons as in interrupting their continuity, making them play roles in which they no longer recognise themselves, making them betray not only commitments but their own substance, making them carry out actions that will destroy every possibility for action'.[1] In metaphysics, one denies the alterity of the other; one 'tries to integrate the other into [one's] project of existing as a function, means, or meaning'. In so doing, one thereby risks 'reduc[ing] the other to his countenance',[2] which, in turn, risks forcing the other to play a role in which the other can no longer recognise themselves. In this way, the reduction of the other to the Same is an exercise of power over the other.[3]

> Philosophy as ontology is thus, for Levinas, ultimately narcissistic and egotistical. Philosophy is 'egology' since it gives priority to the self rather than the other. This priority of the self, this violence, leads to the death of the Other in the assertion of the self. He writes: 'in society such as it functions one cannot live without killing, or at least without taking the preliminary steps for the death of someone. Consequently, the important question of the meaning of being is not: why is there

---

1. Ibid., 21.
2. Roger Burggraeve, 'Violence and the Vulnerable Face of the Other: The Vision of Emmanuel Levinas on Moral Evil and Our Responsibility', *Journal of Social Philosophy* 30 (1999), 30.
3. As Burggraeve puts it:

   In [reducing the other to myself] I approach the other not according to his otherness itself, but from a horizon or another totality. . . . I look the individuality of the other, so to speak, up and down, forming a conception of him not as this-individual-here-and-now but only according to the generality of a type, an a priori idea, or an essence. . . . The 'comprehending' I, or ego, negates the irreducible uniqueness of the other and tries to conceive of him in the same way as he does the world. Comprehensive knowledge is thus also no innocent phenomenon but a violent phenomenon of power. By my 'penetrating insight' I gain not only access to the other, but also power over him.

   Ibid., 30, 36.

something rather than nothing – the Leibnizian question so much commented upon by Heidegger – but: do I not kill by being?'[1]

Rather than making ontology or epistemology primary in philosophy, Levinas argues that philosophy must begin with ethics. Levinas urges us to move from an 'economy of the same' (totality) towards the other (transcendence), something which can only happen in an encounter with the other, to bring us out of ourselves, as

> a calling into question of the Same – which cannot occur within the egoistic spontaneity of the Same – is brought about by the Other. We name this calling into question of my spontaneity by the presence of the Other ethics. The strangeness of the Other, his irreducibility to the I, to my thoughts and my possessions, is precisely accomplished as a calling into question of my spontaneity as ethics.[2]

This happens through encountering the face of the Other, which for Levinas is 'the way in which the other presents himself, exceeding *the idea of the other in me*'.[3] For Levinas:

> the epiphany of the Absolutely Other is a face by which the Other challenges and commands me through his nakedness, through his destitution. He challenges me from his humility and from his height. . . . The absolutely Other is the human Other. And the putting into question of the Same by the Other is a summons to respond. . . . Hence, to be I signifies not being able to escape this responsibility.[4]

In all of this, 'the Other (*Autrui*) remains infinitely transcendent, infinitely foreign; his face in which his epiphany is produced and which appeals to me breaks with the world that can be common to us'.[5] The command that the face of the Other gives us is 'you shall not kill', and not just that, but 'make space for me'; 'feed me'; 'reduce my suffering, share the world with me'. In this encounter, you are 'infinitely responsible' for the Other: 'The I before another is infinitely responsible.'[6] In his thought, with respect to

1. Emmanuel Levinas, *Ethics and Infinity: Conversations with Philippe Nemo*, trans R.A. Cohen,(Pittsburgh: Duquesne University Press, 1985), 85-7.
2. Levinas, *Totality and Infinity*, 43.
3. Ibid., 50.
4. Emmanuel Levinas, 'Transcendence and Height' in *Basic Philosophical Writings* (Bloomington: Indiana UP, 1996), 17.
5. Levinas, *Totality and Infinity,* 168, 194.
6. Levinas, *Trace of the Other*, 353.

our encounters with the Other, Levinas also talks about desire. For Levinas, desire must be distinguished from need. Need seeks to fill a negation or lack in the Subject; need is using the Other for oneself and thereby inflicting violence upon the Other. Desire is positively attracted by something other not yet possessed or needed, but not in as selfish and self-fulfilling a way.

Conclusion

The similarities between the thought of Yannaras and Levinas are manifold. There is the starting point of Heidegger's critique of previous accounts of being, but both go beyond Heidegger in ways that emphasise the relationality and the apophaticism of the Other. Within that, there is the desire that the Other remain Other, that they should let the Other be Other. Moreover, there is the sense in which desire is a positive part of our relationality to others, but that our relationality to others can never involve fully knowing or categorising the Other. Levinas seems to have his own apophaticism of the person.

However, the difference that I noticed in particular, and that I would like to tease out here, is that of vulnerability. This focus becomes particularly important when one considers the work of the late Pamela Sue Anderson. In Yannaras, the preservation of the otherness of the other becomes a means to an end; a means of maintaining and emphasising the otherness of God. In Levinas, regardless of his thoughts on how God is known in the trace of the Other, glimpsed in the face-to-face encounter, the question of philosophy is that of ethics, and the question of philosophy is how do I not kill; how I am responsible for the Other. Levinas is wary of the term 'love' to the extent that he treats 'love' as 'responsibility', and 'the neighbour' as 'the Other (who commands the I)': where 'the I before the Other is infinitely responsible',[1] and the face of the Other commands you in its alterity.[2]

It is this acceptance of the vulnerability of the person and the responsibility for the other that surpasses the work of Yannaras, although some have argued that Levinas takes it too far. This responsibility is taken to an extreme in Levinas. Levinas understands that we are even responsible for the responsibility of the other to us.[3] Using Anderson's

---

1. Emmanuel Levinas, 'Existence and Ethics' in *Proper Names*, trans. Michael B. Smith (Stanford: Stanford University Press, 1996), 74.
2. Emmanuel Levinas, *Otherwise than Being, Or Beyond Essence*, trans. Alphonso Lingis (Pittsburgh: Duquesne University Press, 1997), xiv.
3. 'In my analysis. . . the relation to the Face is the relation to the absolutely weak. . . and there is, consequently, in the Face of the Other always the death of the Other and thus, in some way, an incitement to murder, the temptation

work on vulnerability, a middle path can be proposed. Echoing the critique of individualisation in Heidegger and Yannaras, Anderson writes that autonomy is often held up as an ideal without an examination of what it should entail.[1] Anderson sees that the Kantian ideal of self-authorship can only be partly true, as 'inevitably the self is vulnerable also to the demands of time and variables of gender in shaping the stories of our lives'.[2] If this view were accepted more widely, it would challenge decisively the still dominant, liberal idea of autonomy as, straightforwardly, the ability to "write my story."[3] Anderson proposes a paradigm wherein the Kantian ideal is transformed by facing up to our vulnerability, read through Ricoeur, where 'in the face of vulnerability due to our neediness and contingency, we seek a common humanity in aspiring to be autonomous selves, while nevertheless remaining dependent on others to a certain degree'.[4] She argues for vulnerability due to the impossibility of full knowledge of others, informed by the impossibility of full knowledge of the self.[5]

---

to go to the extreme, to completely neglect the other – and at the same time (and this is the paradoxical thing) the Face is also the "Thou Shalt not Kill". A Thou-Shalt-not-Kill that can also be explicated much further: it is the fact that I cannot let the other die alone, it is like a calling out to me. . . at the outset I hardly care what the other is with respect to me, that is his own business; for me, he is above all the one I am responsible for.' Phillippe Nemo: 'But is not the Other also responsible in my regard?' Levinas: 'Perhaps, but that is his affair. . . I am responsible for the Other without waiting for reciprocity, were I to die for it. Reciprocity is his affair. It is precisely insofar as the relationship between the Other and me is not reciprocal that I am in subjection to the Other; and I am "subject" essentially in this sense. It is I who support all. You know that sentence in Dostoevsky: "We are all guilty of all and for all men before all, and I more than others".' *Ethics and Infinity*, 98.

1. '[T]here is one prominent claim, which has become the object of feminist and post-modern critiques: that autonomy is a personal ideal, according to which individuals are authors of their own lives.' Pamela Sue Anderson, 'Autonomy, vulnerability and gender', *Feminist Theory*, vol. 4(2) 2003, 150.
2. Ibid, 153.
3. Ibid.
4. Ibid.
5. 'We have no direct knowledge of a perfectly ethical act; we have no fully adequate self-knowledge. Instead we have only the continual process of endeavouring to make intelligible what remains unintelligible. In the case of our lived experiences, knowledge is always potentially possible in so far as we have phenomenological access to our lived body.' Ibid., 157. Anderson utilises but distinguishes her own project from Judith Butler's accounts of vulnerability. Butler explicitly bases her account of vulnerability on Levinas in 'Giving an Account of Oneself'. She writes that 'whether or not the Other is singular, the Other is recognized and confers

Anderson thus suggests that what must happen is the creation of a new narrative, 'as finite authors of our own acts and principles, we would have to gain new knowledge by creating narratives out of the phenomenologically accessible, yet never fully intelligible dimensions of our bodily and relational lives. These dimensions include our physical condition, marital or other relational dependencies, emotional health and rational capacities.'[1] Anderson stresses the embodied person in her work,[2] and through her use of Michèle Le Doeuff there is also a stress on the collective, which moves one from beyond oneself.[3] Reading Yannaras in conjunction with both Levinas and feminist philosophy, I argue that Levinas' account of vulnerability and responsibility can inform and prevent exploitation of the erotic desire and drive in Yannaras, and Yannaras can allow for more positive accounts of social relations. This

---

recognition through a set of norms that govern recognizability. So whereas the Other may be singular, if not radically personal, the norms are to some extent impersonal and indifferent, and they introduce a disorientation of perspective for the subject in the midst of recognition as an encounter.' Judith Butler, 'Giving an Account of Oneself', *Diacritics*, 31.4 (2001), 22. It is in an encounter with the Other that we realise our vulnerability; because the Other defies our account of ourselves and our account of them, they interrupt our own self-narrative. However, self-narrative itself is never complete, and its incompleteness is more fully revealed in the encounter with the Other.

1. Anderson, 'Autonomy, vulnerability and gender', 160.
2. 'The openness of corporeal vulnerability, which is like "a throbbing pulse" and "a trembling thing", is deeply relational; and for this reason, it can involve a becoming in the sense of enhancing life relationally; here my concept would be "mutual affection". Thus, I recognise my ongoing challenge is to confront the restrictive – strictly negative – uses of "vulnerability". This concept tends to be understood in contemporary, social and political worlds as negative; it is "the hurt", which Plath describes, but without the capacity to "sing". Corporeal vulnerability has been referred to by Christian theologians as "the flesh" of the body which needs to be discarded and replaced with "the spiritual" body. As a result, those associated with the flesh – like fleshy female bodies, or the failing flesh of the injured, ill, and dying – are treated as less capable than those who are thought to have achieved invulnerability.' Pamela Sue Anderson, *The Transformative Power of Vulnerability*. Available at: http://enhancinglife.uchicago. edu/blog/the-transformative-power-of-vulnerability. Accessed on 19 May 2017.
3. '[C]ollective work is necessary for women's access to the philosophical, enabling a mutual vulnerability in philosophical relations . . . [using] Michèle Le Doeuff's provocation for collective work in gaining access to philosophy, the unknown and the unthought, which need to be reintroduced continually, in order to avoid a fixation on the completeness of one's knowledge.' Pamela Sue Anderson, *Silencing and Speaker Vulnerability: Undoing an Oppressive Form of (Wilful) Ignorance.* Available at: https://womeninparenthesis.wordpress.com/2016/03/25/read-pamela-sue-andersons-iwd-keynote. Accessed on 19 May 2017.

more positive account of social relations, where we are not so responsible for the other's responsibility towards us, can be further augmented by Anderson's embrace of vulnerability and her emphasis on both the care of the self, in allowing for autonomy of self, and the power and importance of the collective. There can be a preservation of alterity whilst embracing relationality, and the apophaticism of the person enables us to always move beyond ourselves; out into nothing but never lost in it.

Chapter Six
Relation, Activity and Otherness in Christos Yannaras' Propositions for a Critical Ontology
Sotiris Mitralexis

Christos Yannaras has written extensively on ontology, epistemology, ethics, theology and politics. It is good fortune that a significant number of his books have recently become available in English thanks to Dr Norman Russell's translation of the bulk of Yannaras' work, including his magnum opus *Person and Eros*, the German edition of which bears a subtitle that describes it most abundantly: *A Comparison of the Ontology of the Greek Fathers and the Existential Philosophy of the West*.

In his work, Yannaras applies certain stable criteria emerging from his philosophical understanding of the world to a variety of categories, unveiling the vital connection between branches of philosophy and the world we live in. Thus we may classify the works *Person and Eros*, *Relational Ontology*, *Propositions for a Critical Ontology* and others under ontology/metaphysics, the works *On the Absence and Unknowability of God: Heidegger and the Areopagite* and *The Effable and the Ineffable: The Linguistic Limits of Metaphysics* under epistemology, and, finally, *The Freedom of Morality* under moral philosophy. The application of the criteria emerging from these works leads to his treatises on social philosophy (*Rationality and Social Practice*), political economy (*The Real and the Imaginary in Political Economy*), the relationship between contemporary physics and philosophy (*Postmodern Metaphysics*), the philosophy of religion (*Against Religion*) and the historical background of the clash of civilisations (*Orthodoxy and the West*).

Returning to Yannaras' critical ontology,[1] it is interesting to note that

---

1. With the kind permission of Wipf and Stock Publishers (www.wipfandstock. com), I am reprinting here with some revisions the chapter on Yannaras' critical ontology from my book *Ever-Moving Repose: A Contemporary Reading of Maximus the Confessor's Theory of Time* (Eugene, OR: Cascade, 2017), 29–40, first

Propositions for a Critical Ontology[1] (not yet translated in English) is one of the few philosophical books by Yannaras which does not explicitly mention theological notions *at all* – it seems to emphasise the fact that it is meant as a *philosophical proposition* in the strictest sense, with none of the traits of what we term and categorise under 'theology' – despite the fact that Yannaras absolutely does not believe in the exclusion of the ecclesial body's ontological testimony from the field of philosophy. The fact that the *structure* of the book follows the pattern of Wittgenstein's *Tractatus* and the *method* of the book is reminiscent of Karl Popper's insistence on falsifiability (although here employed in a different context) does also suggest this. One could perhaps explain that by saying that the book is also directed towards people who *do* believe in such a contrast between theology and philosophy, but we would have to disagree: *Propositions for a Critical Ontology* attempts to trace the *preconditions* for an ontological enquiry that would be free from philosophical dead ends and contradictions arising from traditions of thought that are, in Yannaras' view, characterised by arbitrary apriorisms and axiomatic certainties (which would be the case with not only e.g. idealism or monism, but also with empiricism or materialism) – to 'clear the ontological path', so to speak. His proposal for the *content*, not merely the preconditions, of an ontology freed from problematic starting points, of a truly *critical* ontology, is to be found in the book's sister volume published twenty years later, Yannaras' *Relational Ontology* – or, for that matter, in his magnum opus *Person and Eros*, where Patristic literature is studied and employed much more extensively.

This later book, *Relational Ontology*, opens with a phrase from Ludwig Wittgenstein's *Vermischte Bemerkungen* (1930): 'Every proposition that I write always means the whole, and is thus the same thing over and over again. It is as if they are only views of a single object seen from various angles.'[2] The same could be said of *Propositions for a Critical Ontology*: here Yannaras applies some very specific criteria to a multitude of categories (ontology, epistemology, even society) and arrives at an ontological proposition that calls for communal empirical verification and validation.

presented at the 2013 Oxford conference on Yannaras. A revised version of my 2016 Cambridge paper at the 'Polis, Ontology, Ecclesial Event' conference will appear in *Christos Yannaras: Philosophy, Theology, Culture* (London: Routledge, 2018, forthcoming), ed. Andreas Andreopoulos and Demetrios Harper, as this will serve the balance of each volume much better.

1. Christos Yannaras, *Προτάσεις κριτικῆς ὀντολογίας* [*Propositions for a Critical Ontology*] (Athens: Domos, 1985 & Ikaros, 2010).
2. The phrase is here taken from Christos Yannaras' *Relational Ontology* (Brookline, MA: HC Press, 2011), v. The Greek original, Ὀντολογία τῆς Σχέσης, was published in 2004 in Athens by Ikaros Publishing.

Preconditions for a Critical and Relational Ontology: λόγος, Relation, Consciousness

According to Yannaras, we can name *critical ontology* the answer to the ontological question that is subject to critical evaluation and verification, subject to the principle of the falsifiability of knowledge (the second proposition).[1] Answers to the ontological question can only then be subject to critical and empirical verification or refutation, 'if we affirm the cognitive access to the existential event as an experience of *relation*'. 'A *critical* ontology is possible, if we affirm the experience of the subject's consciousness of self as a starting point for the interpretation of the existential event' (7.3).

This experience of the self's consciousness of self is the only cognitive event that is truly, universally verified by all human persons – and 'this experience is only constituted through *relation*, which means that the experience of relation and its *referential widening* (i.e. the communal verification of the relation) constitutes the prerequisite for the cognitive access to the existential event'. Knowledge is the experiencing of relation and the nexus of shared experiences validates and verifies knowledge (7.3). The criterion thereof is the communal verification of knowledge, which can never be finite or taken for granted. This verification is an 'attainment' (κατόρθωμα), and by 'attainment' I mean it is always open to a fuller, a more complete communal verification, excluding the possibility of certainties or apriorisms (2.1). Linguistic and semantic formulations 'signify the experience of relation without being able to exhaust it, as a relation is actualised [ἐνεργεῖται] as the manifestation and unveiling of the subject's existential otherness' (2.11).

Consciousness of self is a prerequisite for this. The subject's consciousness, the consciousness of the fact that it exists, is the first and only certainty. The reality of consciousness precedes every assertion concerning reality (1.41). The existence of consciousness, of the Self, can be the only constant of a critical epistemology and ontology, as it is a cognitive event that precedes any epistemological stance, method, or assertion, even a *critical* stance. Consciousness of the self, the consciousness of one's existence and otherness, cannot but be *the only*

---

1. For practical reasons, in this chapter I will not cite the book's pages in footnotes, but its propositions in parentheses, which are hierarchically numbered statements in the style of Wittgenstein's *Tractatus* – thus, numbers in parentheses point to statements in Προτάσεις Κριτικῆς Ὀντολογίας. An elaboration of each point I make can be found in the book's cited proposition, which is also the case with the quotes mentioned.

certainty of a critical ontology (1.42). However, this does not lead us to forms of solipsism, as it is the relation to other realities that reveals our consciousness of Self.

The semantic function, not only in its linguistic meaning but in every relation of signifier and signified, is a cornerstone of the actuality of relations. The word Yannaras uses to denote all facets of the semantic function is the word λόγος, with all of its multiple meanings (and, sadly, any translation of the word in English would annihilate this polysemy). Λόγος is the manifestation of a signifier, which in turn signifies a presence. To be signified is to be manifested as a presence, and this referential function of λόγος turns it into the first precondition and manifestation of *relation*. A relation is *logical* as it pertains to λόγος (1.3). Each manifestation of something in the horizon of consciousness is a λόγος, a revealing of the Other to the subject, to the subject's consciousness. It is a referential revealing; a relational revealing (1.31). For Yannaras, 'λόγος is the subject's ability to *relate*, to manifest a perceptual relation to existence. The subject perceives existence as a revealing, as a manifestation which signifies the *otherness* of each phenomenon' (1.33).

I am not referring to abstract conceptions of relation. The physical impression constitutes a relation, as it functions as a signifier representing something for someone. Λόγος is the term we use for each and every semantic function: it creates the distinction between the two constituents of the relation, and in doing so constitutes the relation (1.332).

To perceive a λόγος (whether visual or auditory, sensible, or intelligible etc.) and to experience a relation to and connection with something or someone is to become conscious of one's individuality, as one perceives the other part of the relation as an otherness. Consciousness of the self is the consciousness of a difference, of an otherness, which is revealed in the relation. But the *fact* of consciousness precedes this: the *event* of consciousness is the prerequisite for every relation, it is manifested through relation but it precedes it, thus making it possible (1.341).

Yannaras maintains that the word λόγος signifies every referential activity which manifests the subject's otherness. (A similar definition of λόγος that he often employs is that λόγος is the mode in which everything that *exists* is *manifested*, becomes *known*.)[1] In different contexts, λόγος can mean a word, a meaning, 'an image, a sound, a visual representation, form, shape, a musical melody, a painting, etc. The polysemy of λόγος allows us to say that the mode in which λόγος informs us of the subject's

---

1. Cf. Christos Yannaras, *Σχεδίασμα εἰσαγωγῆς στὴ Φιλοσοφία [An Outline of an Introduction to Philosophy]* (Athens: Domos, 1988), 20: 'τὸν λόγο τοῦ κόσμου, τὸν *τρόπο* μὲ τὸν ὁποῖο ὅ,τι *εἶναι* γίνεται φανερό, *φαίνεται.*'

otherness is the mode of λόγος (ὁ τρόπος τοῦ λόγου) – that the subject itself is actualised (ἐνεργεῖται) as λόγος.' This would mean that λόγος is the *mode of relation*. 'The *mode of relation* in the subject's ability to make the participation in its otherness possible, as well as the *mode of relation* in the subject's ability to participate in the activities that manifest the other subjects' othernesses' (6.13).

Ontological Categories: Substance, Particulars, Activities

What would be the meaning of *truth* in a critical ontology? The notion of truth as a static and finite formulation, either known or unknown, would surely be excluded, together with the notion of truth as stemming solely from the individual's rational faculty. For a critical ontology, truth is not an *object*, but an event in which we participate: truth is the mode of reality. For Yannaras, it is the fullness of the subject's participation in existence that is the criterion of truth (2.3). It is an empirical truth, the knowledge of which can never be finite and consists of the nurturing of the subject's relationship with reality. However, the subjective experience of the individual is not enough: the cognitive event of individual experience is to be validated intersubjectively. The fullness of this communal verification is also a criterion of truth (2.31). For Yannaras, if truth is the mode of reality, then every true knowledge has a sound ontological starting point: he excludes the possibility of relativism or scepticism concerning the existence of truth itself (2.32).

It is in recognising truth as the mode of reality and reality as manifested through relation that we are led to an anti-essentialist notion of substance (οὐσία). Yannaras traces in the etymological implications of the Greek word οὐσία a relational conception thereof. Stemming from the feminine participle of the verb *to be* (εἰμὶ – οὖσα),[1] it signifies the event of participating in being. It defines existence as the mode of participating in being, which is even more the case when the word οὐσία is used to specify a specific substance, the qualities that manifest something as different from something else. Something is different from something else (in this context, a stone from a horse, not this horse from that horse), because it has a different mode of participating in being, and this is what defines its substance. In this, the *substance* (οὐσία) is the mode of participating in being – the substance not as a *what*, but as a *how* (4.13).[2]

---

1. Cf. *Scholia in De Divinis Nominibus*, CD4.1 313C, 'ἀπὸ γὰρ τοῦ εἶναι τὸ ὄνομα παρῆκται τῆς οὐσίας.'
2. Yannaras also illustrates notions such as the body and soul as modes and not

This understanding of substance (οὐσία) as the mode of existence dictates a corresponding understanding of a particular existence. Excluding an understanding of substance as an entity in itself, we have cognitive access to the substance only through its particular actualisations and manifestations – through the mode in which they are different, through the mode in which they manifest otherness.

> Every particular actualisation of the substance recapitulates the substance in its universality without exhausting it. A piece of stone embodies the universal truth of 'stone', by coming to know this particular piece we come to know *what stone is*, but the reality of 'stone' is not limited to that particular piece. That piece of stone manifests the totality of the mode in which something is a stone, it manifests the *substance* (οὐσία) of stone. However, this mode has also other, possibly infinite, manifestations. (4.131.)

We can only know the substance through its particular manifestations.

The Greek word for 'mode' (τρόπος, from the verb τρέπω, i.e. to turn, to turn in a certain direction, to alter, to change) does also have a dynamic meaning: it presupposes action/activity (ἐνέργεια) and an actualised relation. Substance (οὐσία), *the mode of participating in being*, is an event of perpetual becoming (it is interesting to note the Patristic identification of οὐσία with φύσις, nature, which stems from φύεσθαι, to grow, to become). It is known to us through the subject's perceptive activity (ἐνέργεια). Substance as the mode of participating in being *is* and *is manifested* as a whole set of activities and realised relations (4.133).

The Activities (ἐνέργειαι) as a Primary Ontological Category

According to Yannaras, the activities (ἐνέργειαι) are to be ascribed to the substance, to the mode of existence – they constitute each hypostasis, each particular existence, and manifest its substance. For him, 'the activities constitute an *ontological category* – the third ontological category together with the *substance* and the particular existence (καθέκαστον)', which is more commonly termed the *hypostasis* (4.2).[1]

---

as entities, modes that are revealed and manifested as relations through the activities. To conceive of these sums of actualized relations in a perpetual becoming as things, as some sort of material or immaterial objects, would be a grave misunderstanding (2.372-3.1).

1. For an account of the philosophical importance of the *activities* (ἐνέργειαι)

The notion of *activities* (ἐνέργειαι) emerges as a key term in Yannaras'
propositions for a critical ontology, a criterion for the existential
realism of said propositions. For Yannaras, the *activities* are not just a
'third term', an elucidation of previous terminology, but another way of
perceiving and analysing reality. By approaching the existential event
through the relations of (a) substance and activities, (b) substance and
the particular (the hypostasis), and (c) the particular and the activities,
our terminology acquires the prerequisites for a realism that is not to
be found in the common distinction of substance and hypostasis. As
Yannaras writes:

> We acquire cognitive access to the *substance* through its
> *activities* as its common mode of participating in being, as the
> sameness of the particulars' nature.
>   We come to know each *particular*, each hypostasis, as a
> manifestation of its *substance*, while the substance itself is
> known through its particular existential realisations.
>   We come to know the *activities* as the *modes* that signify
> the *substance*, but also as the othernesses which constitute the
> particular as particular (4.21).

'The *substance* is distinct from both the activities *and* the particular, as
it is *through the activities* that the substance's sameness of nature and the
otherness of the particular is manifested, and as it is *through the particular*
that the substance is recapitulated and manifested but not exhausted.'
To mention an example, *smiling, to smile*, or *laughing, to laugh*, is an
activity of the human substance and nature; it is to be found in every
human being, in every particular manifestation of 'humanity'. But each
human person manifests smiling or laughing, or *smiles* and *laughs*, in
a completely unique way, in a way that actualises (not merely *reveals*,
but *actualises*) their substance as a hypostasis, in a way that *actualises
complete otherness*. The activities, being distinct from both the substance
itself *and* the hypostasis itself, belong to the substance but actualise
the hypostasis. The activities (ἐνέργειαι) are hypostatically manifested
activities of the substance (4.211).

These signifiers, together with their signified realities, cannot
function as apriorisms, as axiomatic statements and certainties,
because their definitions emerge from their intertwined relations,
relations that 'signify the realised manifestation of the existential

in Patristic thought and related matters, see also Yannaras' *Person and Eros*
(Brookline, MA: HC Press, 2007), 43-70 (in which ἐνέργειαι is rendered as
energies).

event'. That is why the notion of activities as an ontological category is a prerequisite for the articulation of a critical ontology, if it is to be truly critical (4.212).

It is the interference of the notion of *activities* that subjects this ontology to the critical (intersubjective and communal) validation or rejection of its empirical testimony. For it is the notion of *activities* that demonstrates the contradictory character of a perception of either the substance or of the particular as existences-in-themselves, thereby transcending ontological categories such as the *phenomena* or the *noumena,* materialism and idealism, etc. (4.213).

Otherness (ἑτερότητα) and Artistic Expression

The absolute otherness of each human person and its indeterminacy in language is not an abstract concept. Even the physical form of each particular person is impossible to describe exhaustively in language – and by physical form I am referring to 'the way (τρόπος) in which [each person's] bodily otherness is actualised (ἐνεργεῖται) – from the fingerprints and the exact shape of the body to his gaze, his smile, his hand gestures'. Even an exhaustive description of a person cannot but correspond to more than one human hypostasis, as the function of each separate specification is to objectify the specified so it can be understood by more people – whereas shared, common experience affirms that each human being constitutes a whole of absolutely unique and unprecedented mental and physical activities and actualisations (ἐνέργειαι), 'an absolute existential otherness' (6.11).

We come to *know* this otherness, we have cognitive access to it, but we cannot *define* it, exhaust its reality in formulations of language. We come to know each otherness through the manifestation of its activities (ἐνέργειαι), through the mode in which they are actualised. To directly experience a personal otherness is to participate in the activities and actualisations (ἐνέργειαι) that manifest it, in the way in which this otherness becomes known. 'And that is why the recognition of another subject's otherness is a *relational* event, a *relational experience*' (6.12). Descriptions, however exhaustive, cannot contain, manifest or reveal a person's otherness. However, the participation (μετοχή-μέθεξη) in the λόγος of a person's creations can and does reveal it. A painting, a musical symphony, a poem or a sculpture *can* and *do* reveal the otherness of their creators – 'only the creation's λόγος can "signify" the reality of the subject, its otherness' (6.321).

It is in artistic creations we can most clearly discern this reality, but every act, creative activity and creation (πρᾶγμα, πεπραγμένο) has the subject's otherness imprinted in it and is manifesting it – however evidently or subtly. Human action is not merely contrasted with theory, it manifests and preserves the λόγος of the personal otherness; the reality of the personal otherness. As such, 'every human action is a relational event, a communal event' (6.322). Yannaras mentions the example of man's ability to discern the otherness of the poet in his poetry, or of the musician in his music – to be able to recognise Baudelaire's poetry and to distinguish it from Eliot's poetry, to be able to recognise the otherness of Mozart in his music and to be able to discern it from Bach's music. The fact that man is led from the information gathered by the senses to the 'empirical recognition of the otherness of the artist's creative λόγος is a cognitive event that is valid and true while annulling the "objectivity" of perceptible information', as it cannot really be demonstrated scientifically or formulated linguistically in its fullness, but can be only experienced and never defined, only inadequately signified through language, science or by other means. In the communal validation of experience, experiences of different persons *do* overlap, but this does *not* constitute 'objectivity', 'as the affirmation of the difference between Bach's music and Mozart's music is not adequate to transmit the knowledge of this difference' (7.2201).[1]

Axiomatic Dichotomies and Problematic Ontologies

A critical ontology is an attempt to transcend philosophical apriorisms and dichotomies of the past, which were based on a lack of realism. Philosophical contemplation has at times identified the *abstract* with the *non-existent*, or the *abstract* with the *truly existing*. However, both theses

1. Art, usually not a subject directly pertaining to ontology, gives me the opportunity to comment on ontology's relation to *society*, there are ontological preconditions, whether clearly articulated and widely known or not, behind each collective approach to the *meaning* of reality, each approach to organising society, each choice in living collectively. A particular interpretation or reality, a particular ontological approach is to be discerned even in facets of life or in disciplines where one would not suspect the direct presence of ontology – perhaps due to the absence of articulated ontological reasoning (8.11). Yannaras discusses Karl Marx's insights on several occasions in his *Propositions for a Critical Ontology* (mostly in 6.2-6.613). In these pages, Yannaras does not only demonstrate Marx's vital and radically new ideas concerning the core of Western philosophy's dead ends, but also the inner contradictions of Marx's own system – contradictions which pertain to its implied or explicit ontological basis.

overlook the fact that every abstract formulation functions as a signifier and every signifier constitutes a relation. This relation is an empirical reality in cases of both sensible signified realities and abstract/intelligible notions. For Yannaras, the question is not if the signified is sensible or abstract/intelligible, but if the relation between the subject and the signified is real or imaginary – and this is to be verified communally, not individually; it must be judged from the wholeness of relations (2.35). To equate the abstract with the non-existent or with the truly existing is to impose apriorisms and axiomatic certainties to reality, giving birth to dichotomies such as materialism and idealism, whereas the basis of a critical ontology would be the realism of relation (2.351).

In a critical ontology, both the reality of sensible and abstract/mental signifiers and manifestations are subject to intersubjective, communal experience, to the 'cognitive widening' of experience (2.36). 'Knowledge can neither be solely objective (independent of the subject) nor solely subjective (irrelevant of the object). The contradistinction of objectivity and subjectivity divorces and contrasts the object from the subject, it ceases to accept them as partners and constituents of a cognitive relation' (2.361).

It is not only philosophy as an isolated 'discipline' that gives birth to the need for a critical ontology. Yannaras maintains that the profound changes in the scientific worldview during the twentieth century and up to the present cannot but change the way we see philosophy. Our perception of reality cannot be the same as the one offered to us by Newtonian physics, Euclidian geometry and the Cartesian 'cogito'. Yannaras discerns in science's recent developments that our perception of reality as a sum of separate entities in a given structure must be substituted with a perception of reality as a sum of relations and relationships that cannot be understood and explained in a singular and given way. 'Relation emerges as both the *mode* of reality and the *mode* of *knowing* reality,' of having cognitive access to it (4). In this it is *physics* that traces new paths for *metaphysics*.

For Yannaras, the sharp distinction between physics and metaphysics that is taken for granted in mainstream philosophy seems to be the corollary of a specific understanding of λόγος as individual *ratio*, as *facultas rationis*. The cognitive access to reality is thus limited to the formulations stemming from method, ideology, and proof, giving birth to dualisms such as matter and spirit, dualism, and monism, physics and metaphysics, science, and ontology (7-7.023). However, the antithetical distinction between physics and metaphysics (ontology) seems to exclude the possibility of a *critical* access to the ontological question, the possibility of a critical ontology. For this contradistinction to exist:

every anti-thesis presupposes a definitive thesis, a thesis not subject to critical evaluation. In terms of the distinction between physics and metaphysics, the position (thesis) that is not critically examined and evaluated is the assumed axiom of either matter, or mind, or both. Because of that, the contrast between physics and metaphysics is always subjecting ontological reflection to the dogmatic apriorism of either dualism or monism (7.1).

The focus of critical ontology on experience and consciousness does not lead to empiricism or mysticism. The experience of (self-)consciousness transcends the information gathered by the senses. Consciousness of the self 'is not the only cognitive event that arises from experience without being limited to the information that is gathered by the senses'. Yannaras maintains that 'every relational experience, every experience of relation is a cognitive event which may arise from the information of the senses, but the relation as a cognitive event is not limited to this information' and transcends it (7.22).

Different Accesses to Reality:
A Personal Causal Principle and the Fullness of Participation

Every subject is participating in reality, but to what extent does one participate in the *fullness* of reality? Yannaras illustrates how a different stance towards reality produces seemingly equally valid conclusions in their inner logic, which are, however, radically different from one another. For example, while contemplating a painting by Van Gogh, a strict positivist would acknowledge the reality of it as a sum of canvas and oil paint. A different access to the reality of the painting would be to recognise the image it depicts. A third possibility would be to define the painting by its subjective aesthetic integrity, mastery of technique, etc. A fourth and different type of access to the reality of the painting would be one which is actualised by the degree of the subject's participation in the observed reality:

> to recognise in the painting the visual λόγος of the person that
> created it, the otherness of the creative activity (ἐνέργεια) of this
> particular artist, whom we today have never met as a tangible
> presence, but the existential otherness of whom is 'defined' by
> the reality of his painting. Neither of these four interpretations
> is false concerning the description of the painting's reality, but
> the description and definition of reality differs according to the
> fullness of the subject's relation to it (7.4101).

Yannaras applies the same approach to the subject's perception of reality as a whole. There are approaches to reality as a whole which only recognise the constituents of reality, matter and energy, or even the beauty of the cosmos. However, another approach to accessing reality – an approach signified by the fullness of one's personal participation in the world, to reality as a whole – would be 'to recognise in cosmic reality the otherness of a personal creative activity (ἐνέργεια), the "bearer" of which we have never encountered as a sensible presence, but whose personal existence is signified by the world's reality'. The fullness of one's personal participation in the aforementioned painting or in reality as a whole is that which distinguishes these different paths to accessing reality, none of which is false in itself, even if they represent different degrees of personal participation in the fullness of reality (7.411).

If it is the experience of relation that constitutes the cognitive event, if reality is known and is manifested and revealed through relation and the dynamic of relation, then 'the hermeneutic access to the [philosophical] problem of the *causal principle* of reality can be freed from the dualism and contrast between physics and metaphysics', between science and ontology (7.43). The dynamic of each person's (and humanity's) relation to reality is an actual event, 'which cannot be subjugated to neither the natural "objectivity" of the sensible', to the natural sciences, 'nor to the abstract (mental, reductive) nature of metaphysical enquiry' (7.4202). This is in no way to be understood as a 'proof of God's existence' or even 'proof of God's inexistence' or anything of the sort: the very notion of a critical ontology is constituted against 'proofs' as compulsorily convincing constructs of the logical faculty. However, it recognises the communal affirmation of the presence of the relationship's Other. The personal discovery of a creative activity (ἐνέργεια) beyond physical reality, which constitutes physical reality, 'is a hermeneutic access to reality that cannot be confined or subjugated to the "extra-subjective" (objective) certainties of science and metaphysics. It remains a hermeneutic proposal that differs from other hermeneutic proposals in the fullness of the personal relation to [and participation in] the cosmic reality that it actualises' (7.43). The fullness and realism of the subjective cognitive participation in reality is to be judged by 'the wide referentiality of relation, its *communal* validation' (7.44). There is also a very real and practical difference in the *meaning* that each person's participation in reality grants to his life, or the *meaning* that each society's or community's collective participation in reality grants to each facet of human coexistence (7.45).

The recognition of a personal causal principle of the world in the field of ontology has direct implications for our human coexistence. If the universe in its infinite complexity and vastness is not a product of randomness but the outcome of a personal activity (ἐνέργεια), if the world is a manifestation of God's activity (ἐνέργεια), then 'the principle of conscious experience (consciousness), freedom and creativity is not an inexplicable exception pertaining only to the human subject, but the causal principle of existence' – the causal principle of existence as the existential otherness arising from consciousness and freedom. If that is the case, freedom and otherness must be recognised as 'real (and not evaluative, i.e. arbitrary) criteria for the genuineness of history and society: dependence, subjugation and oppression are to be recognised as very real forms of existential corruption', not merely as the corruption of social relations. (5.22)

Ultimately, the question of a critical ontology is a question of meaning, a question of truth. This question is not limited to the world of philosophy, but extends to the world of human coexistence, of civilisation and history.

> Philosophical *ontology* is a proposal concerning the *meaning* of man's existence and its relations – a proposal of meaning concerning the mode of existence. And *critical* ontology builds its proposal on the subject's existential self-awareness as an experience of freedom and otherness. Freedom and otherness become accessible to us as a cognitive and empirical event through relation and the dynamic indeterminacy of relation. The criterion of reality is the experience of relation to reality and the verification of the relation's genuineness through its collective widening – i.e. the equally indeterminable dynamics of the social event that constitutes history and civilisation (8.21).

Yannaras ends his *Propositions for a Critical Ontology* with proposition number 9: 'For a critical ontology, truth is relation. And relation – i.e. truth – is never taken for granted. It is an attainment' (9). If Ludwig Wittgenstein has completed his *Tractatus Logico-Philosophicus* with the famous phrase 'Whereof one cannot speak, thereof one must be silent,' I could say that Yannaras' answer would be: *Whereof one cannot speak, therein one must participate.*

We hope that this short exposition concerning the possibility of a critical ontology will help the reader who wishes to explore Yannaras' philosophical work in acquiring a fundamental knowledge concerning it, as the continuous publication of newer translations of Yannaras' works seems to kindle an ever-growing interest in his thought.

Chapter Seven
As for God, So for Sound:
Engaging with Yannaras' Philosophy of Language
Marcello La Matina

My aim in this paper[1] is to engage with Yannaras' thought by connecting his concept of knowledge-as-relation to a problem often neglected by the philosophers of language: the ontology of the musical sound. The main question might be formulated as follows: what would happen if Yannaras' view of relational ontology were applied to investigating the ontological status of the musical sound? This attempt puts the investigator in a position very close to that of a theologian dealing with ontology. Sound and God – the Christian God – are similar in this respect: neither is reducible to concepts and neither is reducible to a mere content of experience. Consequently, both require an ontological effort. Taking for granted the relevance of Yannaras' work for both theologians and Patristic scholars, I shall refer in the present paper to just two of Yannaras' topics: first, the Eastern challenge to the Occident as far as knowledge is concerned, and the project of an integrated ontology which he has been developing throughout his work as a legacy of the late antique and late modern philosophy. I also hope to highlight the significance of Yannaras' framework for the students of the philosophy of language who are attracted by the philosophy of music too.

1. Allow me to show my gratitude to the professors of the Department of Greek Philology at the University of Palermo, which shaped the 'cultural womb' of my education. This had a role in my discovery of both Yannaras and his effort to reconcile the theoretical and the erotic content of relationship. My presence here is also in the name of the professors who introduced me to the fascinating world of the present and the past Greek language and culture, particularly Professors Gennaro D'Ippolito and Salvatore Nicosia. Let me likewise thank Dr Sara Marilungo and Dr Barbara Osimani for their wise help in revising my English.

Some Preliminary Troubles

To begin with, allow me to define a term. By 'musical sound' one commonly means the *product* – and/or the *process* – of a performance through which a musician 'rescues' a given written score in a public context. We used here very common words as *definientia*: i.e. terms as 'product', 'process of production' and 'rescue'. Their indefiniteness furnishes evidence of a malaise that one would attribute to our current lexicon of musical matters. Indeed, almost all literate cultures do prefe to categorise in terms of durable objects rather than in terms of passing and unstable things. Insofar as sounds are transient phenomena, they seem not to fit the philosophical framework. The question thus arises whether it is possible to finitely differentiate the product from the producing-process; that is, to distinguish the concrete object from the abstract category it belongs to. In the affirmative, we could have something as a (modest) concept of sound; we could then capture the sound by use of the concepts a musical sound falls under.[1] Nonetheless, why should the quest for concepts seem to be such a relevant point in a discussion about a physical phenomenon after all? The analytic philosopher may answer that having a concept for some objects – for some or any class of objects – should give us a powerful grammar and a consistent basis to support valid inferences, thus improving our investigation. By applying to music such an account, our knowledge about sounds shall be expressed through sentences like the following: 'ξ falls under the concept Φ.'

Note that the concept *sub* 'Φ' is *true of* any given object substitutable for ξ, provided the interpreters are able to judge whether that single sound is a true *token* of the Φ-*type* it falls under. Consequently, knowledge holds in a matter of definite concepts and truth is more than the coincidence of *intellectus* and *res*. We should ask ourselves nevertheless whether this is what we want our philosophy of music to do. In fact, as other philosophers sometimes claim, such an understanding of music and sounds has

---

1. The expression 'falling-under' [*sc.* a predicate] is of common usage among the analytic philosophers (and among German people). Gottlob Frege introduced such terminology in paragraph 3 of his germinal work, *Begriffsschrift: A Formula Language, Modeled upon that of Arithmetic, for Pure Thought*, trans. Stefan Bauer-Mengelberg in *From Frege to Gödel: A Source Book in Mathematical Logic* ed. Jean van Heijenoort (Cambridge: Harvard University Press, 1967), 1-82, originally published as *Begriffsschrift. Formelsprache des reinen Denkens* (Halle: Nebert, 1879). See also Gottlob Frege, 'On Concept and Object' in *Translations from the Philosophical Writings of Gottlob Frege*, ed. Peter Thomas Geach and Max Black (Oxford: Blackwell, 1960), 42-55: In this writing Frege argues against the psychological account of concepts endorsed by his interlocutor Benno Kerry.

already proved to be useless and illusory, because it traces by stipulation what should be traced by investigation, i.e. through the installation of a discursive space between what, on the one side, one accepts as a problem and what, on the other, he accepts as a solution for that problem. It goes without saying that the question and its solutions are not always to be found in one and the same theoretical field.[1] This is especially true when it comes to music, a phenomenon supposedly inexplicable in terms of just *one* (and only one) aspect of human society or language or mind.

The State of the Art

Our present difficulties, however, could be due to bigger obstacles: for instance, it could be a malaise springing not only from a terminological uncertainty but from theoretical causes having to do with the format of the ontology we usually commit to in a large part of the cultivated West.[2] By 'ontology' I refer here not only to Quine's criterion for the 'ontological commitments' of a language, but rather to a set of questions that arise from participation in the life of the world. Understood in this way, the ontological question is the problem itself of being or, still better, our being amazed at the fact that *the referential character of the human being is not reducible to a mere intellectual question.* Yannaras argued persuasively on this subject:

> I am aware of objects, and with the help of the 'semantics' which language offers me, I define a stone, a river, or a child, and yet the information or sense arising from consciousness which makes the content of cognition common knowledge has its origin in my 'personal' cognition (or experience) of these common objects. That is to say, cognition differs from one human being to another. The objectivity of the cognitive content of consciousness is not primordial.[3]

1. See Nelson Goodman, *Fact, Fiction and Forecast*, 4th ed. (Cambridge: Harvard Univ. Press, 1983): 31-3.
2. Since his PhD thesis Yannaras evidenced some differences between the Greek and the Latin philosophical and theological traditions. Yannaras' most relevant claim tends to correct the solely conceptual definition of truth endorsed by the Western thought under the influence of both the Scholastic and the rationalistic dominance. Namely, Western 'scholasticism' departed from the 'immediacy of relationship,' whom he takes as the key to hypostatic knowledge. See Yannaras, *On the Absence and Unknowability of God. Heidegger and the Areopagite* (New York: T. & T. Clark, 2005), 27-9.
3. Christos Yannaras, *Person and Eros* (Brookline, MA: HC Press, 2007), 7.

What remains of this personal dimension in many of today's philosophical perspectives? Why repeatedly listen to musical sounds, if knowledge is identified with just concepts? Finally, what one might learn from one's own efforts to form music from noises? If, according to Quine's view, 'ontology recapitulates philology',[1] or if 'the shaping of a person's *Weltanschauung* does happen through grammar, syntax, and other formal aspects of his language',[2] there is no need at all for philosophical investigations on the role of music all along the process of anthropogenesis. On the contrary – as Yannaras claims – '[i]f we now accept the human *person* as the "horizon" of the disclosure of beings (their rising up from oblivion to truth), knowledge becomes the experience of the disclosure within the context of the person's relation to objective beings'.[3] From Yannaras' perspective – one is tempted to say – 'person does recapitulate ontology'. What you need to understand is how to reconcile the freedom of the person with the formal constraints that every superordinate system of rules involves. This means reconciling the subjective experience of sounds with the objectivity of common knowledge.

As it will be shown later, such a concern could benefit from a more analytical attention to Yannaras' approach to otherness, to the alternation of presence and absence as a way of experiencing person and, not least, to space and time as measure of personal relation. Analytic philosophers of the recent past typically paid scarce attention to such themes, as well as to the ontological commitments of musical sound. It was through the efforts of phenomenology that the question was first posed from a more significant perspective, where the logical form of human experience had a prominent role. The phenomenologist Giovanni Piana – the most influential among modern philosophers of music – considers the musical sound not as 'givenness', but as a sort of *affected* object. Sounds do not refer to the things they are produced by or through. Sounds are rather taken as such only by listeners, who 'put somehow in brackets the world'.[4] Music and sounds are thus involved in the phenomenological discourse mostly as a complex of possibilities (or atmospheres) which the subject is affected by.

---

1. This sentence later became a summary of Quine's approach; it appeared as an exergue on the flyleaf of Willard Van Orman Quine, *Word and Object* (Cambridge, MA: The M.I.T. Press, 1960). Quine attributed the statement to James Grier Miller, though without indications of page and book. Inspired by this quotation, some students wrote about this puzzling saying.
2. Theodore Sarbin, 'Ontology Recapitulates Philology: The Mythic Nature of Anxiety', *American Psychology*, Jun. 23, 6 (1968), 411-18.
3. Yannaras, *Person and Eros*, 176.
4. See Giovanni Piana, *Filosofia della musica* (Milano: Guerini & Associati, 1991), 131.

Unlike phenomenologists, analytic philosophers mostly tended to dismiss any concerns about the personal or existential sphere of sounds; their main question might be stated as follows: 'Provided that human experience is expressed as propositional knowledge, which place, if any, should be assigned to the terms denoting musical sounds in any sentence about sound?' Such a formulation indeed transposes our conundrum – without however solving it – into a broader context, the boundaries of which are those of the so-called 'linguistic turn'. In so doing, a concern for language is introduced as such in our discussion about the ontology of music, having already removed from investigation any metaphysical appeal. Consequently, other questions arise, such as whether we should take sounds as *effected* or as *affected* objects. In short, is sound rather *a* physical event among others? Or is it, still better, *the* event itself of giving lawlikeness (τὸ νομικόν) to other physical events?[1] Similar perspective fluctuations could be observed among scholars of the analytical aesthetics not only as far as sound is concerned, but also in relation to the musical artefacts.[2]

Jerrold Levinson studied the ontology of musical works and proposed four different responses one can use relative to the present question. A musical work – and *a fortiori* a musical sound – could be identified (1) in a set of performances or tokens; (2) in a pure structure made of universal properties. Moreover, a work (a sound) can exist (3) as a context-bound structure belonging to a given culture, or, finally, (4) as a mental event occurring as a process.[3] Depending on which ontology one chooses, six different (and alternative) forms of theory are possible. Nominalists, for example, could imagine their world crowded with individuals, Platonists with pure forms; furthermore, Physicalists and Phenomenalists colonise

---

1. Reference is made here, on the one side, to Davidson's 'anomalous monism' and, on the other side, to various forms of dualism, mostly present in the cognitive approach to the philosophy of mind. Against the latter I have argued that the musical event escapes this dichotomy, for it does not acquire its lawlikeness – as any other measured phenomenon, but seems to possess lawlikeness (the νομικόν). This is perhaps why Greeks did term their musical tracks νόμοι. See, respectively, D. Davidson, *Essays on Actions and Events*, (Oxford; New York: Clarendon, 2001), 207-27, and in M. La Matina, *Notes on Sound: Philosophy of Languages and Forms of Life*, forthcoming. Orig. ed. which I quote from: *Note sul suono. Filosofia dei linguaggi e forme di vita* (Ancona: LeOssa, 2014), 56-8.

2. A panoramic view on this is offered by Alessandro Arbo, 'Que ce qu'un "objet musical"?', *Les cahiers philosophiques de Strasbourg*, II (2010), 225-47.

3. Jerrold Levinson, 'What a Musical Work Is?' *Journal of Philosophy* 77 (1980), 5-28.

their worlds with percepts and *qualia* respectively. Thus, if *qualia* are time-bound, then the system will be a Particularist one; if, on the contrary, they are time-free, the system shall be a Realist one.[1] More recently, the philosophical debate set in opposition supporters of a dualistic view of musical 'properties' and supporters of a monistic reductionism that abandons sound and its problems to the kingdom of Nature with its 'strict laws'. As an exception, we would mention the position of Donald Davidson who theorised the notion of 'anomalous monism'. Although Davidson neither handles *expressis verbis* musical objects or sounds nor admits to music as a special class in his ontology of events, we consider his attempt as a really useful one in the present discussion, because he emphasises the role of actions and events as a matter of semantics and ontology.[2]

There is room at this point for a significant remark. In the approaches mentioned above no explicit mention was made of the role of matter in the constitution of music. Still better, matter is very often involved in explanations of music insofar as a form captures it, so it becomes a mere vehicle or support for morphologic or syntactic operations. One can see in this model some residue of the attitude that so irritated Martin Heidegger e.g. in his profound meditation on the origin of the work of art:

> The matter-form-structure [*Stoff-Form-Gefüge*], however, by which the being of a piece of equipment is first determined, readily presents itself as the immediately comprehensible constitution of every being.... The inclination to take the matter-form structure [*Stoff-Form-Gefüge*] to be *the* constitution of every being receives, however, particular encouragement from the fact that, on the basis of religious – biblical – faith, the totality of beings is represented, in advance, as something created [*Geschaffenes*]. And here, that means 'made' [*Angefertigtes*].[3]

---

1. This detailed differentiation among theory-formats is due to the philosopher Nelson Goodman, *The Structure of Appearance* (Dordrecht: Reidel, 1977), 135-48.
2. As to Davidson's account on events see the essay 'Mental Events' in Donald Davidson, *Essays on Actions and Events* (Oxford; New York: Oxford University Press, 2003), 215-25. The question whether mental events are identical with physical event is a crucial one for the present debate; an examination of it, in connection with the notion of *supervenience* is given in La Matina, *Notes on Sound*, 203. The reason why I pay attention to Davidson's anomalous monism lies in the fact that, on the one side, it 'rejects the thesis, usually considered essential to materialism, that mental phenomena can be given purely physical explanations', and, on the other side, he states that 'the mental is nomologically irreducible'.
3. Martin Heidegger, 'The Origin of the Work of Art' (1935-6), *Off the Beaten Track*, ed. and trans. Julian Young and Kenneth Haynes (Cambridge: Cambridge

Heidegger's claim, as everyone knows, was directed against the then dominant conception of artworks in terms of a duality between *materia* and *forma*. As has been shown by the studies of Panayiotis A. Michelis,[1] Erwin Panofsky,[2] and Christos Yannaras, such a view can be traced back to the Gothic – and the Scholastic too – thought of art, which tended to subjugate matter to form. Unlike the Latin world, Yannaras argues, these phenomena of subordination of matter to form are mostly unknown to Byzantine artists and craftsmen:

> The first characteristic one might note in the architecture of the 'Byzantine' church, as we now call it, is *respect for the building materials*; an attempt to manifest *the inner principle of the material*, the 'rational' potentialities of the matter, and to bring about *a 'dialogue' between the architect and his material*. . . . The Byzantine architect seems free and untrammelled by any a priori ideological aim.[3]

A very similar divide, it might be noted, exists today between, on the one side, philosophers who address sounds through a conceptualistic perspective and, on the other side, philosophers who refuse any dualism of matter and form. As an example of the former, think of the *Begriffsschrift* or Ideography sketched by the German logician Gottlob Frege.[4] Any building materials of language are dismissed; there is no dialogue at all between the logicians and the living language they analyse: '[O]nly the conceptual content is of significance for our ideography,' Frege said.[5] On the contrary, scholars like Yannaras propose to acknowledge as a theoretical step the 'respect for the peculiar "reason" in the natural material',[6] for it manifests the artist's improvement in personal knowledge as well as in love for the created world.

University Press, 2002), 10-11. German ed., *Der Ursprung des Kunstwerks* (Frankfurt am Main: Klostermann, 1950), 28.

1. Panayiotis A. Michelis, *An Aesthetic Approach to Byzantine Art* (London: Batsford, 1955), 57-65.
2. Erwin Panofsky, *Gothic Architecture and and Scholasticism*, Wimmer Lecture, 1948 (Latrobe: Archabbey Press, 1951), 10-21.
3. Christos Yannaras, *The Freedom of Morality*, trans. Elizabeth Briere (Crestwood, NY: St Vladimir's Seminary Press, 1984), 237, 244; my italics.
4. See Frege, *Begriffsschrift*. It goes without saying that by conceiving of an 'Ideography' the philosopher can easily dismiss any concern about the Signifier and its time-bound body.
5. Frege, *Begriffsschrift*, 12.
6. Yannaras, *Freedom of Morality*, 246.

Whatever one may think of this divide, it drives us to the point of taking seriously the ontological questions relative to so neglected a topic as musical sound.

Our last remarks do not mean the recent studies went blank; they only aim to stress that no one among these analytic moves obtained a really significant progress. On the contrary, the superfoetation of formal constraints made it more and more evident that the Western paradigm is struggling with some crucial limits of the mere conceptual analysis. Now, the radical hypothesis is to assume that neither music nor musical sound could be reduced to both their intensional and/or intentional features. Leaving aside for a moment the quest for propositional meaning, a supposition is taking shape gradually: the musical sound looks like 'something' (of course, not necessarily a thing) neither reducible, on one hand, to its conceptual features nor, on the other hand, to simple phenomenal sense data. Currently, philosophers have no shared ideas about how sounds (be they objects or events or whatever else happening in the world) should be captured in the context of a sentence regarding the ontology of music.

Transition: Escaping Conceptualism and Semantics

Wittgenstein once wrote that understanding a musical phrase is the same as understanding a verbal sentence.[1] One might wonder how this similarity could be expressed through use of some logical notation. What would a musical phrase made of sounds without meaning would look like? During the last few decades, philosophers and semiotics came across such a puzzle. To summarise in a few words a long and varied debate, two distinct patterns can be identified: structural theories and evidence-oriented theories. The former assumed language expressions mostly as sign complexes, not affected *per se* by time. Interpretation was considered to be a systemic relationship that depended on previously shared codes; the latter provided a stable link between signifiers and denotations. In these methods there was no room for time or history, to the extent that one could now term them all *timeless* accounts of signs and languages. Code-based theories could not be applied to musical works, for each musical sound emerges in time and cannot be reduced to a mere pattern of timeless pitches and rhythm or quality. Evidence-

---

1. See Ludwig Wittgenstein, *Philosophische Untersuchungen* (Oxford: Blackwell, 1953), ii, 527: 'What I mean is that understanding a sentence lies nearer than one thinks to what is ordinarily called understanding a musical theme.'

theories (also termed inductive theories) did seem to be more powerful than code-bound semiotics, for induction makes substantial use of time. A significant breakdown of time is introduced: the present sound is not only the content of one's attention, but also the result of a categorisation of any previous sound and a prefiguration of any future sound. Sounds are affected as both instances examined *before a certain time t* and instances *not already given at t.*

Listening to any of Mozart's *Sonatas for piano* is not unlike the guessing of a possible relationship between present and absent sounds. The splitting point of time introduces each *passing* instance as a possible new case relative to one's expectations. Time is a twofold divide: it is passing evidence of present and coming of possible future sounds. However, one might wonder if any new instance of sounds really a *new* event. As Augustine once wrote, '*praesens de futuris expectatio*' ('expectancy is the present of future times'). Splitting time by induction is not yet being in the time. Time, Yannaras would say, involves relation to the Other within a personal event. If so, we can now understand what troubled us in both the structural and the inductive accounts; troubles spring, on the one side, from the absence of any concern for time, and, on the other side, from the uncertainty relative to the distinction between the *ontic* and the *ontological* dimension of both present and future. This now evidenced limit cannot be exceeded, unless the inductive account of time takes into consideration the personal dimension of the other by its alternation of presence and absence: 'beings are *disclosed* as presence and *are* as presence and absence. As presence, beings are conceived of as *phenomena*. As presence-absence, beings *are*, conceived of through intellect and word.'[1]

This easily applies to music: one might take the experience of disclosure as the passing of sounds from silence to noise, or from noise to shaped sounds. Music emerges as this movement of rising up, through which something as a chain of beings takes place in time and space. Sounds do exist as a *mode* of being. They come into light. Nevertheless, how to conceive of such beings now as ontic and now as non-ontic categories? Is there a comprehensive framework where sounds as *phenomena* and sounds as *concealment* could be conceived of, without being reduced to the mere ontic dimension? The laws of induction are too strict to satisfy this requirement. Moreover, they are unaware of the human angst before such a thing as the *disclosure* (according to Yannaras: φανέρωση). Neither the semiotic codes nor the inductive classes of instances prove to be useful in front of the emptiness, or the uncertainty, of non-being.[2]

1. Yannaras, *Person and Eros,* 13; author's italics.
2. Ibid.

On another side, the phenomenological approach – as Yannaras himself evidenced – ends in an ontological void. To overcome this impasse, he proposes a different ontology providing 'a distinction of essence from persons, and also a distinction of essence from the essence's *energies*, which are always personal. These two distinctions respond to the question concerning the *mode* by which that which exists *is*.'[1] According to this terminology, the essence of sounds – *per se* unattainable – lies in the *mode* of existence, *i.e.* in the disclosure itself of sounds. This experience remains conceptually indefinable, but results from time as the *ek-static* mode of being of the person. Accordingly:

> Essence can only be known within the context of the existential fact, the *mode of existence*, and this knowledge constitutes a possibility of potentiality, not the delineation of a given objectivity. The ontological problem is summarised exhaustively in the reality of the person (a reality never circumscribable linguistically), which is the only possible way in which essence is disclosed, essence's *mode of existence*.[2]

Even with these limits, however, the mentioned approaches are capable of suggesting a path. Induction offered more powerful tools than semiotics insofar as it took time into consideration; its power lay in the possibility of introducing a *splitting point* in a continuous line of phenomena, unlike a large number of the semiotic or analytic attempts, which mostly consisted of translating (and thus interpreting) a given notation into a different system of symbols. However, it gradually appeared that, though perfectible, each tested notation displayed inconsistencies which resisted any adjustments. How to explain this deficiency? In a sense, Western logic expresses a well-definite model of human reason; a model based upon the structural distinction between the concept part of a proposition and the object part.[3] Moreover, the prominent element is the former, not the latter.

---

1. Ibid., 176.
2. Ibid., 177.
3. Yannaras opposes the dichotomy of '*Begriff*' vs. '*Gegenstand*', a different view of matter and logic, grounded on the thought of the Cappadocians. See Yannaras' account of the 'logical' constitution of matter in his book *Elements of Faith*, trans. Keith Schram (Edinburgh: T. & T. Clark, 1991), 39-42. In another book – *Against Religion* (Brookline, MA: Holy Cross Orthodox Press, 2013), 150 – Yannaras marks the counterposition between Greek and Latin attitudes to objectification of the world in connection with Augustine's theory of knowledge: 'Augustine found himself in a hermeneutic impasse. He was attracted by the Platonic invention of the Ideas, which predetermine the form/mode and the end/goal of the existence of sensible things, but he was unable to accept their

Steps towards a New Ontology

Hans Blumenberg once observed that, after Kant, human Reason was mostly taken as a matter of just Concepts;[1] even better, reason is the human capacity of creating concepts and in this respect it characterises the vertex of the progress of human knowledge. This supremacy of conceptuality as such, however, is not without puzzling consequences for the ontology, because 'Der Begriff vermag nicht alles, was die Vernunft verlangt.' As a consequence of this, as philosophers we must consider 'ob die Vollendung des Begriffs nicht die Erfüllung der Ansprüche der Vernunft behindert oder gar inhibiert'.[2]

For instance, the logical concept of man works as an umbrella under which any individual that is a man takes place. Many other concepts are built up in the same way. Could we conceive musical sounds as we do with man? In the affirmative, for example, the concept 'being-a-sound-X' could be used as a basket where different sound-tokens could be placed as fair samples of X. In other words, the concept 'being-a-sound-X' could be used to collect single events of X-sound, irrespectively of the matter and the instruments and the ambience they are performed through. It goes without saying that such features can vary from context to context. In a logical sense, variances are not the clue of a semantic approach to sounds: thus, being a sound is the same as being a genuine member of the set of sounds. The same applies to the concept of 'man': being a man is the same as being a fair sample of any other object *falling-under* the concept of man.[3] Properties of sounds as well as of men are viewed in

ontological autonomy and transposed the Platonic world of the Ideas into the divine intellect identified with the divine essence.'

1. Hans Blumenberg, *Theorie der Unbegrifflichkeit, aus dem Nachlaß hrsg. von Anselm Haverkamp* (Frankfurt a. M.: Suhrkamp, 2007), 9. See the *incipit*: 'Der Begriff gilt als ein Produkt der Vernunft, wenn nicht sogar ihr Triumph, und ist es wohl auch. Das läßt aber nicht die Umkehrung zu, Vernunft sei nur dort, wo es gelungen oder wenigstens angestrebt sei, die Wirklichkeit, das Leben oder das Sein – wie immer man die Totalität nennen will – auf den Begriff zu bringen.'
2. Blumenberg, *Theorie*, 11; To translate, 'the concept cannot do everything that reason demands'; we must consider 'whether the completion of the term hinders or even inhibits the fulfillment of the claims of reason'.
3. As to the necessity of a differentiation between the concept-word Man (relative to the *essence*) and the non-conceptual plural-of-men (relative to the *existence*) see M. La Matina, 'Oneness of Mankind and the Plural of Man in Gregory of Nyssa's Against Eunomium book III. Some Problems of Philosophy of Language' in *Gregory of Nyssa's Contra Eunomium III), Supplements to Vigiliae Christianae*, edited by Matthieu Cassin and Johann Leemans (Leiden: Brill, 2013), 552-78.

terms of simple membership. Of course, phrasing things this way does not mean that sound and humans should have something in common. Logic just aims at evidencing the very entities admitted into an ontology in one and the same conceptual form. Insofar as we say that '*x* is a man', we say that '*x* is a sound'. From a philosophical point of view, Yannaras' appeal to the dimension of personal relation can be understood as a happy move for restoring an ontological approach to the relationship, regardless of whether such a relation is meant as holding between only divine (or only human) persons or both. Moreover, Yannaras' search for truth as a communion event can also be taken as another crucial move criticising the model of rationality that sprang out of the Scholastic views on theology and philosophy: up until now, this model has been the dominant one in many areas of our own philosophical studies, sometimes unawares.[1]

Indeed, as long as we use the predicative logic as a notational device to order our own thoughts and languages to say something about the world, there is nothing – or almost nothing – we should worry about. However, if we think of philosophy as a theoretical device for assessing our commitments while using things in our common world, while introducing things or persons in our ceremonies, in our 'musical offerings', or while entering some special liturgies, then things do change. Further questions should be posed about the way sounds do exist. Suppose that we accept sentences about groups of men as expressing a meaning equivalent to the meaning of sentences about 'individuals falling under the predicate "man"'; in so doing, a true sentence about 'many men' as a plural results from a chain of conjunct sentences which are individually true of single men. Sentences of this kind about the man *a*, the man *b*, the man *c* are shown in the following strings:

$$(a \text{ is a man}) \cap (b \text{ is a man}) \cap (c \text{ is a man}), \text{ etc.}$$

Suppose that one now introduces the predicate 'Rational' and then applies it to the previously delimited plural of 'Man'; then, imagine that one uses the pair of predicates, Man and Rational being, to form the more complex pair of predicates: '*x* is a man' and '*x* is a rational being'. In the above-mentioned notation, the rationality of man appears as the character imposed to each individual belonging to the extension of the 'Man' predicate; we might write this formula in quasi-symbols:

$$(x) (\text{Man}, x) \rightarrow (\text{Rational}, x)$$

---

1. As already said, the ontological approach to art is a mark of the Byzantine civilisation all along its history. See Yannaras, *Freedom of Morality*, 231-63.

This means that *for any x, if x is a man, then x is rational.* If *a* is a man, and if *b* is a man, and if *c* is a man etc., then *a* is a rational being, and *b* is a rational being and *c* is a rational man, etc. However, according to this notation, every rational creature, one would say, becomes rational *on its behalf*, i.e. without any contributions by any other conspecific individuals. This happens because of our own, often unwitting, ontological commitments. Working in our languages as a sort of *a priori*, such naïve ontology does force us to conceive and represent human rationality as a distributive property of the man species. As a consequence, human rationality is viewed as an innate capacity and consequently as something each of us is born with.

Such a *distributive* and innatist view of human reason stems from the standard interpretation of the famous statement claiming 'Rationale *enim est animal homo.*' Any propositional representation according to this statement necessarily *says* that 'man is a rational being'; however, the logical form *shows* something else. Namely, it shows that the variable bound by the universal quantifier ('for any *x*, such that *x* is a Man') is connected to the 'Man' concept and to the 'Rational-Being' concept in a distributive way. What is amazing here is that humaneness and rationality do take place in the living being without any contribution of other sensitive beings. Human Reason is something each single man is born with. No other man contributes to this possession by any other man. Reason is human in a distributive way. The being-a-man of the one does not participate in the being-a-man of the other (or of any other sensitive beings). *What remains unthought-of in this form is the being-together of men.* As I argued in my book,[1] men are not the plural of the man species. Bertrand Russell once wrote: 'Whatever is, is one, but whatever are, are many.'[2] This is not a *boutade*, but it seems an objection *in embryo* to the Western model of rationality. In fact, apart from some exceptions, any propositional representation does oblige the analyst to distribute properties and to take relationships as having nothing to do with the foundation of *being-a-man* and *becoming-a-rational-being*. This distributive view of human reason seems to be the missing point of the human condition. On the contrary, the relational ontology offered by Christos Yannaras in his books persuasively capsizes, in my opinion, the Aristotelian separateness of the humans as rational creatures that become humans humanising each other.

---

1. Marcello La Matina, *Notes on Sound,* 199.
2. Bertrand Russell, *The Principles of Mathematics* (Berlin: Norton, 1903), 43 f.

The Emergence of Sound as Signifier

Let us return to the musical sound. If Yannaras is right – and I think he is – and the heritage of the Greek Fathers is preserved and improved by his concept of relation, we must wonder whether the Occidental logic, presupposed in any propositional form, could be an adequate framework for assigning the right semantics and the right ontological state to the musical sound. *As for God so for sound*: what is given in experiencing sounds is not the concept of a given sound or the notion of the so-called 'supervening' properties of the aesthetic object as such.[1] The propositional form – elaborated in the Occidental analytical tradition since Frege and Russell – does not capture what is interesting in sounds. This does not happen because certain representations are imperfect or lack details: such imperfections, if any, could be due to transitional limits. Rather, the reason driving us to judge inadequate any predicative representation of the ontology of sounds springs from the incapacity of that model (in German terms: *Begriffswort* and *Gegenstandswort*) to capture sounds as 'signifiers emerging from the field of the Other', as Yannaras would himself say, and coming to us before we were born as subjects. This is why, though produced by my own hands, the musical sound always surprises me. Sound is not the *hypokeimenos* expecting to receive a form (an *eidos*); nor is it the accident of a substance. Perhaps an approach close to the Eastern 'apophaticism' would be preferable here; it would be also a method characterised by an undeniable ontological parsimony. The music sound is a *signifier*, which expresses (i.e. instantiates) and shows the relational ontological status of the participants in the process of the enunciation. It has an indexical function; it is a sort of deictic body suspended in the betwixt of the *I* and the *Thou*. Approaching the music sound as the expectancy of a relationship is very close to Yannaras' way of sketching any possible, original, relationship with God. Sounds do come as God is coming: they are unconceivable as such, even if they call us to a common life in the inner of a *tintinnabulatio*.[2]

---

1. A panoramic view of the current theories of 'supervenience' is offered by Brian McLaughlin and Karen Bennett, 'Supervenience', *The Stanford Encyclopedia of Philosophy*, ed. Edward N. Zalta, Spring 2014 edition, accessed 7 March 2017, https://plato.stanford.edu/archives/spr2014/entries/supervenience.
2. I refer here to the well-known technique of composition elaborated by the music composer Arvo Pärt and called *tintinnabulatio*. This name derives from the set of small bells used in the Russian Liturgy (the *zvon* of Russian bells). See, for example, Paul Hillier, *Arvo Pärt* (New York: Oxford University Press, 1997), 20-3.

In sum, the relevance of Yannaras for scholars interested in the ontological perspective seems to be very hard to deny. He indicates a path not only to theologians, but also to philosophers and scholars of human sciences. His quest for sense calls philosophy to its heritage: we all are born in the sound of a womb. We all become subject through the relationship with the mother, in a process of nourishing and of discovering the signifier offered as a rhythm and a sound. The human infant is not yet a subject or, at least, does not have markers of his own subjectivity, apart his and his mother's sounds, on the one side, and its ancillary gestures relative to sounds, on the other. Yannaras stresses that when he meets the mother's breast he does not see in this epiphany only the opportunity to satisfy his desire for nourishment, but also something coming over and beyond that desire. On the contrary, the animal puppy tries the breast to obtain food. The philosopher Christos Yannaras persuasively argues:

> In the human infant, the dominant desire for life-as-relation is mediated by the need for food. That is why in the human infant alone, the sensory location of the power to respond to the need for food (i.e. the location of the mother's breast) leads not to reactions of Pavlovian type, but to the appearance of the first signifier of relation: a rational signifier. The signifier of response to the desire for food is the starting point for the introduction of an invitatory call to relation, the starting point for constituting the relation as language – and, consequently, also for constituting thought).[1]

The desire for food arouses an expectation of satisfaction both in animals as in humans; in the latter, however, the epiphany of the breast works like a call for relation. That is because reference is given not as a 'natural lawlikeness', but as the *metrical clause* of human desire. The starting point of Reason is just the possibility for a *non-semantic reference*. If we transfer this description to the dynamic of the musical sound, we realise that the existence of each performed sound does not depend on a physical law rigorously deducible on the basis of its mental or conceptual properties. Music is for us the extension of an original relational reference emerging as the possibility for a human way of existence (in Yannaras' words, a τρόπος της υπαρξη) in an ontological sense. Sounds give form to such a relationship by suspending the indexical values of *Thou* and *I* to the coming time of the *Other*.

---

1. Yannaras, *Relational Ontology*, 20 ff.

From Reference to Desire

It must be emphasised that this relation – the food, the foetal sound – is
not formed amid two individuals, each one already existing on its behalf.
The indexical signifier emerging as sound is not a logical function. On
the contrary, it gives evidence for an indexical reference (in Goodman's
terms: a *non-semantic reference*) that does not distribute the subjectivity
among the individuals affected in the context. One might even say that
what we find attractive in the sound is not the non-personal matter from
where it comes, but a personal presence transcending the ontic plan.
We primarily meet the sound in the womb. Every future experience
is influenced by the foetal environmental soundscape. Moreover, this
'erotic' relationship is maintained even in the adult, to the extent of
producing significant modifications in the dyadic interaction among
humans. Evidence for this, for example, is given by the recently published
researches of two biologists working at the Department of Psychology at
the University of California, Davis.[1] It is the mother-to-child relationship
that we must scrutinise in order to see if rationality and relationship
work together. If this is correct, then rationality does not emerge when
one learns to formulate concepts, but at an earlier stage, i.e. when we
start expecting our desire to be satisfied. Such a rhythmic alternation of
silence and sound, of beats and pauses, does arise as a metrical rationale,
a sort of pulsatile alternation of demand and response, an amoebic pair
of possible *arsis* and *thesis*. Yannaras argues: '[T]ime exists not when
change as movement from before to after *counts* the personal relation,
but when movement as change from before is after is counted.'[2] Finally,
I would add that what counts time is nothing but *rhythm*. Insofar as
persons know time as their own mode of existence, time is *rhythm* of
presence-absence, of παρουσία-ἀπουσία.

In conclusion, we are born from nature and we are certainly members
of a species. However, our birth *qua* rational subjects does not coincide
with our biological birth. The birth of human rational subject is connected
with the context of personal *enunciation*. This relation is a matter of
indexical expressions and of signifiers, rather than of meanings and
semantic categories. The primary human reference is of the type which
Goodman called *non-semantic reference*.[3] The voice that calls to relation is

1. I refer here to Emilio Ferrer and Jonathan L. Helm, 'The dynamical systems
   modeling of psychological co-regulation in diadic interactions', *International
   Journal of Psychophysiology,* 88, 3 (2013), 296-308.
2. Yannaras, *Person and Eros,* 137.
3. See 'Routes of Reference' in Nelson Goodman, *Of Mind and Other Matters*

the mother's voice. Consequently, the voice is not just reference but also desire, as Yannaras stresses. My effort in these pages was first aimed at evidencing Yannaras' account of knowledge as an original and extended contribution to contemporary philosophy, namely the philosophy of music. Any occasional reader who picks up a book by Yannaras may easily find more than singular concepts, ideas or arguments in his thought. The very patient reader will discover an original account and a portrait of both late antique and late modern philosophy. Yannaras' work could be valuable not only for scholars who deal with Patristic studies or with theology but also for scientists and philosophers involved with investigations into the ontological commitments of languages and symbolic systems. Indeed, Yannaras is an exciting thinker particularly for those scholars who work in the frontiers between traditionally separated areas of knowledge. Let me briefly discuss, as an example, the following three cases. At the beginning of his path, he investigated thoroughly Heidegger's approach to ontology; more recently he dedicated his attention to Wittgenstein,[1] so conjugating – without labels – the philosophy of being to the philosophy of meaning and language. His recent books on relational ontology – where Yannaras' point of reference is not only the philosophical tradition but also the psychoanalytic understanding of the signifier promoted by Jacques Lacan – does prompt a method offering guidance for anyone who thinks of philosophy (and theology) not especially as a theoretical shrine of certainties, but rather as a possible engagement within a form of life where the usual separateness between *conceptual* knowledge and *erotic* knowledge collapses.

The courageous reversal of the dominant paradigm achieved by Yannaras is this: we are not living rational beings before the emerging of the signifier in the field of the other. Reason is this call; reason is the expectation and the desire the other can answer. This simple pulse, the

---

(Cambridge: Harvard University Press, 1984), 54-71. I dealt with this form of reference in my paper by title, 'Esemplificazione, Riferimento e Verità. Il contributo di N. Goodman ad una filosofia dei linguaggi' in *Nelson Goodman e la filosofia dei linguaggi*, eds. Marcello La Matina and Elio Franzini (Macerata, Quodlibet, 2007), 109-55.

1. As an interesting line of investigation one should take the recent book on Wittgenstein edited by Sotiris Mitralexis. As explained in the author's introduction, the concern of his book is a comparison 'between Ludwig Wittgenstein's "analytic stance" towards philosophy and the inherently apophatic nature of his epistemology'. See Sotiris Mitralexis: 'Introduction – An Apophatic Wittgenstein, or a Wittgensteinian Apophaticism' in Mitralexis (ed): *Ludwig Wittgenstein between Analytic Philosophy and Apophaticism* (Newcastle: Cambridge Scholars Publishing, 2015), vii-xiii.

beat of call and response – and not the concept – is the original form of our own reason. Yannaras oriented our attentiveness to this truth of the person. As a consequence of this, I stressed here that music and sounds are correctly understood only if framed in their ontological dimension. Sound does not appear in our ontology, unless our ontology is relational.

Chapter Eight
Yannaras' and Marion's Overcoming Onto-Theology: On the Way of St Dionysius the Areopagite
Daniel Isai

The Problem of Onto-Theology
in the Work of Jean-Luc Marion

There is a close relationship between the theological project of Hans Urs von Balthasar and the phenomenology of Jean-Luc Marion. I will start treating the problem of onto-theology, referring to a text of Balthasar's – 'A Resume of My Thought' – from which we might see the close connection between the Swiss theologian and the French phenomenologist. Balthasar underlines, in this summary of his thinking, the phenomenalisation of God in history:

> God appears. He appeared to Abraham, to Moses, to Isaiah, finally in Jesus Christ. A theological question: How do we distinguish his appearance, his epiphany among the thousand other phenomena in the world? How do we distinguish the true and the only living God of Israel from all the idols which surround him and from all the philosophical and theological attempts to attain God?[1]

Balthasar's answer comes explicitly a few phrases below in the same text where he refers to God as One in being and threefold in person: 'In the Trinitarian dogma God is one, good, true, and beautiful because He is essentially Love, and Love supposes the one, the other, and their unity.'[2]

I appeal to this text from Balthasar because the phenomenological project of Marion starts from this interrogation and reaches the same answer through the erotic reduction. This does not belittle the project of

1. Hans Urs von Balthasar, 'A Résumé of My Thought' in *Hans Urs von Balthasar: His Life and Work*, ed. David L. Schindler (San Francisco: Ignatius Press, 1991), 4.
2. Balthasar, 'A Résumé', 4.

the French phenomenologist who outlined his philosophical thinking in the *nouvelle théologie,* which was expected to be a reaction to the Catholic Neo-scholastic theology and has promoted the return to the Patristic Eastern sources. For this reason, the theologians and philosophers who took part in this current can enter very easily into a constructive dialogue with Eastern theology. I have made this reference to Balthasar in order to be able to show that there are voices in the theology of the West which signal the necessity of an approach to Christian revelation starting from the phenomenon of embodiment and from a vivid revelation of God. At the same time, Marion's phenomenology, as we shall see, embraces this vision. Here I claim that similarities may be seen between some of Marion's emphases and those expressed through the modern Greek philosopher Christos Yannaras' ontology of personhood.

In light of this, we will move to the problem of onto-theology, referring especially to *The Idol and Distance,* in which Marion highlights the bifurcation in Western thought between the philosophical concept of 'God' and the God of Christian revelation. What happened was an extension of the influence of the antique Greek ontology of monistic style, in which matter is eternal, and in which the god, the demiurge, is simply the organiser of this. From here appeared the idea of the Supreme Being, interpreted as an operative concept for the integrality of beings in the world. St Dionysius the Areopagite defined God as being beyond being, precisely to note a distinction from monistic ontology. This detail fits with the Christian doctrine of creation *ex nihilo* and facilitates a surpassing of the monistic ontology that had gone before. Hence, it follows that any theology which remains under the influence of an ontology or another form of Greek philosophy leaves itself open to the danger of overlooking God's freedom of self-manifestation through a theology subsumed by discourse about being. The Church Fathers show us that God's being is incomprehensible. That is why reference to Him cannot be made by way of a strict ontological discourse in which 'God' plays a role as a fundamental cause of the world or *causa sui.* Instead, we have to relate to God through the hypostatic way He opened to us. Indeed, Father Stăniloae says that being is manifested and appears in hypostasis.

Returning to the problem of onto-theology, we notice that Marion rehearses the way in which the philosophers speak of the divine:

> Plato speaks about Good, Aristotle about νοήσεως νόησις, Plotinus the One, Kant about a 'moral founder of the world', Thomas Aquinas about the five ways (the first mover, efficient cause, necessary cause, cause of perfection, and the ultimate

aim), Melebranche about *Infinite, Human being in its totality, Human being infinitely perfect*, Descartes speaks about *Infinite substance*, as wise as possible and almighty, Spinoza about *absolutely infinite human being.*[1]

The examples continue, but we pause here in order to let Marion express himself regarding the ease of the philosopher concerned with metaphysics to formulate concepts regarding God without the legitimacy of such concepts coming from God's self-revelation. In such cases, concepts have the potential to do violence to the incomprehensibility of God's being. While the concept may lay claim to a near identification, delivering the impression of cognition, in reality the concept does not capture the thing itself. It is helpless; it offers us at most a simulacrum of this cognition. Conceptual discourse reduces the distance between the actual being of God and the constructed concept, which, without this distance, would eventually replace the living God of revelation. A dimension of Marion's claim is that, in opposition to the idol, the icon maintains distance and may be identified specifically with the desire to avoid the idol of onto-theology in which the concept claims the ability to encounter God through cognition.

Marion explains the relationship between the categories of Being, beings, and Supreme Being by a relation in which Being is made present through beings, but this existence in itself is not eternal, and therefore it needs a foundation. The role of Supreme Being supplies this foundation which 'in its turn, delivers the most present [and lasting] figure of the presence which only it allows to each [non-supreme] being.'[2] On the other hand, Being finds its foundation in beings, because otherwise it does not have another form of presence. Marion shows that there is a 'mutual game of the Being of beings in general (ontology, general metaphysics) with supreme being (special metaphysics, theology),'[3] in which a mutual foundation is realised. The Supreme Being establishes the beings, and the beings offer to Being access to presence, established on the Being of beings. More precisely again, Marion says: 'the supreme being is conscious of its existence in its being, but manifests in this way the being in action, included and first of all in itself', at which point he adds that 'the supreme being is not summoned only for ensuring the foundation.'[4] The Supreme Being plays the role of a metaphysical

---

1. Jean-Luc Marion, *The Idol and Distance*, trans. Tinca Prunea Bretonnet şi Daniela Pălăşan (Bucharest: Humanitas, 2007), 33-5.
2. Ibid., 39.
3. Ibid., 40.
4. Ibid.

construct that is necessary from the logical point of view, but it does not have existential relevance. Marion says that this onto-theological constitution was brought into play before the Christian revelation by the famous representatives of ancient Greek philosophy, and the Supreme Being functions as a *causa sui*. Thus, metaphysics 'must think beyond God, because the thing that concerns it is Being, and this comes into being in an essential way as a basis'.[1] About this needed basis, Marion says that 'it refers to the cause as first understood as a *causa sui*. This is the name which "God" bears in philosophy'.[2]

Before this metaphysical concept of *causa sui* or foundation of existence, with a role of pure conceptual operativity, Marion says that we have no way of relating to it existentially; it does not have a face, because it is a conceptual idol that 'not only does not point, as does the icon, to the invisible, but even offers a face like the icon, in which the divine can watch us and give itself in order to be contemplated'.[3]

The English translation of Marion's essay 'Thomas Aquinas and Onto-theology' in *The Essential Writings* provides some useful shades of meaning. Here the distinction between the terms of onto-theology is described between Being, entity and the supreme entity.[4] Marion notices in this text that we deal with two foundations: one is of a conceptual nature and the other is of a causal nature.[5] The logical need to deal with these foundations led to the intersection of these two foundations. In light of this, we attend to a form of fusion, or conceptual coincidence, and we do not talk about the supreme entity, but about the Supreme Being, as that who keeps in existence not only the entities, but also the Being of entities or of beings.

Marion does not simply consider the onto-theological constitution of the conceptual idol, but also looks for a way out of this horizon, not only effectively making a step outside this approach, which is not possible in reality because there is the risk of repeating the same mistake again and again, but also investigating from the inside at the maximum the limits of this constitution. He looks for the achievement of the distance towards this ontological coincidence and theology, and he makes a journey through Nietzsche's thinking as a perspective outside onto-theology.

---

1. Ibid.
2. Ibid.
3. Ibid., 41.
4. The terms which I used normally are Being, beings, supreme being, but for the purposes of clarity I have used some equivalent terms, such as Being, entity, and supreme entity.
5. Jean-Luc Marion, *The Essential Writings*, ed. Kevin Hart (New York: Fordham University Press, 2013), 290.

Then he examines the 'distance received in a filial way of the presence of a God found as a fatherly face in retreat, per Hölderlin, and as distance covered liturgically by the discourse of the beatification of those who ask for the One asked, per Dionysius'.[1]

In *God Without Being*, Marion speaks about a liberation of God from the horizon of metaphysics. This is a liberation of 'the existence of being'; from the ontological discourse about being. Here we must make a clear distinction between God's being (the one above all the beings) and the concept of the ontology of Being as a foundation of existence. The question that arises is this: Is it possible to think outside the Being of the ontological horizon that functions as a screen? Marion, following Heidegger's thinking on this, will say that this approach is not only possible, but also necessary. This is because Being is not identical with God, and for theology this term of Being is not necessary, because it functions, at least in the case of Heidegger's thought, in a register of methodological atheism in the way that the question about God is cancelled. The ontological term of *Being* is separated from God by an entire abyss. The Being of all Existence is put in function through interrogation, while God is looked for through faith.[2]

In Marion's most recent work, we notice a revised position in regard to the affirmations made in *God Without Being*, in which Thomas Aquinas was seen as one of the initiators of onto-theology. Marion says that Thomist theology has rejected from the very beginning any type of concept of univocity regarding the relation between entities and the supreme entity, keeping the ontological difference between created and uncreated. This is because he observes that Thomas 'denies the essence of any onto-theology according to which the theological and ontological functions could mutually establish one another in a common determination'.[3] The responsibility of constituting the onto-theology in the scholasticism of the Middle Ages is now placed with Aegidius of Rome, who reintegrates God into metaphysics, and with Duns Scotus, who consolidates this understanding, talking about the univocity of the concept *ens* for the created and the uncreated, arguing that the experience of God is possible only on the basis of this univocity.[4] Marion adds that using the doctrine of *analogia entis*, starting with Duns Scotus until Suarez, produced a real inflation regarding the univocity of the concept of existence (*ens, entity*).

1. Marion, *Idol*, 48.
2. Jean-Luc Marion, *God without Being*, trans. Thomas Carlson, with a foreword by David Tracy (Chicago: The University of Chicago Press, 1991), 62.
3. Marion, *Essential Writings*, 296.
4. Ibid., 294.

Also, Marion advances the thesis that the idea of cause in Thomas does not fall under the doctrine of univocity because it highlights the idea of God as Creator, which in itself ensures the necessary distance.[1] What we can remember from the approach of Marion regarding Thomas Aquinas would be just what Yannaras reproaches scholastic theology for: that it is a strictly rational way of knowing God. From the perspective of Eastern theology, this is nothing more than failing to know God and runs the risk of building mental idols.

Yannaras and the Difficulty of Onto-Theology

In order to see how Marion's discourse meets the discourse of the Greek philosopher it will be necessary to continue the present approach exactly from the problem of *the analogy of being*. More precisely, from the way Yannaras considers that the scholastics used Aristotle's categories in ontology, in the relationship between Being and beings. We have two of Aristotle's texts from which Yannaras starts his analysis. The first text refers to the way in which being is defined: '[B]eing is discussed in many ways, but in relation with a certain point of view and regarding a certain condition.'[2] The second text of Aristotle makes reference to the categories with which the concept of being relates:

> The meanings of Being are as many as these categories. Because, therefore, among the categories one indicates the substance, another one the quality, another the quantity, another one the relation, another the action or passion, and others the place and the time, the Being tends to be the same thing as each of these categories.[3]

To simplify, the categories we have to take into consideration are quality, quantity, place, time, and relation. Yannaras, referring to these categories, uses the following example: the horse is white; the horse is two meters long; and the horse is here. Consequently, 'we always use the verb to be in relation with a principle: *the horse is white*, in an analogic relation with white in general or the tree is tall, in an analogic relation with height in general,'[4] and about the existence in itself of one thing, Yannaras claims,

---

1. Ibid., 302
2. Aristotle, *Metaphysics*, IV.2, 1003a, Translation St Bezdechi, Notes and alphabetic index, Dan Bădărău, (Bucharest: Publisher IRI, 1996), 118.
3. Aristotle, *Metaphysics*, V.7, 1017a, 184.
4. Christos Yannaras, *Person and Eros*, trans. Zenaida Luca, with an introduction by Mihai Șora (Bucharest: Anastasia, 2000), 219.

'[T]he proper definition of the fact of a being's existence is always accomplished by a reference to a single principle, that is by referring to the essence...of a subject: we say, basically that this is a horse and this is a tree.'[1] What Yannaras underlines further is the fact that Aristotle considers the two elements that are the determination of the subject based on analogy, the properties refer, and through referring to the definition of its essence, they consume the analogic relation as a possibility of the definition; that is, of knowing the being. Thus, according to Yannaras, what Aristotle does is to use the analogy concept in order to ensure the unity of the thing; he does not extend the analogy as a relation of the ontological identity, as a participation of the beings in Being. The relation of the beings with Being for Aristotle is a relation between the cause and effect – a relation of passing from *being as possibility to being as an act*, a relation between the moved things, put into movement and moving.[2] In order to explain movement, the first scholastics used the analogical relation between the beings and the Being when it was about defining the Being in itself; that is, God, the first engine, the First transcendental cause of his To Be. Every being that participates in Being, is *ens per participationem*, while God, the first and last being, the eternal one and the good one, does not participate in Being, but constitutes Being in itself, *being per essentiam*, the proper existence, in relation with which is what it is.[3]

For the sake of clarity, the term being is used by Yannaras with the meaning of the universal Being of nature. For the Greek thinker, 'the analogical participation of beings in Being constitutes the key to the analogical understanding of the Being of all beings as it relates to the Divine cause. And God, the Cause of Being, is analogically determined in relation to the Being of all beings.'[4] Using analogy, the characteristics of the particular beings, through *reductio ad absurdum* of the rationalistic way, 'in an analogical way the transcendental characteristics of God can be made known to us. Albert the Great and Thomas Aquinas synthesised these characteristics that can constitute the foundation of the transcendental analogy: *Unum, verum, bonum, res, aliquid* (one, true, good, thing, something).'[5] The transcendental analogy thus constitutes a mental extension of these five categories beyond the reality of the tangible world, that 'we can' by means of the intellect know the characteristics of God's essence.

---

1. Ibid., 219.
2. Ibid., 220.
3. Ibid.
4. Ibid., 220-1.
5. Ibid., 221.

For Yannaras, two major consequences follow from this way of knowing God. The first consequence would be that the analogical cognition

> is used up in the rational approach of the true essence of God, that is transcendental, but which, anyway, is ontological essence, with a real existence – a transcendental object (*objectum*) of the intellect. The scholastic analogy ignores the personal existence of God, the Third of divine persons, the way of existence of the Divine Essence, which is personal. Thus, it introduces into the Christian theology's space not only the 'poverty' of Judaic monotheism, but also a conception incomparably lower than God: They replace the personal God of biblical revelation and of the ecclesiastic experience with an impersonal concept (*conceptio*) of a transcendental 'object', of a Cause in itself in a rational way, necessary and the Cause of beings.[1]

The second consequence, suggested already in the first, refers to the fact that the *analogia entis* of scholastic theology makes God into an *object* that is known through human cognition. In reality, however, God is fundamentally personal, and so must be revealed to us through the mystery of personal encounter.

The problem of onto-theology is addressed by Heidegger in his work *Identität und Differenz*.[2] In this text Heidegger underlines the necessity of separation and defining the two discourses of philosophy as a rational discourse and of theology as a discourse of faith, because the overlapping of the two led in time to outlining onto-theology as an abstract, purely rational discourse about an existential reality, about a relation that should have been based on the complete revelation of the Gospel (that is, on love), so that God came to be treated as a simple principle: the first mover, *causa sui*, foundation, the supreme being, etc.

Like Jean-Luc Marion, Christos Yannaras notices that the 'death of God' declared by Nietzsche is nothing else than the death of a concept, identified by Heidegger as the being of onto-theology. Yannaras claims that the death of this concept is a fulfilled fact for those 'who refuse to prefer an abstract notion to a present person, an intellectual certainty to a direct relation. These refuse to identify the reality of God with the necessity of the First Cause (as rationalist metaphysics suggests) or with the Supreme Value (as utilitarian ethics suggests).'[3]

---

1. Ibid., 222.
2. Martin Heidegger, *Identity and Difference [Identitat und Differenz]*, trans. Joan Stambaugh (New York: Harper & Row, 1969), 70.
3. Christos Yannaras, *On the Absence and Unknowability of God: Heidegger and the*

Referring to the same text from Heidegger, *Identitat und Differenz*, Yannaras and Marion notice the fact that 'the human being cannot pray, cannot even bring human sacrifices, to this God'[1] is seen as a *causa sui*. That is why Marion applies to the concept of cause, *aitia*, used by St Dionysius the Areopagite through the One invoked, because He is the One called, summoned in the prayer of the human being who looks for Him. Marion speaks about *the third way*, as a passing of the predication through *hymnein*, beyond affirmative and negative theology. Yannaras formulates an ontology of the person in order to go beyond the dilemma of onto-theology and appeals to the resources of Eastern apophaticism as being the true way of getting closer to God, the personal and Living One, One in being and three *hypostases*. Yannaras sees in nihilism 'a radical negation of *the mental idols* of God' and sees in this the adumbration of two possible consequences of nihilism: '[T]he affirmation of the *absence* of, or the acknowledgment of not knowing, God.'[2]

Why in particular is scholastic theology called rationalist? One part of the answer comes to us from the way in which scholasticism related itself to St Dionysius the Areopagite – more precisely, from the way in which the representatives of this method used his writings while remaining in the paradigm of Aristotle's philosophical thinking related to the analogy of being. Vladimir Lossky says that Thomas Aquinas 'reduces to only one the two ways of Dionysius making from the negative theology a correction of the affirmative theology'.[3] Attributing to God all the perfections which we find in created beings, we use the negations in order to show that these perfections are limited and then we return to say that these perfections are found in God in a sublime way. We assert, then we deny, in order to say again the same thing at a sublime level. All this endeavour remains in the field of the language or rational discourse. Lossky wonders himself if this is really what St Dionysius wanted to realise. He notices that for St Dionysius the negative way is higher than the affirmative one, and it is not a concealed apophasis as it appears from the critique of Derrida. Christos Yannaras will enumerate also the three ways of the scholastic theology, from which we can notice the difference in relation to the third way of St Dionysius. Thus, we have *triplex via*: '[T]he way of abstraction or the negations (*via negationis*), the way of superiority (*via eminentiae*) and

---

Areopagite, trans. Nicolae Șerban Tanașoca, (Bucharest: Anastasia, 2009), 48.

1. Heidegger, *Identity and Difference*, 72.
2. Yannaras, *On the Absence and Unknowability of God*, 62.
3. Vladimir Lossky, *The Mystical Theology of The Eastern Church*, trans. Fr Vasile Răducă (Bucharest: Anastasia, 1990), 55.

the way of causality or of affirmations (*via causalitatis* or *afirmationis*).'
What can be noticed is that Thomas does not respect the order of the
three ways from St Dionysius, more than that all the three ways remain
ways of predication. In this way, Yannaras will say that theological
apophaticism 'constitutes a transcendence of the methodology of the
speculative knowledge, not only the analogical approach of cognition
through affirmations and negations, but also of the inductive approach
of causality'.[1]

For St Dionysius, the third way after affirmation and negation is the
one of comprehension through prayer and purifying in the overluminous
cloud, abandoning any discursiveness, entering there through the
quietness of the mind. Yannaras underlines the fact that 'theological
apophaticism, giving up any rational necessity, determines the eradication
of idols of God shaped by the human intellect'.[2] This claim is based on the
writings of the Cappadocian Fathers. St Basil the Great says that there are
some people who have false beliefs about God, 'serving in themselves a
noetic idolatry';[3] and St Gregory of Nyssa, who inspired Marion in what
we could call the rejection of conceptual idolatry, says very relevantly to
the problem of analogy, '[T]he divine word prohibits firstly to look upon
God with something from the things known by the people, given the fact
that any meaning which comes up in the contemplation or the reasoning
of the temper through a representation includes and invents an idol
about God and does not announce God.'[4] The divine word about which
St Gregory speaks here is the one which Moses used to hear after he
entered the cloud on the mountain of Sinai. St Gregory says that analogy
ceases its function the moment in which Moses enters the cloud. Lossky
says that apophaticism is:

> a disposition of the mind which refuses to form concepts
> regarding God. This thing excludes firmly any abstract and
> purely intellectual theology, which would like to adapt at the
> limits of human thinking, the mysteries of God's wisdom. This
> is the existential attitude which engages the man entirely: there
> is no theology besides experience: you must change, to become
> a new person. In order to know God you must get closer to

1. Yannaras, *On the Absence and Unknowability of God*, 74.
2. Ibid., 78.
3. St Basil the Great, *Commentary on Isaiah*, 96, trans. Alexandru Mihăilă
   (Bucharest: Publishing House of Romanian Patriarchy, 2009), 114.
4. St Gregory of Nyssa, *The Life of Moses*, PSB 29, trans. Fr Dumitru Stăniloae and
   Fr Ioan Buga (Bucharest: Publishing House of Biblical and Missionary Institute
   of the Romanian Orthodox Church, 1982), 74.

Him; you are not a theologian if you do not follow the path of
the union with God. The path of God's knowledge is necessarily
the one of deification.[1]

Concerning entering the overluminous dark, 'the unapproachable light'[2] in
which God lives, Father Dumitru Stăniloae speaks in further detail about
the three steps of apophaticism, which culminate with an apophaticism
of third rank, in which the human person sees the uncreated light of
God's blessing. After the first step of apophaticism, which is a negative
intellectual theology as a reply to affirmative theology, leaving any
consideration of concepts, follows 'a state of silence produced by prayer' and
'a sensation in the dark of the divine energies'.[3] This would be the second
step of apophaticism. Father Stăniloae says that not even St Dionysius
takes this into consideration, as a supreme step, when he talks about the
overluminous dark. In this way, Father Stăniloae will say that St Gregory
Palamas in his polemic with Varlaam showed that 'the Areopagite texts
refer to other darkness, that is an overluminous darkness which does not
mean even a negative theology, not even a certain sensation in the dark of
God. . . . [It is] darkness not because there is no light in it, but because it
is an overabundance of light.'[4] From this point of discussion appears the
distinction of background between the Eastern tradition and the Western
one, because St Gregory Palamas rejected the idea of Varlaam 'that after the
created nature nothing else follows but the divine nature, which is totally
unapproachable and unknowable'. In the same fragment, Father Stăniloae
will underline also the fact that Lossky, although he knew this distinction
between essence and energies, 'is not concerned with seeing the divine,
but he speaks only in general that by not knowing God, God is somehow
experienced, something also admitted by recent Catholic theology'.[5]

    Yannaras underlines the fact that Western theology, through its focus
on God's nature, gave birth to a form of apophaticism of essence, a thing
that in reality does not involve a cognition, but rather a recognition
of reason's inability to form a cognition. The human being cannot
penetrate God's being in any way, because this remains unknowable to
him. This apophaticism of 'the scholastics does not oppose the rational
conceptualisation and confirmation of the demonstrative way of the

1. Lossky, *Mystical Theology*, 67.
2. St Dionysius the Areopagite, *Full Works and Scolia of Saint Maximus the
   Confessor*, trans. Fr Dumitru Stăniloae (Bucharest: Paideia, 1996), 258.
3. Dumitru Stăniloae, *The Orthodox Ascetics and Mystics*, Vol. II (Alba Iulia: Deisis,
   1993), 54.
4. Ibid.
5. Ibid., 53.

notion of God as another possibility of cognition. It underlines only the relative character of the rational determinations and of the analogical inductions from the created to the uncreated.[1] About this apophaticism of essence, Yannaras says that it facilitates the appearance in the West of relativism, scepticism, and agnosticism. Why? Because the human being needs a living relation, direct and personal with God (the one and only), who is love. The Trinity as a source of love cannot remain in isolation in relation to beings, in relation to man, and the most clear demonstration of this fact is the incarnation of the Son who assumes our human nature in the hypostatic union, and on Tabor discloses the brightness of His divine blessing to his disciples.

From the desire to get beyond the Western essentialism situated at the diametrically opposed pole, under the influence of existentialism and of the personalism influenced by the existentialist philosophy in which the existence precedes the essence, Yannaras came to give priority inside the Trinity to the hypostatic relation, leaving the being on a secondary plane. In reality, God is one in Being and three Persons. The metaphysical principle that essence precedes existence or the reverse formulation of this cannot abide when we talk about God. The Father from eternity begets the Son from whom proceeds the Holy Spirit, having a common divinity as an element of their unity. The Trinity have in common the being in which they embrace in everlasting love. Any overemphasis on the being or hypostases moves away from the spirit of the Cappadocian Fathers. In this way, Jean-Claude Larchet shows us that Yannaras, from the desire to establish an ontology of the person, modifies the authentic intentions of the Trinity of Patristic theology and leads to the problem of knowing 'which of them constitutes the ontological principle through excellence, person or nature'.[2] Additionally, in order to carry forward with the metaphysical principle of existentialism, Yannaras overemphasises the hypostasis of the Father and the role of the Father as cause. Larchet underlines a distinction in Patristic thinking between the idea of a cause and that of a principle necessary for the present discussion:

> We must note that the notion of cause also inspired the fear
> of many of the Fathers, for the fact that it could suggest the
> disputable idea of an intra-divine creation. This explains why
> Saint Epiphanius or Saint Maximus the Confessor preferred it

---

1. Yannaras, *On the Absence and Unknowability of God*, 20.
2. Jean-Claude Larchet, *Person and Nature: The Holy Trinity, Christ, and the Human Being: Contributions to Contemporary Interorthodox and Interchristian Dialogues*, trans. Dragoş Bahrim and Marinela Bojin (Bucharest: Basilica, 2013), 376.

the notion of 'principle' (ἀρχή) and why the Greek Fathers in general have applied it only when it is about a creative work and the providence of God.[1]

In order not to remain stuck in this never-ending polarisation between Western theology and Eastern theology, consider the Jesuit monk Balthasar's criticism of neo-scholastic theology at that time. The Swiss theologian said regarding this period of his studies that he felt a never-ending thirst for God in the wilderness of neo-scholasticism.[2] In another place he described his entire period of study with the Society of Jesus as being chained to a sad and dark theology, towards which he felt the anger of Samson, who demolished the temple to which he was chained.[3] Not accidentally, the current of *nouvelle theologie* was strongly criticised within the Catholic Church, this criticism culminating with the 1950 encyclical *Humani generis*. Today, the epic repeats with Marion, who in his turn received hard criticism, so that he ended up formulating the ideas in a remote way himself, using the authority of Augustine in order to criticise all those theologians from the West who introduced the metaphysical discourse about being into theology. Marion says about the theological approach of Augustine that 'he does not ask questions about Being, not even about the being, he thus does not refer to God in terms of Being, not even in those of the being by excellence. . . . [He] does not investigate a foundation, nor even look for it in any ways; he does not belong to metaphysics.'[4] Moreover, referring to the *Confessions* of Augustine, he underlines the fact that he does not employ any of the rational ways to come closer to God, but only the anthem of praise: 'Praise offers us the only way, the only royal way of access to His presence.'[5]

The approach of Marion as coming from Western culture while also being an attentive and faithful reader of the Eastern Fathers, meets Christos Yannaras in the sudden way that they mutually complement one another. The phenomenological project and the theological one of Marion can be a good tool for reading the prosopocentric ontology of Yannaras. Meanwhile, the shades of Yannaras' prosopocentric ontology can contribute to breaking the dilemmas of onto-theology that the phenomenological project confronts in Marion, while, at the same time, clarifying what Marion calls the *third way* and the *saturated phenomenon*.

1. Larchet, *Person and Nature*, 390.
2. Peter Henrici, S.J., 'A Sketch of His Life' in Schindler, *Hans Urs von Balthasar*, 12.
3. Henrici, 'A sketch', 13.
4. Jean-Luc Marion, *In the Self's Place: An Approach of Saint Augustine*, trans. Jeffrey L. Kosky (Stanford: Stanford University Press, 2012), 9.
5. Marion, *Self's Place*, 14.

The value of Eastern Patristic thinking to both of these two thinkers indicates to us the fact that phenomenology, through its appeal to observing to what it shows as such and the person's ontology as probe into the depths of human being, can achieve the outreach of the rationalist discourse about God. The human should thus be concerned with a real mystical knowledgein the manner of the Eastern Fathers, of The One who is the Spring of life and which lets itself be known and even sent from this world.

Chapter Nine
Education as Freedom:
An Attempt to Explore the Role of Education through Christos Yannaras' Thought
Nikolaos Koronaios

Introduction

Throughout the voluminous oeuvre of Christos Yannaras one finds many references to education. These are scattered, however, since they do not form part of a work exclusively written to present Yannaras' general views on education. Of course, there is the feuilleton collection *Παιδεία και Γλώσσα [Education and Language]*, published in 2000, which along with his public lectures (plenty of which are available on the Internet), constitute a criticism on the Greek educational system. Both these sources and some other aspects of his philosophical work will be the basis of this paper. Most of Yannaras' comments about the Greek educational system cover the historical period from 1974 (the year of the fall of the Greek military junta) to the present. Of course, one can discover earlier references[1] in his autobiographical work and in some public lectures and interviews, but I will not concentrate on them here.

In this paper, I will explore Yannaras' opinion about the role of education. Firstly, I will explain his view on the 'meaning' of education. Then, I will present one of his distinctions related to the 'meaning', namely that between 'utilitarianism' and 'relations of communion'. After that, I will argue that Yannaras' insistence on 'relations of communion' stems from his peculiar, apophatic definition of freedom. From the link between education and freedom I will deduce that the role of education is to serve the 'relations of communion' in such a way that human beings

---

1. Christos Yannaras, '14-11-1994 The ecumenical dynamics of Hellenism'. YouTube video, 02:13:58. Available at: https://www.youtube.com/watch?v=Kvt-eJdHVX0&t=829s.

can preserve their freedom. At this point, I will turn to the literature, and, more specifically, to the famous text by Gert Biesta and Karl Anders Säfström, 'A Manifesto for Education'. This is an interesting and provocative text because it contains an acute critique of the way that most people think about education today. The authors present the two most dominant ways of thinking: the 'idealistic' and the 'populistic', and they raise questions about the relation between freedom and education. In this sense, the main goal of this paper is to highlight that, apart from Yannaras' relevance as one of the most important Orthodox theologians of his time, aspects of his thought can also be expanded to other fields, such as the philosophy of education.

The Meaning of Education

Christos Yannaras' references to education almost always include the question about the 'meaning' of education. Whether one examines his opinions about the Greek educational system (as they appear in his book 'Paideia and Language') or his suggestions about what education is in general,[1] the question about the 'meaning' is always there. Yannaras would say that the 'meaning' of education lies in its 'aim', and more specifically, in the criteria which favour one 'aim' over another. In his book *Education and Language* he declares one aim for education to be the fulfilment of human needs. He also thinks that education should aim at the happiness, satisfaction and preparation of the child in order to help them live a happy and dignified life:

> 'Meaning' means: What is the aim and does [this aim] correspond to real needs of the human being? [Does this aim] supply [the human being] sufficiently in order to participate in life? [Does this aim supply him] with completeness and satisfaction in his every-day life?[2]

From the very first line, Yannaras refers to 'needs'. I will give a further explanation for this term, since it is important for the clarification of his understanding of 'meaning'. Although the limits of this paper do not

1. Christos Yannaras, 'Democracy: A function of education'. Vimeo video, 48:05. Available at: https://vimeo.com/22238481.
2. Christos Yannaras, Παιδεία καὶ γλῶσσα , Ἐπικαιρικά παλινωδούμενα [*Education and Language: Timely Recantations*] (Athens: Patakis, 2000), 23. The English translation of the quotation is mine and the same applies to all of the quotations from Yannaras' work in this paper.

allow me to analyse both uses of the term 'needs'[1] throughout his work, I will mention that in many cases where he uses it he means 'what makes the human being happy, complete'. This specific meaning can motivate the careful reader of Yannaras to explore many interesting distinctions throughout his work, either implied (i.e. this understanding of 'needs' is absolutely different from that of 'impersonal, instinctive needs') or explicitly stated, like the distinction between 'needs' and 'values'. The latter distinction is crucial in elucidating Yannaras' conception of the 'meaning' of education.

Yannaras will persistently refuse to accept 'values' as something 'valuable' or even useful for the human being. This is due to the fact that, in the core of the term, Yannaras discerns a deontological element which presupposes an authority that determines what should be done or not: 'values' are set as goals that one 'should' achieve. Thus Yannaras will wonder: Who has the authority to determine a goal that we 'should' achieve? Who has the authority to define certain 'values' as 'values'?[2] More importantly, who is going to impose these 'values' on everybody else? As is clear to the careful reader, many of the terms which are often highlighted as 'values' (like 'democracy') have a very different meaning in Yannaras' work. It would certainly require a deeper analysis to explain that, in his opinion, the notion of 'value' comes out of the notion of 'ideology', and in Yannaras one can find many arguments against ideology (both as a political phenomenon and as a mode of thinking).[3] What is important here, however, is precisely to become clear that for Yannaras the 'meaning' of education, the 'aim' (as we saw in the aforementioned quote), cannot be identified with 'values' but only with 'needs'. 'Needs' represent the reality of the human being, and that is why they are the dominant motive powers of human history: *'History doesn't*

---

1. The term 'needs' has two different meanings in Yannaras' work. On the one hand it means 'what makes people happy' and it is used mostly in his theory of civilisation when he explains that every civilisation is determined by a specific hierarchy of 'needs' (see Christos Yannaras' interview with Evi Kyriakopoulou. Youtube video, 49:39. Available at: https://www.youtube.com/watch?v=Dsf837drFdo&t=1572s). On the other hand, the term 'needs' is closer to 'necessities' (often encountered also as 'impersonal, instinctive needs') meaning the egocentric elements, that often prevent the human being from establishing free relations with the other people (see Christos Yannaras, Ὀρθὸς λόγος καί Κοινωνική Πρακτική [*Right Reasoning and Social Practice*] (Athens: Domos, 1984), 284.

2. Christos Yannaras' interview with Babis Papadimitriou. Youtube video, 12:05. Available at: https://www.youtube.com/watch?v=ePqE5p-1pu0&t=2s.

3. Christos Yannaras, *Postmodern Metaphysics,* trans. Norman Russell (Brookline: Holy Cross Orthodox Press, 2004), 39.

*move forward with ideologies, values or idealism. It moves forward with
needs.*[1] Given this standpoint, a realistic aim or meaning for education
would, for Yannaras, certainly focus on 'needs' and not on 'values.'

At this point, I will attempt a summary of this short chapter: in most
of Yannaras' references to education, one encounters the question about
the 'meaning' of education. The 'meaning' is the 'aim' of education and,
more specifically, the answer to the question of whether education can
create happy, complete people. This aim cannot be identified with any
'value'; rather, it refers to real human 'needs'. One interpretation of
the term 'need' in his work is also 'that which makes the human being
happy'. I will now proceed to the next chapter, where I will elucidate
the distinction between 'utilitarianism' and 'relations of communion'.
This distinction is closely related to the topic of 'joy' or 'happiness' and,
subsequently, to the topic of 'meaning'.

'Utilitarianism' versus 'Relations of Communion'

The predominant reason Yannaras criticises the Greek educational
system is because, in his view, this system has a utilitarian character. By
the term 'utilitarian' Yannaras means that, in this system, knowledge is
viewed exclusively as something that the child can use in order to make
money in the future. As we will see, his criticism focuses on the fact
that, under the Greek educational system, a child goes through all the
educational stages in order to reach a specific goal: to consume as much
as possible. Alternatively, Yannaras proposes an educational system that
would serve the 'relations of communion' and introduce the child to a
mode of living different from the 'utilitarian' one. This mode of living
requires the child to do the difficult task of establishing relations:

> The contemporary rationale of . . . all educational practices
> is absolutely utilitarian: [The final goal is for] the child to
> get a 'piece of paper' [a diploma/degree]. [For] the child
> to have a weapon in his/her hands; [for the child] to be a
> good student in order to go to the next class and then to the
> next class, to graduate from the gymnasium [Greek middle
> school], to enter the university, to take this 'piece of paper'
> in order to make money. The whole rationale tends towards
> this end: how, finally, the knowledge can be used, how [the

1. Christos Yannaras, 'Αρκεί η παιδεία για ανακαμψή; 1ο μέρος ΧΡΗΣΤΟΣ
ΓΙΑΝΝΑΡΑΣ' ['Is education sufficient for the recovery?']. Video Serres TV,
52:19. Available at: http://www.serrestv.gr/tv/musicvideo.php?vid=ec3d277e6.

child] will be able to transform . . . all the knowledge they obtained into material success. . . . The knowledge given from kindergarten until the PhD is absolutely subjugated to the utilitarian priority and mentality. . . . What could [the school] serve? [It could serve] the absolute priority of the relations of communion. [In such a case,] the child would not enter the school so that their ego could be armed with weapons to fight more effectively . . . the child would enter the school in order to be initiated in 'communing'. They would [be taught] how our existence is actualised as relation, as communion, and, to use the Ancient Greek word, as 'polis'. The school trains people to be *polítes* [citizens] . . . not consumers.[1]

Another passage:

The goal of school today seems to be exclusively to arm the individual: to arm the ego with knowledge . . . information [and] skills. . . . A psychologist could tell us . . . that the soul of the child . . . [and] their character, namely the prerequisites of their happiness, are mainly developed in kindergarten and in primary school . . . according to [a child's] ability to share their life with the others and establish relations, their ability to co-exist with the others and derive joy from their relations.[2]

Phrases like 'the child would not enter the school so that their ego could be armed with weapons to fight more effectively' are indicative of Yannaras' opinion regarding the identification of utilitarianism with egocentrism. The utilitarian educational system in this sense trains people to be or to remain egocentric. It leads them to take as many 'pieces of paper' as possible so that they will be competitive enough in the future to fulfil the need that the school trained them to prioritise: the need to consume. This prioritisation stems exactly from the utilitarian educational system that presses the child to obtain more now (certifications, diplomas etc.) in order to have more in the future (money, flexibility to consume). In this sense, the political system (always responsible for the educational system in Yannaras' thought) has endowed education with a certain 'meaning'. As I explained in the previous section, the term 'meaning' or 'aim' as it applies to education is related to human 'needs'. I also noted that the term 'needs' often means 'what makes the human being happy,

1. Christos Yannaras, 'The distinction between good & bad as a failed pedagogical principle (Corfu, 30.1.2017)'. Youtube video, 01:15:37. Available at: https://www.youtube.com/watch?v=tr3tdXbxp3A&t=852s.
2. Ibid.

complete'. The answer to the question of 'needs' given by the utilitarian system is this: consumption.[1] The more you consume, the happier you are, or will be.

On the contrary, the educational system that aims to serve the relations of communion answers the question of 'meaning' very differently. Yannaras suggests the school to be a place where the child is introduced to a relational 'mode of living'. In this 'mode of living', the child will experience that establishing relations and sharing can be a source of joy and completeness, higher than the joy that one receives by being egocentric. Of course, this relational approach to education is not just a theory, distinct from the everyday school reality or the subjects of the school. A practical way to explain this is through the subject of language.

In the lecture 'Αρκεί η παιδεία για την ανάκαμψη;' ['Is education sufficient for the recovery?'], Yannaras explains that reading a text is not only about understanding what the text says, or about receiving the information that the text conveys. Reading a text also means establishing a relation with the writer, and this relation means that the reader explores the writer's personal way of writing depicted in the text. In this sense, the text is something that carries, as a stamp, the writer's personal otherness. Yannaras says: 'Can you reduce a Cavafy poem just to the information that it conveys? Of course not!'[2] He means that the Cavafy poem also carries the identity of Cavafy. This identity is something that can be gradually explored by the reader, and, after a long time, the reader can possibly recognise this otherness of the writer. Imagine, for example, someone who has read and explored many poems of Cavafy (but not all of them). If he accidentally finds a poem unknown to him in a book, he is possibly able to recognise whether or not it is written by Cavafy.

This example shows that Yannaras' opinion about 'relations' doesn't refer only to the direct, interpersonal level; it presents a broader challenge to the educational reality as a whole. The language-teaching task in this case is not only to extract some information from a text, but also to experience the joy of discovering the personal otherness of the writer as depicted in the text. While the utilitarian view about language-teaching would focus only on the information[3] that the text conveys, the relational approach would set a different and, of course, more demanding task. This task could, however, offer a joy of higher quality, since the child would become actively involved with the text by developing a relation with the writer. Subsequently, in speaking about

---

1. Christos Yannaras, 'Is education sufficient for the recovery?'
2. Ibid.
3. Ibid.

an education that serves the relations of communion, Yannaras doesn't mean something like 'organising activities that make children happy'. The challenge for this type of education is to lead the child to experience the joy of establishing relations (both with the other people and with the objects of the existing reality) within the framework of the school's necessary activities (subjects, evaluation, etc.).

So far, I have mentioned that in most of Yannaras' references on education, the question about 'meaning' is crucial. The 'meaning' does not refer to a 'value', nor to an ideal; it refers to real human 'needs'. The term 'needs', of course, refers to basic biological needs, but in Yannaras' thought it also refers to 'what makes people happy, complete'. He argues that the Greek educational system has given education a utilitarian 'meaning'. In contrast, Yannaras suggests an educational system that would create a different kind of school. This school would direct all aspects of educational life (subjects, teaching methods, etc.) to serve the relations of communion. Yannaras' suggestion is based on the criteria for the meaning or aim of education that I explained in a previous paragraph: to create a child who can relate with other people means to create a happy and complete person. In the next chapter, I will argue that the reason why Yannaras persists in the opinion that the 'relations of communion' can be a source of happiness is because there is a strong link between relation and freedom.

Freedom and Education

Combining education with freedom in a paper about Yannaras was not an arbitrary decision. Although he hasn't written any work to specifically analyse the link between these two, he often refers to it either implicitly or explicitly. For example, when he uses the Greek word 'καλλιεργημένος' (cultured, well-educated) he is not referring to a 'wise' person, or even to a person with impressive academic qualifications, as sometimes we do in Greek. For Yannaras, 'καλλιεργημένος'[1] means the person who is capable of being free from his egocentric, instinctive, 'impersonal needs', in order to establish relations. This is, of course, something that a completely illiterate person can achieve too. But at the same time for Yannaras the creation of such capability is the final goal, the aim of education.[2] The problem of freedom in general is one of the most crucial subject matters of Yannaras' work. In this chapter I will focus on the way in which freedom is described in one of his books, titled Ὀρθός λόγος

1. Christos Yannaras' interview with Evi Kyriakopoulou.
2. Ibid.

καί Κοινωνική Πρακτική' *[Right Reasoning and Social Practice]*. I will
start by explaining that 'freedom' is defined in an apophatic[1] way, before
arguing that through the apophatic definition of freedom Yannaras is led
to the apophatic definition of the identity of the subject (human being).
Then, from the apophatic definition of the identity of the subject I will
reach the notion of 'relation'. I will explain that according to Yannaras, the
notion of 'relation' is a presupposition for the emergence of the identity of
the subject. At this point it will become clear that, for Yannaras, freedom
is only possible as a relational fact. I will emphasise that 'freedom' is
something 'dynamic', not 'static'. Towards the end of this section I will
argue that *because* the 'relation' is a presupposition of freedom, Yannaras
referred to 'relations' as an answer about the 'meaning' of education.
Finally I will discuss the role of education.

In the book Ὀρθός λόγος καί Κοινωνική Πρακτική *[Right Reasoning
and Social Practice]*, Yannaras describes freedom in an apophatic way.
Freedom is the denial of necessity. Necessity is the imposition of power
over the subject that does not allow it to be completely itself. Necessity is
the deprivation of the capability of the subject to be 'what it is'. Necessity is
thus an alienation of the subject. The denial of this alienation is freedom.
Since freedom is the denial of all elements that do not allow the subject
to be itself, we could say that freedom refers to the dynamic actualisation
of the subject's identity. But what is the identity of the subject?

Yannaras will define the identity of the subject again in an apophatic
way: the identity of the subject is the subject's being completely different
from everything that is not itself. In this sense, the identity of the subject
is the fact of its being totally unprecedented: it is the absolute otherness of
the subject. Yannaras goes deeper: if we define the subject as an absolute
otherness, we presuppose a relation. A subject is completely unique only
if it is related to something else that the subject is not. If the subject is
an absolute otherness, and the otherness presupposes a relation, then
the relation is the 'place' in which the subject actualises its identity. The
otherness of each subject is revealed in the relation.

I shall now get back to the concept of freedom. In the second
paragraph, I explained that the apophatic definition of freedom refers
to the actualisation of the subject's identity. Yannaras argues that since

---

1. Yannaras is well known amongst theologians for his conception of apophaticism
   as something more than the scholastic 'via negativa'. Apophaticism is, according
   to Yannaras, a general epistemological stance and more specifically it is the
   denial to exhaust truth in its formulations .See more in Christos Yannaras, *On
   the Absence and Unknowability of God: Heidegger and the Aeropagite*, trans.
   Haralambos Ventis (London: T. & T. Clark International, 2005), 59-60.

this actualisation happens only through relation (because we talk about an otherness), then freedom, in the apophatic sense, is the dynamic fact of relations that secures the otherness of the human being. This means that the human being is free when in the relations by which he actualises his existence (cohabitation, production, consumption, religion etc.), he preserves his absolute otherness. To 'preserve my absolute otherness' means not to be subjugated to any elements that alienate my otherness.

A relation in which each pole preserves its 'absolute otherness' is not something easy or given. The subject can indeed be subjugated to elements that do not allow it to be itself: '[W]e are talking about codependent relationships, relations of subjugation to necessity, authoritative relations, unfree relations....'[1] Apart from that, Yannaras adds that the alienation of the subject's otherness can also come from 'inside' the subject. This alienation derives from the 'impersonal instinctive needs, the uncontrollable passions, the unconscious impetus'.[2] If these elements dominate, they render the subject impersonal; incapable of establishing relations that preserve freedom. In this sense, freedom as a denial of necessity also means the struggle of the subject to be free from such elements. Again, however, this happens in the relation. In other words, when someone wants to be free he can only achieve it through relation. Each pole of the relation that aims at freedom tries not to alienate the otherness of the other pole by allowing egocentric elements to invade relation. Each pole actualises its identity by protecting the otherness of the other pole.

Freedom is thus a dynamic fact, which is why Yannaras also uses the term 'dynamics of freedom'. The term 'dynamics of freedom' refers to the constant struggle of the poles of the relation to prevent any type of necessity from alienating the otherness of one another. Of course, this path is full of both progress and failure. But even failure is part of the dynamics of freedom, if the poles of the relation realise it as failure. The absence of freedom starts when the necessity, the state of alienation is 'passively accepted'[3] and becomes natural and usual. Imagine, for example, the case of an authoritative husband and his wife, in which both have reconciled themselves to the relation between master and servant. In this sense freedom can only be conceived as a 'γίγνεσθαι'[4] – 'becoming'. It cannot be conceived as something static or as something that one possesses at a certain moment, but

---

1. Christos Yannaras, *Right Reasoning and Social Practice*, 283.
2. Ibid., 284.
3. Ibid., 285.
4. Ibid., 284.

as something dynamic in which someone participates. As Yannaras describes, it is not a subjective but a collective achievement, since it stems from the relation.

Having clarified the strong link between the 'relation' and freedom, I shall now return to the problem of education. This strong link, I would say, is the reason for Yannaras' insistence on an education in the service of the relations of communion. To serve the relations of communion means to serve freedom, and freedom in the apophatic definition, as I explained, means one's being oneself. This dynamic actualisation of one's identity corresponds to the idea of joy, happiness and satisfaction because it refers to the fulfilment of one's fundamental need to be oneself without any restrictions. In this sense, the subject derives its happiness and satisfaction from actualising its identity through the relations[1] that it establishes in the educational environment. The meaning of education, and the aim of education, is to cover this specific need of the person. The meaning of education is freedom.

If the meaning or the aim of education is freedom then the role of education is to introduce children to the mode of freedom. The role of education in this sense is to serve the relations of the children. To 'serve' a relation means to gradually guide the poles of the relation into the dynamics of freedom: to guide children through experiencing the difficult but great satisfaction of being themselves and through the struggle to respect each other's otherness completely. I use the word 'struggle' here in order to emphasise that the role of education is difficult. The education introduces children to a mode of living which is not easy or always joyful. Many children will find it difficult to prevent their egocentric elements from appearing in their relations. It is this continuous effort, however, which keeps the relation into the dynamics of freedom, even if it is not always successful. The role of education is to help the child recognise their egocentric elements that doesn't let them relate with the other people and to encourage the child to remain in the path of freedom so they can gradually experience the real joy derived from the relational self-actualisation: the real joy of freedom. In this sense education is not a static thing

---

1. From now on when I refer to *relations* in education, I mean *interpersonal* relations between students. In the previous chapter I mentioned the example of relational language-teaching that is not directly interpersonal but which deals with the relation of a child to an object of the existing reality, namely a text. Examining the relations of the subject with the objects of the existing reality in the light of apophatic freedom would require a specific analysis beyond the scope of this paper.

since it follows this 'becoming' (γίγνεσθαι) by trying to redress the balance in the relations that it serves. This service, I would say, is the role of education.

The Role of Education and the 'Manifesto of Education'

In this chapter I will argue that the role of education as derived from Yannaras' conception of freedom can contribute to some interesting points raised in the field of philosophy of education. More specifically, I will focus on the paper of Gert Biesta and Karl Anders Säfström, 'A Manifesto for Education'.[1] This paper, first published in 2011, has since been translated into many languages, republished in many journals of teacher unions and triggered the interest of some academics of education.[2] The reason for my focus on this paper is because it is a criticism of the way in which we think about education today. At the same time, this paper can be seen as a call for participation in a dialogue about education.[3] I will concentrate on the introduction, written by both authors, and the first part of the 'Manifesto', written by Biesta. I will present their opinion about two different contemporary critiques of education. They say, as I will show, that these critiques represent two ways of thinking about education that both distinguish it from freedom.[4] They emphasise the lack of an educational theory with freedom as its central interest. At this point, I will argue that a possible answer to this problem could be the role of education as it stems from the apophatic definition of freedom.

In the introduction, one finds a distinction between two types of current criticism of education. According to the authors, both types diagnose that education fails to accomplish its goals. The first type of criticism the authors call 'populism.' This type of criticism ties education to 'what is' – something that the authors explain as follows:

> Education under the aegis of 'what is' can . . . be an adaptation to the 'what is' of society rendering education socialisation . . . or it can be adaptation to the 'what is' of the individual child or

1. Gert Biesta and Carl Anders Säfström, 'A Manifesto for Education', *Policy Futures in Education* 9 (2011), doi: 10.2304/pfie.2011.9.5.540. Accessed 20 May 2017.
2. Sunnin Yun, 'Education, Freedom and Temporality: A Response to Biesta and Säfström's Manifesto', *Journal of Philosophy of Education* 48 (2014), 385, doi: 10.1111/1467-9752.12086. Accessed 20 May 2017.
3. Biesta and Säfström, 'A Manifesto for Education', 544.
4. Ibid., 541.

student, thus starting from certain 'facts' like the gifted child, the child with attention deficit hyperactivity disorder, the student with learning difficulties, and so on.[1]

Alternatively, we have 'idealism'. This type renders education a utopian dream, since it always links it to future projects like democracy, justice, peace, solidarity, inclusion, tolerance, etc. Idealism thus ties education to 'what is not yet';[2] namely, to something which is not real but which is expected to become real in the future. They explain:

> If we go there, we tie up education with utopian dreams. To keep education away from pure utopia is not a question of pessimism but rather a matter of not saddling education with unattainable hopes that defer freedom rather than making it possible in the here and now.[3]

For both Biesta and Säfström, what really counts for education is freedom, to such an extent that they believe that speaking about education *educationally*,[4] as they say, is the same as expressing an interest in freedom; specifically, the freedom of the 'other' – for example, the freedom of the child or the student. After correlating education with freedom, the authors observe that both 'idealism' and 'populism' render freedom an illusion.

On the one hand, populism that ties education to either the 'what is' of the society or the 'what is' of an individual child 'loses its interest in freedom . . . [in the sense that it] loses its interest in an "excess" that announces something new and unforeseen.'[5]

This happens because even the idea of education being an adaptation to 'something' doesn't allow the 'something else' to appear, meaning that populism already denies education as a historical fact – something always open to the new and unexpected. Education in this sense cannot be or bring something new.

On the other hand, we have idealism that ties education to the 'what is not yet'. In this case, given that freedom is what matters for education, we conceive education as something that will deliver its promises in the future. Thus, freedom becomes a future subject matter, running the

---

1. Ibid.
2. Ibid. The authors identify idealism both with a 'what is' and with a 'what is not yet'. Here I am examining the 'what is not yet' part, although the difference between them is not important for this paper.
3. Ibid.
4. Ibid.,542.
5. Ibid., 541.

risk of always being postponed. It is interesting that Biesta expresses the opinion that in the previous important connections between education and freedom[1] (e.g. through the notions of 'emancipation', 'enlightenment', 'liberation' etc.), freedom was something 'always to arrive, but to arrive later'.[2] This conception of freedom could on the one hand 'disconnect' education from the current state of affairs (from the 'what is') and thus create hopes for the 'new'; on the other hand, freedom was not here and now but always in the future.

The problem of 'what is' and 'what is not' also creates a problem of language. The authors question the ability of the academic disciplines that conduct research in education (educational sociology, developmental psychology, etc.) to talk about education in such a way that freedom will be included in the 'educational moment'.[3] Including freedom in the 'educational moment' means neither to operate in the field of 'what is' (the view that would deal with education as an adaptation to something) nor the field of 'what is not yet' (that would run the risk of postponing freedom forever). For example, they express the opinion that educational sociology operates in the field of 'what is' because it explains how education reproduces already existing inequalities. Talking about education (which is always identified with freedom) through this specific discipline, 'runs the risk of turning the individuals towards what is, rather than promoting freedom'.[4] On the other hand, talking about education through the discipline of developmental psychology, which understands the future as a 'what is not yet',[5] we run the risk of 'subjecting current freedom to a freedom-to-be that may never arrive'.[6]

The authors thus call for the development of a purely educational theory that will straightly refer to a purely educational 'object'. This means that they seek a theory of education that would include freedom in 'now' without adapting education to 'now' (i.e. society, individuals). Including freedom in 'now' without adapting education to 'now' means that education is a historical fact; always open to the new and unforeseen. At the same time, this theory will not operate in the domain of 'what is not yet' (in which freedom would always be placed in the future).[7] I

1. Ibid., 543.
2. Ibid.
3. Ibid.
4. Ibid., 542.
5. Ibid.
6. Ibid.
7. One very interesting response to this text came from Sunnin Yun. Yun focused on the relation between temporality, freedom and education. He proposed

would argue that the link between education and freedom extracted from Yannaras' work would actually be a good starting point for referring to such an educational 'object'.

Yannaras' understanding of education is certainly compatible with the criticism of the authors against idealism. Idealism, as we said, reveals itself by tying education to future projects like democracy, justice, peace, solidarity, inclusion, tolerance, etc. I will remind you of a distinction that I described in the chapter about the 'meaning' of education: the distinction between 'values' and 'needs'. Tying education to goals like democracy or peace would not agree with Yannaras' thought as they represent 'values', meaning that they are based on deontology. In Yannaras' case, the future goals of education do not refer to 'values' of unspecified or at least debatable content like democracy or solidarity but to certain, realistic 'needs'. Thus, in this sense, the meaning of education always refers to 'needs'.

Let us turn to the idea of freedom. In the previous section, I mentioned that, according to the apophatic definition, freedom is the refusal of all elements that do not let the subject be itself; to actualise its identity. I also explained that Yannaras defines the identity of the subject in an apophatic way, too, as an absolute otherness, which means as something that is revealed in a relation. Subsequently, the subject is free when it establishes relations in such way that both poles of the relation preserve their absolute otherness. The otherness is preserved through a constant struggle: both poles try not to let egocentric elements invade the relation and reduce it to a relation of exploitation and subjection. This constant struggle, as I said, that contains both successes and failures, is the 'dynamics of freedom'. The failures are also included in the 'dynamics of freedom', given that the two poles of the relation 1) recognise these failures and 2) do not accept them passively. This apophatic definition of freedom does not let us understand freedom as something that someone possesses in a 'certain moment'. Freedom, in the apophatic sense, is a collective achievement – a constant struggle in which someone participates.

---

a Heideggerian view of the relation between freedom and temporality that understands freedom as *possibility*, by analyzing Martin Heidegger's conception of this term. Deriving his stance from Heideggerian terminology, he defines education as a *project*, and by this definition he escapes the problem of 'what is' and 'what is not'. This specific definition of education actually 'secures' freedom in the 'educational moment' and at the same time is a very interesting criticism of the modern conception of temporality. See Sunnin Yun, 'Education, Freedom and Temporality: A Response to Biesta and Säfström's Manifesto', 391-7. In this chapter I will show that despite the Heideggerian response we can have a 'Yannarian' solution, too, mainly based in the role of education.

I then came back to Yannaras' suggestion about an education that serves the relations of communion. The suggestion he made is based on his understanding of freedom; thus, I tried to give my interpretation of what serving the relations of communion means if we take that apophatic freedom into account. Serving the relations of communion means 'a guidance'; the continuous attempt of education to keep the relations of the children in the dynamics of freedom. Education tries to make the child experience that actualising their personal identity as a complete otherness, in the relation, is a need the fulfilment of which will offer the child real happiness. I concluded by saying that education that serves freedom cannot be conceived as something static or as a specific formula. This means that serving the relations of the children in order to be in the dynamics of freedom is not something that can be absolutely pre-designed or pre-defined; every type of relation that appears between the children needs specific guidance so as to not be alienated. Every child is a different person with different capabilities of controlling their egocentric elements in order to establish relations which include freedom.

I think the view of an education that serves the relations of communion in order to keep these relations in the apophatic freedom could offer a good answer to the Manifesto's quest for the construction of a theory about education that will include freedom in 'now'. On the one hand, this view doesn't operate in the field of 'what is not' because freedom is not something to be achieved in the future, as an affirmative (cataphatic) definition could probably show. Freedom is the struggle itself, here and now, with success and failure inherent in it. This co-existence of failure and success makes freedom dynamic. On the other hand, this view doesn't tie education to the 'what is'. The type of education that tries to guide the relations of the people in such a way that each person preserves their absolute otherness is the only type of education that is really open to the new and unforeseen. This type of education does not homogenise people, because its very goal is the dynamic actualisation of each person's unique and unprecedented identity. Since this actualisation is dynamic it is always open to the new and unforeseen. Education serves the dynamically actualised identity by helping the relations (in which this identity is actualised) to remain in the dynamics of freedom. Education secures in this sense the probability of the new to appear. Subsequently, it seems that through the apophatic definition of freedom we have a view about education that brings freedom to 'now' without tying education to 'now'. In the apophatic view of freedom, education and history[1] seem to be reconciled with each other.

1. Ibid., 543.

Conclusion and Final Remarks

In this paper I tried to give an answer to the question about the role of education based on Yannaras' thought. I began with the problem of the meaning/aim of education, I continued with Yannaras' distinction between 'utilitarianism' and the 'relations of communion' and I reached the 'apophatic freedom': I argued that because the 'aim' or 'meaning' of education is to create free people, the role of education is to serve this freedom. The role of education is thus to serve the relations of people by trying to keep these relations in the dynamics of freedom. Based on this role of education, I suggested an answer to the question of Biesta and Säfström: can we create an educational theory that would be really based on freedom? We can if we think about an education that plays this role.

Thinking about education through Yannaras' work is creatively rewarding. For example, his peculiar definition of 'apophaticism', his theory about 'civilisation' or his comments about the 'pedagogical relation' are definitely some sources by which one can enrich his opinions about education. At the same time, such elements of his thought can be the starting point for serious contributions to many dialogues in the contemporary philosophy of education, such as the relationship between education and the meaning of life, the link between education and freedom, and the peculiarity of the pedagogical relation, and this is important, too.

Part III
ECCLESIA

Chapter Ten
In Conversation with Christos Yannaras:
A Critical View of the Council of Crete
Andreas Andreopoulos

Much has been said and written in the last few months about the Council in Crete, both praise and criticism. We heard much about the issues of authority and conciliarity that plagued the council even before it started. We heard much about the history of councils, about precedents, practices and methodologies rooted in the tradition of the Orthodox Church. We also heard much about the struggle for unity, both in terms of what every council hopes to achieve, as well as in following the Gospel commandment for unity. Finally, there are several ongoing discussions about the canonical validity of the council. Most of these discussions revolve around matters of authority. I have to say that while such approaches may be useful in a certain way, inasmuch they reveal the way pastoral and theological needs were considered in a conciliar context in the past, if they become the main object of the reflection after the council, they are not helping us evaluate it properly. The main question, I believe, is not whether this council was conducted in a way that satisfies the minimum of the formal requirements that would allow us to consider it valid, but whether we can move beyond this administrative approach, and consider the Council within the wider context of the spiritual, pastoral and practical problems of the Orthodox Church today.[1]

Many of my observations were based on Bishop Maxim Vasiljevic's *Diary of the Council*,[2] which says something not only about the official

---

1. Some approaches, however, such as the short book written by John Chryssavgis, *Toward the Holy and Great Council: Retrieving a Culture of Conciliarity and Communion* (Department of Inter-Orthodox, Ecumenical & Interfaith Relations, 2016), make a good effort to explore some of the issues that the council started considering, but which were quickly dropped from the agenda.
2. Bishop Maxim (Vasiljevic) of Western America, *Diary of the Council* (Los Angeles: Sebastian Press, 2017).

side of the council, but also about the feeling behind the scenes, even if there was a sustained effort to express this feeling in a subtle way.

Many of the ideas that I start with here, however, are based on the ideas of Christos Yannaras, some of which were published in *Kathimerini* around that time,[1] and some of which I came to understand through an exchange with him during 2016-17. It is for this reason that this essay is titled 'In Conversation with Christos Yannaras'. Nevertheless, this should not be taken as a presentation of his own views (by which I mean that he should not be blamed for any ideas expressed here in a stronger form than he himself would present them, or for any opinions of mine with which he may disagree), but rather as a reflection on the significance and the role of the Council, using some of his concerns as an entry point.

Browsing through Bishop Maxim's *Diary of the Council*, we can certainly discern a lot of good will among the participants of the Council, something that may be seen in, among other things, the practical difficulties involved in the preparation of the Council and the participation and the co-ordination of the several Orthodox Churches that eventually took part. We can also see this good will at work in the way that the Council tried to encourage unanimity of decisions with a light rather than a heavy hand, trying not to give the impression of a centralised event organised by a strong vertical hierarchy – something that was a sensitive point regarding the relationship between Constantinople and other Churches. My concern here, however, is not whether there was enough good will and desire for cordial relationships among the bishops who participated, but whether or not the framework of the Council was problematic enough to urge serious ecclesiological questions, as well as with questions about what constitutes a dialogue and a Council, what the urgent problems facing the Orthodox community are, and what may (or may not) be the way forward.

Before discussing the council itself, we have to take a step back and look at a number of pastoral, ecclesiological, administrative, and theological problems in the Orthodox world. Let us begin with an idea that was fundamental for the Council, even in the discussions that preceded it: the idea of unity. According to the historical guidelines that were discussed

---

1. Cf. Christos Yannaras, '«Μεγάλη Σύνοδος»: ἡ Ἀντίφαση Ἐγγενής' ['Great Synod': A Contradiction in Terms]. Available at: http://www.kathimerini.gr/864266/opinion/ epikairothta/politikh/megalh-synodos-h-antifash-eggenhs. Accessed 4 April 2017. See also Christos Yannaras, 'Ρεαλισμός Μαρτυρίας –'Ὀχι Ἰδεολογήματα'. Available at: http://www.kathimerini.gr/865107/opinion/epikairothta/politikh/pealismos-martyrias--oxi-ideologhmata. Accessed 4 April 2017.

in the context of the council and which are mentioned by Bishop Maxim in the *Diary of the Council*,[1] despite the historically understandable absence of Rome and the unfortunate self-exclusion of Antioch, the Council came close to having the authority of an Ecumenical Council. Nevertheless, reality is different. The first idea for a Panorthodox Synod may be found in two encyclicals of Ecumenical Patriarch Joachim III in 1902 and 1904, while there have been many preparatory meetings in Constantinople, the Holy Mountain and Chambesy since 1923.[2] The need for a Panorthodox Council has been acknowledged for over a century, and the anticipation for the meeting of Orthodox bishops has lasted as long. The Panorthodox community, therefore, in one way or another, has repeatedly expressed the need for a wide council that would address many of its practical and theological difficulties.

In terms of participation, the most notable absence from the Council was the absence of Russia and two of the Churches that are closest to it. The absence of Russia has significant ripples everywhere, especially in the diaspora, where the unity of the Orthodox world is more visibly tested. There has been a tension here between Constantinople and Moscow for quite some time, because of the lack of clarity (or rather consensus) over ecclesiastical jurisdiction in the diaspora as well as in other places (something we can see in the troubled history of the OCA, its emancipation from Moscow and the subsequent question of Constantinople as to who can grant autocephaly, but also in the difficult divisions of the Ukrainian Church), the question of the ethnic identity of several Western Orthodox Churches that consist of largely non-ethnic members notwithstanding. Incidentally, the Orthodox Church in North America, and the OCA in particular, is an interesting case study in itself: while the laity are largely united by the (now mostly) common language of worship, and it is not unusual to see Greeks worshipping in OCA churches and vice versa, the OCA itself is still caught in the struggle of power between Moscow and Constantinople. Although it emerged as a serious attempt to emancipate itself from Moscow and help create an autocephalous, indigenous American Church (regardless of how

1. Bishop Maxim mentions the canonical criteria set by the 7th Ecumenical Council for a council to be recognized as ecumenical: participation (even by representation) of the Patriarchates of Rome and Constantinople, and agreement (also even by representation) of the Patriarchates of Alexandria, Antioch and Jerusalem. Bishop Maxim, *Diary of the Council*, 26.
2. Cf. Ioannis Sideras, *Τὸ Ὅραμα τῆς Ἁγίας καὶ Μεγάλης Πανορθοδόξου Συνόδου [The Vision of the Holy and Great Pan-orthodox Synod].* Available at: https://www.scribd.com/doc/314615368/ Πανορθόδοξη-Σύνοδος-2016. Accessed 4 April 2017.

successful it was in this direction), caught between its Russian past and its not yet fully recognised autonomy, the church of Schmemann and Meyendorff was not represented in the Council.

How serious is the tension between Moscow and Constantinople? There is a level of political antagonism, or struggle for authority, understandable in the simple observation that while Constantinople demonstrates and guarantees the continuity with the historical past and the age of the Fathers, Moscow is much more powerful and rich at the moment, and yet, there is another level beyond the dynamics of the last few decades. The most pessimistic reading of this situation is the one that Christos Yannaras has expressed several times: that in the last five centuries the Russian Church has gradually created a distinct and autonomous religious culture, something that Yannaras observes in its distinct style of music, the specifically Russian vestments for priests and bishops, and the modification of ancient symbols and images. In the list of such specifically 'Russian' symbols we could also add the Russian Cross, which has its footstool directed in the opposite way from what it was in antiquity, something that has given it a very different meaning (predated by the attempt of Ivan the Terrible to create a national cross that echoed his victory over the Tatars and Islam in Kazan in 1552),[1] and even the particular directions of Russian architecture. Ultimately, along with different liturgical and pastoral practices, such as confession just before communion, kneeling during the Liturgy, the insertion of the prayer of the Third Hour in the epiclesis and the insertion of the precommunion prayers (normally read individually at home) just before communion, such differences may constitute a distinct and separate ecclesiastical ethos. Some of the changes that originated in Russia, such as the emergence of the high iconostasis that divides completely the nave and the altar, have spread, perhaps unfortunately, to the rest of the Orthodox world, while others have not. While many such particular characteristics simply reflect the local culture and ultimately the openness of Orthodoxy (the Orthodox Church in the past not only did not oppose the translation of Scripture and the liturgical texts to different languages, but encouraged the creation of writing in the case of the Slavic-speaking people so that the Gospels and the services could be written down, as opposed to the practice of the medieval Roman Catholic Church, which systematically imposed its own style of worship in lands under its jurisdiction), they become problematic when they stress an otherness, and especially when

1. Cf. Didier Chaudet, 'When the Bear Confronts the Crescent: Russia and the Jihadist Issue', *China and Eurasia Forum Quarterly*, Central Asia-Caucasus Institute & Silk Road Studies Program, 7/2 (2009), 37-58.

they produce a distinct theological strand, which stands in opposition to the attitudes, the sensitivities and the views of the rest of the Church. The onion dome, for instance, came about as a combination of the traditional use of the dome as a symbol of heaven (something that may be traced to pre-Christian civilisations)[1] and the Gothic spire – something quite natural for the time, the place and the influences that Russia accepted. When Evgeny Trubetskoi, on the other hand, tried to explain it as a result of a different theology (the flame of prayer), he did so carving a special place for the Russian Orthodox identity, equally distinct from the West and the Orthodox world.[2] Likewise, there are modern Russian iconographers, accustomed to flat surfaces and to a strict symbolism of colours, who do not recognise the sixth century Pantokrator of Sinai as an image that complies with the definition of an icon. In other words, while the multiple local experiences are a wide base for the ecumenical experience of the Church, they become problematic if they start producing separate theologies.

Perhaps this view sounds too extreme or unfair within a context of ecclesiastical cultures that have seriously attempted to move beyond the historical stumbling blocks of the past. What we see in the North American experience, for instance, where Greeks, Russians, Serbians, Romanians, Arabs, Albanians, as well as Orthodox from non-traditionally Orthodox backgrounds have worshipped together for generations, such symbolic language has been generally embraced by all, and any critical approach to their significance and use can only be done from the inside, pertaining to symbols that may have a distinct origin, but nevertheless belong to all ethnicities. When Alexander Schmemann says that he is not fond of Byzantinisms,[3] he does so at a level beyond the old oppositions of the historical past, as a way to look into the liturgical experience beyond the weight of history – and it is precisely in this way that Orthodoxy can absorb particular cultures, but not to be tied to any one of them – Greek, Russian, or anything else. Nevertheless, while this promising syncretic view can be seen in multi-ethnic societies at the level of the laity (but not usually at the level of the higher clergy), the European experience has not yet caught up with it.

Yannaras observes, quite poignantly, that this alienation of religious culture preceded, in very similar steps, the historical separation between East and West, and warns against the danger of a future schism between

---

1. Cf. the seminal article by Karl Lehman, 'The Dome of Heaven', *The Art Bulletin*, 27/1 (1945), 1-27.
2. Eugene Trubetskoi, *Icons: Theology in Colour* (Crestwood, NY: SVS Press, 1973), 17.
3. Cf. Alexander Schmemann, *The Journals of Father Alexander Schmemann, 1973-1983* (Crestwood, NY: SVS Press, 2000).

the Russian Church, along with any Orthodox Churches that may follow it, and the rest of the Orthodox world on the other side. Indeed, by the time Sylvester Syropoulos describes the theological and political difficulties between the East and the West in the context of the Ferrara-Florence Council in the fifteenth century, he also records the great divide in the culture between the two parties, to the extent that he did not recognise the worship space as consistent with his own experience.[1] In contrast, although the Greek and the Coptic Church have been formally separated five centuries more than the Latin West and the Greek East, both sides hold a mutual recognition of the sacred space in each other.

Here we could also remember the idea of Moscow as the Third Rome, a concept that emerged in the sixteenth century during the time of Ivan the Terrible.[2] This idea has been put forth since then, even in the twentieth century by people who were influential in the diaspora, such as Nicholas Zernov,[3] which furthered the divide between Russia and the rest of the Orthodox world, and encouraged mistrust between the two sides for a long time. Perhaps the current reluctance of Moscow to recognise the title of the Ecumenical Patriarch is the result of some residual tension. What is disconcerting about the idea of the Third Rome is that as with the alienation between the East and the West, the creation of a different religious and cultural identity may eventually lead to an antagonism of primacy, power struggles, and eventually the exploration of opposing worldviews or theologies.

This is the elephant in the room of Orthodox ecclesiology, and although the prestige of the Council of Crete suffered from the absence of the Russian Church, the Council was not able to solve or even to address the problem. While at a first reading the absence of the four Patriarchates (especially of Antioch) seems to be caused by a circumstantial disagreement, it brings forth important ecclesiological questions, which may not be solved by an attempt to find the middle way between two different centres of power. We need to look for a deeper spiritual principle here, rather than appeal to the politics of compromise. In this case, we have two basic questions. The first question, as Yannaras has posed it, has to do with the meaning of a Patriarchate today, and whether its

1. V. Laurent, ed., *Sylvestre Syropoulos: Les Mémoires du grand ecclésiarque de l'Église de Constantinople Sylvestre Syropoulos sur le Concile de Florence (1438-1439)* (Lutetiae: Éditions du Centre national de la recherche scientifique [CNRS], 1971).

2. Cf. Alar Laats, 'The Concept of the Third Rome and its Political Implications' in *Religion and Politics in Multicultural Europe: Perspectives and Challenges* ed. Alar Kilp, Andres Saumets (Tartu University Press, 2009), 98-113.

3. Nicholas Zernov, *Moscow: The Third Rome* (MacMillan, 1937).

meaning, especially after the emergence of the newer Patriarchates in the Balkans, has drifted to signify the official state religion, and ultimately to legitimise the *de facto* ethnophyletist structure of the modern Orthodox Church. Second, whether the independence of the Patriarchates, and the autonomous and autocephalous Orthodox Churches, is such that in effect we operate on the principle of the branch theory within the Orthodox communion, and in this way our ecclesiology in practice has drifted to a mutual recognition of independent churches, most of which are defined by national characteristics, rather than criteria of faith and tradition. Bishop Maxim, in his *Diary*, expresses repeatedly the view, or perhaps the hope, that this is not the case, but after the Council of Crete, which relied so heavily on national representations, it is becoming increasingly difficult to see the difference.

All of the important sees in early Christianity, Patriarchates and Metropoleis, emerged as such because they had apostolic foundation, administrative significance, and were pioneering theological thought – although we see that perhaps the strongest criterion quickly became the administrative one, and the structure of the Church mirrors the structure of the state cities or prefectures. In the beginning this did not reflect the need for a system of global (ecumenical) co-ordination or governing, something that happened after the fourth century. The addition of Constantinople introduced the Constantinian model of the relationship between the Church and the state, and the addition of Jerusalem, a city which was not important in terms of administration, was made mostly for symbolic reasons. Already at the time we can start questioning what the meaning of a Patriarchate is, because of the proximity of Antioch and Jerusalem, but nevertheless the system of the ancient pentarchy was understood and functioned as an actualisation of community at the global level. Pentarchy certainly never implied the balance of five separate parties, and certainly there was nothing that looked like national representations, as the ecclesial unity expressed in each Patriarchate was inspired by the inclusive vision of Pentecost, where the first Christian community was made by 'Parthians, Medes and Elamites, residents of Mesopotamia, Judea and Cappadocia, Pontus and Asia, Phrygia and Pamphylia, Egypt and the parts of Libya near Cyrene, visitors from Rome (both Jews and converts to Judaism); Cretans and Arabs' (Acts 2:9-11).

Over the last few centuries this principle has been eroded, first by the emergence of national churches in lands that were becoming Christian, and wished to assert their ecclesiastical authority and independence from Constantinople, and, second, through the establishment of national churches in lands that had formerly belonged to the spiritual and ecclesiastical oversight of Constantinople, following the establishment of national states. The first such national church was the Church of Greece, which, although it never proceeded to the establishment of another yet Patriarchate, as the Churches of Serbia, Bulgaria and Romania did, was reformed under the guidance of the Bavarian regency of King Otto in the nineteenth century. Other churches followed quickly, sometimes using financial pressure against Constantinople, or confiscating its dependencies. In this new order, it is interesting to note that although the normative criterion of pre-eminence in the ecumenical conciliar hierarchy – whatever this may mean – traditionally had been the antiquity of each Church, we see that this principle was not always observed, but had been taken into account along with political power. The Patriarchate of Moscow, for instance, although established five centuries after the Patriarchate of Georgia, occupies a higher place of honour in the hierarchy of Orthodox Churches.

The independence of the Church of Greece from the Patriarchate of Constantinople in 1833 and subsequently, one by one, of all of the other Balkan nations, either as autonomous or autocephalous Churches or as Patriarchates, was defined according to national criteria. Despite the repeated condemnation of ethnophyletism in theory, the practice of the Orthodox Church since the nineteenth century has resulted in a communion of fourteen or fifteen (depending on whether the OCA is one of them) national self-governing Churches, each of them administratively independent of the other. The Patriarchate of Constantinople, as Yannaras reminds us, as it is based in a land and a surrounding culture that is not Orthodox or even Christian, is certainly as far as possible from the idea of a national state church, but I am afraid that, while it maintains a historical *raison d'être* as to what a Patriarchate is because of its particular historical circumstances, it is the exception rather than the rule when compared with the majority of the Orthodox national churches. With the exception of Constantinople, the ecclesiological structure of the Orthodox Church is similar to the landscape we encounter in the Protestant world, which consists of several different state churches that may be defined by different national or spiritual trajectories, and yet they largely recognise each other, denying any kind of central co-ordination. While the pre-eminence of Constantinople is generally recognised in the Orthodox world, its role is certainly nowhere close to the strong vertical authority of Rome. Moreover, this pre-eminence is not understood in the same way in the Orthodox world, as for some churches its position is mostly a memory of the glorious past, without any executive or spiritual powers, and as the case of Crete showed, there is no way to enforce any meaningful unity co-ordinated by it. One of the differences however, is that while much of the Protestant world in the past had been shaped by a climate of war (political and religious), clash and differentiation, this is usually not the case any more: today in the Protestant world we see a large mutual recognition and intercommunion at the level of laity and clergy, among churches that had previously been separated by national as well as spiritual differences.[1] In this way, the national factor has become increasingly important in the Orthodox world, where the diaspora has still not yet been able to develop an ecclesiastical structure defined by local/geographical criteria rather than by national criteria, despite the significant spread of Orthodoxy beyond ethnic groups, and also despite the gradual assimilation of these ethnic groups into the wider culture. Unfortunately, Orthodoxy in the New World is still divided and defined by ethnic lines. The effort to create an American Church beyond and above ethnic lines started in a very interesting way with the weaning of the OCA from Moscow, but in the end the OCA did not move much beyond its Russian roots, nor was this move followed by any similar moves in the other ethnic jurisdictions in North America.

To return to the question of the co-ordination of the entire Orthodox world, since many things have changed since the fourth century, and since the geopolitical map has changed significantly since the time of the foundation of the ancient Patriarchates, I think it is no longer practical or possible to keep considering the question of the entirety of the representation of the Orthodox or Christian world, as we see repeatedly in Bishop Maxim's *Diary*, measured by the historical participation of the two more senior Patriarchates (Rome and Constantinople), or the five (or four) ancient ones. This narrow historical approach effectively limits the definition of Orthodoxy as the religion that looks to the glory of Byzantium as its 'classical period', and makes sense primarily within the historical, cultural, technological, and spiritual context of the period between the fourth and the fifteenth centuries. On the other hand, a wider understanding of Orthodoxy, not tied to a specific memory of a former glory, would remind us that Christianity, rather than an organised religious structure, is the celebration of the presence of Jesus Christ among us and the continuous communion of the Church with him, as it is reflected in the Gospel, and as it is attested and experienced by the Fathers and the saints of every age and of every place, equally in the past, in the present and in the distant future.

1. An example is the sharing of communion between the Anglicans, the Lutherans, the Methodists, the URC, the Old Catholics, and other churches.

The highest-level authority of the Orthodox Church in the present is a committee of fourteen (mostly national) representations. However, there is no clear mechanism that can protect or enforce this unity. While it is generally recognised that the role of the Ecumenical Patriarchate is to convene or preside over Ecumenical Councils – something that has not always been the case, incidentally – it has no power to enforce participation or agreement. The absence of an Emperor, the person who often demanded and enforced conciliar unity, sometimes using not very Christian methods, shows a gap in Orthodox ecclesiology – the system cannot work very effectively without an Emperor. Here we need to remember that although from the point of view of the citizens of the Roman Empire it made little difference if the head of the state was an Emperor or a King, in the wider context of the Christian world it did make a difference for a long time, at least in terms of symbolism and protocol: for many centuries, the heads of Western European kingdoms sought the recognition and confirmation of their title by the Emperor of the Eastern Roman state when they ascended to power. Even if this was a mere formality, it shows that the role of the Emperor was properly understood beyond and above ethnic lines.

Lacking this kind of unifying agent, there was no way to coopt the participation of Russia, Bulgaria, Georgia, and Antioch in the Council of Crete. But beyond questions of authority, representation, and ethnophyletism, we must askabout how we understand unity and distinctiveness: can we understand the unity of the Orthodox Churches at the level of the minimum common ground, or should we understand it as the sum of their experience, considered as a shared experience? Simply put, the first approach would consider normative only what is happening everywhere, whereas the second would consider normative anything that a local Orthodox Church, with its own circumstances, would consider normative. While the first approach seems particularly suited for the exploration of faith and doctrinal thought (which is why it resonates in the interesting, yet problematic, formula of Vincent of Lerins 'everywhere, always, and by all'),[1] the second is suitable for the practical and pastoral challenges that need to be considered within their time and place. The Council of Crete did not make this distinction, and took the conservative approach in pastoral matters. Instead of the richness of the ecumenical Orthodox experience, which would urge us to look at the local experience through the lens of the timelessness and the boundlessness of the eternal Church, in the case of mixed marriages, for instance, the decision was to fall back to the

1. *Commonitory* chapter 2, 6; NPNF Series 2 Vol. 11, 132.

safety of the letter of the law, and to understand the eternal through local criteria instead of the other way round: what was perhaps true for the majority of the Christian world several centuries ago, and still holds true in the mountains of Georgia, has to remain the norm in the rest of the Orthodox world.

From this point of view, perhaps one of the most problematic themes that were discussed in Crete was the question of the pastoral and practical difficulties of marriage in the present age, especially in the context of the modern, multicultural world. Marriage was discussed extensively, both in Crete and in the pre-conciliar discussions, and as we have already mentioned, despite the pastoral difficulty of mixed marriages, the Council had the chance to explore its meaning in the context of Orthodox spirituality, and shed some light to its practical difficulties. There is a serious problem with the way the question was approached: beyond a token presence of a few non-voting female and lay consulting theologians, this discussion involved no women at the highest level, and no men who had had the experience of marriage themselves. It seems to me that the bishops and monks who attempted to explore the spiritual, the theological and the pastoral aspects of marriage should have kept a humble silence on a matter on which, with the rare exception of bishops who were widowed before they ascended to the episcopacy, they had no experience. Instead, the proper procedure would be to refer the matter to committees of married priests and lay men and women. The Orthodox Church, at least in theory, recognises that both the way of the parish and the way of the monastery lead equally to salvation (although it is hard to remember even more than a handful of saints who were not monastics),[1] and that the monk is no closer to salvation than the layman. As Maximus the Confessor reminds us, commenting on the Transfiguration, the presence of Elijah and Moses signifies, among other things, the equality of the celibate and the married life, since Elijah was celibate, and Moses was married (indeed more than once).[2] Therefore, as it would be inappropriate for a parochial committee to draw up the regulations of a monastery, it is inappropriate for a community of monks to draw up the regulations of married life. The practice of the Church, however, does not usually follow suit, as it is usual for people who live in the world, married or not, to seek the advice of monks. Married priests often confess to monks,

1. One study in this vein is David and Mary Ford's *Marriage as a Path to Holiness: Lives of Married Saints* (South Canaan, PA: St Tikhon's Seminary Press, 1995).
2. Maximus the Confessor:,*Ambigua* 10, 31, PG 91, 1161-1169B.

but the reverse does not happen very often. Finally, the majority of books and articles on marriage in the Orthodox tradition are written by people who have no relevant experience.[1]

To push this to an extreme, in order to illustrate the depth of the difficulty, we must discuss the case of the second marriage of priests, a topic that was dropped from the agenda before the beginning of the Council, although it touches on the lives of thousands of priests. I am afraid that this intended omission shows a serious vacuum of theological methodology and thought. The Council in this case acted as a timid administrative structure, closing the door to a huge pastoral problem, by choosing to simply ignore the spiritual and pastoral dimensions of the issue. Acting in a pietistic manner, without exploring the theological, anthropological and pastoral dimensions of the issue, the Council did not find any compelling evidence against the marriage of widowed priests, but decided that since it was not going to be accepted by all Orthodox Churches (for cultural rather than theological reasons, although we have to note that the Church has a strong hand in creating local culture, as much as it is shaped by it), it could not proceed with this line of exploration. In addition, without giving a convincing reason, it did not even consider the much bigger and more theologically challenging issue of divorced priests. Yet, it is this case – extreme, perhaps – that tests the limits of our understanding both of the priesthood and of the nature of marriage. We could mention here three reasons qualifying this, as an attempt to explore the practical and the spiritual depth of this issue:

First, in widowhood the bonds of love may not be shattered, and therefore the spiritual and psychological union between the husband and the wife, although not physical, may continue even after the death of one of the two. The separated couple does not have this privilege: here it is recognised that not only that the bond of love is no longer present, but also

---

1. Perhaps it is necessary to mention here that I am not trying to criticize monasticism as a movement or as a constituent part of the Church. My criticism, on this and on other similar points, perhaps reflects an impatience with the kind of monasticism that betrays its own calling: monks who have spent only a short time in a monastery, and then become spiritual guides, archimandrites or bishops, being scandalized by the world, and also scandalising it, instead of living in 'their repentance'; the monastery of their tonsure, to use the monastic expression that Papadiamantis uses in his story entitled *The Monk*, which explores precisely these problems, which have not changed in the last century. Monasticism is exemplary as an act of love, repentance and asceticism, beyond rationality, but I believe it is problematic when it asserts itself as the normative, or highest form of Christianity, and when it tries to impose the particularity of its struggle (such as against sexuality) on the rest of the Church.

that the marriage may be detrimental to the psychological and even the spiritual life of the spouses. While a widowed priest with children may face a heavier practical load (in terms of raising the children as a single parent), the divorced priest may face a heavier psychological and spiritual load.

Second, the Orthodox Church recognises marriage as an ascetic challenge. The theological implications of this are twofold: first, that while there may not be such a thing as a perfect and carefree marriage, marriage is not founded on pleasure, but on a continuous attempt to be drawn beyond the limits of the ego and to urge us to become more than we are. A successful marriage is not necessarily one that makes life easier for the spouses, but one that leads to their psychological and spiritual maturity – and conversely, we need to recognise that a marriage where the spouses become increasingly antagonistic, defensive, and duplicitous is harmful to them and to the family, and it may be necessary to dissolve it in order to prevent its harmful effects from being perpetuated, and to make sure that the children are not affected. The second point is that, as with any ascetic ascent, if a marriage fails irrevocably, in the Orthodox Church the people are allowed a second and a third attempt, rather than giving up after the one and only attempt; yet this premise of trying again is not extended to priests. The de facto fallback status of a widowed or divorced priest is monkhood, although the calling and the roles of the priest and the monk are quite different and should not be confused.

Third, even if we consider a failed marriage a moral stain, it is a personal stain, rather than one that would necessarily impede the ability of the priest to act as the father of a community – to extend this metaphor, life shows us that a divorced biological father or mother may be still a good parent to a child; and also that a father or a mother do not usually lose their status as parents and the parental relationship with their children. The analogy here is that the defrocking of a priest who remarries after the death of his wife is analogous to social services taking away children from their parents if they divorce. In addition, to insist on a legalistic reading of 1 Timothy 3:2, which mentions that the priest should be the husband of one wife, is simply bad exegesis – not only for the legalist attitude, but also because 1 Timothy simply finds concubinage and polygamy incompatible with the most basic understanding of love as understood in the Christian tradition, which does not distinguish between spiritual and corporeal attraction, but is based on the imagery of the Song of Songs, and the complete union of the spouses. 1 Timothy, and the New Testament in general, shows a new direction, speaking of the union of the husband and the wife as a union of two equals, two beloveds given to each other completely, rather than as a social contract. This was revolutionary at the time, and even after many centuries of Christian formative education, issues surrounding the union of the beloveds that are based on social economy, such as property, social status, lineage, taxation benefits, and so forth, often take precedence over the meaning of the marital union. To draw from all this a legalistic instruction goes against the spirit of the commandment itself. In contrast to Donatism, for the Christian Church after the fifth century it is clear that the moral status of a priest does not affect his priestly role, and the Biblical spirit of such prohibitions (usually Pauline rather than from the Gospels) has to do with the general concern of St Paul to avoid schisms caused by scandals. The experience of the Anglican Church, where priests are allowed to remarry (something that did not meet with much contention), has shown us that society at large is ready for it. Moreover, if we think of scandals and pastoral sensitivity, the Church, or perhaps more correctly, a certain part of the hierarchy in our day, scandalises more people by expressing extreme conservative positions, usually articulated in a fundamentalist, legalistic language. Its involvement in political life is greatly reduced to an extreme conservativism leaning towards the extreme right political wing, or often preaching a sermon of intolerance and hatred, as we see in the case of the bishops of Peiraias and Kalavryta. If scandal is to be considered within the Pauline context of 1 Corinthians 8:13, where the apostle explains that while he naturally has the right to eat meat, he would rather never do it if this caused a difficulty to his fellow Christians (and therefore avoiding scandal is not a matter of observing laws and regulations, but an act of love), we certainly need to discern whether people today are scandalised by a priest who remarries, or by a bishop who directs his flock to spit on homosexuals on sight.[1]

Overall, although it is often said that Orthodoxy also means Orthopraxy, and that there is no distance between doctrine and practice, in the Orthodox Church there is a serious lack of what has elsewhere been developed as practical theology. The systematic examination of practical and pastoral issues, and the recognition of several problems that flow from them, which may be illuminated by theological thought, implies a bottom-to-top approach, which has not been developed satisfactorily. For this reason there is often a significant gap between akriveia and oikonomia. However, when the exception is more frequent than the rule, it may be a good sign for us to reconsider our theological thought about such matters in depth.

---

1. Cf. Metropolitan Amvrosios of Kalavryta and Aigialeia, Ἀποβράσματα τῆς κοινωνίας σήκωσαν κεφάλι᾽ ['The Scums of Society Raised their Head']. Available at: http://mkka.blogspot.gr/2015/12/blog-post_9.html. Accessed on 18 May 2017.

These views, which admittedly only scratch the surface of an issue that unfortunately affects a good part of the clergy nowadays, serve only as an example of how such a case may be explored in a spiritual and pastoral way. Likewise, issues that may be explored in a similar light include the ordination of women and the anthropology or symbolism behind it, a more sustained discussion on fasting, bioethical questions, and liturgical literacy. Some of these areas have been explored to some extent, whereas others not sufficiently so. The anthropology of gender and sexuality has certainly not been explored satisfactorily, at least not much beyond the level of canon law. While Yannaras in his *Freedom of Morality*[1] has expressed some interesting concerns about the archetypal symbolism behind the maleness of the priest, it is not certain that this symbolism has the same meaning today as it did two thousand years ago. As Carl Jung has repeatedly shown, while archetypes generally express a pattern beyond time and space, it is nevertheless possible for them to evolve and give their place to new archetypes over time. While social changes within the last few decades may have influenced the way we think, unless we extend our gender research to the dynamics of sexuality, it won't be possible to consider the weight of the symbolism of gender. Interestingly, this also shows that the discussion on the gender of the priest needs to be connected not simply with the examination of anthropology in general, but more specifically with a deeper examination of love and sexuality. It is unfortunate that many spiritual guides cannot distinguish between lust and love, and the fallback position of safety is to judge a relationship based on its legal status, i.e. whether sexuality is expressed within the confines of a legitimate marriage or not. An example that is often used to demonstrate this absurdity is that, technically speaking, sex five minutes before the wedding ceremony is a sin, while five minutes afterwards is legitimate. Obviously it is an absurd approach either way, because marriage is the self-offering of love that includes the two spouses and also God. While there has always been a legal dimension to marriage, long before the Christian wedding ceremony was established, I think it is more appropriate to look at the sacrament of marriage in a way similar to the canonisation of saints, where the Church recognises the sanctity that is already there, rather than conferring it on a person as one would do a promotion, thus 'making' a saint. In the case of the sacrament of marriage, I think it is equally sensible to avoid the legalistic question, and think of the recognition of the commitment and the wish for an ascetic self-offering that has taken place even before the blessing itself – not that this would make the blessing itself irrelevant, as this too would be part of the commitment, and the wish of

---

1.   Christos Yannaras, *The Freedom of Morality* (Crestwood, NY: SVS Press, 1984).

the couple to present themselves as a new family in front of God and the people. Be this as it may, these are questions that need to be explored much further than they have been before.

There is much more that needs to be said here. Asceticism has been explored, almost exclusively, within the context of a willing self-limitation, an abstinence from material pleasures. This useful training of the self, which we owe to the monastic tradition, is nevertheless only half of the way. The other half is the offering of the self to the Other, personally, willingly, and without an expectation of a reward. Without this actualisation of love, and without a relationship with the Other, one's relationship with God may become ideological, abstract, and ultimately self-serving. The most essential Biblical images of the relationship of the Church with God take precisely this kind of love as a model. The image of Christ as the Bridegroom of the Church, and the imagery of the *Song of Songs*, which was used as a catechetical text both in Judaism and in the early Church,[1] show that this kind of asceticism of love was understood very clearly in early Christianity, before it was obscured by the asceticism of self-castration, found figuratively and literally in Origenism. It is certainly interesting that Yannaras has explored the *Song of Songs* as a source of theological inspiration, in one of his most fascinating books.[2] But here we need to point to a serious gap in Orthodox theology. In the eighteenth century, Nikodemos the Hagiorite and Makarios of Corinth compiled the *Philokalia* of monastic asceticism, a collection of texts that is by no means a systematically solid Patristic collection (it does not include any of the writings of Basil the Great, for instance), and has no place for the ecclesial communion, but reflects the despair of the people who saw the collapse of the Church structure around them, and tried at least to find salvation individually, through the way of personal ascetic ascent. Influence of this text has been such that several theologians, ignoring these problems, have argued that after the age of the Fathers we live now in the age of *Philokalia*. While the *Philokalia* of monasticism has helped us preserve the tradition of the individual ascetic ascent, it has preserved only half of the meaning of asceticism. The other half would consist of texts that follow the tradition of the *Song of Songs*, or the imagery of the Christ Bridegroom and his love for the Church, the image of God as the passionate lover as we find it in the thirtieth step of the Ladder of

---

1. Cf. Andreas Andreopoulos, 'The Song of Songs: an Asceticism of Love', *The Forerunner* (No 57, Summer 2011, Orthodox Fellowship of St John the Baptist), 17-26.
2. Christos Yannaras, *Variations on the Song of Songs* (Brookline, MA: Holy Cross Orthodox Press, 2005).

John Klimakos[1] and in the writings of other saints, or of the lives and experiences of saints such as Boniface of Tarsos and Aglaia of Rome, who found salvation through their love for another human being rather than in the desert, fighting against acts of selfishness rather than against bodiless temptations. Furthermore, it would include texts that illustrate the experience of the sacrament, the significance of the *communitas* with the living and with the dead, the Church as a hospital and workshop of love instead of a court of ideas and behaviour. The *Philokalia of Love* has not yet been written, and perhaps in our days we need it much more than the compilation of Makarios and Nikodemos.

I admit that my views on many of these matters sound quite bleak. I am afraid that we are witnessing the potential beginning of two different schisms within the Orthodox Church. The one, as already mentioned, concerns any independent Church that creates its own, distinct religious culture, and gradually separates itself from the dialogue that the rest of the churches engage in, something that can happen because of the lack of a clear ecclesiological model of global communion. As Yannaras reminds us, it is sufficient to look at the trajectory the Franks followed in their alienation from the Roman Empire, first culturally and subsequently theologically, which prepared the schism between East and West, and draw our conclusions about how much this pattern is repeated in our days. To compare the situation with what happens in other Christian denominations, the Papist model may be successful in terms of its administrative effectiveness, but the centripetal force of this model is too high a price to pay. The imperial model, where unity was forced upon the Church by the political power, is also a memory from a different time, which cannot work in our days. The Protestant model of the parallel churches seems to be closest to what we are facing, or rather to what we are practicing today. Still, while that model is not concerned about an overall unity of the constituent churches, for better or worse, it is much more inclusive in practice, more permissive in variance and in pastoral sensitivity than the Orthodox communion.

Next to this 'vertical' schism, we can observe a 'horizontal' schism. There is a great number of people who are disappointed by the Church, and who although may be nominally Orthodox, in reality they feel they have been marginalised by their own Church, and in the end they are

---

1. 'Μακάριος ὅστις τοιοῦτον πρός Θεόν ἐκτήσατο ἔρωτα, οἷον μανικός ἐραστής πρός τήν ἑαυτοῦ ἐρωμένην κέκτηται.' In the translation of Liubheid and Russell, 'Lucky is the man who loves and longs for God as a smitten lover does for his beloved.' John Climacus, *The Ladder of Divine Ascent* [The Classics of Western Spirituality] (New York: Paulist Press, 1982), 287.

not active members. An even greater number of people may not even consider themselves faithful, but simply accept their Orthodoxy as part of their cultural identity, as there is nothing else (yet) that could replace it at the spiritual level – because the disappointment of our time with the failure of the hierarchies has led to a quite robust post-Marxist materialism, in the East and in the West.

These people, who have been left out, form the silent majority of the laity in Orthodox countries, and I am afraid that the percentage is growing. While Orthodox ecclesiology in theory is based on the community of the faithful, where all the people have a place and they contribute in distinct yet equally important roles, what we see in practice is a solipsistic clericalism. The Church generally keeps a distance from the wider cultural, academic, scientific, and political life, and its recurrent role in the last few decades is to express and cultivate fear of almost everything new. While the entanglement of Church and politics has generally been disastrous wherever it has been attempted, the quasi-monastic, withdrawn image of the Church vis-a-vis the other aspects of communal life, has rendered it irrelevant for larger society. With a very small number of notable exceptions, by and large, Orthodox higher and middle clergy is absent from cultural, academic and scientific life. We may simply remember the animosity of the clergy towards Nikos Kazantzakis, both during his lifetime, when he was almost excommunicated by the Church of Greece in 1954 (an attempt that was stopped in its rails only because of the decisive action of Patriarch Athenagoras), and even much afterwards, when Metropolitan Augustine of Florina organised rallies in 1988 against the screening of Martin Scorcese's *The Last Temptation*, based on Kazantzakis' book.[1] In both those cases, the laity and the political leadership stood firmly by the side of Kazantzakis. Here is precisely the problem: that the organised Church has, more readily, identified itself with people such as Augustine of Florina, rather than with the author of *Spiritual Exercises*, and has identified with the side of fear and ideological fanaticism instead of the side of hope.

There is a visible and growing alienation between the clergy and the laity. Symptoms of this alienation, from both sides, include the contempt of many clergymen, especially monastics, for anything 'secular', and likewise, a rising social anticlericalism, among people from various socio-economic strata, who nevertheless consider themselves Christian, and also

---

1. Cf. Ὁ «Τελευταῖος πειρασμὸς» ποὺ ἔφερε τὸν Καζαντζάκη ἕνα βῆμα πρὶν τὸν ἀφορισμὸ' ['The "Last Temptation" that brought Kazantzakis on the verge of aphorism']. Available at: https://fouit.gr/2017/04/15/ ο-τελευταῖος-πειρασμός-που-έφερε-το. Accessed on 20 May 2017.

a growing percentage of people in traditionally Orthodox countries, who do not consider themselves Christian. As an indication for this alienation we can look at the statistics that describe church attendance: In Greece the percentage of people who claim that they attend church regularly is 27%,[1] compared to a 51% in Ireland,[2] 47% in the USA,[3] and 20% in the UK.[4] In Russia, the percentage is 8%[5] – and we also know that most of even these percentages in Orthodox countries reflect the participation of the elderly, while the younger generations are even more dramatically absent from the life of the Church, or hostile to it. In this case, the historical pattern and precedent that should concern us is that of the Reformation, which, among other factors, was caused by a sharp contrast between the clergy (or Rome) and the laity (or the local authorities), despite an overall zeal for Christianity on both sides. In contrast to ancient Christianity, and with very few exceptions (such as in Cyprus), in most Orthodox countries there is no participation of the laity in the election of bishops. In addition, although the tradition of married bishops is ancient, and accepted even among the apostles, the Church decided to ordain to the episcopate only monks, at a time when monasticism was becoming a spiritual model for all Christians, another practice that must be questioned.[6] Therefore, the entire administration of the Church has been transformed to a closed, self-selected club, consisting only of monastics. Nevertheless, to return to the Council, in the context of what we know and what we have experienced in the last few centuries, a larger Church gathering, such as an important council, cannot be limited to a gathering of a small number of bishops who act as representatives of their constituencies, even if these bishops are accompanied and assisted by lay theologians. Mutatis mutandis, we can see that Vatican II, which played a significant role in the regeneration of Roman Catholicism in the middle of the twentieth century, faced some

1. Pew Research Center, 'Global Attitudes Project Spring 2013 Topline'. Available at: http://www.pewglobal.org/category/datasets/2013/?download =31111. Accessed on 20 May 2017.
2. Know Your Faith, 'Mass Appeal – Church Attendance in Ireland'. Available at: http://knowyourfaith.blogspot.co.uk/2009/11/mass-appeal-church-attendance-in_20.html. Accessed 20 May 2017.
3. Pew Research Center, 'US Public Becoming Less Religious'. Available at: http://assets.pewresearch.org/wp-content/uploads/sites/11/2015/11/ 201.11.03_ RLS_II_full_report.pdf. Accessed 20 May 2017.
4. Pew Research Center, 'Global Attitudes Project Spring 2013 Topline'.
5. Pew Research Center, 'Global Attitudes Project Spring 2013 Topline'.
6. Cf. Sotiris Mitralexis, 'A Return to Tradition? The Marriage of Bishops in the (Greek) Orthodox Church', *International Journal of Orthodox Theology* 7:4 (2016), 205-18.

of the same problems that Orthodoxy is facing now: the antagonism with liberation movements (in our case also with ultra-nationalist or pagan revivalist movements), the need to assert the position of the laity within the Church, the need to foster dialogue with the modern world, and the need for internal evangelisation. Since in the Orthodox world we face deeper and more urgent challenges than these, we need and should expect a Council with at least comparable impact as that of Vatican II for the Catholic Church.

Is there a way forward here? I am obviously disappointed with the way our hierarchy understands the structure and the voice of the Church. The ancient Church Councils were not meant to be instruments of *potestas* and *magisterium*, but a framework that would allow a pluralist rather than an exclusivist dialogue, which would address every view and practice that could divide the Church, and it would try to consider these problems in the context of theological reflection, thus finding and showing the way forward to all involved parties. Simply put, heresy was nothing else than the *choice* (which is what the word αἵρεσις means) to leave the conversation, and to establish a separate community. At the dawn of Christianity, the examination of such issues started at the local level, but for matters of consequence to the entire Church, this meant an as complete representation as possible, with ideally the participation of all bishops from across the entire Christian world, for an extended amount of time – sometimes years. The bishops, all of them equal to each other, contributed the testimony of their direct liturgical and communal experience, rather than represent national or local interests in carefully considered and agreed groups. Basil the Great, as we can remember, divided several of the dioceses under his care, ending up in some cases with extremely small dioceses, in order to take more bishops with him in the Second Ecumenical Council – we can perhaps say that he tried to play the system, but the point is that the system was disposed to accept all the voices it could possibly accommodate.

Many centuries after the last Ecumenical Council, in anticipation of what could be one notch less than an Ecumenical Council for the Orthodox Church, we can look into what motivated early Christianity and what, at the same time, the practical and pastoral hopes and challenges of our time are. Although the Orthodox Church is sadly disfigured by centuries of ethnophyletist practice, and this is a reality we cannot ignore, I believe it would be wrong to give in to an Orthodox version of the branch theory, as the Council of Crete effectively did, by allowing itself to be defined by participating national Churches, each of which brought a carefully considered number of delegates.

The branch theory is inconsistent with Orthodox sacramental theology, for which it is essential that we recognise the entire sacramental presence of Jesus in a gathering of two or three people in his name, following Matthew 18:20. In order to appreciate this, however, we need to look at its implications in some theological depth, rather than as a matter of administrative co-ordination. Tangentially, another question which has not been adequately examined is that if we accept this catholicity (if by catholicity we imply that the gathering of the faithful in one place around one chalice manifests the complete Church) at the level of the Eucharistic gathering, we either need to consider the entirety of the sacramental presence of Jesus Christ at the level of the parish rather than at the level of the diocese (which is consistent with ancient Christianity), or to recognise that something is missing from the Eucharistic gathering. Our ecclesiology has not yet defined clearly the difference between the parish and the diocese, or the celebrant-priest from the celebrant-bishop, the primary role of both of whom is to preside over the Eucharistic gathering.[1] Nevertheless, the fragmentation of Orthodoxy into national state churches, sanctioned by the Council in Crete, can only be explained on the basis of a version of the branch theory within the limits of the Orthodox cultural tradition. Sadly, although Orthodox ecclesiology has given us several theological gems in the twentieth century, there is a great difference between Orthodox ecclesiological theology and practice.

All these problems, however, mean that we need to consider a much more open, much more public, and much more extended dialogue than ever before, which will transcend ethnic lines, make obsolete the concept of the ethnic state Church, and revitalise the entire Eucharistic community. The formula of a Council consisting of national representations of bishops, in the context of a local synodal and hierarchical system that has not operated very well for centuries, is an attempt to use a modified fourth century structure in order to address twenty-first century problems. This will not be sufficient.

Despite the decades-long hype and the non-conclusions of the Council in Crete, there are many real theological as well as practical questions that need to be addressed, the first two of which have been posed by Yannaras:

---

1. This is essentially the observation of Demetrios Bathrellos on the episcopocentric ecclesiology of John Zizioulas. Demetrios Bathrellos, 'Church, Eucharist, Bishop: The Early Church in the Ecclesiology of John Zizioulas' in *The Theology of John Zizioulas: Personhood and the Church* ed. Douglas Knight (Routledge, 2007), 133-46.

1. What is the meaning of a Patriarchate today (and therefore how can we address the discrepancy between Orthodox ecclesiology and ethnophyletist practice)?

2. Can salvation be considered an individual achievement or a communal struggle (which touches on pietism and a judicial approach to Christianity)?

3. We could also add a question about the Orthodox understanding of belonging to the Church. Too often the approach we encounter nowadays reflects the reduction of Christianity into an ideology, of a religious correctness that is more precisely defined as Orthodoxism rather than Orthodoxy. This may be seen in the last few decades in the question of millenarism and the end of the world, especially as expressed through literal interpretations of the Apocalypse encouraged by bishops and elders, and which usually reduces salvation to 'belonging to the correct party or ideology', against any serious interpretation of the Book of Revelation. Although this may be a question of lesser theological value, there is a great need for clarity among the faithful, since the numerous ideological, 'Orthodoxist' approaches in circulation, in print or on the internet, articulate fanaticism using Biblical and theological terms.

4. As discussed above, it is necessary to start an examination of anthropology, with particular emphasis on sexuality, and on gender differences and similarities, which would go well beyond citing Biblical passages out of context. The discussion on marriage and its impediments that took place in Crete has nowhere near the depth of the exploration that is needed.

5. It is necessary to conduct a discussion about liturgical practices, which would include corrections of the text (such as the quite important προσφέροντες which has become προσφέρομεν, something that changes dramatically the meaning of one of the most important prayers of the liturgy),[1] parts that have been interjected into the text relatively recently (such as the individual prayers before communion), a discussion and enforcement of the twentieth canon of Nicaea I about kneeling, which is still prevalent in many Orthodox countries, and other liturgical matters. Of course the list can go on and on. It is important that we look at things like that very seriously though, because the Liturgy is, practically and theologically, a product as well as a source of our theological understanding, and of our attitudes concerning communion and salvation. For many people it is the

---

1. A succinct survey of this problem can be found in the late Archimandrite Ephrem Lash's writings. Cf. Ephrem Lash, *The Central Part of the Byzantine Anaphora: a Translator's Notes.* Available at: http://www.thyateira.org.uk/docs/Articles/FrEphrem_KataPanta.pdf. Accessed on 20 May 2017.

only, or at least the main source of theological thought. Therefore, liturgical matters, in the Orthodox Church more than anywhere else, should not be allowed to collapse because of indifference or limited understanding.

I believe that it is necessary to have an extended and prolonged discussion and exploration of such matters that could last two or three years rather than two weeks, with the full participation of bishops, priests, lay theologians and professors, and scientists. This is the kind of theology in the public square that would allow us to air the pastoral and theological issues that threaten to repeat history either with a vertical schism between Greeks and Russians (as took place between Greeks and Franks in the past), or with a horizontal schism between the clergy (especially the higher clergy) and the laity (as it took place in the Western Reformation). The Council of Crete at least succeeded in reminding us that we need to carry on with such discussions, and one of its concluding remarks was indeed that it will be good to continue further after this first step. I believe that this needs to be done at a much larger scale than ever before. Otherwise, I am afraid that history will look on this Council as one of the last opportunities to prevent the fragmentation of Orthodoxy.

In the end, there is only so much we can do. To close with a thought that Christos Yannaras has expressed repeatedly in the face of bleakness, solutions to our most difficult problems often come from unexpected places, not as a credit to our diligent efforts, but as a result of the presence and the operation of the Holy Spirit. To this effect, he cites two examples. First, in the 1960s it seemed certain to everyone that the thousand-year old history of Mount Athos had come to an end, as only a handful of aging monks had remained in these monasteries. But generations of younger monks, many of them educated, with a zeal for the contemplative life and a passion for theology, appeared out of nowhere, manned the dilapidated monasteries and gave a new, unexpected and vibrant life to the monastic peninsula.

The second example is something we see frequently nowadays. Without any apparent clear co-ordination, without the encouragement of a figure such as Nikodemos the Hagiorite who were advocating frequent communion, in the last few years we can see a rising number of frequent communicants, most of them young, in places such as Greece, where the norm among the previous generation was to receive communion only two or three times a year. There is something acting beyond our intellectual discernment here, something that moves despite our best or our worst efforts. It is in the life-giving energies of God that we must place our trust. At the same time, I believe that we need to look at the theological, practical, pastoral and ecclesiological challenges we face, and start talking about them in depth, even if our first reaction is that of despair.

Chapter Eleven
Orthodoxy and the West: The Problem of Orthodox Self-Criticism in Christos Yannaras
Brandon Gallaher

It's time we admitted the truth:
we're Greeks also – what else are we? –
but with Asiatic tastes and feelings,
tastes and feelings
sometimes alien to Hellenism.

C.P. Cavafy[1]

Master and Lord, there was a
measure once.
There was a time when man could say
my life, my job, my home
and still feel clean.
The poets spoke of earth and heaven. There were no symbols

Dennis Lee[2]

'How My Mind Has Changed'

This essay might be called 'How My Mind Has Changed', or, perhaps, 'Why Yannaras is somewhat right about the West and I was somewhat wrong'. I have written about Christos Yannaras' work on a number of occasions including a book review of his great *Orthodoxy and the West* (1992/2006).[3] Until now, I have always argued that Yannaras creates in

---

1. C.P. Cavafy, 'Returning from Greece' in *C. Cavafy: Collected Poems*, trans. Edmund Keeley and Philip Sherard, ed. George Savidis (Princeton: Princeton University Press, 1980), ll.11–15, 187.
2. Dennis Lee, 'Civil Elegies' in *Civil Elegies and Other Poems* (Concord, Ontario: Anansi Press, 1994 [1968]), 2, ll.40-45, 32.
3. See Brandon Gallaher, 'Review of Christos Yannaras', *Orthodoxy and the West:*

regard to Orthodoxy and the West a sterile antinomy between Orthodoxy as Eastern-mystical-communitarian-Greek and Western-rationalist-individualist-Barbarian. In short: Orthodoxy=good; the West=bad. But I was wrong. I have changed my mind. I now think Yannaras' argument is more complex and even nuanced than I formerly gave him credit for, as I mean to show, though I do still think he does slip into language and characterisations of certain thinkers and periods that very easily leads to my previous conclusion. Moreover, part of my former difficulty with his opposition of Orthodoxy and the West was that I have for many years focussed on the continuity between the Orthodox Church and Western Christianity. I now believe I had, as it were, the wrong end of the theological stick. Orthodoxy is not Western in its ecclesial consciousness and part of the challenge of contemporary Orthodox theology is articulating its distinctness, its Easternness, its salt, light, and difference in a wholly Western context. Inevitably, when you are acknowledging that you were wrong, there enters in an element of autobiography about why you made a mistake and of just how precisely you came to be wrong and I shall allude to this element later in the paper. This paper is a personal meditation of sorts on Orthodoxy and the West, laying out what I now think is more accurately the position of Yannaras on this subject, pointing out where I think he is right and where I still depart from his reading of this theme. At the close of this study, I will lay out some basic principles or (in a Lindbeckian vein) 'grammatical rules' which will acknowledge the difference between Orthodoxy and the West without falling into a false opposition between the two, with the denigration of the second and the apotheosis of the first.

Hellenic Self-Identity in the Modern Age, trans. Peter Chamberas and Norman Russell (Brookline, MA: Holy Cross Orthodox Press, 2006), *Logos: A Journal of Eastern Christian Studies,* 50:3-4 (December 2009), 537-42; 'Μιὰ ἐπανεξέταση τῆς Νεο-πατερικῆς σύνθεσης: Ὀρθόδοξη ταυτότητα καὶ πολεμικὴ στὸν π. Γεώργιο Φλωρόφσκυ καὶ τὸ μέλλον τῆς Ὀρθόδοξης Θεολογίας' ['A Re-envisioning of Neo-Patristic Synthesis?: Orthodox Identity and Polemicism in Fr Georges Florovsky and the Future of Orthodox Theology'], trans. Nikolaos Asproulis, Lambros Psomas and Evaggelos Bartzis, *Theologia* 84:1 (2013), 25-92; and 'Eschatological Anarchism: Eschatology and Politics in Contemporary Greek Theology' in *Political Theologies in Orthodox Christianity,* ed. Kristina Stoeckl, Ingeborg Gabriel and Aristotle Papanikolaou, 135-49 (London: Bloomsbury; T. & T. Clark, 2017 [drafted in 2013]).

Christos Yannaras and the Critique of the West

Yannaras repeatedly insists throughout his work that 'the West' has, in a favourite phrase, 'distorted the Christian Gospel'.[1] Here Yannaras consciously builds on the legacy of the Greek American theologian John Romanides (1928-2001)[2] whom he regards as the purest standard of Orthodoxy.[3] Romanides in turn was himself indebted to the (considerably more nuanced) anti-Western polemicism of his teacher Georges Florovsky (1893-1979).[4] Romanides developed an elaborate historical 'myth' of the corruption of Western theology. He argued that Western theology was originally broadly Hellenistic but was tainted by the conquest of the Barbarian tribes of 'Franks' of the Western 'Roman' (=Byzantine Orthodox) Empire in the eighth and ninth centuries. For Romanides, there are neither Latin nor Greek Fathers but only Orthodox 'Romans' in the West and the unsubjugated East who taught 'Roman Orthodox theology' (which is various forms of Palamism) rather than 'Carolingian Frankish' heresy. The fall of the West to the Franks leads to all sorts of heresies, but especially the *filioque* (echoing Vladimir Lossky (1903-1958), another great influence on Yannaras) which 'is as bad as Arianism' and is a sort of corrupt root of Western Christianity, and most of these errors (especially the *filioque*) can be traced to Augustine (354-430) who differed from the 'Roman' St Ambrose (337-397).[5]

---

1. Christos Yannaras, *Orthodoxy and the West*, trans. Peter Chamberas and Norman Russell, (Brookline, MA: Holy Cross Orthodox Press, 2007), 33, 41, 51 etc. and earlier Christos Yannaras, 'Orthodoxy and the West', *Eastern Churches Review* 3:3 (Spring 1971), 286-300.
2. See Marcus Plested: *Orthodox Readings of Aquinas* (Oxford: Oxford University Press, 2015), 205-7.
3. See Yannaras, *Orthodoxy and the West*, 278.
4. See Brandon Gallaher, '"Waiting for the Barbarians": Identity and Polemicism in the Neo-Patristic Synthesis of Georges Florovsky', *Modern Theology*, 27:4 (October 2011), 659-91 (and see the expanded version: 'Μιὰ ἐπανεξέταση τῆς Νεο-πατερικῆς σύνθεσης', 25-92). For texts and commentary, see *The Patristic Witness of Georges Florovsky: Essential Writings*, eds. Brandon Gallaher and Paul Ladouceur (London: Bloomsbury; T. & T. Clark, *forthcoming*).
5. John Romanides, *Franks, Romans, Feudalism, and Doctrine Doctrine: An Interplay between Theology and Society*, Patriarch Athenagoras Memorial Lectures (Brookline, MA: Holy Cross Orthodox Press, 1981), 4ff, 53, 63ff. and 95. Romanides first developed his myth of the Fall of Western theology in *The Ancestral Sin: A Comparative Study of the Sin of Our Ancestors Adam and Eve According to the Paradigms and Doctrines of the First and Second Century Church and the Augustinian Formulations of Original Sin*, trans. George S. Gabriel (Ridegewood, NJ: Zephyr, 2002 [1957]). See also *An Outline of Orthodox Patristic*

Yannaras, like Romanides before him, develops in all his books this 'Fall of the West', this *mythos* or tragic horizon of modern Western self-captivity. I want to trace this *mythos* in some detail in what follows. The discussion of Yannaras' critique of the West has a definite purpose: it is in order to reveal his thought's (often overlooked) self-critical *telos*, the extent to which Orthodox critiques of the West are really attempts to self-critically distinguish the pre-modern vision of Orthodoxy (call it 'East') from its own self-captivity within modernity (call it 'West') and, then, on this basis, to propose some basic theological rules for future Eastern Orthodox (self-) critiques of 'the West.'

Yannaras sees the 'Western deviation' as going back to its roots in Augustine who, he opines, would have remained 'a solitary heretical thinker... if in the 9th century the Franks had not discovered the meaning of his teaching'.[1] Augustine, we are told, is replete with 'numerous examples of legal formalism, absolutised intellectualism, and utilitarian positivism' seen, for example, twelve centuries before Descartes, with the identification of both knowledge and existence with intellection.[2] Indeed, Yannaras even sees in Augustine a sort of proto-utilitarianism (seen as the quintessence of Western thought): 'Knowledge is now linked definitively with the need for a useful result; it is turned into a utilitarian object, subject to the demands of the self-assertion and comfort of the individual.' Here there is a fair bit of conflation of any number of contradictory trends and ideas but the key thought is that Augustine is the polluted origin or, better, the core of the West pictured as a negative spiritual-intellectual vortex sucking all life down into its depths. Augustine is said to be

> commonly recognised as the fountainhead or father of this new era – the Father of Western European philosophy and the civilisation that depends on it – regardless of the viewpoint, ideological principles, or methodological presuppositions with which one approaches history. As the foundation both of Scholasticism and of the Reformation; as the theoretical source of political, religious, and ideological totalitarianism and individualism; as the forerunner both of Descartes' *cogito*

Dogmatics, ed. George Dion Dragas (Rollinsford, NH: Orthodox Research Institute, 2004). There is also The Romans, available at: http://www.romanity. org/index.htm. Accessed on 16 February 2018.

1. Christos Yannaras, *The Elements of Faith: An Introduction to Orthodox Theology* (Edinburgh: T. & T. Clark, 1991), 154-5.
2. Christos Yannaras, *The Schism in Philosophy,* trans. Norman Russell (Brookline, MA: Holy Cross Orthodox Press, 2015), 92.

and Kant's critique and ethics; and as the inspirer of the leading exponents of intellectualism and also mysticism and pietism, Augustine summarises in a single root and principle the many branches and frequently conflicting offshoots of European civilisation – of the only civilisation that embodies a dynamic globalism and constitutes, in relation to every other cultural phenomenon, a new era.[1]

Even stronger yet, Yannaras traces the origins of 'what we now call totalitarianism' to high scholasticism and Aquinas in particular.[2] He claims that from Augustine 'to Thomas Aquinas and up to Calvin' there was completed a new version of 'ecclesiastical orthodoxy' where Orthodoxy becomes a 'religion'.[3] This religion is founded on subjectivism or what he likes to call (especially in his popular *I Kathimerini* columns) 'atomocentrism' which is the turn in scholasticism from reason as a common logos of communion, a participation in the realised community and cosmos to the 'era of *subjective reason*, of the absolute and self-evident priority of the subject' where it 'defines and exhausts the presuppositions for the knowledge of the truth'. This truth, Yannaras argues, was the metaphysical ideology of nascent Roman Catholicism with its elevation of papal authority; that is, this truth is objectively obligatory and focussed in one sole bearer who is the totalitarian ruler of the known world, namely, the Pope of Rome.[4]

Yannaras asserts that scholasticism – despite the fact that scholarship has shown that Aquinas drank deeply of the Greek Fathers and his work has profoundly marked modern Orthodox theology[5] – entirely abandoned the ontological theories of the Greek Fathers of the Christian East in their pursuit of the construction of modern European philosophy on 'the basis of the ontological priority of substance or essence, the logical predetermination of existence, and the restriction of knowledge to the limits of the intellectual capacities of the subject'.[6] In other words, the West and Western theology, from Augustine to Aquinas on down, is characterised by subjectivism, essentialism and hyper-rationalism. It should be noted that there is very little direct engagement of Yannaras – no exegetical engagement of specific works, let alone *ad litteram* commentary – with

---

1. Ibid., 95.
2. Yannaras, *Orthodoxy and the West,* 12 and *Elements,* 158.
3. Yannaras, *Elements,* 156, 158.
4. Yannaras, *The Schism in Philosophy,* 98-9.
5. See Plested, *Orthodox Readings of Aquinas, passim* (and on Yannaras: ibid., 207-8).
6. Yannaras, *The Schism in Philosophy,* 210.

the figures he attacks, such as Augustine and Aquinas. Yannaras even repeatedly attacks throughout his corpus the Gothic Cathedrals as giving material artistic expression to the techniques of scholastic reasoning insofar as they are the first examples of the 'technological violation of natural matter and its subjection to the human understanding, while at the same time being wonderful artistic expressions of the autocratic and emotional imposition of ecclesiastical power and majesty on the human individual'.[1]

What we immediately find puzzling in such broad-brush critiques of medieval cathedrals, which assume that a sort of direct line can be drawn from the rarefied dialectic of the scholars to the workshops of the masons, is why precisely Hagia Sophia (or, say, the Dome of the Rock) does *not* fall under this same critique. Is it somehow artistically a perfect expression of the epistemological universe of Hellenism? If so, how? But to ask such questions is to miss the point of an historical *mythos* of the Fall of the West. The point of such myths is to provide us with a narrative explaining the origins of our own inner spiritual malaise as Westernised beings through a totalising description, what Nietzsche called a 'horizon', of a civilisational vision that is tragically ravaged by a sort of ontological-cum-spiritual virus. We are thereby directed to another mode of life, another horizon and vision, one of health and joy, which supposedly existed before the Fall and of which we can barely conceive as it goes beyond our present horizon's limitations, the absolute presuppositions of our present existence.[2] Historical myths of this sort are goads to action, tools of self-critique, and inspirers of transformation spiritually and politically. The mistake is in thinking of the historical myths found in Yannaras' work as akin to any other contemporary historical interpretation or account of past events. Yannaras' mythologising of the history of the Fall of the West has more in common with the sort of polemical and nostalgic narrative seen in Edward Gibbon's *The History of the Decline and Fall of the Roman Empire* (1776-89) than it does with the portrayal of the gradual, highly ambiguous, as it involved 'curious synchronisms',[3] divergence from a common Christian way between the paths of the very different Christian civilisations of Greek East and Latin West found in more contemporary works of history.[4]

---

1. Ibid., 100.
2. See George Grant, *Time as History*, Massey Lectures, Ninth Series (Toronto: Canadian Broadcasting Corporation, 1974 [1969]), 29-30.
3. Andrew Louth, *Greek East and Latin West: The Church AD 681-1071*, The Church in History, Volume III (Crestwood, NY: St Vladimir's Seminary Press, 2007), 6.
4. E.g. Henry Chadwick, *East and West: The Making of a Rift in the Church, from Apostolic Times Until the Council of Florence* (Oxford: Oxford University Press, 2003) and Louth, *Greek East and Latin West: The Church AD 681-1071*.

For Yannaras, Western Christianity as a religion puts the individual at its core and religion becomes an 'individual event' which is subject to the whims and desires of each person and, above all, the natural need to appease 'the unknown and transcendent – it is an individual effort towards individual faith, individual virtues, individual justification, individual salvation'.[1] With this Western medieval focus on the individual comes man's theorisation in the early modern period (later set out systematically in the Enlightenment) as a rational subject set by nature over and against other such subjects who then calculate their own needs amongst the plurality of subjects. Religion births a new political order as equally diseased as the form of life of the Church and the art that expresses it. First they deduce normative moral principles for all from a logical definition of the common good which is in their interest and then, having accepted this good, they enter into a 'social contract' or mandatory code of law which outlines certain normative rights or powers (a 'claim-demand') to protect them both from other individuals encroaching on them and from the arbitrary use of power from above.[2] The code of law assures the individual that their rights are legally enforceable or mandatory upon all as individual claims.[3] Rights were applied to man regardless of their social class or economic status, or indeed any other difference that marked them out as persons. Here the collectivity of '*societas*' is simply the 'blending together of individuals in the pursuit of common interests . . . an arithmetical sum total of non-differentiated individuals . . . human co-existence as a simple cohabitation on the basis of rational consensus . . . the ideal of societies of unrelated individuals'.[4] In this way, a secular modern realm where the individual was the central focus was fenced off from a sacred realm where there was a meeting of all in a communion of persons. The individual is deprived of his existential difference and uniqueness found in the event of truth which is the community and, above all, the person has taken from him the innermost 'knowledge of subjectivity and identity that comes with reference to a creator God who exercises providential care over his creation'.[5] Secularism is born out of this state of affairs and faith becomes a private mute grasping after transcendence since the 'advancement of

1. Christos Yannaras, 'Human Rights and the Orthodox Church' in *The Orthodox Churches in a Pluralistic World: An Ecumenical Conversation*, ed. Emmanuel Clapsis (Geneva/Brookline, MA: WCC Publications/Holy Cross Orthodox Press, 2004), 83-9. See also Christos Yannaras, *Postmodern Metaphysics*, trans. Norman Russell (Brookline, MA: Holy Cross Orthodox Press, 2004 [1993]), 25.
2. Yannaras, 'Human Rights', 84.
3. Ibid., 83.
4. Ibid., 88.
5. Yannaras, *Postmodern Metaphysics*, 28.

individualism, a characteristic element of modernity, functions as the inexorable alienation of humanity' with ideology taking the place of religious faith, the sacred being eclipsed and substituted by the political rationalisation of the subject.[1] There is, Yannaras argues, a direct line from Western religion's 'individual metaphysical salvation' to the eighteenth century 'secularised (legal) protection' which is the origin of 'the political system of so-called "representative democracy".[2] In modern societies power frees itself from social control and becomes 'technocratic' and subject to the rationalisation of technological and market logic regardless of social needs and national budgets: '"Democratic" government decisions which change people's lives are dictated by considerations freed from all legal control and are sometimes defended on the inviolable grounds of "national security".[3] If this seems to be a rejection of modernity or anti-modern, then that is because it is. Yannaras writes of 'modernisation' as a form of 'fundamentalism':

> One could maintain that the brightest minds in the West are now gathering up their belongings and getting ready to leave the train of Modernity, which is plainly heading for a complete dead end. And it makes no sense at all for us, the peoples of the Balkans and the Middle East, to insist even today on belatedly joining the train of Modernity which intelligent people are hastening to abandon.[4]

Thinking Beyond the West: Hellenism

Yannaras contrasts this apotheosis of egoism and individualism in the West – which birthed modern liberal democracy, modernity, secularisation and the culture of human rights – with Hellenism.[5] Yannaras' vision

---

1. Ibid., 27, 29.
2. Yannaras, 'Human Rights', 87.
3. Yannaras, *Postmodern Metaphysics*, 22.
4. Christos Yannaras, 'The dilemma: modernization-fundamentalism' in Yannaras, *'Generous in Little': A User's Guide* (Athens: Patakis, 2003), 264-76, especially 271, cited in Pantelis Kalaitzidis, 'Orthodox Theology and the Challenges of a Post-Secular Age: Questioning the Public Relevance of the Current Orthodox Theological "Paradigm"' in *Proceedings of the International Conference Academic Theology in a Post-Secular Age* (Lviv: Institute for Ecumenical Studies, UCU/St Andrew's Biblical Theological Institute/DEL, 2013), 4-25 at 6, n. 9.
5. See Demosthenes Gaveas, 'Interview with Christos Yannaras, 24.03.2016'. Available at: http://www.huffingtonpost.gr/2016/03/24/giannaras-sinedeyxi-elliniki-taytotita_n_9517726.html Accessed on 17 February 2018.

of Hellenism can only be described as a sort of idyll of a lost political, liturgical and ontological paradise which inspires us to renew our world, to change society, the Church and, above all, ourselves for the better. It is the lost paradise of the myth of the Fall of the West. This comes out strongly in his description of ancient Greek democracy. In ancient Greece, he argues, there was no need for rights of individuals and, indeed, rights were only applied to social groups and this was because the collectiveness of the citizens, as persons not individuals, were transformed into an 'exercise' or 'event' of truth which is the city. All citizens in this democratic paradise held power together as an event of communion between persons so there was no need to be protected from the arbitrary exercise of power between individuals.[1] The assembly of people, the ancient Greek citizens, did not meet primarily to discuss, judge and take decisions on the ordering of their common life 'but mainly to constitute, concretise and reveal the city' as a way of life according to the truth. This is the direct forebearer of the Eastern Orthodox Church or *ecclesia* (taken from the ancient Greek *polis*) which meets to constitute and reveal itself in the Eucharist according to the truth and after the image of the Trinity where many are one.[2] Politics in such an ethos is a common exercise of life according to the truth where one is 'constituted around the axis of ontology (and not self-interested objectives)'.[3]

Put more theologically, Yannaras holds that Orthodoxy teaches that Christ reveals the mode of God's existence, which is a sheerly free and personal or hypostatic movement of loving communion, and He invites us to share in this gift of grace through incorporation into a loving communion of persons, His Body, the Church as an event of communion. Personhood presupposes a common nature but this common nature does not necessitate our existence, for each person hypostatises himself uniquely in a mode different from any other through his common energies of judgement, will etc. In existing so uniquely, we 'stand out' (*ek-stasis*) from our common nature by revealing who we are in an ecstatic desire to and for an Other whom accepts our disclosure. We are revealed, therefore, as we are in intra-personal loving encounters where we participate in the life of the Other – existing because we love. This self-disclosure is inexhaustible, for we are always learning more of the Other in this loving communion. The Eucharist is the realisation in Christ through the Spirit towards the Father of this experience of loving participation in the Other.

1. Yannaras, 'Human Rights', 85.
2. Ibid., 86.
3. Ibid., 88.

Yannaras and the Critique of the West as Self-Critique

It would be very easy to conclude from much of what has gone before in our exposition that Yannaras is simply and crudely opposing Orthodoxy, understood as what is taught, celebrated and lived in traditional Orthodox countries like Greece, Romania and Russia against the West, understood as the UK, the USA and even Japan. But to conclude this would be an error, albeit one that is understandable, for 'the West' continually seems to be identified in his writings with foreignness[1] and the triumph of the Barbarian German tribes in the Western Roman Empire (the 'Franks'),[2] Western churches,[3] various presuppositions that define Western Christianity culminating in secularism[4] and, as we saw, it is traced by him to Western 'scholasticism', whose poisoned well is Augustine and his 'teachers' (Tertullian and Ambrose).[5] He attacks various eminent Greek theologians such as Nikodemos of the Holy Mountain (1749-1809) as 'Westernised', by which he means *inter alia* that they are guilty of a rationalism that treats God as an Object, a Being amongst beings thus ignoring apophaticism, individualism denying the person, ethical pietism focussed on prescriptive legal codes, a denial that the truth is given in experiential encounter (so ignoring the Palamite distinction of essence and energies) and a forensic approach to the mystery of salvation.[6] In contrast, the 'East' or Orthodoxy, with a seeming Romanticism and blindness to its complex history, seems inevitably tied to the 'Greek spirit',[7] by which he seems to mean not only the Greek Fathers and their characteristic teachings[8] but a uniquely Greek approach to reality[9] expressed in Christian Hellenism[10] and which has its origins in the Greek-speaking Eastern empire.[11]

Is this a wholly accurate reading of Yannaras? Well, yes and no. Yes, insofar as Yannaras all too often reads Western philosophy, religion and art polemically and mythically, resorting to sweeping generalisations and

1. Yannaras, *Orthodoxy and the West*, 184-5.
2. Ibid., 14.
3. Ibid., 184-5.
4. Ibid., 246.
5. Ibid., 16-17.
6. Ibid., 33ff, 49-50, 135, 195, 200-3, 208, 210.
7. Ibid., 126.
8. Ibid., 47ff., 131.
9. Ibid., 8-9, 66-7.
10. Ibid., 251-2.
11. Ibid., vii-viii, 18-19.

ignoring the messiness of its history, its discontinuities where no clear narrative can be traced as he is concerned with his myth of the Fall of the West; say, joining Augustine to Donald Trump and Theresa May. But we must also say 'No', this is not a wholly accurate reading of Yannaras on Orthodoxy and the West, for it leaves out one absolutely crucial element. All that Yannaras writes on the West, he writes as self-critique, self-criticism as reflection on an Orthodoxy that has capitulated to the West, has become Westernised. In a way, the mythic narrative we have just related is an explanation of the decline of contemporary Orthodoxy; its becoming a form of Western religion. A key passage deserves to be quoted at length:

> Let me therefore make one thing absolutely clear. The critique of Western theology and tradition which I offer . . . does not contrast 'Western' with something 'right' which as an Orthodox I use to oppose something 'wrong' outside myself. I am not attacking an external Western adversary. As a modern Greek, I myself embody both the thirst for what is 'right' and the reality of what is 'wrong': a contradictory and alienated survival of ecclesiastical Orthodoxy in a society radically and unhappily Westernised. My critical stance towards the West is self-criticism; it refers to my wholly Western mode of life. I am a Western person searching for answers to the problems tormenting Western people today. The threats to the environment, the assimilation of politics to business models, the yawning gulf between society and the state, the pursuit of ever-greater consumption, the loneliness and the weakness of social relations, the prevailing loveless sexuality – all these seem to go back to the theological differences that once provoked the 'Schism' dividing Christendom into two. Today's individualism and absolute utilitarianism appear to have theological origins.[1]

Westernisation is not only an historical process but also above all an interior and mythic process which defines the malaise of the thinker drowning in the totalising horizon of this age with its individualism, rationalism and essentialism exemplified by Augustine, Anselm, Aquinas, and Descartes. Yet this means the Orthodox thinker is also Western and that his Orthodoxy is split down the middle by the West. We all are Western. The West is in us and is us. It is not elsewhere and outside, for it is the modern and we are the modern. As Yannaras puts it:

---

1. Ibid., viii-ix.

The West in Modernity is no longer the portion or party that at the time of the Schism cut itself off from the body of the One Catholic Church. Now the whole of Christendom is the West, since all of us who bear the name of Christian live integrally and self-evidently within a Western cultural context; we embody the Western mode of life. Our routines, our mental outlook, our reflexes, our prioritisation of needs, the way our social institutions are formed and function are all absolutely obedient to the Western-individualistic not the social-ecclesial model. We live, we think, and we act in the mode fashioned by Augustine, Anselm, Aquinas, and Descartes.[1]

To criticise the West is to trace one's own psychic and personal history, one's place in the common myth, with all its sin and brokenness. It is, in the midst of the Fall, to turn in repentance from this distorted mode of life and attempt to grasp after another horizon beyond one's present which is a sort of civilisational paradise but a paradise that is a living goal for transforming and transfiguring every aspect of reality from the self to the monetary system. Here one might see the weaving of the *mythos* of the Fall of the West and the vision of Hellenism lying just beyond the present horizon as akin to Dante's allegorical narrative of the ascent of Mount Purgatory with the earthly Paradise at its peak, from which one jumps off to heaven, ready for the stars. Yannaras describes this self-critical process of purgation, or *metanoia*, as a turning from the West to Orthodoxy, exemplified by the Orthodox theological focus from the 1960s onwards on individuation as seen through person and eros, and ecclesial life as seen through Eucharistic ecclesiology:

> The incontrovertible fact of the Westernisation of Christians in the Modern age leads us to understand that the ecclesial critique of the errors that led the West to break away from the body of the One Catholic Church cannot today (in the nature of things) be anything but self-criticism (that is, repentance – *metanoia*). There is no entity called the West 'confronting' Orthodoxy; the West is 'within us' and Orthodoxy is the common nostalgia of all who perceive the falling away of both East and West. . . . An attempt to express a criticism of the West in the form of Christian self-criticism began with sincerity and with no little risk in the 1960s on

1. Christos Yannaras, '2011 Commencement Address at Hellenic College and Holy Cross Greek Orthodox School of Theology'. Available at: http://www. hchc.edu/about/news/news_archive/1548 Accessed on 17 February 2018.

two fundamental levels of interconnected topics: On the
level of ontology, . . . [a] hermeneutic of the existential event
on the basis of the reality of *person* and *eros*. And on the
corresponding level of the reconnection of the ecclesial event
with the chiefly existential problem, on the basis of the so-
called *eucharistic ecclesiology*.[1]

We also see this self-critical aspect of Yannaras' critique of the West
in his scathing attacks on Orthodoxy and its expressions in historical
and contemporary Greece. Yannaras claims, as we said earlier, that
from Augustine 'to Thomas Aquinas and up to Calvin' there was
completed a new version of 'ecclesiastical orthodoxy' where Orthodoxy
becomes a 'religion' and is now 'the confirmation to institutionalised
ideology – which is sovereign because it is logically and socially and
metaphysically obligatory'.[2] The contemporary Orthodox Churches, he
claims, are examples of precisely such Westernisation in turning the
Church into a religion, 'religious Orthodoxism'.[3] In his *Against Religion*
(2006/2013) and in newspaper columns in the well-known daily *I
Kathimerini*, he relentlessly chronicles the 'religionisation of the ecclesial
event' which is its refocusing on individualism and objectification. He
relates how Orthodoxy has become 'Orthodoxism' from seeing salvation
as a reward for individual moral effort and the reduction of the ecclesial
event of the liturgy to a 'sacred rite' to the idolisation of tradition,
worship of bishops and monastic elders and the promotion of a false
asceticism which demonises all sexuality: 'The Orthodox version of the
Church's catholicity seems now to have been replaced by an ideological
and radically religionised understanding of Orthodoxy'.[4] One of the most
Western manifestations of the West today, Yannaras contends, can be
found in the 'ideological anti-Westernism of the "Orthodox" opponents
of the West, the individualism of the "Zealots" of Orthodoxy' such
as the monks of Athos who turn the event of truth and communion
into an intellectual certainty.[5] In a startling critique, he even attacks
the individualistic piety of the selection of texts in St Nikodemos the
Hagiorite's *Philokalia*, regarded by many as the quintessence of Orthodox

---

1. Ibid.
2. Yannaras, *Orthodoxy and the West*, 156, 158.
3. Christos Yannaras, *Against Religion,* trans. Norman Russell (Brookline, MA:
   Holy Cross Orthodox Press, 2013), 183.
4. Ibid., 182.
5. Christos Yannaras, '2011 Commencement Address at Hellenic College and Holy
   Cross Greek Orthodox School of Theology'.

spirituality,[1] as yet more evidence of Orthodoxy's failure, its missing of the target of the ecclesial struggle for free ecstatic love in communion with the Other:

> We Orthodox like to accuse the West of institutional rigidity and of imposing religionisation on the ecclesial event, of submitting it to intellectualism, moralism, and legalism. But the case of the *Philokalia* proves rather that the 'West' is within us – its historical outgrowths dwell in an obscure way in the 'inward' instinctive need of every human being for the individualistic self-protection and assurance.[2]

Orthodoxy and the West: A Personal Account

Though I now acknowledge that I previously misunderstood Yannaras on Orthodoxy and the West, I continue to be unhappy with any *sterile polarity* between East and West which his work all too easily slips into in its polemicism. Part of what has led to my reappraisal of Yannaras is in more clearly seeing – after reaching the date at which I had spent more than half of my life as Orthodox which coincided with my working at the Holy and Great Council of Crete in June 2016 – that Orthodoxy or the Faith of the Orthodox Church is *not a product of the West*. By the West I mean the culture and civilisation of the modern age, what Heidegger called the 'Age of the World Picture',[3] and I would agree with Yannaras that at its core is a vision of individual reason as an abstract power that posits that which is before it as an object of enquiry, its relentless gaze stripping that which is thought down to its essentials, to each of its distinct parts that are known, with all mystery and dark depths eliminated by the klieg lights of rationality. That which is exists, then, in thought as an object of subjectivity, which is thrown forward and interrogated to explain its secrets. This is a challenging of both beings and ultimately Being to reveal its *reasons* for being. It is a reification of existence to the end that reality can be used as a means to empower the self who is supreme and defines existence by his ratiocination of it. This way of thinking was something relatively new in history when it was

---

1. See Brock Bingaham and Bradley Nassif, eds., *The Philokalia: Exploring the Classic Text of Orthodox Spirituality* (Oxford: Oxford University Press, 2012).
2. Yannaras, *Against Religion*, 196.
3. See Martin Heidegger, 'The Age of the World Picture', in *The Question Concerning Technology and Other Essays*, trans. William Lovitt (NY: Harper & Row, 1977), 115-54.

first developed through the nascent movement of scholasticism, though one can no doubt find traces of it in earlier periods. It was developed systematically in the Renaissance, with its understanding of man as the rational measure between heaven and earth, and from it blossomed the age of the revolutions. The focus on instrumental abstracting reason, and with it the slow turn to the cosmos being defined by the gaze of the individual, is thus the basis of technology, not merely as bits of machinery from my Apple Mac computer to a dishwasher but as a way of thinking which takes political and economic shape in representative democracy, mass capitalism and industry from the steam engine to Twitter. We see this type of instrumentalising Western modern reason in Milan Kundera's *The Unbearable Lightness of Being* where the Don Juan of the book – and Kundera is echoing Kierkegaard's Johannes the Seducer in *Either/Or* – is the Czech surgeon Tomas who pursues women not for love or the pleasure of sex, but for the sake of the will to power:

> Tomas was obsessed by the desire to discover and appropriate that one-millionth part; he saw it as the core of his obsession. He was not obsessed with women; he was obsessed with what in each of them is unimaginable, obsessed, in other words, with the one-millionth part that makes a woman dissimilar to others of her sex. . . .
>
> So it was a desire not for pleasure (the pleasure came as an extra, a bonus) but for possession of the world (slitting open the outstretched body of the world with his scalpel) that sent him in pursuit of women.[4]

If this is the West, then it differs from the faith of the Orthodox Church, Orthodoxy, as it still can be glimpsed in its tradition of liturgy and hesychastic prayer and is still available through the cycle of its services and its fasts and feasts as well as, acknowledging its problems, the ascetic life lived with greatest intensity in places like Athos, Sinai and Archimandrite Gregory Papazian's Holy Transfiguration Hermitage in Lone Butte in the interior of British Columbia, Canada. Orthodoxy comes from, was forged in and, in a way, maintains a perpetual memorial of a Christian civilisation which remains a sort of alternative narrative of Christianity to the one found in so many diverse forms in the West (and by West I include traditional Orthodox countries). Call it, if you must, the 'Christian East'. Western Christianity, which has given birth to the paradigm of modernity found in Western European culture

---

4.   Milan Kundera, *The Unbearable Lightness of Being*, trans. Michael Henry Heim (New York: HarperCollins, [1984] 1991), 200.

and civilisation, has a strong, and much needed, emphasis on rational symmetry, legal, ecclesial and liturgical order while the individual Christian is faced in faith with the awesome gift of the grace of Christ for salvation.

Orthodoxy, and here I want to emphasise that it can, although all too often does not, stand in creative not sterile polarity with the West, speaks in poetry, is chaotic and messy, is concerned with the upholding of particular community visions that often will clash with what is held as universal, is often just offensive and illiberal and always sides with drama over reason. Orthodoxy needs the gifts of the West and Western Christianity, above all Roman Catholicism. Its emphasis on particular community visions often leads to chaos and a complete internal breakdown in decision making as was seen at the Holy and Great Council of Crete in June 2016. Here a spiritual primacy of Peter, but a primacy with juridical teeth, far away from papal infallibility and universal jurisdiction, would be a gift in allowing the Orthodox Church to express its mind in a new context and age, helping it to balance its particular ecclesial and cultural visions with the universal whole. We need a creative, not a sterile, polarity: an interpenetration of East in West and West in East.

In some ways, Western Christianity needs Orthodoxy more than Orthodoxy needs it, for so much contemporary Western religion is, in its modernisation, chatty, tidy, moralistic and abstract like the secular sphere it engendered. Orthodoxy can help contemporary Western Christianity to remember its own pre-modern roots. It of course shares the essentials and much besides with modern Western Christianity but it retains other key elements of a pre-modern, non-Western spirituality still seen in religions like traditional non-Wahhabist Islam and much of Japanese Buddhism, amongst which I include: its doxological and sacrificial way of reasoning; its belief that the cosmos is filled with 'gods' or 'spirits', some malevolent (call them devils) and others good (call them saints), and that these spirits can be communicated with for good or ill; its belief that creation and God inter-penetrate and that creation is a theophany of the divine glory; that God and the world are one differentiated reality (whose unity and difference is unperceived); that in order to perceive this unity one must cleanse the senses through ascetic labours and this presupposes a normative behaviour; that through grace and a spiritual *podvig* one can realise in one's body and consciousness God's union with His creation (call this *theosis* or enlightenment); that religion is not privatised but speaks to the minutiae of life, including the ordering of society which in every part is called to transfiguration and thereby secularism in its popular sense of a 'neutral sphere' is a lie; that the cosmos is structured in a hierarchy where each level mediates love and light to the one below; and that the heart of reality is light and silence. I find that many of these themes have been lost in Western Christianity – including, sadly, portions of Latin Catholicism – though it certainly still retains the Christian distinctives of the centrality of Christ, God as Holy Trinity and the Church as the Body of Christ. Lacking so much of the ancient context, however, it becomes at times hard to see the connection to classical Christianity and the links to other classical/traditional religious traditions.

Part of the reason I have come to this position is the June 2016 Holy and Great Council of Crete where I worked for my church, the Ecumenical Patriarchate, in its Press Office as a Subject Expert in Theology.[1] Crete was the first modern ecclesial meeting of Orthodoxy on a universal level, which brought together hierarchs from as many contexts and churches as possible. The Council of Crete – in being a universal modern Church council – was the first stop along the way for Orthodoxy of coming to accept on a universal level that Byzantium is no more. Byzantium has a sort of liturgical afterlife in Orthodoxy, like Yeats' 'sages standing in God's holy fire/As in the gold mosaic of a wall'.[2] At Crete you begin to have a faint recognition by the Orthodox Church that Constantinople has fallen and will never return and never be revived. We are all, in some sense, Western now. What was clear in the documents and the discussion of the hierarchs is that Orthodoxy was elaborating itself in a post-Byzantine modern context. This explains much of the reactionary quality and the apologetic tone of many of the council documents, which both attacked modern Western ills like 'secularism' and 'globalisation' (which, it was alleged, give birth to things like genetic experimentation and same-sex marriage), and which simply stated in a sort of summary form the status quo of Orthodox practices post-Byzantium. But if Crete was the beginning of an attempt to articulate an Orthodox world after Byzantium then it was also the first universal conciliar attempt to acknowledge that it now finds itself in a new Western order that it has not created but which it now must respond to creatively.

---

1. See Brandon Gallaher, 'The Orthodox Moment: The Holy and Great Council in Crete and Orthodoxy's Encounter with the West: On Learning to Love the Church', *Sobornost*, 39.2 (2017), 26-71.
2. W.B. Yeats, 'Sailing to Byzantium', *The Collected Poems of W. B. Yeats*, 2nd Ed., ed. Richard J. Finneran (NY: Simon & Schuster Inc., 1996), ll.17-18, 193-94.

A Grammar for Orthodox Critiques of the West

In order to respond creatively to this new Western order, Orthodox theology needs to avoid falling into anti-Western polemicism without in any way denying that Orthodoxy at its core is not the West, even if it has in the modern period succumbed to Westernisation or its own religionisation. Here, briefly, in light of the study of Yannaras and in conclusion, I want to lay out a number of grammatical rules for Orthodox theologians when they discuss Orthodoxy's relationship with the West that both avoid a polemical attack on the West and a concomitant glorification of contemporary Orthodoxy. These rules would also help Orthodox theology not to fall into the trap of simply seeing the contemporary neo-liberal Western order as something for which Orthodoxy should strive. I am referring to the contemporary theological tendency of some Orthodox to call for 'reformation' or 'liberalisation', to call for Orthodoxy to update itself and seeing it as irredeemably irrelevant and out of step with the spirit of the age.

Rule 1: What should be clear from everything we have stated so far is that any Orthodox position on the West needs to lead with its weakness and begin with self-critique. Humility is endless and an Orthodox world that can look at itself and see its flaws, its need for repentance, renewal and even reformation, is one which people will be attracted to rather than repulsed by. What was most evident in the Crete documents – which were largely drafted by a small coterie of academic theologians trained at Athens and Halki and then revised by the representatives of the other local churches – was their triumphalistic and reactionary anti-Western tone.

Rule 2: Any discussion of Orthodoxy and the West, especially if it tries to give an historical account of this relationship, should acknowledge the discontinuity of history, its sharp breaks, its clashes and contradictions and, above all, its ambiguity. This means it will be more difficult to trace a sort of founding narration of the West with a clear break at the eleventh century, perhaps ending up showing how the sort of instrumental and subjective reasoning we have discussed can be seen much earlier in certain Greek Fathers. In emphasising historical discontinuity over continuity, however, it will be far more honest, and indeed persuasive. By identifying certain trends that are distinctively Western, arguing that these trends would grow into the civilisation that is archetypically modern, and by not immediately placing them in one era and with one intellectual movement, this will bolster the plausibility of the historical story, especially if we see Western tendencies of thought at work in non-Western contexts but still leading to modernisation (e.g. Japan in the late 1860s).

Rule 3: Just as I have said that one should focus on historical discontinuity over continuity, so, too, one should avoid writing great thinker narratives that offer only one origin or root for complex historical phenomena. It is not plausible to see Augustine or Aquinas or, if you like, Duns Scotus (as in some thinkers of Radical Orthodoxy) as a sort of epistemological villain to whom one can trace everything from nominalism, the *cogito ergo sum* and Google to Mill's principle of utility, purgatory and, say, social media. Moreover, if we are to have a focus on such great thinkers then any discussion of their work must be grounded in *ad litteram* commentary and historically informed exegesis. It is not enough to attack Augustine's philosophical essentialism without a discussion in detail of Book 14 of his *De Trinitate* and showing how this tendency of thought was appropriated differently (but commonly) by both Aquinas and Palamas.

Rule 4: Any account of Orthodoxy and the West should be one where if it discusses East and West then it should do so by showing how these two realities exist in dialectical interpenetration. Each is dependent on the other and each touches the inner life of the other.[1] Orthodoxy cannot be creatively modern until it acknowledges that in some sense all are Western now and that there is no hermetically sealed Easternness to which one can flee, whether it be Athos or Holy Russia.

Rule 5: To understand the West in its difference from Orthodoxy – a non-Westernised Orthodoxy retained in the liturgical consciousness of the services of the Church and the tradition of the 'prayer of the heart' – one should focus less on the slippery and easily polemicised terms of 'East' and 'West' (or 'Greek' and 'Barbarian') but on the various notions of the 'modern'. We need to ask to what extent we can say that Orthodoxy has retained some sense of the Christian form of pre-modernity. In asking this sort of question, one will inevitably look at the West or Western European Civilisation less monolithically but as the wellspring of a paradigm of the modern which has been pluralised throughout the world from Indonesia to Japan. There is no one West, just as there is no one form of the modern, but instead 'multiple modernities' (Eisenstadt),[2]

---

1. See Gallaher, 'Μιὰ ἐπανεξέταση τῆς Νεο-πατερικῆς σύνθεσης', 82-92.
2. See S.N. Eisenstadt, 'Multiple Modernities' in *Comparative Civilizations and Multiple Modernities*, 2 Vols. (Leiden/Boston: Brill, 2003), 2, 535-60. See also *Comparing Modernities: Pluralism Versus Homogenity: Essays in Hommage to Shmuel N. Eisenstadt* ed. Eliezer Ben-Rafael and Yitzhak Sternberg (Leiden/Boston: Brill, 2005).

contradictory and competing. If there can be a Japanese form of modernity (rather, there are many forms), then why cannot we speak of an Orthodox form of modernity? Why cannot Orthodoxy creatively appropriate and adapt modernity, allowing for an 'alternate modernity'?[1]

Rule 6: Lastly, if Orthodoxy retains to some extent a vision of the premodern which is apart from the West in all its sundry forms, including the religionised or Westernised forms of Orthodoxy, then surely we should be looking to compare it to other non-Christian civilisations that have also retained to some extent a form of non-Western spirituality. Here we are laying out the first portion of the argument as to why it is imperative for the Orthodox to have some engagement with other religions; specifically, an Orthodox comparative theology.[2]

Conclusion: The Fate of Orthodox Theology

The significance of our study of Yannaras on 'Orthodoxy and the West' the problem of Orthodox self-criticism goes far beyond simply understanding better a great but much maligned contemporary thinker. It has a universal dimension for contemporary Orthodox theology. Orthodox theology contains both polarities of East and West, Orthodoxy and Western thought in a ceaseless creative tension, which illumines the fate, cultural tragedy and opportunity/crisis of Orthodox theology in the contemporary West: to find itself unhappily Westernised in a new modern Western order that its Christian vision has not created, but which it now must respond to and shape creatively from the depths of that living tradition.

---

1. See Brandon Gallaher, 'A Tale of Two Speeches: Secularism and Primacy in Contemporary Roman Catholicism and Russian Orthodoxy' ed. John Chryssavgis, *Primacy in the Church: The Office of Primate and the Authority of the Councils, Volume 2: Contemporary and Contextual Perspectives* (Crestwood, NY: St Vladimir's Seminary Press, 2016), 807-37.
2. See 'International Consulation on "Eastern Orthodoxy and Inter-Religious Encounter in a Secular Age"', available at: http://www.acadimia.org/en/news-announcements/press/477-international-consultation-on-eastern-orthodoxy-and-inter-religious-encounter-in-a-secular-age. Accessed 17 February 2018.

Chapter Twelve
The Theology of Personhood: A Study of the Thought of Christos Yannaras
Rowan Williams

Reprinted and adapted from Sobornost 6 (1972), 415-30.

This article will be devoted chiefly to an examination of Christos Yannaras' doctoral thesis presented to the University of Salonika ('The Ontological Content of the Theological Notion of Personhood', Athens, 1970), a remarkable essay in 'theological personalism'. Those of us familiar with the work of the late Vladimir Lossky, especially his various studies of the significance for Christian theology of the Chalcedonian distinction between 'nature' and 'person', will recognise familiar themes in Dr Yannaras' book, though here they are given a philosophical grounding, of great subtlety and sophistication, which would have been somewhat alien to Lossky's general style of doing theology. Indeed, Lossky's near-Barthian hostility, during most of his career, to secular philosophy makes it very hard to assess the extent to which, consciously or unconsciously, he utilised motifs from his philosophical contemporaries: there are times when a reader of Lossky (especially of his work in the early 1950's)[1] will catch some quite pronounced echoes of Merleau-Ponty, even of Sartre; but one can hardly doubt that Lossky would have repudiated indignantly any suggestion of 'influence'. This consideration gives Dr Yannaras' work an added interest for the student of Lossky: a glance at the bibliography shows us Lossky (represented by the 'Theologie mystique', and the posthumous collection, 'A l'Image et a la Ressemblance de Dieu') side by side with Heidegger, Husserl and Sartre. What Dr Yannaras has attempted, in fact, is a synthesis of what may loosely be called the Greek Patristic tradition (conceived of as including Palamas and other medieaevals) and

---

1. See especially Vladimir Lossky's articles on 'Rédemption et Déification', 'La notion théologique de la personne humaine' and 'La théologie de l'image' in the collection *A l'image et à la ressemblance de Dieu* (Paris: Aubier-Montaigne, 1967).

modern phenomenological thought. An earlier work ('The Theology of
the Absence and Ignorance of God', Athens, 1967; now available in a
French translation)[1] provided a basis for this in a comparison between
the Byzantine apophatic tradition, and the confrontation with 'Nothing'
in the philosophy of Heidegger: this study also made extensive use of
Nietzsche, and attempted to present the 'Death of God' and existential
nihilism as a logical and inevitable growth from the rationalism of the
Western theological tradition. It is a highly provocative work, and one
may, I think, legitimately object to the vast sweep of its generalisations;
but it is undeniably a very significant essay in what does appear to be
genuinely an alternative theological language to that which has become
customary in the Latin tradition and its offshoots. I hasten to add that
the fact that it is an alternative does not automatically guarantee its
superiority: in assessing Dr Yannaras' work, as in assessing that of other
Eastern theologians, it is important not to be hypnotised by sheer novelty
into suspending our critical faculties.

On the whole, the present work seems less determined in its expression
by a desire to present a sharp contrast to 'Western' theology: Aristotle
is quoted fairly frequently as a spokesman for 'classical metaphysics', but
Latin theologians are hardly ever referred to by name. The argument of
the book is positive rather than controversial in character, and exhibits
a remarkable integration of sources and authorities into the body of the
thesis: there are long sections devoid of footnotes or quotations, but no less
rigorous and precise for that. However, I must register a complaint about
the rather annoying repetition of 'Leitmotif' phrases in Heideggerese 'the
potentiality for universal ek-static personal relatedness' (or variants of
this wording)[2] recurs time and time again. Granted that, for those with
some acquaintance with Heidegger, it is the most exact statement possible
of what is involved in the concept of 'relation', must it be used *every* time
this concept is under review? Perhaps, however, this is simply the reaction
of a mind acclimatised to the pedestrian phraseology of Anglo-Saxon

1. Christos Yannaras, 'An Orthodox Comment on "The Death of God"' in *Sobornost*
    5:4 (Winter 1966) and in *Orthodoxy and the Death of God*, ed. A.M. Allchin
    (Studies Supplementary to Sobornost 1. London: Fellowship of St Alban and St
    Sergius, 1971), 40-9, gives what amounts to a summary of the conclusions of this
    book.
2. E.g. μοναδικὴ δυνατότης εἶναι ἔναντι τῶν ὄντων (Christos Yannaras, 'Τὸ
    Ὀντολογικὸν περιεχόμενον τῆς θεολογικῆς ἐννοίας τοῦ προσώπου' ['The
    Ontological Content of the Theological Notion of Personhood'] (PhD diss.,
    Aristotle University of Thessaloniki, 1970), 17), ἡ διάστασις τῆς καθολικότητος,
    ἡ ἐκστατικὴ φορὰ τοῦ προσώπου (21), δυνατότης προσωπικῆς ἀναφορᾶς,
    προσωπικῆς σχέσεως (23), and so on.

philosophy to what appears to be Teutonic mystification. Certainly, the dialogue with Heidegger is the main them of the whole work; and it might be of some interest and value to compare Yannaras' use of Heidegger with Rahner's.[1] On a superficial examination, they would appear to have a good deal in common; but a detailed study of this lies outside the scope of the present paper (and the abilities of the author!).

It may be as well, at this point, to attempt a summary of Dr Yannaras' argument. He begins by noting the relational element in the Greek πρόσωπον (person), the aspect of πρὸς – ὦψ/ὠπός, the existence of person only over-against, in relation to someone or something; 'We know being as presence (παρουσία), not essence (οὐσία)',[2] we cannot know 'Being-in-itself' as *such*. Our acts of knowing, then, are not merely intellectual, they are an orientation of our personhood in *relation*, the outgoing openness to other realities which Heidegger calls 'ek-stasis'. The reality or unreality of entities depends on their relatedness or not-relatedness to persons; personhood, then, is the 'horizon' (ὁρίζων in Greek means 'that which determines or defines') upon which all beings manifest themselves, and so it may be said to have a 'universal' character. Personhood is not a part of human nature, it defines nature, it is the 'ontological starting-point' for understanding nature. Not that it is (in Sartre's sense) the 'source' of existence: rather, existence is to be perceived only *in* persons. One consequence of this is that we cannot properly conceive of God as a 'First Cause', external to His effects: if He is personal, we must see Him as creative energy relating to creation in the present, establishing communion between Himself and His creatures. Another consequence is that any idea of the image of God as residing in a 'part' of man must be abandoned: the person is a unity, not merely a synthesis (as in the Aristotelian system), the body is not a component in man, it is his mode (τρόπος) of existence, the manifestation to the outside world of the 'energies' of his nature, that through which personal presence or absence may be apprehended. The image of God is the whole man; and it is the whole man who enters into relation with God. He may know God by way of 'absence', that is, he may know him through the manifestation of His energies in creation (as one 'knows' the absent artist through his work); or he may know Him as personal presence, as Christ in the Church. Outside the Church, only the former way is possible; yet

---

1. It is interesting to note that John Meyendorff (*Christ in Eastern Christian Thought*, 165-6) suggests some points of contact between Rahner and the Greek Patristic tradition.

2. Yannaras, 'Τὸ Ὀντολογικὸν περιεχόμενον', 13: the responsibility for translation of quotations from the Greek is the present writer's.

even here, the absence is personal, the absence of someone, and so it is painful. Within the Church, this experience is familiar to the man of prayer – hence the πένθος ('compunction', 'lamentation') associated in the East with the ascetic life.

The emergence of beings into personal relation can thus be seen as an emergence into order, unity, the formation of a *cosmos,* in fact: Anaximander was essentially right in comparing cosmic order with moral and social order. Contemporary science has abandoned any crude notion of absoluteness or necessity in physical 'laws', and has stressed indeterminacy and asymmetry in things: the concept of a closed and regular system governed by immutable laws is as untenable as the concept of an 'Unmoved Mover' as the first term of such a system. Both alike are based on an objectification of reality which scrupulously avoids the personal. The cosmos much now be seen as 'a universal harmony in an infinity of indeterminate distinctions',[1] a manifestation of personal being in a set of unique, unrepeatable realities.

The awareness of this multiplicity as a harmonious set leads us to the apprehension of universal objective 'beauty', of 'reason' (λόγος) in creation, to the person of the Logos, in fact, manifested through life-giving energy, the Spirit.

Our categories of space and time are dependent on the ideas of personal presence and absence, also. The 'personal dimension of space' appears in awareness of personal absence, where 'distance' has nothing to do with 'geometrical', objectively measurable space: we are dealing with a non-objectified, *relational* space. This experience of absence, as Sartre makes clear,[2] is tragic, it is 'agony'; yet at the same time, it presupposes and establishes the possibility of relation to an authentic reality. Thus Heidegger can speak[3] of death as a phenomenon of life, a final personal revolt against the constant failure to achieve authentic personal relation in 'geometric' space: 'Death is the apophatic definition of personhood.'[4] Similarly, time is to be regarded as the recognition of outgoing ('ek-static') relation as *change,* not as an external computation of movement, but as a dimension of relation itself, a part of the *being* of things. In our experience, however, awareness of continuity is awareness of 'corruption', of movement towards death; so that again death appears as, in some way, the vehicle of the possibility of 'total' relationship, because it

1.   Yannaras, 'Τὸ Ὀντολογικὸν περιεχόμενον', 37.
2.   Jean-Paul Sartre, *L'être et le néant* (Paris: Gallimard, 1976), 44f.
3.   Martin Heidegger, *Sein und Zeit* (Tübingen: Walter de Gruyter, 1969), 245-6; quoted in Yannaras, 'Τὸ Ὀντολογικὸν περιεχόμενον', 44.
4.   Yannaras, 'Τὸ Ὀντολογικὸν περιεχόμενον', 45.

manifests the finally limited character of merely individual, 'atomistic' existence. In human life, we are aware of personal energy as 'enduring', as extending individuality into totality, outside the limits of temporal succession and death: this is what we experience through the work of art, a communion with the artist unconditioned by the circumstances of his or our individual historical circumstances, an awareness of *presence*. So the relation of man to the cosmos which we measure as 'time' has its real end beyond time, limitation, corruption, death, in a duration of presence. And at this point, we may introduce the Person of the Logos again, as the person to Whom *all* realities are 'present', in this sense, and Who is present in all realities (as the artist is in his creation). The presence is made experienced reality in the sacraments of the Church; which is why we may speak of the establishment of a 'liturgical time' in the Church, the union of past, present, and future in the presence of the Word – the Kingdom of God, eternal life – which gives us the ground for a faint apprehension of the 'time' of the Holy Trinity, which is eternity, the measure of *perfect* personal communion.

'Logos' is therefore never merely a detached statement, but is an attitude, an involvement in 'what there is'; it is at the same time a gathering up of diverse elements in a universal (because personal) unity, and a definition of the distinct modes in which this unity exists. It is the medium through which things are manifested to, brought into relation with the person: the uniqueness of the word is the uniqueness of the relation it 'names' (the uniqueness of the work of art). The word reveals personhood through the outgoing creative 'energies' of nature, nature's capacity to show itself as personal. We are again led to the theological notion of a cosmic personal Word, establishing the reality of all things in relation to the Person of God. The 'expressive energy'[1] of the human word reveals the cosmic Word, and reveals Him as a second partner in a 'dia-logical' relation, the encounter of two persons in outgoing reciprocity, κοινωνία.

However, the capacity for this sort of relatedness is a possibility, not an automatically realised necessity: we must reckon with the fact of human *fallenness*, the empirical fact that man exists in a state of 'atomistic' self-consciousness, connected to other such consciousnesses solely in virtue of a shared objective relation to the 'world', or to 'absolute reality'. The idea of Being is thereby reduced to that which exists, opposed to that which does *not* exist – Nothing (Μηδέν, Sartre's 'Neant'): nothingness is, as it were, introduced into the definition of Being, as a possibility; the possibility of the universality of Being-as-relation is denied. There are only individual entities existing in 'distance' (ἀπόστασις) from the whole:

---

1. Ibid., 63.

mutual absence is the basic ontological category, Being is identified with Nothingness. Hence the problem in contemporary art and philosophy of 'one-dimensional man', existing in alienation, in the absence of relation: the reality of the person is wholly obscured, and there is thus nothing to bridge the gulf between the individual and the whole, the mass. Yet we can only understand this 'fall' as a *personal* decision, the result of the ability of freedom to deny itself, to subordinate itself to 'nature'. We are bound to presuppose some degree of awareness of our impotence, awareness of failure, and thus of the possibility of something different. Nothingness, then, is not an empty concept, known only as the opposite of existence, it is a personal experience of the absence of relation: and the necessity ('ontological', not conceptual) of the universal second person again appears. Man experiences a divine call, an invitation to enter into relation, and so to become truly personal: personhood is known as response to the invitation of the Divine Person, its 'truth' is to be found outside the mere 'givenness' of finite facts. In this invitation, this outgoing of personal energy, the unknowable Divine essence becomes known as content of person (not known 'in itself'): the mode of God's being is personal communion.

What we are talking about is the *perfect* revelation of personhood; and so we must say that God does not 'emerge' into personhood, He *is* personal. And since fullness of personal being-in-communion is beyond singularity and duality, we are right to think of Him as Trinity: in our relation to God, our response to His call, we apprehend His energy as triadic, and, at the same time, as kenotic: each Person 'witnesses' to the others in continual περιχώρησις. This personal energy is the foundation of finite, created personhood: the Godhead 'comes out of' Its Essence, in free exercise of will, to establish a new reality possessed of the power of standing-over against God in personal freedom, the capacity to affirm or to deny God's call. To deny it is to be condemned to 'atomic' individuality, the condition in which 'Hell is other people', when 'every "other" is a direct confirmation of the failure of the person to deny ... the fragmentation of nature into self-sufficient individuals'.[1] And it is this which the Church asserts that Christ has overcome, not simply by 'volitional' response to God's call, but by the union of the Divine and human natures: the possibility is opened to man of existing as truly personal nature, being-in-communion. This change in nature is conveyed to us through the Sacraments, but it should not be seen as in any way an obliteration of created freedom: rather is it the attainment of true freedom by on-going 'conversion' (μετάνοια). And so the experience of 'Nothing' is revealed

1. Ibid., 81.

finally as a confirmation not only of human freedom but also of the personal reality of God: Christ's descent into Hell is 'the transformation of Nothingness, of the abyss of human failure, into a triumph for the love and benevolence (φιλανθρωπία) of God'.[1]

If God is personal, κατ' οὐσίαν, we cannot speak of Him in ethical terms as they are normally employed, since the concept of an ethic presupposes a *fall*. Morality properly considered is the measure of a person's 'fullness of personal existence', existence in communion, and, as we have seen, God is not *becoming* personal, as we are, He *is* the fullness of personal existence. This means that morality is intimately related to Being, it is an ontological idea: a failure to consider it ontologically leads to the idea of some absolute division between 'principles' of good and evil, a dualism in creation. The identification of Being with the 'Idea of the Good' is really nothing other than a vast absolutisation of concepts; and talk of good as not being 'for' anything or anyone reduces it to a purely intellectual abstract, unconnected with the business of life in communion or relation. We must refuse to give an ontological content to the concepts of 'good' and 'evil' (paradoxically, this always leads eventually to a 'socialised' utilitarian idea of good): the refusal of the Eastern theological tradition to allow ontological reality to evil implies a complete rejection of the dualism, distinguishing not good and evil, but Being and Nothing, life and death, affirming morality as a mode of personal being. Μετάνοια is a conversion of man's *whole* being from failure to be what he *is* (from sin, which is again a mode of being) into true personhood: the experience of sin is not primarily an experience of the violation of law, but an experience of Nothing, as existence-in-isolation, the 'outside' (ἐκτός) of communion. We may say, therefore, that morality and ontology are identical (Heidegger points to the original Greek meanings of ἦθος δαίμων, 'God', in Heraclitus, 'place of residence' in Homer and Herodotus – both ideas connected with 'modes of being'), and that an individually orientated ethic inevitably involves an ontology based on encapsulated individual entities. 'Ontological morality' for the Christian, however, is an affirmation of personal freedom in the fullest sense, presupposing an ontology of personal, relational existence, being-in-communion, the dialogue of God with man.

I hope I may be pardoned for having set out Dr Yannaras' argument at some length, but I think a briefer summary would do it less than justice. An adequately detailed examination of it is really beyond the scope of this article, but I propose to select a few points of significance for discussion, in an attempt to relate the book to the wider background of Eastern theology

---

1. Ibid., 85.

in general, and, to a lesser extent, to certain aspects of Western theology. I have already remarked on the points of contact between Yannaras and Lossky, and I think it is worth commenting a little further on this. Students of Lossky will be aware of two parallel models for a 'personalist ontology' in his work, the Chalcedonian nature-person schema, and the essence-energies distinction of Gregory Palamas: both are intended to guard against a static essentialism, a cosmos of enclosed substances incapable of acting upon one another. However, there seems at times to be something of a gulf between the two models in Lossky's writings: the Palamite scheme clearly poses some difficulties in a Trinitarian context, since the temptation is to contrast an *impersonal* essence with *personal* energies, and thus to put the Persons of the Trinity on the same plane as the energies (as I think Pseudo-Denys does). Now indeed Palamism is not so simple as that, and the Palamite certainly *can* state his distinction intelligibly in a Trinitarian scheme; but I am not sure that Lossky always succeeds in doing so, and I suspect that, finally, it is the nature/person distinction which is of more central importance to his theology.[1] What Dr Yannaras has brilliantly succeeded in doing is to integrate these two models in a synthesis which clearly distinguishes 'nature', 'person', and 'operation', but which demonstrates the close interrelation of the three. As a model for Trinitarian theology (including a theology of the *operationes, Trinitatis ad extra*) it is, in many ways, admirable; but, later on, I should like to question its usefulness for Christology.

Dr Yannaras very frequently refers to 'ek-static' relationship as something essentially 'pre-conscious' (προσυνειδησιακή); and his examination of the implications of this marks something of an advance from Lossky's very definite emphasis upon the importance of 'consciousness' in personal relation. Although Lossky grants that person is by no means identical with consciousness and that 'la conscience n'est plus limitee comme sujet connaissant et agissant',[2] he is equally emphatic that inter-personal union 'ne peut etre non plus inconsciente'.[3] Consequently, he asserts that the characteristically 'Western' (so he considers it) experience of the 'Night of the Spirit', and the idea of 'passive purgation' in St John of the Cross are wholly alien to the spirituality of the Christian East, because they deny the free *personal* co-operation of

---

1. See especially the articles quoted above, and the articles on Dogmatic Theology published posthumously in the *Messager de l'Exarchat du Patriarche Russe en Europe Occidentale,* Nos. 46-47, 48, 49 and 50 (1964-65).
2. From an unpublished lecture (in a course on Dogmatic and Comparative Theology) given on 8 March 1956.
3. Ibid.

man in the work of salvation, leaving him in darkness and ignorance while God proceeds to purify man's nature. Now it is not difficult to show that Lossky's account of Western, especially Carmelite, spirituality is in very many respects seriously misleading, reflecting a fundamental misunderstanding of the terminology and presuppositions especially of St. John of the Cross; but the point I wish to make is that Dr Yannaras recognises – as Lossky does not – that the 'experience of the absence of God' is by no means the same thing as the 'absence of the experience of God'. Dr Yannaras' exposition of the experience of personal absence as establishing the possibility of total authentic communion by a sort of via negativa is, I would suggest, very close to the Carmelite tradition; and his connexion of this with the Eastern ascetical tradition, with the idea of πένθος in the Fathers, provides a most valuable bridge between the two 'schools' (can one really call them that?) of spirituality. Of course, a very great deal depends upon what meaning one gives to 'consciousness': Lossky probably has a considerably less 'intellectual' (or even perhaps 'conceptual') idea of it than Yannaras, and it is hard to see why he should reject the idea of a consciousness of personal absence.[1] It is words like 'consciousness', one often feels, which bedevil the study of theology, because there is nothing easier (and nothing more fatal) than to assume that all theologians using such a word mean roughly the same thing by it; but that is another story.

To leave Lossky aside for the moment, and to move into the very different sphere of British philosophy of religion: a recent issue of *Theology*[2] contained a paper by Professor John Macquarrie entitled 'God and the World: One Reality of Two?' and a comment on this paper by Mr Brian Hebblethwaite of Queen's College, Cambridge. Dr Macquarrie suggests that without dispensing with the idea of transcendence, it is time that we began to think of the God-world relation as 'in some respects' symmetrical or reciprocal: this position, sometimes described as 'pantheism', particularly characterises 'those theologians who have been influenced by such philosophers as Alexander, Whitehead, Bergson, Heidegger' (p. 395). He goes on to suggest some possible models for the expression of such a relation. Mr Hebblethwaite's comments are extremely interesting in the light of Dr Yannaras' book: Professor Macquarrie, he says, 'is constantly inclined to identify God's immanence

1. Cf. P. Miguel ('La conscience de la grâce selon Syméon le Nouveau Théologien' in *Irenikon* 42 (1969), 314-42); 'La sécheresse l'absence et la nuit sont aussi des expériences : ce'st pressentir qu'il y a . . . une Présence qui ne se peut encore révelér, un Jour qui ne finira pas et dont on attend l'aurore', 342.
2. 75:626 (August, 1972).

with some structural aspect of the created world. . . . The reason seems to be that, for Macquarrie, traditional theism has posited a purely *external* relation between God and the world, which fails to do justice to the intimacy and involvement which biblical religion attributes to the living God in his dealings with the world. . . . But at least one might think that a doctrine of *creation* is better expressed in terms of an external relation between God and the world, without prejudice to God's further involvement in his creation. The old theology distinguished between the inter-trinitarian processions and the *operationes Trinitatis ad extra;* and it is hard to see how one can abandon some such distinction and yet retain the concept of creation' (p. 404). What Mr Hebblethwaite is objecting to is any attempt to solve the problem of the God-world relation, the problem of the action of the infinite in and upon the finite, by making the relation internal to God (or internal to the 'world', depending upon one's point of view), 'And you'll agree, as I expect, that he was right to so object.' Yet, as he admits, 'externality' is a notion which has acquired 'pejorative connotations when predicated of the relation between God and the world' (p. 405); one cannot help feeling that Professor Macquarrie's plea for a recognition of genuine reciprocity is justified (I do not think that the term 'symmetry' is really very helpful here). And it seems to me that at this point Dr Yannaras' synthesis of Heidegger and Palamas provides a possible solution. The most cursory reading of the book will impress upon the reader that one of Yannaras' central concerns is to establish that the relation between God and man is personal and reciprocal, a relation of *communion,* a 'real' (as opposed to a logical) relation: thus far, he is as much Heidegger's pupil as is Macquarrie. However, precisely by underlining that it is a communion of *persons,* and therefore a confluence of personal energies, he succeeds in avoiding any notion of the 'involvement' (in Macquarrie's sense) of the Divine Essence in the finite world: the energies of God, manifesting the Person of the Word, create and preserve the world, and are fully involved in it, there is no 'external' relation in question, nor any identification of the Divine Essence with a causal abstraction. But it is only in this personal 'mode' that we can apprehend the Essence of God at all: we do not and cannot know It in Itself, but only as content of the Persons of the Trinity, it is not and cannot be 'involved' in creation except through the outgoing of personal energy, in Itself It remains beyond all finite being. The personal energies freely 'come out of' the unapproachable, transcendent Essence, so that the relations ad extra established by the energies are not internal (in the sense of 'natural' or 'necessary') to the Essence. So (as Lossky would no doubt have delighted to point out) the Eastern theological tradition, here as elsewhere, proposes a satisfactory via media whereby Western theology may escape from a choice between two ultimately unacceptable alternatives.

It is, as I have said, a *possible* solution; not necessarily an adequate one, though, because its validity depends upon the validity of the whole essence-energies schema. Plainly this is far too large a question to embark upon in detail here, but it may be worthwhile to raise one or two issues which seem to be of some importance. In the first place, I am never quite certain what Dr Yannaras (and his predecessors in the East) are saying about the incomprehensibility of the Divine Essence. There are times when Orthodox theologians seem to be asserting this simply because *all* essences (considered as Aristotelian individual essences) are incommunicable and imparticipable,[1] and therefore (since knowledge involves some sort of participation of knower in known) unknowable. Whereas at other times, the Divine Essence is held to be unknowable because it is Divine, and therefore beyond the capacity of the finite mind. These two approaches – need I add? – are not incompatible, but I think it is helpful to recognise that they are different. The trouble with the first approach is that inevitably it tends to make God a member of a class of essences, *closed* essences: and the theological problem then is to think of something in God which is 'not-essence' and therefore not incommunicable and enclosed. The result is the classical statement of Palamism, which encounters severe difficulties in reconciling this distinction with the doctrine of the absolute simplicity of God. The latter approach, however, leaves the door open to a more open-minded notion of essence: Aquinas, who is just as ready as any Easterner to assert the incomprehensibility of God, succeeds in avoiding a system of closed essences by *revising* the Aristotelean notion of essence,[2] so that *ens* or *esse*, the 'essence-in-its-act-of-existing' is seen as primary. On this basis, it is possible to assert a real communication with the Divine Essence *in actu*, while still denying that, even in the Beatific Vision, a finite intellect can *comprehend* the Essence, can know It as It knows Itself.[3] Thus, we

---

1. Cf., in this context, Philip Sherrard's assertion in his *The Greek East and the Latin West* (Limni, Evia: Denise Harvey, 1995), 38: 'We can conceive neither of the relationships of God to creation, nor of how all things participate in His divinity, except by distinguishing His entirely *simple, immutable, and incommunicable* Essence from His multiple and communicable powers and energies' (my italics). Surely, in a conservative Aristotelian system, the properties here enumerated would not be peculiar to the *Divine* Essence as such.

2. See E.L. Mascall, *The Openness of Being: Natural Theology Today* (Philadelphia: Westminster Press, 1972), Appendix III, *Grace and Nature in East and West*.

3. *Summa Theologica*, I, xii, 7.

continue to affirm that essences are not 'interchangeable': *'participate* in this context never means to have part in another entity.'[1] This would be absurd, as it would necessarily presuppose an abstraction of the entity (*essentia*) from its act of existing (*ens*), which is metaphysically impossible if we are speaking of actual essences. Yet we can also maintain real, 'existential' communication, mutual accessibility, between essences as they *in actu:* we are not making any awkward division between 'essence' and 'not-essence' in a thing, rather are we defining the mode in which essences exist.

It should by now be clear that this is not an irrelevant digression: the position we have arrived at is very close to that proposed by Dr Yannaras, it seems, and once again he appears to have given us an invaluable link between East and West. Professor E.L. Mascall has suggested more than once that the essence-energies distinction is – at least in intention – parallel to the essence-existence distinction in St Thomas;[2] and not only do we find Dr Yannaras coming to conclusions fundamentally very close to those of Professor Mascall, we even find a fairly clear identification of the 'energies' with 'existence' throughout (they are 'the mode in which entities exist', εἶναι a frequently repeated formula, and God is 'revealed as personal existence',[3] ὑπαρκτικότης, in the relation established by the energies). Dr Yannaras quotes Palamas' dictum that God did not say to Moses 'I am Essence', but 'I am that I am', 'I am He Who Is', ἐγὼ εἰμὶ ὁ ὤν;[4] and it is precisely this 'existentialist' point which Aquinas makes in his comment on the text from Exodus.[5] It is curious that Orthodox theologians (including Dr Yannaras at some points in his book) persist in regarding Thomist thought as basically essentialist: there is a tendency either to assimilate the Angelic Doctor to Augustine and Anselm (Paul Evdokimov is inclined to do this), or to view him through the medium of late scholastic thought, or, worse, Cartesianism (Lossky is often guilty of this) in apparent oblivion of the copious expositions of Thomist existentialism provided by Gilson, Maritain, Mascall and others. And in this connexion, one may ask whether Dr Yannaras' strictures[6] on the use of analogy in Western

1. Per E. Persson, *Sacra Doctrina: Reason and Revelation in Aquinas*, trans. Ross Mackenzie (Oxford: Blackwell Publishers, 1970), 130.
2. e.g. Mascall, *The Openness of Being*, 222.
3. Yannaras, 'Τὸ Ὀντολογικὸν περιεχόμενον', 77.
4. Palamas, *On the Hesychasts*, in vol. A of P. Christou's edition of Palamas' work, 66; quoted Yannaras, 'Τὸ Ὀντολογικὸν περιεχόμενον', 79.
5. *Summa Theologica*, I, xiii, 11; See E.L. Mascall, *Existence and Analogy* (New York: Longmans, Green and Co., 1949), 10-12.
6. E.g. Yannaras, 'Τὸ Ὀντολογικὸν περιεχόμενον', 74.

theology are really justified: if Professor Mascall is right in affirming the existential character of analogy in Aquinas,[1] I think one might be able to state a doctrine of analogy giving a satisfactory degree of priority to the reality of God over the reality of man. Mascall's suggestion[2] that the 'energies' of Palamism are parallel not simply to Aquinas' *esse* but to *analogia* as well seems to merit further examination (which I cannot give it in the present article, unfortunately).

The question of analogy brings us to a (brief) consideration of Dr Yannaras' methodology. I suppose this book would be classified by most Western readers as an essay in 'natural theology,' though it is a natural theology with a Trinitarian sting in the tail: it is an attempt to show how personhood as we know it is grounded in Being, and so in God, and because we begin from a particular notion of personhood (existence-in-communion) we are obliged to postulate 'internal' personal communion in God. And this, like any attempt to explicate the relation of finite to infinite, is inevitably an essay in *analogy*; which does not necessarily mean that we take finite existence as a starting-point which is 'more real' or 'more certain' than infinite existence. At one level, we are not 'starting from' either the finite or the infinite pole, we are presupposing *both*; while at another level – as it is almost trivial to point out – of course we are beginning from finite existence, simply because we are finite existents. It is important not to confuse ontological priority with epistemological priority: when the late Austin Farrer said,[3] 'This problem of analogy is in principle prior to every particular relation,' he was (as a reading of 'Finite and Infinite' shows) very far from claiming any *real* priority for a knowledge obtained outside revelation; rather was he insisting, I believe rightly, that any talk about the content of a revelation necessarily requires some underlying theory of what it is that enables us to talk about a revelation as the revelation of *God*. It is only fair to add that there is a world of difference between Dr Farrer's brilliant essay in 'voluntarist metaphysics' and Dr Yannaras' book: Farrer, in fact, represents precisely that intellectualist strand in Western theology which Yannaras condemns so frequently and strongly. What Dr Yannaras – like some of the theologians of the Reformation – has done is to set the doctrine of analogy in the context of the *totality* of God's action upon the world, so that we are not obliged to make a distinction in kind between our knowledge of God in creation and our knowledge in revelation: one is ἀπουσία, the other παρουσία, but in both it is the same

---

1. E.L. Mascall, *Existence and Analogy*, passim, especially chapter 5.
2. Mascall, *Existence and Analogy*, 154.
3. Austin Marsden Farrer, *Finite and Infinite: A Philosophical Essay* (New York: Seabury Press, 1979), 2.

sort of relation with the Person of the Word that we apprehend. If one may so express it, Dr Yannaras has 'theologised' the concept of analogy very thoroughly. Though perhaps, in one way, not thoroughly enough: one misses in the book any real integration of the idea of the Holy Spirit as illuminator, mediator of the knowledge of God (this, interestingly enough, is a far more prominent theme in Lossky's theology)[1] the Person through Whom 'analogical' participation in God, participation in the Divine energies, becomes a reality here and now. (On this subject, much of the work of Professor T.F. Torrance is highly suggestive; I would refer particularly to his essay on 'The Epistemological Relevance of the Spirit.')[2] In the light of all this, I feel that Dr Yannaras is wrong to use the terms like 'analogy,' as he does, in a consistently negative and derogatory way, as if analogy necessarily involved a methodological doubt of non-finite reality. After some sixty pages mainly devoted to an essentially philosophical analysis of the structure of human personhood, the reader may well raise his eyebrows at a statement like this: 'In the theology of the Christian East, we approach the reality of human personhood on the basis of the revealed Truth of the Person of God, in contrast to the theology of the West, which seeks the Truth about God analogically and anagogically, concentrating basically on the reality of man.'[3] And as to the use made of Heidegger's system and terminology throughout, one may be forgiven for wondering whether it is perhaps a little uncritical: it is reminiscent of the use made of Hegel by Russian theologians at the end of the nineteenth and the beginning of the twentieth century; a writer in *Istina*, introducing an article by Dr Yannaras,[4] remarked on the possible danger of an 'Hellenic Slavophilism,' and this seems to me fair comment as dependence upon a particular system of secular philosophy is concerned.

It should be clear by now that Dr Yannaras is far less of a 'revelationist' than Lossky, and it is significant that he devotes very little space to Christology as such (as opposed to what might be called 'Logology', the theology of the cosmic Word). As I have already indicated, I find his remarks on Christology[5] cryptic and rather unsatisfactory. The fall, we are told,[6] is a diminution of personal capacity for relation, it is not an 'essential' change, an alteration in the underlying structure of human

---

1. See Vladimir Lossky, *The Mystical Theology of the Eastern Church* (Crestwood, NY: St Vladimir's Seminary Press, 1997), chapter 9; also 'La Tradition et les traditions', in *A l'image et à la ressemblance de Dieu*, 139-66.
2. In *God and Rationality* (Oxford: Oxford University Press, 2000), 165-92.
3. Yannaras, 'Τὸ Ὀντολογικὸν περιεχόμενον', 74.
4. *Istina*, 1971, 130: the article (131-50) is on 'La théologie en Grèce aujourd'hui'.
5. See especially Yannaras, 'Τὸ Ὀντολογικὸν περιεχόμενον', 82.
6. Yannaras, 'Τὸ Ὀντολογικὸν περιεχόμενον', 71-2.

existence, except insofar as it means that 'nature' has become incapable of *expressing itself* personally.[1] We should expect to be told that Christ restores this power of 'personal expression' to nature; but what does Dr Yannaras mean by saying that the capacity for ek-stasis has, in Christ, become proper not merely to the person, but to the nature of man? If nature is, in any case, only capable of ek-stasis through the person, does this statement have any content? It is not difficult to see why Dr Yannaras should feel obliged to make it: the great *betes noires* of Orthodox theology seem to be, on the one hand, any doctrine of man's total depravity (i.e. a radical obliteration of God's image in man by the Fall), and, on the other, any 'moralistic' approach to soteriology, which neglects the ontological side of salvation, the restoration of man's nature.[2] Obviously Yannaras is trying to state the Eastern position as fully as possible over against these distortions: but the soteriological passage on pp. 82-83 gives the impression (all the stronger for being so rare in the book) of being insufficiently carefully thought out. If Dr Yannaras means that Christ, and man-in-Christ, are removed from the condition of 'becoming' personal to a state of simply *being* personal, the state enjoyed by the Persons of the Trinity, have we not arrived at a sort of Monophysite position, in which human, finite nature as such has no real place? Clearly this is not at all what Dr Yannaras means: but we do need a sharper distinction between the Union of the Trinity, the Hypostatic Union, and the Union of Grace. Here, I think, we have much to learn from Lossky,[3] with his carefully worked-out theory of redemption as consisting in the restoration of nature in Christ and the *personal* realisation of this in the Holy Spirit, in Whom, by Whose indwelling, men become truly persons, truly human. This is a system which, I believe, does justice to both the primacy of God's action in salvation and the distinctness of human response. Now this is more or less implicit in what Yannaras says, but, again, I believe that a more positive pneumatology would have clarified matters.

The clue to Yannaras' Christological remarks may lie in his assertion[4] that the union of humanity and divinity in Christ is 'not only volitional'; that is, we are to regard it as 'natural' *as opposed* to volitional, and presumably should regard the communion of man with God in Christ

---

1. For a parallel insistence that the Fall does not produce an alteration in man's *nature,* see Paul Evdokimov, *L'orthodoxie* (Paris: Desclée de Brouwer, 1992), 88-92.
2. See, for instance, Evdokimov, *L'orthodoxie,* 93 ff.
3. See especially *The Mystical Theology of the Eastern Church,* chapters 8 and 9, and the articles in *A l'image* already referred to.
4. Yannaras, 'Τὸ Ὀντολογικὸν περιεχόμενον', 82.

as equally 'natural' (a union of φύσεις) rather than volitional. This looks back to the venerable Byzantine doctrine of the absence of the 'gnomic' or 'dispositional' will in Christ: in the system of Maximus the Confessor, man has two wills, 'natural', and 'dispositional', of which the latter is solely a consequence of the contingencies of human action after the Fall. Ideally, man exercises only a 'natural' will, he wills to do only that which is an accord with his nature (as God's image); but after the Fall, he can will this only at the result of moral decision between two alternatives which are, at one level, equally attractive. Only by good 'habit' (γνώμη) does he choose the good. For Maximus, Christ has no gnomic will, but exercises natural will alone; so that one might conclude that the end of the redemptive process is for the saved man to exercise only such a will (one still needs a satisfactory doctrine of the indwelling of the Spirit to account for this). This, I think, is what lies behind Yannaras' statements; to rephrase Maximus in Yannaras' more usual terminology we may perhaps say that, 'since the Fall', man has been capable of ek-stasis, of genuine personal communion, only by conscious exercise of his will to escape 'atomicity'. In Christ, the possibility of existence-in-communion which is *not* merely dependent on our continuing struggle against atomicity is established. There is still an ongoing μετάνοια;[1] but what we are given is authentic personal freedom, freedom to *be* persons, freedom from the threat of existence-in-isolation. This seems to be what Yannaras means: but I, for one, should be grateful for an exposition, at some future date, of how this is to be related in detail to the Chalcedonian definition, and, indeed, to the general Byzantine tradition in Christology. The main points of contact are clear enough, and a fuller integration into the Eastern tradition certainly seems possible.

This has brought us into the sphere of Dr Yannaras' ethics and the identification of ethics with ontology. It occurs to me that it would be most interesting to compare this with Wittgenstein's insistence that ethics should only be spoken of – indeed, are only intelligible – within the context of a total world-view: ethical belief and ethical practice are 'forms of life' (modes of being?), we can begin to consider them only as they are seen to be a facet of a whole approach to living. Moral debate is debate about world-views.[2] There is more to it than that, of course, and perhaps the differences are more significant than the parallels; but it is worth noting. Again, is Dr Yannaras really fair to the 'Platonic' tradition? The kind of Platonism proposed by, say, Miss Iris Murdoch in 'The Sovereignty of Good' seems to me to have a certain amount in common

---

1. Ibid., 83.
2. See, for example, D.Z. Mounce and H.O. Phillips, *Moral Practices* (London: Routledge & K. Paul, 1969), especially chapter 9.

with Yannaras' outline, and not to deserve his sharper strictures on Platonism.[1] However, an examination of all this would probably double the length of an already overlong essay, and I must leave it aside for now.[2]

In summary, it seems that Dr Yannaras' book is one of the most important theological studies to come from the Orthodox world in recent years. It often exhibits a certain degree of onesidedness in its argument, but is rarely actually polemical; and one might well concede that a measure of onesidedness is perhaps necessary to provoke Western readers to question the presuppositions of their own theology. It is a profoundly 'traditional' theology, obviously rooted in the Fathers and in Byzantine theology; yet this very fact prompts me to ask how necessary to Dr Yannaras' case the explicitly Heideggerian framework is. Could this development and maturation of Lossky's ideas have been successfully carried through without such heavy dependence on a particular system of secular metaphysics? I should be the first to grant that Christian faith has ontological corollaries, that in this sense it is 'in search of a metaphysic'; but this is rather different from claiming one metaphysic as against all others as 'the' Christian metaphysic. I doubt whether Yannaras would seriously claim this; and I hope it is not presumptuous to suppose that in future works from his pen we shall see a gradual diminution of dependence on Heidegger. Dr Yannaras' case can stand well on its own theological feet; Western theologians have much to lose by neglecting it.

---

1. We should also note that, in some significant aspects, Miss Murdoch appears to have been influenced by Heidegger.
2. Dr Yannaras has more recently produced an extended exposition of his ethical theory in Ἡ Ἐλευθερία Τοῦ Ἤθους [*The Freedom of Morality*] (Synoro. Athens: Athina, 1970).

Bibliography

'Countries of the World', run by Information Technology Associates. http://www.theodora.com/wfbcurrent/greece/greece_economy.html.

'The Naked Capitalist', run by Yves Smith: http://www.nakedcapitalism.com/2013/12/yanis-varoufakis-confessions-erratic-marxist-midst-repugnant-eurozone-crisis.html.

'Trading Economics', run by IECONOMICS INC, New York. http://www.tradingeconomics.com/greece/households-debt-to-gdp.

Allchin, A.M., ed. *Orthodoxy and the Death of God*. Studies Supplementary to *Sobornost* 1. London: Fellowship of St Alban and St Sergius, 1971.

Anderson, Pamela Sue. 'Autonomy, vulnerability and gender'. *Feminist Theory* 4:2 (2003), 149-64.

–––. *Silencing and Speaker Vulnerability: Undoing an Oppressive Form of (Wilful) Ignorance*. Available at: https://womeninparenthesis.wordpress.com/2016/03/25/read-pamela-sue-andersons-iwd-keynote. Accessed on 19 May 2017.

–––. *The Transformative Power of Vulnerability*. Available at: http://enhancinglife.uchicago.edu/blog/the-transformative-power-of-vulnerability. Accessed on 19 May 2017.

Andreopoulos, Andreas. 'The Song of Songs: An Asceticism of Love'. *The Forerunner*. Orthodox Fellowship of St John the Baptist, 57, Summer (2011), 17-26.

Angelov, Dimiter G. 'Byzantinism: The Imaginary and Real Heritage of Byzantium in Southeastern Europe'. In *New Approaches to Balkan Studies,* ed. Dimitris Keridis, Ellen Elias-Bursac and Nicholas Yatromanolakis, 3-23. Dulles, VA: Brassey's, 2003.

Anonymous. 'Mass Appeal – Church Attendance in Ireland'. *Know Your Faith.* Available at: http://knowyourfaith.blogspot.co.uk/2009/11/mass-appeal-church-attendance-in_20.html. Accessed on 20 May 2017.

–––. Ὁ «Τελευταῖος πειρασμὸς» ποὺ ἔφερε τὸν Καζαντζάκη ἕνα βῆμα πρὶν τὸν ἀφορισμό.' *Φούιτ.* Available at: https://fouit.gr/2017/04/15/ο-τελευταίος-πειρασμός-που-έφερε-το. Accessed on 20 May 2017.

Arbo, Alessandro. 'Que ce qu'un "objet musical"?' *Les Cahiers Philosophiques de Strasbourg* 2 (2010), 225-47.

Aristotle, *Metaphysics*, trans. Şt. Bezdechi. Bucharest: IRI, 1996.

Aulen, Gustaf. *Christus Victor*. Oregon: Wipf & Stock, 2003.

Basil of Caesarea. *Commentary on Isaiah* 96, trans. Alexandru Mihăilă. Bucharest: Publishing House of Romanian Patriarchy, 2009.

Bathrellos, Demetrios. 'Church, Eucharist, Bishop: The Early Church in the Ecclesiology of John Zizioulas.' In *The Theology of John Zizioulas: Personhood and the Church*, ed. Douglas Knight, 133-46. London: Routledge, 2007.

Berger, Peter L. *Facing Up To Modernity*. New York: Penguin, 1979.

Betz, John. *After Enlightenment*. Oxford: Wiley-Blackwell, 2009.

Biesta, Gert and Säfström, Carl Anders. 'A Manifesto for Education.' *Policy Futures in Education* 9 (2011): 540-47. Available at: doi: 10.2304/pfie.2011.9.5.540. Accessed on 20 May 2017.

Blumenberg, Hans. *Theorie der Unbegrifflichkeit, aus dem Nachlaß hrsg.* von Anselm Haverkamp, Frankfurt am Main: Suhrkamp, 2007.

Boff, Clodovis and Leonardo Boff. *Introducing Liberation Theology*. London: Burns & Oates, 1987.

Burggraeve, Roger. 'Violence and the Vulnerable Face of the Other: The Vision of Emmanuel Levinas on Moral Evil and Our Responsibility.' *Journal of Social Philosophy* 30 (1999), 29-45.

Butler, Judith. 'Giving an Account of Oneself.' *Diacritics* 31:4 (2001), 22-40.

Cavanaugh, William T. *Theopolitical Imagination: Discovering the Liturgy as a Political Act in an Age of Global Consumerism*. London: Bloomsbury; T. & T. Clark, 2002.

–––. *Migrations of the Holy*. Grand Rapids: Eerdmans, 2011.

Cavafy, C.P. *C. Cavafy: Collected Poems*, trans. Edmund Keeley and Philip Sherard, ed. George Savidis. Princeton: Princeton University Press, 1980.

Chaudet, Didier. 'When the Bear Confronts the Crescent: Russia and the Jihadist Issue.' *China and Eurasia Forum Quarterly* 7:2 (2009), 37-58.

Chryssavgis, John. *Toward the Holy and Great Council: Retrieving a Culture of Conciliarity and Communion*. Department of Inter-Orthodox, Ecumenical & Interfaith Relations, 2016.

Coffey, John. 'Puritan Legacies.' In *The Cambridge Companion to Puritanism*, ed. John Coffey and Paul C.H. Lim, 327-45. Cambridge: Cambridge University Press, 2008.

Cole, Jonathan. 'Personhood, Relational Ontology, and the Trinitarian Politics of Eastern Orthodox Thinker Christos Yannaras.' *Political Theology*. Published online 22 February 2017. Available at: http://dx.doi.org/10.1080/146231 7X.2017.1291127.

–––. 'The Communo-Centric Political Theology of Christos Yannaras in Conversation with Oliver O'Donovan.' In *Mustard Seeds in the Public Square*, ed. Sotiris Mitralexis. Wilmington, Delaware: Vernon Press, 2017.

Das, Satyajit. *Extreme Money*. USA: Financial Times Press, 2011.

Davidson, Donald. *Essays on Actions and Events,* Oxford and New York: Clarendon, 2001.

'Depoliticization.' *Décalages* 1 (2014). Available at: http://scholar.oxy.edu/decalages/vol1/iss3/4. Accessed on 5 February 2018.

Desmond, William. *The Intimate Strangeness of Being*. Washington D.C.: Catholic University of America Press, 2012.

Dionysius the Areopagite (ps.). *Complete Works and Scholia,* trans. Dumitru Stăniloae. Bucharest: Paideia, 1996.

Dragoumis, Ion. Ὁ Ἑλληνισμός μου καὶ οἱ Ἕλληνες [*My Hellenism and the Greeks*]. Athens: Pelekanos, 2014.

Ellul, Jacques. *Money and Power*. Southampton: Marshall Pickering, 1986.

---. *The Presence of the Kingdom*. Colorado Springs: Helmers & Howard, 1989.

---. *The Technological Society*. New York: Vintage, 1964.

Eurostat, run by the European Union, Luxembourg. http://ec.europa.eu/eurostat/ statistics-explained/index.php/File:Unemployment_rates,_seasonally_ adjusted,_January_2017_(%25)_F2.png. Accessed on 20 November 2017.

Evdokimov, Paul. *L'orthodoxie*. Paris: Desclée de Brouwer, 1992.

Farrer, Austin Marsden. *Finite and Infinite: A Philosophical Essay*. New York: Seabury Press, 1979.

Ferrer, Emilio and Helm, Jonathan L. 'The dynamical systems modeling of psychological co-regulation in dyadic interactions.' *International Journal of Psychophysiology* 88:3 (2013), 296-308.

Ford, David and Ford, Mary. *Marriage as a Path to Holiness: Lives of Married Saints*. Waymart, PA: St Tikhon's Seminary Press, 1995.

Frege, Gottlob. 'On Concept and Object.' *Translations from the Philosophical Writings of Gottlob Frege*, ed. Peter Thomas Geach and Max Black, Oxford: Blackwell, 1960: 42-55.

---. *Begriffsschrift. Formelsprache des reinen Denkens*. Halle: Louis Nebert, 1879.

Freud, Sigmund. *Civilization and Its Discontents*, trans. James Strachey. New York: W. Norton & Company Inc., 1962.

Gallaher, Brandon. 'Eschatological Anarchism: Eschatology and Politics in Contemporary Greek Theology.' In *Political Theologies in Orthodox Christianity: Common Challenges – Divergent Positions*, ed. Kristina Stoeckl, Gabriel Gerda and Aristotle Papanikolaou. New York: Bloomsbury; T. & T. Clark, 2017.

---. '"Waiting for the Barbarians": Identity and Polemicism in the Neo-Patristic Synthesis of Georges Florovsky.' *Modern Theology* 27:4 (October 2011), 659-91.

---. 'Μιὰ ἐπανεξέταση τῆς Νεο-πατερικῆς σύνθεσης: Ὀρθόδοξη ταυτότητα καὶ πολεμικὴ στὸν π. Γεώργιο Φλωρόφσκυ καὶ τὸ μέλλον τῆς Ὀρθόδοξης Θεολογίας' ['A Re-envisioning of Neo-Patristic Synthesis?: Orthodox Identity and Polemicism in Fr Georges Florovsky and the Future of Orthodox Theology'], trans. Nikolaos Asproulis, Lambros Psomas and Evaggelos Bartzis. *Theologia* 84:1 (2013), 25-92.

---. Review of *Orthodoxy and the West: Hellenic Self-Identity in the Modern Age*, by Christos Yannaras, trans. Peter Chamberas and Norman Russell. *Logos: A Journal of Eastern Christian Studies*, 50:3-4 (December 2009), 537-42.

Gavrilyuk, Paul. 'The Reception of Dionysius in twentieth century Eastern Orthodoxy.' *Modern Theology* 24:4 (2008), 707-23.

George, Susan. *Shadow Sovereigns*. London: Polity Press, 2015.

Goodman, Nelson. *Fact, Fiction and Forecast*. Cambridge: Harvard University Press, 1983.

---. *Of Mind and Other Matters*. Cambridge: Harvard University Press, 1984.

---. *The Structure of Appearance*. Dordrecht: Reidel, 1977.

Gounopoulos, Angelos. 'The Common Path of Ontology and History: Orthodoxy and Theology of Liberation in Dialogue.' In *Mustard Seeds in the Public Square: Between and Beyond Theology, Philosophy, and Society*, ed. Sotiris Mitralexis, 165-89. Wilmington, Delaware: Vernon Press, 2017.

Gregory of Nyssa. *The Life of Moses.* Vol. 29, trans. Dumitru Stăniloae and Ioan Buga. Bucharest: Publishing House of Biblical and Missionary Institute of the Romanian Orthodox Church, 1982.

Hamann, Johann G. *Writings on Philosophy and Language.* Cambridge: Cambridge University Press, 2007.

Hauerwas, Stanley. *After Christendom? How the Church is to Behave if Freedom, Justice, and a Christian Nation are Bad Ideas.* Nashville: Abingdon, 1991.

Hauser, Michael. 'The Twilight of Liberal Democracy: A Symptomatic Reading of Depoliticization.' *Décalages* 1:3 (2014). Available at: http://scholar.oxy.edu/decalages/vol1/iss3/4. Accessed on 20 May 2017.

Heidegger, Martin. *Identity and Difference (Identitat und Differenz),* trans. Joan Stambaugh. New York: Harper & Row, 1969.

———. *Introduction to Metaphysics,* trans. Gregory Fried and Richard Polk. Yale: Yale University Press, 2000.

———. *Sein Und Zeit.* Tübingen: Walter de Gruyter, 2006.

———. *What is Metaphysics?* Available at: http://naturalthinker.net/trl/texts/Heidegger,Martin/Heidegger.Martin..What%20Is%20Metaphysics.htm. Accessed on 19 May 2017.

Hillier, Paul. *Arvo Pärt.* New York: Oxford University Press, 1997.

Huntington, Samuel. 'The Clash of Civilizations?' *Foreign Affairs* 72:3 (1993), 22-49.

John Climacus. *The Ladder of Divine Ascent.* The Classics of Western Spirituality. New York: Paulist Press, 1982.

Kalaitzidis, Pantelis. 'The Image of the West in Contemporary Greek Theology.' In *Orthodox Constructions of the West,* ed. George Demacopoulos and Aristotle Papanikolaou, 142-160. New York: Fordham University Press, 2013.

———. Ἑλληνικότητα Καὶ Ἀντι-Δυτικισμὸς Στὴ Θεολογία Τοῦ '60' ['Greekness and Anti-Westernism in the Theology of the '60s']. PhD diss., Aristotle University of Thessaloniki, 2008.

———. *Orthodoxy and Political Theology,* trans. Fr Gregory Edwards. Geneva: World Council of Churches Publications, 2012.

Karambelias, Yorgos. Ἡ Ἀποστασία Τῶν Διανοουμένων *[The Intellectuals' Apostasy].* Athens: Enallaktikes Ekdoseis, 2012.

Kierkegaard, Søren. *Concluding Unscientific Postscript to Philosophical Fragments.* New Jersey: Princeton University Press, 1992.

———. *Sickness Unto Death.* New Jersey: Princeton University Press, 1980.

———. *Two Ages.* New Jersey: Princeton University Press, 1978.

Kokkolis, Giorgios. Τὸ νομικὸ καθεστὼς τῶν σχέσων ἐκκλησίας-κράτους: εἰσαγωγή στὶς νομικὲς διαστάσεις τῶν σχέσεων ἐκκλησίας-κράτους στὴν Ἑλλάδα καὶ στὴν Κύπρο' ['The legal framework of Church-state relations: introduction to the legal dimensions of Church-state relations in Greece and Cyprus']. In Ἀπελευθέρωση τῆς Ἐκκλησίας ἀπὸ τὸ Κράτος: οἱ σχέσεις Ἐκκλησίας-Κράτους καὶ ἡ μελλοντικὴ μετεξέλιξή τους *[Liberating the Church from the State: Church-State Relations and Their Future Development],* ed. Sotiris Mitralexis, 57-85. Athens: Manifesto, 2015.

Kundera, Milan. *The Unbearable Lightness of Being,* trans. Michael Henry Heim. New York: HarperCollins, 1991.

La Matina, Marcello. 'Esemplificazione, Riferimento e Verità. Il contributo di N. Goodman ad una filosofia dei linguaggi.' In *Nelson Goodman e la filosofia dei linguaggi*, ed. Marcello La Matina and Elio Franzini, 109-55. Macerata: Quodlibet, 2007.

———.'Oneness of Mankind and the Plural of Man in Gregory of Nyssa's *Against Eunomius* Book III. Some Problems of Philosophy of Language.' In *Gregory of Nyssa's Contra Eunomium III), Supplements to Vigiliae Christianae*, ed. Matthieu Cassin and Johann Leemans, 552-78. Leiden: Brill, 2013.

———.Note sul suono. Filosofia dei linguaggi e forme di vita. Ancona: Le Ossa-Anatomie dell'ingegno, 2014.

Laats Alar. 'The Concept of the Third Rome and its Political Implications.' In *Religion and Politics in Multicultural Europe: Perspectives and Challenges*, ed. Kilp Alar and Saumets Andres, 98-113. Tartu: Tartu University Press, 2009.

Larchet, Jean-Claude. *Person and Nature, Holy Trinity–Christ–Human Being. Contributions to the contemporary inter-orthodox and inter-christian dialogues.* Translation by Dragoş Bahrim and Marinela Bojin. Bucharest: Basilica, 2013.

Lash, Ephrem. *The Central Part of the Byzantine Anaphora: a Translator's Notes.* Available at: http://www.thyateira.org.uk/docs/Articles/FrEphrem_KataPanta. pdf. Accessed on 20 May 2017.

Laurent, V., ed. Sylvestre Syropoulos. 'Les Mémoires du grand ecclésiarque de l'Église de Constantinople Sylvestre Syropoulos sur le Concile de Florence (1438-1439).' Lutetiae: Éditions du Centre national de la recherche scientifique (CNRS), 1971.

Lehman, Karl. 'The Dome of Heaven.' *The Art Bulletin*, 27:1, (1945): 1-27.

Lenis, Amvrosios Metropolitan of Kalavryta. Ἀποβράσματα τῆς κοινωνίας σήκωσαν κεφάλι.' Available at: http://mkka.blogspot.gr/2015/12/blog-post_9. html. Accessed on 18 May 2017.

Levinas, Emmanuel. 'Ethics of the Infinite.' In *Debates In Continental Philosophy: Richard Kearney in Conversation With Contemporary Thinkers*. New York: Fordham University Press, 2004.

———. 'Existence and Ethics.' In *Proper Names*, trans. Michael B. Smith. Stanford: Stanford University Press, 1996.

———. 'The Trace of the Other.' In *Deconstruction in Context*, ed. Mark C. Taylor. Chicago: University of Chicago Press, 1986.

———. 'Transcendence and Height.' In *Basic Philosophical Writings*. Bloomington: Indiana University Press, 1996.

———. *Difficult Freedom*, trans. Sean Hand. Baltimore: Johns Hopkins University Press, 1997.

———. *Ethics and Infinity: Conversations with Philllipe Nemo*, trans. R.A. Cohen. Pittsburgh: Duquesne University Press, 1985.

———. *Otherwise than Being, Or Beyond Essence*, trans. Alphonso Lingis. Pittsburgh: Duquesne University Press, 1997.

———. *Totality and Infinity: An Essay on Exteriority*, trans. Alphonso Lingis. Pittsburgh: Duquesne University Press, 2005.

Levinson, Jerrold. 'What a Musical Work Is?' *Journal of Philosophy* 77 (1980): 5-28.

Lewis, C.S. *Mere Christianity*. Glasgow: Fount, 1977.

Lossky, Vladimir. *A l'image et à la ressemblance de Dieu*. Paris: Aubier-Montaigne, 1967.

———. *The Mystical Theology of The Eastern Church*, trans. Vasile Răducă, Bucharest: Anastasia, 1990.

———. *The Mystical Theology of the Eastern Church*. Cambridge: James Clarke, 1957.

Loudovikos, Nicholas. 'Person Instead of Grace and Dictated Otherness: John Zizioulas' Final Theological Position.' *Heythrop Journal* 52 (2011): 684-99.

Louth, Andrew. 'Some Recent Works by Christos Yannaras in English Translation.' *Modern Theology* 25:2 (2009): 329-40.

MacKridge, Peter. *Language and National Identity in Greece, 1766-1976.* Oxford: Oxford University Press, 2009.

Maddox, Marion. 'Prosper, Consume and Be Saved.' *Critical Research on Religion* 1 (2013): 108-115.

Makrides, Vasilios N. 'Orthodox Anti-Westernism Today: A Hindrance to European Integration?' *International Journal for the Study of the Christian Church* 9, no. 3 (2009): 209-24.

Marion, Jean-Luc. *God Without Being*, trans. Thomas Carlson, with a Foreword by David Tracy. Chicago: The University of Chicago Press, 1991.

———. *In the Self's Place. An Approach of Saint Augustine*, trans. Jeffrey L. Kosky, Stanford: Stanford University Press, 2012.

———. *The Essential Writings*, ed. Kevin Hart. New York: Fordham University Press, 2013.

———. *The Idol and Distance*, trans. Tinca Prunea Bretonnet şi Daniela Pălăşan, Bucharest: Humanitas, 2007.

Mascall, E.L. *Existence and Analogy*. New York: Longmans, Green and Co., 1949.

———. *The Openness of Being: Natural Theology Today*. Philadelphia: Westminster Press, 1972.

Maximus the Confessor. *Mystagogy*, trans. Ignatios Sakalis. Introduction by Dumitru Staniloae. Athens: Apostoliki Diakonia, 1973.

McLaughlin, Brian and Karen Bennett. 'Supervenience,' *The Stanford Encyclopedia of Philosophy* (Spring 2014). Available at: https://plato.stanford.edu/archives/spr2014/entries/supervenience. Accessed on 7 March 2017.

McGrath, S.J. *Heidegger: A (Very) Critical Introduction.* Grand Rapids, Michigan: William B. Eerdmans, 2008.

Metallinos, George D. 'Θεολογία Ἐλευθερίας καὶ Θεολογία Ἀπελευθερώσεως' ['Theology of Freedom and Liberation Theology']. Available at: http://www.kostasbeys.gr/articles.php?s= 3&mid=1096&mnu=1&id=24187. Accessed on 4 January 2016.

Metz, Johann Baptist. 'Two-Fold Political Theology.' In *Political Theology: Contemporary Challenges and Future Directions*, ed. Francis Schüssler Fiorenza, Klaus Tanner and Michael Welker, 13-20. Louisville, KY: Westminster John Knox Press, 2013.

Meyendorff, John. *Christ in Eastern Christian Thought*. St Vladimir's Seminary Press, 2011.

Michelis, Panayiotis A. *An Aesthetic Approach to Byzantine Art.* London: Batsford, 1955.

Milbank, John and Adrian Pabst. *The Politics of Virtue: Post-Liberalism and the Human Future.* London: Rowman & Littlefield, 2016.

Mitralexis, Sotiris. 'A Return to Tradition? The Marriage of Bishops in the (Greek) Orthodox Church.' *International Journal of Orthodox Theology* 7:4 (2016): 205-18.

–––. 'An Ontology of the Historico-Social: Christos Yannaras' Reading of European History.' In *Mustard Seeds in the Public Square: Between and Beyond Theology, Philosophy, and Society*, ed. Sotiris Mitralexis, 93-112. Wilmington, Del.: Vernon Press, 2017.

–––. 'Introduction – An Apophatic Wittgenstein, or a Wittgensteinian Apophaticism,' in *Ludwig Wittgenstein between Analytic Philosophy and Apophaticism*, vii-xiii.

–––. 'Person, Eros, Critical Ontology: An Attempt to Recapitulate Christos Yannaras Philosophy.' *Sobornost* 34:1 (2012): 33-40.

–––. *Ever-Moving Repose: A Contemporary Reading of Maximus the Confessor's Theory of Time*. Eugene, OR: Cascade, 2017.

Mitralexis, Sotiris, ed. *Ludwig Wittgenstein between Analytic Philosophy and Apophaticism*, Newcastle: Cambridge Scholars Publishing, 2015.

Moltmann, Jürgen. 'Political Theology in Ecumenical Contexts.' In *Political Theology: Contemporary Challenges and Future Directions*, ed. Francis Schüssler Fiorenza, Klaus Tanner and Michael Welker, 1-11. Louisville, KY: Westminster John Knox Press, 2013.

Mpegzos, Marios P. Τὸ Μέλλον τοῦ Παρελθόντος [*The Future of the Past*]. Athens: Armos, 1993.

Nikolaidis, Apostolos, Κοινωνικοπολιτικὴ Ἐπανάσταση καὶ Πολιτικὴ Θεολογία [*Socio-Political Revolution and Political Theology*]. Katerini: Tetrios, 1987.

O'Donovan, Oliver. *The Desire of the Nations: Rediscovering the Roots of Political Theology*. Cambridge: Cambridge University Press, 1996.

Panofsky, Erwin. *Gothic Architecture and Scholasticism*. Wimmer Lecture (1948). Latrobe: Archabbey Press, 1951.

Papagiannapoulos, Ilias. 'Re-appraising the Subject and the Social in Western Philosophy and in Contemporary Orthodox Thought.' *Studies in Eastern European Thought* 58 (2006): 299-330.

Papathanasiou, Athanasios. Ἡ Ἐκκλησία ὡς Ἀποστολή. Ἕνα κριτικὸ ξανακοίταγμα τῆς λειτουργικῆς Θεολογίας τοῦ π. Ἀλεξάνδρου Σμέμαν' ['The Church as a Mission. A Critical Re-evaluation of the Liturgical Theology of Fr Alexander Schmemann']. *Theology* 80 (2009): 67–108.

–––. Χαμένοι στὴν Ἠθική: Στάσεις τῆς Σύγχρονης Ὀρθόδοξης Θεολογίας' ['Lost in Ethics: Stances of Modern Orthodox Theology']. In Ἡ Ἐπιστροφή τῆς Ἠθικῆς [*The Return of Ethics*], ed. Stavros Zouboulakis, 281-318. Athens: Artos Zois, 2013.

Persson, Per E. *Sacra Doctrina: Reason and Revelation in Aquinas*, trans. Ross Mackenzie. Oxford: Blackwell Publishers, 1970.

Petrà, Basilio. 'Christos Yannaras and the Idea of "Dysis".' In *Orthodox Constructions of the West*, ed. George Demacopoulos and Aristotle Papanikolaou, 161-80. New York: Fordham University Press, 2013.

Petrà, Basilio. *Christos Yannaras: L'Orizzonte Apofatico Dell'Ontologia*. Brescia: Morcelliana, 2015.

Pew Research Center. 'Global Attitudes Project Spring 2013 Topline.' Available at: http://www.pewglobal.org/category/datasets/2013/?download=31111. Accessed on 20 May 2017.

–––. 'US Public Becoming Less Religious.' Available at: http://assets.pewresearch. org/wp-content/uploads/sites/11/2015/11/201.11.03_RLS_II_full_report.pdf. Accessed on 20 May 2017.

Phillips, D. Z., Mounce, H. O. *Moral Practices*. London: Routledge & K. Paul, 1969.

Piana, Giovanni. *Filosofia della musica*. Milano: Guerini & Associati, 1991.

Plato. *Theaetetus*, trans. Harold Fowler. Loeb Classics Library. Massachusetts: Harvard University Press, 1921.

Plested, Marcus. "'Light from the West': Byzantine Readings of Aquinas." In *Orthodox Constructions of the West*, ed. George Demacopoulos and Aristotle Papanikolaou, 58-70. New York: Fordham University Press, 2013.

———. *Orthodox Readings of Aquinas*. Oxford: Oxford University Press, 2015.

Romanides, John. *Franks, Romans, Feudalism, and Doctrine Doctrine: An Interplay between Theology and Society*. Patriarch Athenagoras Memorial Lectures. Brookline, MA: Holy Cross Orthodox Press, 1981.

———. *The Ancestral Sin: A Comparative Study of the Sin of Our Ancestors Adam and Eve According to the Paradigms and Doctrines of the First and Second Century Church and the Augustinian Formulations of Original Sin*. Translated by George S. Gabriel. Ridgewood, NJ: Zephyr, 2002.

———. *An Outline of Orthodox Patristic Dogmatics*, trans. George Dion Dragas. Rollinsford, NH: Orthodox Research Institute, 2004.

Ross, Chanon. *Gifts Glittering and Poisoned*. Oregon: Cascade, 2014.

Russell, Bertrand. *The Principles of Mathematics*. Berlin: Norton, 1903.

Russell, Norman. 'Christos Yannaras.' In *Key Theological Thinkers: From Modern to Postmodern*, ed. Svein Rise and Staale Johannes Kristiansen, 725-34. New York: Routledge, 2013.

———. 'The Enduring Significance of Christos Yannaras: Some Further Works in Translation.' *International Journal for the Study of the Christian Church* 16:1 (2016): 58-65.

Sartre, Jean-Paul. *L'être et le néant*. Paris: Gallimard, 1976.

Schindler, David L., ed. *Hans Urs von Balthasar: His Life and Work*. San Francisco: Ignatius Press, 1991.

Schmemann, Alexander. *The Journals of Father Alexander Schmemann, 1973-1983*. Crestwood, NY: SVS Press, 2000.

Shaxson, Nicholas. *Treasure Islands*. London: Vintage, 2013.

Sherrard, Philip. *The Greek East and the Latin West*. Limni, Evia: Denise Harvey, 1995.

Sideras, Ioannis. *Τὸ Ὅραμα τῆς Ἁγίας καὶ Μεγάλης Πανορθοδόξου Συνόδου [The Vision of the Holy and Great Pan-orthodox Synod]*. Available at: https://www.scribd.com/doc/314615368/Πανορθόδοξη-Σύνοδος-2016. Accessed on 4 April 2017.

Simpson, Christopher B. *The Truth is the Way*. Oregon: Cascade, 2011.

Stăniloae, Dumitru. *The Orthodox Ascetics and Mystics*. Vol. II. Alba Iulia: Deisis, 1993.

Steger, B. Manfred and Ravi K. Roy. *Neoliberalism*. Oxford: Oxford University Press, 2010.

Steiris, Georgios, Sotiris Mitralexis, and Georgios Arabatzis, eds. *The Problem of Modern Greek Identity: From the Ecumene to the Nation-State*. Newcastle: Cambridge Scholars Publishing, 2016.

Stiglitz, Joseph. *Globalization and its Discontents*. London: Penguin, 2002.

Stoeckl, Kristina. 'The "We" in Normative Political Philosophical Debates: The Position of Christos Yannaras on Human Rights.' In *Orthodox Christianity and Human Rights*, eds. Alfons Brüning and Evert van der Zweerde, 187-98. Leuven: Peeters, 2012.

Sunnin Yun, 'Education, Freedom and Temporality: A Response to Biesta and Säfström's Manifesto.' *Journal of Philosophy of Education* 48 (2014), 385-99. Available at: doi:10.1111/1467–9752.12086. Accessed on 20 November 2017.

Svoronos, Nikos G. *Τὸ Ἑλληνικὸ Ἔθνος: Γένεση καὶ Διαμόρφωση τοῦ Νέου Ἑλληνισμοῦ [The Greek Nation: The Genesis and Development of Neo-Hellenism].* Athens: Polis, 2004.

Taylor, Charles. 'The Person.' In *The Category of the Person: Anthropology, Philosophy, History*, ed. Michael Carrithers, Steven Collins and Steven Lukes, 257-81. Cambridge: Cambridge University Press, 1985.

Thucydides. *History of the Peloponnesian War,* trans. Rex Warner. London: Penguin, 1972.

Torrance, Alexis. 'Personhood and Patristics in Orthodox Theology: Reassessing the Debate.' *Heythrop Journal* 52 (2011), 700-707.

Trubetskoi, Eugene. *Icons: Theology in Colour.* Crestwood, NY: SVS Press, 1973.

Tziovas, Dimitris. 'Beyond the Acropolis: Rethinking Neohellenism.' *Journal of Modern Greek Studies* 19 (2001), 189-213.

van Heijenoort, Jean, ed. *From Frege to Gödel: A Source Book In Mathematical Logic.* Cambridge: Harvard University Press, 1967.

van Vleet, Jacob. *Dialectical Theology and Jacques Ellul.* Minneapolis: Fortress Press, 2014.

Varoufakis, Yanis. *Economic Indeterminacy.* Abingdon: Routledge, 2014.

Vasiljevic, Maxim. *Diary of the Council.* Los Angeles: Sebastian Press, 2017.

Virilio, Paul. *Negative Horizon.* New York: Continuum, 2005.

–––. *The Administration of Fear.* Los Angeles: semiotext(e), 2012.

Weil, Simone and Rachel Bespaloff. *War and the Iliad.* New York: New York Review of Books, 2005.

Welby, Justin. *Dethroning Mammon.* London: Bloomsbury, 2017.

Williams, Rowan. 'The Theology of Personhood: A Study of the Thought of Christos Yannaras.' *Sobornost* 6 (1972), 415-30.

Wink, Walter. *Engaging the Powers.* Minneapolis: Fortress Press, 1992.

–––. *Postmodern Metaphysics,* trans. Norman Russell. Brookline, MA: Holy Cross Orthodox Press, 2004.

–––. *Παιδεία καὶ γλῶσσα : Ἐπικαιρικὰ παλινωδούμενα [Education and Language: Timely Recantations].* Athens: Patakis, 2000.

–––. *De l'absence et de l'inconnaissance de Dieu d'après les écrits aéropagitiques et Martin Heidegger,* trans. Jacques Touraille. Paris: Cerf, 1971.

–––. *Ἡ Ὀντολογία Τοῦ Προσώπου (Προσωποκεντρικὴ Ὀντολογία) [The Ontology of the Person (Prosopo-Centric Ontology)].* Athens: Ikaros, 2017.

Yannaras, Christos. '«Μεγάλη Σύνοδος»: ἡ Ἀντίφαση Ἐγγενής.' Available at: http://www.kathimerini.gr/864266/opinion/epikairothta/politikh/megalh-synodos-h-antifash-eggenhs. Accessed on 4 April 2017.

–––. 'A Note on Political Theology.' In *The Meaning of Reality: Essays on Existence and Communion, Eros and History*, ed. Gregory Edwards and Herman A. Middleton, 149-52. Los Angeles; Athens: Sebastian Press ; Indiktos, 2011.

–––. 'An Orthodox Comment on "The Death of God".' *Sobornost* 5:4 (Winter 1966).

———. 'Human Rights and the Orthodox Church.' In *The Orthodox Churches in a Pluralistic World: An Ecumenical Conversation*, ed. Emmanuel Clapsis, 83-9. Geneva/Brookline, MA: WCC Publications/Holy Cross Orthodox Press, 2004.

———. Ἀρκεῖ ἡ παιδεία γιὰ ἀνάκαμψη;' ['Is education sufficient for recovery?'],Video Serres TV, 52:19. Available at: http://www.serrestv.gr/tv/musicvideo. php?vid=ec3d277e6. Accessed on 19 May 2017.

———. Ἑλλαδισμὸς τὸ τέλος τοῦ Ἑλληνισμοῦ;' ['Is the Greek nation-state the end of Hellenism?']. In *Ἡ ἑλληνικότητα ὡς ποιότητα καὶ ὡς ντροπή [Greekness as Quality and Shame]*, 287-91. Thessaloniki: Ianos, 2014.

———. Ἡ Δημοκρατία Συνάρτηση Παιδείας' ['Democracy: A function of education (Ch. Yannaras),] Vimeo video, 48:05. Available at: https://vimeo.com/22238481.

———. Ἡ διάκριση καλοῦ καὶ κακοῦ, ἀποτυχημένη παιδαγωγικὴ ἀρχὴ (Κέρκυρα, 30.1.2017)' ['The distinction between good & evil as a failed pedagogical principle, Corfu, 30.1.2017']. YouTube video, 01:15:37. Available at: https://www.youtube.com/watch?v=tr3tdXbxp3A&t=852s.

———. Ἡ Οἰκουμενικὴ δυναμικὴ τοῦ Ἑλληνισμοῦ.' ['14-11-1994 The ecumenical dynamics of Hellenism.'] YouTube video, 02:13:58.Available at: https://www.youtube.com/watch?v=Kvt-eJdHVX0&t=829s.

———. Ὅ καπιταλισμὸς καὶ ἡ συνείδηση τῆς θνητότητας' ['Capitalism and the Consciousness of Mortality']. In *Ἡ Νεοελληνικὴ ταυτότητα [Modern Greek Identity]*, 15-22, 4th ed. Athens: Grigoris, 2001.

———. Ὅξφόρδη, Σεπτέμβριος 2013' ['Oxford, September 2013']. In *Ἡ ἑλληνικότητα ὡς ποιότητα καὶ ὡς ντροπή [Greekness as Quality and Shame]*, 295-302. Thessaloniki: Ianos, 2014.

———. Ῥεαλισμὸς Μαρτυρίας – Ὄχι Ἰδεολογήματα.' *Kathimerini*, 26 June 2016. Available at: http://www.kathimerini.gr/865107/opinion/epikairothta/politikh/pealismos-martyrias--oxi-ideologhmata. Accessed on 4 April 2017.

———. Συνεπάγεται ἀχρείωση ὁ ἀφελληνισμός' ['De-Hellenisation implies infamity'], *Kathimerini*, 10 August 2014. http://www.kathimerini.gr/779516/opinion/epikairothta/politikh/synepagetai-axreiwsh-o-afellhnismos. Accessed on 4 April 2017.

———.'Σωτηρία,ἴσως,ὁ κοσμοπολιτισμός' ['Perhaps our salvation is cosmopolitanism'], *Kathimerini*, 23 January 2017. Available at: http://www.kathimerini.gr/892825/opinion/epikairothta/politikh/swthria-isws-o-kosmopolitismos. Accessed on 4 April 2017.

———. Τὸ Ὀντολογικὸν περιεχόμενον τῆς θεολογικῆς ἐννοίας τοῦ προσώπου' ['The Ontological Content of the Theological Notion of Personhood']. PhD diss., Aristotle University of Thessaloniki, 1970.

———. Τὸ πολιτικὸ περιεχόμενο τῆς θρησκευτικῆς ἀδιαφορίας' ['The Political Significance of Religious Indifference']. In *Ἡ Νεοελληνικὴ ταυτότητα [Modern Greek Identity]*, 40-6, 4th ed. Athens: Grigoris, 2001.

———. Τὸ σήμερα ἔρχεται ἀπὸ τὸ χθὲς' ['Today follows tomorrow'], *Kathimerini*, 12 February 2017. Available at: http://www.kathimerini.gr/896065/opinion/epikairothta/politikh/to-shmera-erxetai-apo-to-x8es. Accessed on 4 April 2017.

———. *Against Religion: The Alienation of the Ecclesial Event*, trans. Norman Russell. Brookline, MA: Holy Cross Orthodox Press, 2013.

———. *Elements of Faith: An Introduction to Orthodox Theology*, trans. Keith Schram. Edinburgh: T. & T. Clark, 1991.

---. *Heidegger şi Areopagitul*, trans. Nicolae Şerban Tanaşoca. Bucharest: Anastasia, 2009.

---. Interview with Babis Papadimitriou. Ὁ Χρῆστος Γιανναρᾶς: Νόημα στὸ νὰ εἴμαστε Ἕλληνες,᾽ ['Is there any point in being Greek?'] YouTube video, 02:11. Available at: https://www.youtube.com/watch?v=ePqE5p-1pu0&t=2s.

---. Interview with Evi Kyriakopoulou. YouTube video, 26:11. Available at: https://www.youtube.com/watch?v=Dsf837drFdo&t=1572s.

---. *On the Absence and Unknowability of God: Heidegger and the Areopagite*, trans. Haralambos Ventis, ed. Andrew Louth. New York: T. & T. Clark, 2005.

---. *Orthodoxy and the West: Hellenic Self-Identity in the Modern Age*, trans. Peter Chamberas and Norman Russell. Brookline, MA: Holy Cross Orthodox Press, 2006.

---. *Persoană şi eros*, trans. Zenaida Luca. Bucharest: Anastasia, 2000.

---. *Person and Eros,* trans. Norman Russell. Brookline, MA: Holy Cross Orthodox Press, 2007.

---. *Person und Eros: eine Gegenüberstellung der Ontologie der griechischen Kirchenväter und der Existenzphilosophie des Westens*. Göttingen: Vandenhoeck & Ruprecht, 1982.

---. *Postmodern Metaphysics*, trans. Norman Russell. Brookline, MA: Holy Cross Orthodox Press, 2004.

---. *Relational Ontology,* trans. Norman Russell. Brookline, MA: Holy Cross Orthodox Press, 2011.

---. *The Enigma of Evil*, trans. Norman Russell. Brookline, MA: Holy Cross Orthodox Press, 2012.

---. *The Freedom of Morality*, trans. Elizabeth Briere. Crestwood, NY: St Vladimir's Seminary Press, 1984.

---. *The Schism in Philosophy*, trans. Norman Russell. Brookline, MA: Holy Cross Orthodox Press, 2015.

---. *Variations on the Song of Songs*. Brookline, MA: Holy Cross Orthodox Press, 2005.

---. *Ἀόριστη Ἑλλάδα: Κοντσέρτο γιὰ δυὸ ἀποδημίες [Indefinite Greece: Concert for Two Emigrations]*. Thessaloniki: Ianos, 2016.

---. *Ἔξι φιλοσοφικές ζωγραφιές: Σύνοψη εἰσαγωγικὴ καὶ πάντως αὐτεξεταστική [Six Philosophical Paintings: Synoptic Self-Examination]*. Athens, Ikaros, 2011.

---. *Ἔξι φιλοσοφικές ζωγραφιές: Σύνοψη εἰσαγωγικὴ καὶ πάντως αὐτεξεταστική [Six Philosophical Paintings: Synoptic Self-Examination]*. Athens: Ikaros, 2011. EPub version.

---. *Ἡ ἀπανθρωπία τοῦ δικαιώματος [The Inhumanity of Right]*. Athens: Domos, 1998.

---. *Ἡ Ἐλευθερία Τοῦ Ἤθους [The Freedom of Morality]*. Synoro. Athens: Athina, 1970.

---. *Ἡ Εὐρώπη Γεννήθηκε ἀπὸ τὸ Σχίσμα [The Great Schism Engendered Europe]*. Athens: Ikaros, 2015.

---. *Ἡ Μεταφυσικὴ τοῦ Σώματος [The Metaphysics of the Body]*. Athens: Dodoni, 1971.

---. *Ἡ Νεοελληνικὴ Ταυτότητα [Modern Greek Identity]*. Athens: Grigoris, 1978.

---. *Καταφύγιο Ἰδεῶν: Μαρτυρία [Refuge of Ideas: Testimony]*. 8th ed. Athens: Ikaros, 2011.

---. *Καταφύγιο Ἰδεῶν: Μαρτυρία [Refuge of Ideas: Testimony]*. Athens: Domos, 1987.

---. *Κεφάλαια Πολιτικῆς Θεολογίας [Chapters in Political Theology]*. Athens: Grigoris, 1983.

---. *Ὀρθὸς λόγος καὶ κοινωνικὴ πρακτική [Rationality and Social Practice]*. Athens: Domos, 2006.

---. *Πείνα καὶ Δίψα [Hunger and Thirst]*. Athens: Grigoris, 1969.

---. *Πολιτιστικὴ Διπλωματία [Cultural Diplomacy]*. Athens: Ikaros, 2001.

---. *Προτάσεις κριτικῆς ὀντολογίας [Propositions for a Critical Ontology]*. Athens: Ikaros, 2010.

---. *Προτάσεις Κριτικῆς Ὀντολογίας [Propositions for a Critical Ontology]*. Athens: Domos, 1985.

---. *Σχεδίασμα εἰσαγωγῆς στὴ φιλοσοφία [An Outline of an Introduction to Philosophy*, translated in English as *The Schism in Philosophy]*. Athens: Domos, 1988.

---. *Τὰ καθ᾽ἑαυτὸν [Personal Matters]* 4th ed. Athens: Ikaros, 2005.

---. *Τὸ πραγματικὸ καὶ τὸ φαντασιῶδες στὴν Πολιτικὴ Οἰκονομία [The Real and the Imaginary in Political Economy]*. Athens: Domos 2006.

---. *Τὸ Προνόμιο τῆς Ἀπελπισίας [The Privilege of Despair]*. Athens: Grigoris, 1983.

---. *Τὸ ρητὸ καὶ τὸ ἄρρητο: τὰ γλωσσικὰ ὅρια ρεαλισμοῦ τῆς μεταφυσικῆς [The Effable and the Ineffable: the Linguistic Limits of Metaphysical Realism]*. Athens: Ikaros, 1999.

Yannoulatos, Anastasios, *Ἱεραποστολὴ στὰ Ἴχνη τοῦ Χριστοῦ [The Mission on the Traces of Christ]*. Athens: Apostoliki Diakonia, 2007.

Yoder, John Howard. 'The Constantinian Sources of Western Social Ethics.' In *The Priestly Kingdom*, 135-47. Notre Dame: University of Notre Dame Press, 1984.

Zernov, Nicholas. *Moscow: The Third Rome*. New York: MacMillan, 1937.

Zizioulas, John, 'Θεία Εὐχαριστία καὶ Ἐκκλησία' ['Eucharistic Event and Church']. In *Τὸ Μυστήριο τῆς Θείας Εὐχαριστίας [The Mystery of the Eucharistic Event]*, 25-47. Athens: Apostoliki Diakonia, 2004.

---. *Ἡ Κτίση ὡς Εὐχαριστία. Θεολογικὴ Προσέγγιση στὸ Πρόβλημα τῆς Οἰκολογίας [Creation as Eucharist: A Theological Approach to the Problem of Ecology]*. Athens: Akritas, 1992.

Zouboulakis, Stavros. 'Τὸ 'Σύνορο' καὶ ὁ Χρῆστος Γιανναρᾶς. Ἡ Θεολογικὴ Πρόταση τῆς Ἀποηθικοποίησης τοῦ Χριστιανισμοῦ' ['The "Border" and Christos Yannaras: The Theological Proposal of Demoralizing Christianity']. In *Ἀναταράξεις στὴ Μεταπολεμικὴ Θεολογία: Ἡ Θεολογία τοῦ '60 [Turbulence in Post-war Theology: The Theology of the 60s]*, ed. Pantelis Kalaitzidis, Athanasios Papathanasiou and Athanasios Abatzidis, 315-26. Athens: Indiktos, 2009.

Index

You might also be interested in:

Ever-Moving Repose:
A Contemporary Reading of Maximus the Confessor's Theory of Time

By Sotiris Mitralexis

PB ISBN: 9780227176849
PDF ISBN: 9780227906804

Sotiris Mitralexis offers a contemporary look at Maximus the Confessor's (580–662 CE) understanding of temporality, logoi, and deification, through the perspective of the contemporary philosopher and theologian Christos Yannaras, as well as John Zizioulas and Nicholas Loudovikos. Mitralexis argues that Maximus possesses both a unique theological ontology and a unique threefold theory of temporality: time, the Aeon, and the radical transformation of temporality and motion in an ever-moving repose. With these three distinct modes of temporality, a Maximian theory of time can be reconstructed. This theory can be approached via his teachings on logoi and deification, as time is more precisely measuring a relationship, the consummation of which effects the transformation of time into a dimensionless present, devoid of temporal, spatial, and general ontological distance. This manifests a perfect communion-in-otherness. In examining Maximian temporality, the author not only focusses on one aspect of Maximus' comprehensive Weltanschauung, but looks at the Maximian vision as a whole through the lens of temporality and motion.

You might also be interested in:

Divine Essence and Divine Energies: Ecumenical Reflections on the Presence of God in Eastern Orthodoxy

By C. Athanasopoulos and C. Schneider

PB ISBN: 9780227173862
PDF ISBN: 9780227900123
ePUB ISBN: 9780227900086
Kindle ISBN: 9780227900109

The result of a colloquium organised by the Institute for Orthodox Christian Studies (Cambridge, UK), Divine Essence and Divine Energies offers a rich repository of diverse opinion about the distinction between essence and energy in Orthodox Christianity – a doctrine which lies at the heart of the often fraught fault line between East and West, and which inspires a lively dialogue between the contributors. In what way were the Aristotelian concepts of ousia and energeia used by the Church Fathers, and to what extent were their meanings modified in the light of the Christological and Trinitarian doctrines? What theological function does the essence-energy distinction fulfil in Eastern Orthodoxy with respect to theology, anthropology, and the doctrine of creation? What are the differences and similarities between the notions of divine presence and participation in seminal Christian writings, and what is the relationship between the essence-energy distinction and Western ideas of divine presence? A valuable addition to the dialogue between Eastern and Western Christianity, this book will be of great interest to any reader seeking a rigorously academic insight into the wealth of scholarly opinion about the essence-energy distinction.

#0014 - 051118 - C0 - 234/156/15 - PB - 9780227176719